Praise for *Romantic Vacancy*

"For some time now there has been what we might call a movement that attends in Romantic writing to affects and states of being we had previously neglected or simply missed altogether. A generation of scholars, junior and senior, is mapping out this uncharted territory in the most original manner, along the way teaching us how to be with Romanticism, and how Romanticism has always been with us, in ways that are teaching all of us in turn how to be with the present. We can put Kate Singer's *Romantic Vacancy*—smart, insightful, beautifully argued—at the vanguard of this movement, proof of the fact that any rumours of the death of our field are not only highly exaggerated but just plain wrong."

— Joel Faflak, author of *Romantic Psychoanalysis: The Burden of the Mystery*

"*Romantic Vacancy* offers compelling close readings of Romantic women poets and two canonical male poets (Shelley and Wordsworth). After reading this book, Romantic-era scholars will no longer be able to read these poets in the same way again—I think this book will be a game changer for scholars working on women poets. This is a very fine work that should have a significant influence on the field."

— Daniela Garofalo, author of *Women, Love, and Commodity Culture in British Romanticism*

ROMANTIC VACANCY

SUNY series, Studies in the Long Nineteenth Century
Pamela K. Gilbert, editor

ROMANTIC VACANCY

The Poetics of Gender, Affect, and Radical Speculation

Kate Singer

Cover art: Sonia Gechtoff, *The Beginning*, 1960. Denver Art Museum: Vance H. Kirkland Acquisition Fund. 2015.62. © Sonia Gechtoff. Photography courtesy of Denver Art Museum.

Published by State University of New York Press, Albany
© 2019 State University of New York
All rights reserved

No part of this book may be used or reproduced in any manner whatsoever without written permission. No part of this book may be stored in a retrieval system or transmitted in any form or by any means including electronic, electrostatic, magnetic tape, mechanical, photocopying, recording, or otherwise without the prior permission in writing of the publisher.
For information, contact State University of New York Press, Albany, NY
www.sunypress.edu

Library of Congress Cataloging-in-Publication Data
Names: Singer, Kate, 1977– author.
Title: Romantic vacancy : the poetics of gender, affect, and radical speculation / Kate Singer, State University of New York.
Description: Albany : State University of New York Press, [2019] | Series: SUNY series, studies in the long nineteenth century | Includes bibliographical references and index.
Identifiers: LCCN 2018040338| ISBN 9781438475271 (hardcover)
| ISBN 9781438475295 (e-book) | ISBN 9781438475288 (pbk.) Subjects:
LCSH: English literature—19th century—History and criticism.
| Sentimentalism in literature. | Senses and sensation in literature. | Romanticism—Great Britian.
Classification: LCC PR468.S46 S56 2019 | DDC 820.9/353—dc23
LC record available at https://lccn.loc.gov/2018040338

10 9 8 7 6 5 4 3 2 1

To my mother, who taught me to read

To my father, who taught me to dream

And to Bue, who teaches me how to be

Contents

ACKNOWLEDGMENTS ... ix

INTRODUCTION   The Poetics of Vacancy ... xiii

CHAPTER 1   Charlotte Smith and the Taste of Aporia ... 1

CHAPTER 2   Mary Robinson's Intensities: Sensation after Oblivion ... 35

CHAPTER 3   Reaping Songs and Ineffable Tales: William Wordsworth and Percy Shelley's Singing Women and the Rave of Affect ... 63

CHAPTER 4   Felicia Hemans's Ruined Minds: Cognitive Overload and the Soul of Freedom ... 95

CHAPTER 5   Maria Jane Jewsbury and the Phantom Feelings of the Moving Image ... 123

CODA   The Phantom Menace and the Spirit of Affect ... 149

NOTES ... 155

WORKS CITED ... 189

INDEX ... 219

Acknowledgments

This book began as a project at the University of Maryland, thanks to the untiring tutelage of Neil Fraistat, whose planetary visions and Shelleyan spirit still revolve and reimagine Romanticism, and of Orrin N. C. Wang, who taught me to read like de Man, to revise like Derrida, and to think poised on the abyss. My many thanks to my other wonderful mentors Jason Rudy, Laura Rosenthal, Bill Cohen, and Tita Chico, who helped me write through and believe in the possibility of this project. I was lucky enough to be aided and abetted at UMD by two writing groups, Radioheadites Heidi Scott, Joseph Byrne, Elizabeth Whitney, and the salvific sisterhood of Kelly McGovern, Sarah Hamilton Kimmet, Joanne Baste, Rebecca Borden, and Caroline Egan. My MFA poet-mentors and grad school friends first taught me, and continue to teach me, about poetics and affect in the thick atmosphere of the Beltway, especially Josh Mensch, Joanna Osborne (aka Nick Flynn), and our 16th-Street corridor family, particularly Alex Orr, Charlie Clark, Paul Bolstad, Emily Manus, the Kahla-Lewandowskis, and the King-Woodses.

I won the colleague lottery when I landed at Mount Holyoke and was gifted an assemblage suffused with brilliant, witty coolness. Thank you Amy Martin for your continuous mentoring and savvy conversation; Elizabeth Young for the graceful, studied advice and encouragement about this book and the project of academia; Iyko Day for your constant intellectual and gourmet generosity, especially all of your theory-infused Noho salons; Wes Yu for your always precise thoughtfulness; Nigel Alderman for your co-processing and literary companionship; Suparna Roychaudry for redirecting my attention to aesthetic beauty; Jenny Pyke for your object lessons, affect playlists, and Eliotesque sympathies; and Amy Rodgers for reminding me to laugh while at the factory and for teaching me independence of thought and true interdisciplinary friendship. I have been doubly blessed to have amazing colleagues in the Five Colleges as well. Romanticism is alive and well in our small band of Joselyn Almeida-Beveridge, Daniel Block, Amelia Worsley, and Lily Gurton-Wachter. Thank you especially to Amelia and Lily for your gifted affective reading and final-stages pep talks. I am irreparably entangled with my truly amazing Mount Holyoke students, especially those who trooped through British Romanticism, Romantic Epistemologies, Feminist Poetics, Posthuman Affect Theory, and Love, Sex, and Death in the Anthropocene. I am forever in your debt for all that you have shown me, taught me, felt with me, and allowed me to attempt to articulate. You are our future-to-come. As if an *alma mater*, Mount Holyoke College has been generous with its fellowship and multiple faculty grants that enabled research in the United States and the UK. Many thanks, as well, to the Keats-Shelley Association of America, which offered a Pforzheimer Grant to support this project and whose continued support of Romantic-era endeavors has been an inspiration and bildung in communicating literary spirits to the wider world.

Somehow, along the first-book Sisyphean road, I have been granted some amazing colleagues and friends. My thanks to Daniel Robinson, Orianne Smith, Noah Comet, C. C. Wharram, Devoney Looser, and Libby Fay for reading and serving as academic GPSes at crucial moments. To Nan Sweet for teaching me the complex intricacies of Hemans, of editing, and of deep scholarship. Thank you to my unpantsed writing group who read many pieces of this project with ever-incisive annotations about Romanticism and writing: Ashley Cross, Yohei Igarashi, Suzanne Barnett, Chris Washington, and Michael Gamer. My new materialist assemblage, Suzanne L. Barnett and Ashley J. Cross—aka the Thunder Bitches—thank you for teaching me to live in the flows of transgressive thinking and brownie being. Thank you Gamer for the twenty-third hour readerly kick in the pants at exactly the time I needed it. Thank you David Sigler for all your insuperable grace in reading, editing, and eloquence. That punning pack of Keatsians cards at the Keats Letters Project, Ian Newman, Anne McCarthy, Brian Rejack, Emily Stanback, and Michael Theune, has taught me new forms of collaboration, friendship, and virtual pleasure. #yykm. A special thank you, Ashley, for your genius-in-a-garret Robinsonian work as you read so much of this, so many times, with your organizational and intellectual superpowers. Likewise, I was able to complete this book thanks to the painstaking work of the readers of the manuscript and to Daniela Garofalo, who read an earlier draft.

My whole heart goes to my extended family of choice, my mom and Milan and all the Steins, especially Sammy, who is a true mensch, and Aunt Lea, Jodie, and Margie, who continue to be models of caring women who work. Thank you Mom for processing all my beta waves, for being there, and for showing me that repair, change, and love are always possible.

My brother, who has given lots of "listen, pal" advice to be weighed and not taken, you carry our father's generosity and corniness, which is only unmasked sentiment and heart. To DLO, all the years of support and triage cannot be erased from this project; I only hope the future will bring new affects for us both. Thank you for teaching me stamina, endurance, and strength, even if these are not the words you would have had me write. Thank you, Ilene, for being a friend, the Blanche to my Dorothy. Long may we eat taco dip and drink champs while sitting on the beach of DC politics. Only good things happen when we're driving in the car to Target.

And, finally, for Chris, who is the trace. If there is any starlight in these words, it is surely yours.

The chapter on Maria Jane Jewsbury is derived, in part, from an article published in *European Romantic Review* on August 29, 2012, and available online at https://www.tandfonline.com/doi/full/10.1080/10509585.2012.709792. A piece of the Mary Robinson chapter was first published in *Literature Compass*.

Introduction

The Poetics of Vacancy

> For one poor moment soothe the sense of pain,
> And teach a breaking heart to throb no more?
> And you, Aruna!—in the vale below,
> As to the sea your limpid waves you bear
> Can you one kind Lethean cup bestow,
> To drink a long oblivion to my care? (5.7–12)
> —Charlotte Smith, "To the South Downs," *Elegiac Sonnets*

> So shall this glowing, palpitating soul,
> Welcome returning Reason's placid beam,
> While o'er my breast the waves Lethean roll,
> To calm rebellious Fancy's fev'rish dream;
> Then shall my Lyre disdain love's dread control,
> And loftier passions, prompt the loftier theme! (43.9–14)
> —Mary Robinson, "Her Reflections on the Leucadian Rock before She Perishes," *Sappho and Phaon*

> And what were thou, and earth, and stars, and sea,
> If to the human mind's imaginings
> Silence and solitude were vacancy?
> —Percy Shelley, "Mont Blanc"

At frequent intervals within their respective sonnet sequences, the speakers of Charlotte Smith's *Elegiac Sonnets* and Mary Robinson's *Sappho and Phaon* enunciate a desire for respite, a vacancy from their feverish passions. The problem, they tell us, is that the heart breaks and throbs with too absorbing a sense of pain, or the soul palpitates with Sappho's "fev'rish dream" of Phaon. As the body stirs with sensations, the mind is filled with the heated cares of adult life and love until it distains their "dread control." The speakers both turn to aqueous bodies of water—the Arun River or what Sappho elsewhere calls the "Leucadian deep"—as a balm, a treatment that will, they hope, calm the intense physiological activity of the body and the mind's frenzied speculations. Quite gone are the celebrations of Hannah More's "Sensibility: An Epistle to the Hon. Mrs. Boscawen" (1782), which lauds the infiltration of body, spirit, and mind by nervous vibrations and thrilling sensations: "where bright imagination, reigns, / The fine-wrought spirit feels acuter pains / [. . .] / There is feeling diffus'd thro' ev'ry part, / Thrills in each nerve, and lives in all the heart" (66–67, 71–72). Despite panegyrics like this one, poets of sensibility occasionally voiced "A Prayer for Indifference" (1750s), as Frances Greville did, asking for the fairy balm of a "juice of western flower" that could temporarily mute sensibility's physical sensations and surging emotion (15). Yet Smith and Robinson turn away from either sensibility's full-bodied incandescence or its dearth. Their limpid, rolling waves instead offer other movements, where intense bodily activity and mental fracas give way to alternative motions that move beyond, and differently from, them. Smith and Robinson answer the sensitive and excessive physiological response that characterizes the discourse of sensibility in the eighteenth century, not with stillness, silence, or emptiness, but with a set of figures I am calling vacancy, that stem the tide of sensibility and open a space for another sort of release—and another sort of affect altogether—into the motion of the waves.

As the speakers drink or jump into the rolling water, something altogether more complicated than simply a resistance to sensibility occurs in the encounter between poet, figure, and landscape. When Sappho and Smith's speakers call specifically upon Lethe, the river of forgetting, as sensibility's cure, they crucially enunciate a figurative dimension to the waves' soothing movements. Both poets summon the mythical river of Hades that, if drunk or waded into, could purge them of woeful memories, dreams, and "sense of pain," those sensations that create memory and consciousness in the first place. As Smith converts the Arun River into the cup of Lethe, she creates a figure for imbibing something that eviscerates the possibility of sensory stimulation, a figure for internalization without content. What the speaker asks to drink, but cannot, is not a thing at all, but Lethe, a classical figure and mythological substance: she consumes a figure. Here Smith transforms the entire bourgeois discourse of taste, so often aimed at sensitive consumers of feeling and luxury goods, into an aporia, a figure for impossible consumption. The mythical cup is hollowed out of the tasteful draught of sensibility. In its place, Smith uncovers a figure for taking in the nonexistent balm, an ineffable, abstract motion of absorption and intermixture. In a sonnet considered to express the height of sensibility, Smith composes another, more complex poetic movement: the vacancy that turns from sensibility's famed responsiveness and its reliance on embodied sensation to unfold an alternative, figurative motion. What she arrives at is a form of affect that is not bounded by bodily sensation but rather by abstract, incorporeal movements of figuration; she jettisons sensibility for a much more complex form of affect that is released from the feeling, gendered body and that is created through the interminable motions of language.

Robinson authors the reverse strategy from Smith's when Sappho is swallowed by the Lethean waves that will eradicate her "fev'rish dream." The Sapphic poet finally takes a plunge not into death but an affective flow where "loftier passions" might roll as the waves do, calmly, without stimulating sensibility's fever. The nonhuman waves, heedless of human romances, overturn Sappho's tragic, womanly love. The poet limns death without resting in its quietude or its absence of sensation, and neither is she reborn as a new subject. In her dissolution as a floating breast amid the Lethean tide, she is released from the confines of the imprisoning body and the frenzied mind, however enlightened. The figure of the Lethean waves shapes repetitive but variable motions, which do not weigh down the sensing, lovelorn woman. Vacancy thus sketches something akin to affects that move beyond the sensate subject and human body, circulating among the Lethean waves and the artist formerly known as Sappho. Such new figural movements provide loftier passions and loftier themes.

Smith's impossible consumption and Robinson's radical immersion emerge from sensibility's concerns with responsiveness, relation, and moral reform, but they trope alternatives to its excessive entrapment within the sensing, gendered body. *Romantic Vacancy* examines how Romantic poets—Smith, Robinson, Felicia Hemans, and Maria Jane Jewsbury as well as William Wordsworth and Percy Shelley—contemplate the philosophical problems with sensibility, and in the process discover the figures of vacancy that move beyond them. These writers find other forms of what we have come to call affect and speculative thinking that revise what we know about the history of sensibility (and its feminization). They, even more importantly, reconceive our current understandings of affect and its relation to language, as well as language's ability to create new ontologies that move beyond the gender and human/nonhuman binaries seemingly endemic to Romantic-era poetry, especially women's verse. So attached have we become to the lens of sensibility that we have been overwhelmingly unmindful of women poets' play with other forms of knowledge and being, which intently speak to the philosophical songs of the Romantic age. Women poets have generally been left behind in studies of philosophical thinking, and we have not yet perused the wide expanse of their serious, speculative poetics, nor for that matter the speculative thinking male writers undertook in response to sensibility.[1]

In grappling with sensibility's translation of empiricism, as a theory about how sensation could be converted into ideas and emotions, poets of vacancy carve out other epistemologies that rewrote some of the period's core philosophies. It is the contention of this book that Romantic poets found other figures to answer the problems with sensibility as they interpreted them: first, its reliance on empirical sensation that trapped them in bodies too sensitive for finer thought, and second, the ideological narratives dictating how bodily responses gender subjects' bodies and minds. Poets of vacancy found a basis for knowledge not in bodily sensation but within the figural movements of language that create conduits among different kinds of things—waves, human bodies, Lethean cups. Responding to eighteenth-century and Enlightenment narratives about affect's genesis in the sensing and emoting human body, Romantic vacancy forms an alternative to sensibility's bodily activity, an affect that is both transcorporeal and incorporeal, material and figural. This propensity to move or be moved within and across bodies, and often before conscious awareness or articulation of these motions, occurs, seemingly impossibly in Romantic poems, through a series of figurative responses and movements.

As they devise a new figurative technique to address sensibility's philosophical problems with sensation, poets of vacancy do not simply turn to figures of absence to void sensation. They do not ask, as Ann Yearsley does in "To Indifference" (1787), for a temporary pause to the constantly sensing, emoting subjectivity: "INDIFFERENCE come! thy torpid juices shed / On my keen sense: plunge deep my wounded heart, / In thickest apathy" (1–3). Smith's plea for "oblivion" may sound as though she longs for this absence of sensation, however temporary, but she in fact calls for the eradication of the entire system of sensation that traps women within bodies that feel too much or not enough. Part of a pattern of excess and lack, the trope of indifference recapitulates the pursuit of mere escape from sensibility, a feeling of insensibility, without any real change to its terms. This dualism echoes the experience of negation, escape, or emptiness—what we might term a precursor to vacancy found in John Keats's plea in "Ode on Indolence" (1819), to "melt, and leave my sense / Unhaunted quite of all but—nothingness" (19–20) or William Wordsworth's remark in *The Prelude* on the "vacancy between me and those days" (2.29). This problem of sensation's boom or bust is exactly the question raised at the end of "Mont Blanc"; however, Shelley, similar to other writers in this study, suggests that what might seem like emptiness or oblivion instead uncovers a "universe of things" flowing, at times, imperceptibly. Permeating through mind and river valley, vacancy's ubiquitous movements offer another figural movement that circumvents sensation's surges and its lyrical excesses that became so feminized within the discourse of sensibility.

Although sensibility was a sociopolitical movement that ideally offered men and women a tool to equalize gender in the public sphere, it did so by privileging women's responsiveness to sensory experiences and emotion—defined as conscious, labeled, and reified experiences of bodily pain and pleasure or bodily states such as anger, sadness, and happiness. Because women were understood to be sensitive to their environments, more liable to sensation, they were seen as naturally more beholden to their physical and emotional experiences—what Robinson condemns as "love's dread control." Many poets claimed sensibility as the source of women's feminine poetic prowess: Helen Maria Williams famously exclaims in "To Sensibility," "In Sensibility's lov'd praise / I tune my trembling reed" (1–2), and Samuel Taylor Coleridge's "Kubla Khan" ends with a damsel with a dulcimer whose "sympathy and song" is called upon to revive his own song. Yet such a "fev'rish dream" of women's poetics resists even "reason's placid beam." The ideological illusion of sensibility's control over women makes it appear natural that Sappho would submit herself to Phaon. Understood as women's purview, such an epistemology binds women to gendered knowledge that could be gleaned only from their too sensitive bodies or from emotional experiences circumscribed by domesticity, social relations, and biographies. Yet women are not the only ones who contemplate vacancy; for Shelley and Wordsworth, bodily sensation too easily genders feeling and thought, infecting everyone with its potential to inscribe inequality. Gender, therefore, as it continually informs both the concepts and realities of sensation and emotion in the period, becomes an important epistemological crux to question reigning ways of knowing and being. Vacancy employs this gender inequality as a staging ground not to eradicate difference but to figure bodies, emotions, and genders as continuously shifting. By breaking free from gendered bodies and poetics, vacancy opens a nonbinary landscape of transgressive figurative motion.

Vacancy's figuration occurs, and recurs, through figural turns, repetitions, and paradoxes—such as catachresis, repetition with difference, and synesthesia. When Smith's impossible consumption critiques sensory modes of consumption and taste, she does not leave us in a no-man's land of oblivion, but rather asks how it might be to move in aporia's circular style, within paradoxes that repeatedly revolve through logical and material impossibility. Vacancy, therefore, enacts tropological movement not merely to eradicate the surety of our sensing bodies and to undermine gender ideology, but to refigure our relation to reality. Without leaving matter behind, vacancy offers poetry's rich attention to linguistic movement as a potent form of material fluidity and figural change.

As I have briefly touched on, affect can be a way to describe vacancy's figural turns as it tracks a set of movements amid the body, the world, and language. As I discuss below, this book intervenes into current accounts of affect—often understood as inchoate, not quite sensed physiological activity—to intertwine bodily change, the motions of nonhuman material world, *and* language's figurative turns. In doing so, these poets irrevocably alter how we understand Romantic-era affect, and how necessary Romanticism is to theorize affect more globally. The Lethean rolls transform Robinson's frenzied passion into the figures of waves that repeat with differences the motion of water over the breast, the ocean's own contingent tides, and a refiguring of the mythical river that forgets old passion for new tropes. Both Smith's Lethean waves and Robinson's Leucadian ones shape figures that are at once linguistic and material; they pose affect as a material motion that occurs through language's turns, repetitions, and frissons. While affect is usually understood as material if not physiological and thus occurring before or beyond language, vacancy uniquely combines language, speculation, materiality, and affect in novel ways. Vacancy enlarges the notion of affect as the movements and rests of human sensation, or even, as Brian Massumi following Spinoza glosses, as the capacity for bodies to affect and be affected by other bodies. It more broadly encompasses those movements of the world and of language, becoming more widely corporeal and eventually incorporeal.[2] When gesturing toward the motions of the nonhuman world, I am especially thinking of Jane Bennett's notion of "impersonal affect," as a materiality and responsiveness shared among groups of humans and things in relation. For Romantic writers, this version of affect includes language as relation, movement, and material. Vacancy initiates a new figurative methodology to track—and construct—material movements outside and through discrete bodies and subjects. In its most radical form vacancy is posthuman—shared among mind, body, figure, and world, beyond the circumference of a self-conscious, consolidated subjectivity.

This book, in effect, intertwines Romantic deconstruction's attention to tropology with notions of dynamic affect developed by affect theory and new materialism. Read this way, the poetics of vacancy rewrites the history of sensibility and the gendering of writing even as it challenges accounts of linguistic impossibility, absence, and contingency written through the Romanticism so imbricated with high theory. Romanticism becomes once again differently capable of reconstituting the figural's ability to create revolutionary ontologies. This book therefore attempts to speak to—and ideally intertwine—two overlapping audiences—those interested in the figural play of gender especially in women's writing and those who study Romanticism's theories about language, knowledge, and being. What have seemed to be deconstructive problems with language, history, materiality, and subjectivity turn out to be even larger problems about finding forms of movement, like affect, that are not generated by the sensing, gendered body but rather created by the playful turns of language itself.[3] Poets of vacancy entangle gender and speculative thought at the heart of Romanticism, as their poems become central to the most interesting debates about how to theorize human language and the material world. By disrupting the solidly empirical, they look askance at linear histories based on clearly gendered subjects, and instead figure newly affective literary histories.

Women's Poetry, Romanticism, and the Ideology of Empirical Feeling

The immense swath of scholarship on sensibility has already duly established how a reform movement that employed the virtues of emotion to chasten male manners and their dominance in the public sphere fell prey to gender ideology. Assumptions that women had more sensitive nerves reinforced sexed and gendered dichotomies. While many writers of the period polemicized the problems of sensibility, poets in particular theorized a dilemma arising from its inheritance from empiricist philosophy that grounded its inquiry on bodily sensation. When the emphasis on sensation drew attention to knowledge drawn from women's bodies, it could likewise underwrite gender difference. We have largely ignored this gender critique of empiricism, mainly because we have inadvertently replicated the period's own gendered readings of women's writing—our assumptions that women writers in the Romantic period were, in fact, more interested in purveying the songs of sensibility and bodily response, as suffering women, mothers of the nation, or troubled denizens of the growing

British empire. For this reason, we have been slow to see women poets' speculative thinking about a variety of the period's philosophical options and bugbears, as well as their thorough contemplation about other ways of thinking and being.

Even at its inception, the embodied and gendered assumptions of the cult of high feeling established sensibility as an increasingly difficult discourse through which to forge any sense of imaginative or intellectual equity—and not simply because its conventions were already overused by the 1790s. Conceived through medical men such as George Cheyne, personal physician to Samuel Richardson, sensibility hails from early scientific understandings of the circulatory and nervous systems as well as empiricism's foundational emphasis on sensory perception as the substrate of all knowledge.[4] G. S. Rousseau delineates how the revolution in physiology—nerves, fibers, and animal spirits—limited the seat of the soul in the brain and subsequently enabled Locke to base his theories on the processing of sensation and reflection (166). Stephen Ahern recapitulates what G. J. Barker-Benfield labels "a new psychoperceptual paradigm," highlighting further the extent to which sensations and nerves defined character and intellectual capacity. He writes, "consciousness becomes an effect of the circulation of volatile animal spirits through the hollow fibers of the nerves, and as a consequence the intensity of a character's emotional and intellectual apperception is reduced to naturalist description of the body as a reactive mechanism" (Ahern 16). As John Mullan writes, eighteenth-century novelists "found it increasingly difficult to distinguish between the figure of the virtuous hero or, more especially the heroine, and that of the sadly distracted and isolated hysteric" (16). Empirical embodiment subjected feeling to the body's mechanical reactions—or supposedly naturalistic descriptions of them.

Though it developed into a discursive, figural practice, sensibility evolved from embodied, gendered epistemologies in which supposedly feminine, and so more sensitive, bodies would become more susceptible to experience apprehended through sense organs, nerves, and blood. Rousseau states quite baldly: "the scientific doctrine of sensibility was soon called upon to legitimate class distinction and gender difference. . . . Sensibility was in this approximate sense a type of eighteenth-century sociobiology" (231).[5] While sensibility granted women both a privileged position from which to profess their feelings and also a subject for their poetry, it also made them seem liable to all the hysterical weaknesses that their supposedly fragile frames might contract. In other words, sensibility both entitled women and made them prey to a gender ideology built on the back of embodiment and difference. As Barker-Benfield delineates in her history of sensibility, the empirical self was thought to be created through processing new sensations, therefore,

> it is not surprising that the fundamental issue for gender would be that of consciousness, of "mind" inevitably associated with feeling.... The revolutionary possibilities for women's consciousness were countered in the same terms, women's subordination naturalized on the basis of their finer sensibility. (3)

Even sympathy, defined by the imagination of another's feelings, nevertheless naturalized women's sensitive bodies. Those with greater sensibility, Adam Smith alleged, were more likely to carry the burden of sympathy.[6] Enlightenment ideas of feeling tended to reiterate this particular strain of embodied, empirical epistemology that put women at risk of becoming both trapped within excessively sensitive bodies too readily gendered, and then corseted within the roles of the suffering mother, consuming wife, and domestic drudge.

Although novels of sentiment, poetry of feeling, and philosophical tracts often employed sensibility as a tool of social reform and although, as Miranda Burgess has argued, sensibility gave voice to the ideas and language of mobility, from its inception the discourse had troubling implications for the ideological construction of women as primarily feeling subjects. While, as Chris Jones attests in *Radical Sensibility*, sensibility pledged to refine men's sympathies, manners, and attitudes toward women in the public sphere, it did so by valorizing women's privileged status as arbiters of feeling. As its role in the Revolutionary debates attests, it promised another avenue for women to assert their social worth.[7] Yet, as Claudia Johnson famously argues, it was notoriously coopted by conservatives such as Edmund Burke, who theatrically depicted how vital were the true feelings of real women to England's social and political inheritance. Women were left without a clear gender site except the hyperfeminine, at least as far as public discourse went.[8]

While historians have been quick to see sensibility as a medical discourse solidifying bodily difference, they have not entirely reckoned with its other foundational discourse, empiricism. When dealing with women or with "the passions," as Hume termed them, certain empiricist lines of thinking had the potential to become shaped by gender. Although for some time scholars opposed sensibility to Enlightenment rationality, more recent discussions of the cult of high feeling have revealed it to be an integral part of

British and Scottish empiricist thought that threads throughout Romanticism as well.[9] Thinkers such as John Locke, David Hume, and Edmund Burke begin with observations about experiential sensation that might lead either to the sensible passions or to rational associations. Romantic poetry has long been understood as growing from—and out of—an empiricist inheritance, when writers work through its ideas about sensation, the categorization of ideas, cause and effect, memory, identity, association, and the passions. Yet when we consider the gendered implications of sensation, Romantic poetry presents some of the most interesting thought experiments with the boons and banes of empiricism. Robinson is quick to remind us, for example, of Hume's dictum that reason holds no quarter against impassioned emotion and of his idea that speculation's dependence on habits of mind can lead to detrimental prejudice. While, as I hope to show, women writers reject passion and sensation, neither do they easily turn to rationality, whether empiricist notions of perfectibility, association, and common sense, or to those forms of reason based on *a priori* concepts, which supplied alternatives to empiricism. Smith and Hemans most intently consider idealism's problems for women, as the rights discourse and legal rules that partook of *a priori* reasoning like Kant's so often excluded them from becoming equal minds and bodies under the crown.

Jerome McGann long ago established sensibility as an extension of empiricism, "a reflection of its thought, and an effort to express that thought in direct ways" (134). Although he lauds sensibility's tendency to erase the difference between matter and spirit, he does not consider how such a seemingly androgynous fusion, as it churned through the eighteenth-century ideological machine, could create problems for women. Although Locke did not gender sensation, because its source of knowledge comes from bodily reaction, it could easily link knowledge to a sexed body, increasingly seen as a second sex.[10] Shelley, in "Alastor" for example, first describes the veiled maiden's effusive song as "woven sounds of streams and breezes," a pervasive and pointedly not gendered metaphor taken from sensibility's troping of vibrations (155). All too soon, however, both the maid and the poet are "stifled in tremulous sobs," and she is "subdued by its own pathos" (164, 165), gendered by the sensation that ties her to her quivering body.

Moreover, when sensation is reflected upon—or in Hume's terminology, when impressions become ideas through habit and custom—sensation again becomes liable to social and political influences that could easily gender acts of perception and reflection. Robinson's *Sappho and Phaon* is a case in point of a poem that begins with a diversity of sensation in the poem entitled "Bower of Pleasure" where "rival flow'rets bloom" (3.12), which all too soon turn into the gendered passion of romance that creates a "fever'd dream" of Phaon (43.12). Such an ideological illusion translates all sensation into women's monomaniacal love. In an attempt to avoid such translation, Felicia Hemans is quick to exclaim that the Widow of Crescentius, paralyzed by her husband's murder, "is no sculptured form of woe" (266). Hemans's line anticipates the ideology her readers would bring to the text, the assumption that the widow's frenzied body and mind would leave her paralyzed by overwhelming emotion. As a figure of both liminal thought and gender when she cross-dresses later in the poem, the widow, Hemans tells readers, should not be easily read as a figure for excessive sensibility.

Poets of vacancy certainly build on these empirical formulations of mental and physical ways of processing self and world. Smith laments sensation's overwhelming tax on her sense of self, and her longing for "oblivion" replays empiricism's inherent skepticism about our ability to know the external world or to compose a consistent identity. Robinson, Hemans, and Maria Jane Jewsbury cite empirical figures for sensory voids such as Locke's "dark room," sleep, forgetting, and the loss of consciousness, while Shelley works through, among other things, David Hartley's notions of vibration. Their figures of vacancy, however, complicate these ideas in the attempt to vitiate empiricism's tendency to understand the passive mind as subject to overwhelming sensation or to the emptiness of oblivion. Instead, they favor proactive movements of language and the material world. The poetic act of making tropes is a kind of constructive, agential movement, a poetic impulse that speaks not simply to the idea of Romantic genius but to a joint posthuman force created by the machinations of language and by its materiality in concert with that of the world and the poet. For this reason, vacancy seeks other forms of mental and bodily movement outside empirical sensation and the subject's gendered sways.

Our neglect of such figures arises from the nature of some twentieth-century feminist efforts to recover Romantic-era women's writing, which, in the attempt to historicize women's verse, replicated the view of women poets as irrevocably embodied beings whose sensitivities dominated their thoughts, feelings, and writing. Many recovery projects used sensibility, sentiment, and sympathy to characterize the appraisal of their verse in ways that have inadvertently but injuriously overfeminized women's poetics.[11] Today, even after nearly forty years of scholarship on women's writers, overviews of Romanticism still persist in this narrow vision of women's poetry. As Michael Ferber writes in *The Cambridge Introduction to British Romantic Poetry*, "Many if not all of the women poets of the Romantic period seem better described as poets of Sensibility than as Romantics, though there is room for debate" (6).[12] Michael O'Neill summarizes a similar received history of women poets: "A major reason for the neglect of Romantic women poets in the twentieth century may be attributed to a radical shift of sensibility in the arts toward a more elitist, Modernist aesthetic. A female sensibility which centered on extended professions of grief became over time associated with over-indulgence in unearned emotion" (561).[13] If an antagonism to undue emotion characterized Modernist canon-makers, then the natural association of women's writing with sensibility has, even in that poetry's recent resurrection, become a Romantic ideology all its own.

Current critical understandings of women's poetry, from both theorists and new historicists, have replicated and validated this Romantic gender ideology when they assume Romantic women poets to be empirical beings writing about embodied sentiment. The context of sensibility has become the default aesthetic and philosophical subtext for many women poets, so inextricably bound have text and context become for women's poetry, which has, in turn, narrowed and skewed our historical and theoretical perspective of Romanticism. Although McGann once argued that we could not understand the culture of sensibility as women's aesthetic achievement because of our tendency to "pre-read" it through a Modernist lens (4), we are now guilty of the other extreme—prereading it under the guise of sensibility and sentiment. Even now, women poets are habitually excluded as if by a theoretical glass ceiling from vital arenas of Romantic criticism—namely, Romantic thinking about the nature of thought, feeling, and being.[14]

The unfortunate legacy of Anne K. Mellor's seminal distinction between masculine and feminine Romanticisms—even if built as a spectrum and not a binary—has bequeathed the construction of women writers as separate but equal to Romanticism, at the very least when it engages in speculative, philosophical thinking and poetics. Although more than two decades have passed since *Romanticism and Gender* (1992) was published, too many Romanticists still assume women writers to be interested more in the concerns of domesticity and the social subject than "masculine" Romanticism's attention to philosophy and language as the main source of revolutionary political and ideological critique.[15] Recent work on sensibility tends to replicate Mellor's divisions when it seeks to sketch a separate female tradition through sentiment, such as Claire Knowles's *Sensibility and the Female Poetic Tradition*, or to valorize sensibility's power to import sexuality and feminine feeling into public discourse, such as Christopher Nagle's *Sexuality and the Culture of Sensibility in the British Romantic Era*. Kari Lokke, Stephen Behrendt, Diego Saglia, and Jason Rudy have each taken the opposite tack of tracing how women adopt a masculine sublime or the transcendent in Charlotte Smith and Felicia Hemans's poems, most often as a dialectical, spiritual critique of the vicissitudes of suffering that they cannot fully escape. There are certainly some agitations of affect beyond binary gender in McGann's pioneering work on the culture of sensibility, for example, when he suggestively offers sensibility as an aesthetics that blends affect and epistemology—"how language as affective thought functions" (6), a constellation Adela Pinch deepens in her seminal work on Romantic-era affect. Yet with the notable exception of studies on millenarian or religious poetry, we have not been able to imagine that Romantic-era women might have conceived of a place and a language for themselves well beyond a supposedly ineluctable empirical standpoint and its historically gendered context.[16] Readers of Romantic women's poetry would do well to return to Hélène Cixous's famous statements about history in "The Laugh of Medusa": the future of our interpretations of women's writing must no longer be determined by the past (857).

While vacancy may have arisen from the problems of excessive sensation and feeling, poets eventually produce an affect that is qualitatively different from empiricism's tendency to dwell on states like indifference or oblivion. Sensibility, like empiricism itself, was certainly a discourse riddled from the start not only with self-critique but also with its antithesis—insensibility, moments of indifference, lack of feeling, or the loss of consciousness. Yet the varieties of empirical escapes from feeling, thinking, or consciousness still very much depend on sensation or its periodic absence, rather than poetry's figural movements, which form the basis of vacancy's epistemology. There have been a variety of attempts to account for these negative responses and critiques to sensibility, and it seems helpful to rehearse them here, to differentiate them from vacancy.

According to Ann Jessie van Sant, women were seen to be most plagued by the physical and emotional excesses of sensibility. Consequently, as Patricia Spacks suggests, eighteenth-century women novelists mount "a critique [of the discourse] occurring at the very moment of the convention's dominance" (506). They depicted a dark side of sensibility, illustrating how responsiveness easily turned into ambivalence, sternness, and ferocity. Women writers established their own critique well before male writers such as Samuel Coleridge and William Gifford protested its feminization and Della Cruscan prostitution of poetry. Sensibility sustains a second vein of critique when it establishes a dialectical relation between feeling and anhedonia, as much as it purveys both sincere emotions and empty, artificial performances of feeling. As McGann declares, "Nothing is more characteristic of the poetry of sensibility than its dialectical relation to 'Indifference'" (50). Ildiko Csengei likewise describes those states of syncope, the fainting or hysterical fits so endemic to eighteenth-century novels, where female characters lose consciousness in protest against feeling too much without the agency to alter their circumstances. Christopher Stokes's notion of "ascesis" suggests that Smith intimates a troubled sense of self that involves dissolution and lack. He develops what Sarah Zimmerman calls "solitude that may lead to a loss of the self," drawing us toward fissures within already lost or incomplete subjectivities (Stokes 144).

These moments of dark excess, indifference, syncope, and ascesis approach sensibility from the point of view of the stable Enlightenment subject disrupted or temporarily lost. The flickering nature of sensations and impressions as well as blockages to their perception that undermine our ready ability to know our own emotions or those of others lead Nancy Yousef to claim, "Skepticism and sympathy are thus bound in a strangely complementary structure in eighteenth-century philosophical discourse" (7). Locke's epistemology certainly gestures toward those interruptions to consciousness, such as sleep, or the mind too slow or confused that it produces obscurity in its ideas—notions that Smith's "unthinking hind" and Robinson's depictions of idiocy certainly work from before attempting to think beyond. Antagonistic to Enlightenment forms of sensation and embodied selfhood, vacancy cannot be absorbed by terms such as psychoanalytic silences, swoons, repressions, abjections, and other subjective voids.[17] Vacancy seeks to replace sensibility (or the sentimental) with more than a negative form of affect, interiority, or subjectivity, as it ultimately proposes a tropic disintegration of the feeling, self-reflexive Romantic subject.[18] Accounts of lack and loss tend, once again, to return us to an analysis of subjectivity and feeling, even when feeling becomes a form of thought.[19]

Because the eighteenth- and nineteenth-century novel is generally concerned with forms of subjectivity, vacancy often doesn't quite manifest in prose. Instead, during moments of difficulty, such as Fanny Price's refuge in the lonely den of Portsmouth, the sensible subject pauses only to resume once again. The novel all too often constructed women as "consuming subjects," to use Elizabeth Kowaleski-Wallace's coinage, with bodies sensitive to all the sensations new commodity markets and shopping venues might furnish. To look beyond subjectivities real or performed, women poets needed to find a linguistic substrate that would not lead directly to bourgeois interiority, feeling bodies, and narratives of the gendered self.[20]

It would be easy to mistake the sublime, perhaps the most famous term identifying the cessation of feeling and thought, for vacancy. However, the Romantic sublime is only an initial and less successful technique to suspend Enlightenment thought. Vacancy does not so much marshal mental cessation as it waylays the sensation that could lead to empirical thought and emotion in order to plot other linguistic movements that might form an alternative basis of knowledge. The sublime, however, ultimately consolidates the Enlightenment subject, either through extreme sensory experience that enlivens the speaker or through rationality that can comprehend, if not apprehend, pleasurable moments of stunning infinitude. At first glance, vacancy might seem to be a version of Burke's aesthetic astonishment, which suspends all motions of the mind. According to Burke the sublime is "productive of the strongest emotion which the mind is capable of feeling" (36). Similarly, Alan Richardson's recent formulation of the neural sublime as the brain's "breakdown" and a "conceptual overload" eventually signals the mind's limits, acquiescing to the "acceptance of rather than wishful freedom from human material embodiment" (29, 31, 35). Feminist accounts of the sublime similarly tend to emphasize the sublime's experiential, ecstatic qualities, as Barbara Claire Freeman glosses it: "neither a rhetorical mode nor an aesthetic category but a domain of experience that resists categorization . . . that is excessive and unrepresentable" (2). By contrast, vacancy distances women poets from embodied experience—representable or not—as well as Burke's emotional surge. Even the accounts of the neural sublime and Romantic brain science similarly revolve around the constitution of the cognitive subject, although their investigation of cognitive activity could lead to other accounts of affect. Vacancy does not amount to "the strongest emotion" (Burke 36) within the human spectrum, nor does it embrace embodied sensation or material embodiment.

Neither does it duplicate Kantian versions of cognitive difficulty, which arguably invigorate the triumphal narrative of the rational human subject in the Romantic period. The third *Critique*'s sublime recuperates man's understanding and his subjectivity when he dynamically judges himself intellectually superior to a sublime object. As Sianne Ngai notes, the sublime plots the triumph of tranquility over fear, one emotion over another, and in doing so "'frees' the subject for other mental activities and thus finds an ally in reason" (269). Kant's critique of the transcendental subject can likewise account for defining vacancy in opposition to melancholy, as the period often invoked a hermetic, secretive form of rational contemplation.[21]

Poets actively elicit figures of sensory cessation as a pointed critique of the gendered body rather than being subject to it, and more importantly, these figures do not end in insensibility or an eternal dark night of skepticism but rather find other models to live on.

Accounts of sensibility that have, finally, broached something like affect do not theorize its potential to travel through both figuration and matter—nor in ways that pointedly exceed binary gender, as vacancy does. McGann's book underlines how sensibility "typically develops through the ethics of loss and suffering" (46), a loss or absence that leads not to abundant recompense but to what he only barely sketches as an epistemology of affect, energy, and passion. James Noggle similarly describes insensibility "not a state of affective lack but a positive process in which affects are added to, built up, or altered without itself being felt," a process that is pointedly "[n]ot theorized" by writers who depict it (125, 126). Both McGann and Noggle lead us to the precipice of affects not yet felt as emotions or feelings, what Brian Massumi calls the "intensity" of embodied movements and rests that occur before language or conscious perception. An important counterclaim comes from Rei Terada, who argues that even a lack of feeling, such as Kant's *apatheia*, dons its own mental sensation, felt through emotions, those physiological states captured through language. Vacancy synthesizes and alters both these views. It pointedly theorizes an *avant garde*, iterative turning of figuration, where rather than sensibility's periodic blackouts, writers find ways to enact and figure new material affects traveling both through and outside the brain, mind, subject, and body.

From Vacant Sensibility to Vacancy's Tropological Affects

Many Romantic poets used the word *vacancy*, often to explore minds and spaces merely emptied of sensation, emotion, and thought, or only to hint at a more nuanced version of the trope that more radically attempts to figure other affective movements. Romanticists have repeatedly been drawn to these moments of absence and the negative, without entirely recognizing their complex linguistic, ontological, and affective work. For instance, Mary Favret, following Kevis Goodman's reading of William Cowper's *The Task*, notes the mental vacuity that occurs in wartime during domestic doldrums.[22] These moments are then filled with conflicting hopes and fears, a welter of information, emotion, and sensation, however inchoate. Wordsworth adjusts this flatter notion of vacancy in "Lines Left upon a Seat in a Yew Tree" to intimate what soft movements might come to enter into such emptiness: "Yet, if the wind breathe soft, the curling waves, / That break against the shore, shall lull thy mind / By one soft impulse saved from vacancy" (5–7). For Wordsworth, the imagination always lurks to fill in these gaps with memories bearing sensation, as the daffodils do in "I wandered lonely as a cloud": "In vacant or in pensive mood / They flash upon that inward eye" (20–21). This thread, from Cowper to Wordsworth, although it evokes vacancy, still largely tracks sensation, and sensation's formulation of memory, whether in fullness or absence. Keats perhaps gets closer to vacancy with the mental voids in the odes, writing of "a drowsy numbness pains / My sense" that acts as an opiate in "Ode to a Nightingale" (1–2). Yet he repeatedly resolves, unlike Smith and Robinson, "No, no, go not to Lethe" (1). In Keats, the loss of consciousness parlays a different type of subjectivity, whether Psyche, Melancholy, or Hyperion's newly embodied states. Lord Byron and Mary Shelley's notions of "peopling vacancy" in *Manfred* and *Frankenstein* likewise recapitulate a feeling subject (however nihilistic) after such affective lack ensues, however doubled or heteroglossic their Byronic personae.

Percy Shelley begins to articulate vacancy's tropological movements when he pointedly uses the term in his late essay "On Life" (1819) to consider acts of linguistic creation that follow from necessary linguistic destruction:[23]

> Philosophy, impatient as it may be to build, has much work yet remaining as pioneer for the overgrowth of ages. It makes one step toward this object, however; it destroys error, and the roots of error. It leaves, what is too often the duty of the reformer in political and ethical questions to leave, a vacancy. It reduces the mind to that freedom in which it would have acted, but for the misuse of words and signs, the instruments of its own creation. (507)

Words and signs, hardened into cliché by their habituated use, must be razed by Philosophy, the pioneer. This impersonal allegory of a metaphorical ground clearing is initiated jointly by the nonhuman force of Philosophy and by human minds that apprehend and create it. Shelley only intimates here how language play might alter the materiality of subject and world in ways that become more complex within his poems.

Poets explicitly do not develop "vacancy" as an official aesthetic term, like the ones that Enlightenment thought sought to codify rigorously. Because the Enlightenment and empiricist philosophers so often atomized nature and philosophical language through distinctive definitions (e.g., the sublime and the beautiful, passion and reason), vacancy operates by lurking below the surface of discursive argumentation in disruptive tropes. Mary Robinson's "Caves of Ice," as a repetitive mimicry of Coleridge's phrase from "Kubla Khan" in her poem "To the Poet Coleridge," broaches this issue of labeling. Her paradise disrupts the causality of influence or terminology, and she constructs vacancy as something other than an empiricist void, vacuum, or empty space through which merely new sensations might flow:

> With thee I'll trace the circling bounds
> Of thy NEW PARADISE extended;
> And listen to the varying sounds
> Of winds, and foamy torrents blended. (5–9)

The poet's tracing of new spaces uncovers a form of movement that is only momentarily captured in a series of bodily boundaries or extensions—winds, torrents, and later fountains, including the poet herself in motion. In this stanza, which becomes a refrain throughout the poem, the poet is ever about to trace those motions that only temporarily solidify into bounds and sounds. The movements proliferate through fluctuations of speed, duration, and rhythm, and become so varied as to be both actual, aural sounds and virtual, nonsonic movements. Robinson repeatedly stacks paratactic descriptions of the scene: amplified by the refrain "'Mid forest gloom, shall slow meander," the moving matter speeds up as "foamy torrents," then becomes completely imaginary as "The mystic fountain, bubbling, panting" (10, 11). She accumulates quickly revolving tonal patterns within the line and through a supply of couplets with different, irregular rhymes. Together, they initiate the swift movements that cannot quite be captured by the language of sensation. The rapid shift from one description to the next eradicates any one reference or physical source (stream, fountain, wind, poetic voice) but evinces an underlying motion actuated by the series of metonymies and slant sounds. To "trace Imagination's boundless space" is to intimate a poetic space housing a plenitude of affect's movements always on the make beyond perception or even bodily movement (26). The poem evokes the "spirit divine" as something much more than the voice of Coleridge or Robinson, or the gendered poetics that his damsel or her nymph might reify, or even the echolalia of nature. Robinson's repetitions with difference trace affect's movements, real and virtual, within an ever-moving, ungendered "boundless space."

Vacancy uses language's peculiar figural movements to approach affect that occurs beyond or before bodily sensation. It therefore departs from

Romanticists who are still fairly dependent on two pieces of the empirical model when they describe affect: the reliance on somatic sensation, however amorphous, and the reliance on the dichotomy between sensation and reflection. In *War at a Distance*, Favret briefly interprets Hume's definition of passion as preceding perception, noting its similarity to Massumi's notion of affect. In this moment, she argues that affect "comprises a welter of unsorted feelings and sensations, often contradictory and contending" (80). Distinct from Hume's passion and Favret's affect, vacancy moves beyond physical sensation and arousal, which must be perceptible in some sense, however "unsorted." All of the poets of vacancy seek to reimagine sensation or move past it without veering directly into Kantian transcendence based on *a priori* concepts. As with Robinson's varying sounds that move between poet and scene as well as within the "mystical foundation," such affect, at times, figures a materiality moving imperceptibly among and between bodies; at others, it includes an incorporeal materiality—an abstraction of all the moves bodies, matter, or—for Romantic poets—figures might make.

Locke and Hume's empirical process, where knowledge is gained by turning sensations into reflections, has tended to influence Romanticist understandings of the similarly dialogic relation between affect and emotion. As sensation would be perceived and categorized into reflection, so affect's physiological movement is often thought to be translated into emotion, or perceptions of physiological states, then articulated through semantic categories such as anger, sadness, and happiness. *Romanticism and the Emotions* has most recently attempted to adjudicate this tension between affect and emotion.[24] Bringing these strands together, the introduction to the volume argues that "[e]motion bears the force of tropes and is in fact . . . constituted by them. Emotion tropes experience, just as language turns, directs, alters emotion, a transfer that is transferrential" (6). *Romanticism and the Emotions* negotiates the feedback loop between precognitive affect and emotion's linguistic expression by positing a transfer between the physiological or material force of affect and the linguistic expression of emotion (7). These dialogic processes retain traces of empiricism's movement from sensation to reflection, through a language of translation or transfer that retains a separation between materiality and figuration. Even Yousef, who describes her own aesthetic approach to affect as "a dynamic interplay that alternately defines and dissolves the conceptual boundaries between feeling and knowing," retains an attention to psychological and emotional structures, such as interest and withdrawal, that reify relations between human subjects, however intersubjective (17). Both studies emphasize language as the realm of emotion.

Romantic vacancy, by contrast, is concerned not with emotion so much as affect, those physiological, material, and figural movements through and beyond a variety of human and nonhuman bodies, including language, that arrive before semantic expression or sensation itself. Current theories of affect, such as Brian Massumi's "intensity," Jane Bennett's "impersonal affect" in *Vibrant Matter*, and the traveling rhythms, vibrations, hormones, and chemical matter in Teresa Brennan's *Transmission of Affect*, have helped to shape how I see Romantic-era affect as moving in the world regardless of human sensation and through multiple kinds of matter. Yet, unlike these theorists who are largely interested in the material world and view affect as occurring before language's translations, Romantic poets figure affect—and not emotion—as arising through language. Vacancy finds affective movements in aporia, refrains, synesthesia, caesura, and repetitive tropic substitution that evince linguistic movement without solidifying into emotions such as love, fear, or even the sensory perception of agitation. This study aims to open up the relationship between affect and language, not as a series of transfers but as one in the same movement—the affect that resides in language's figural play and its dynamic material motions.

Vacancy's mechanics of language, what Paul de Man would call language's automaticity and its materiality, evokes language's affects and asks us to reconsider these two in tandem with much more precision and granularity than de Man's notoriously difficult and nebulous notion of materiality. If some Romanticists regularly read Shelley's final lines of "Mont Blanc" as hinging on the de Manian, deconstructive idea of linguistic impossibility that makes inaccessible the real universe of things that flow through the mind, vacancy's tropic turning at once empties our usual perceptions of things and makes a space for the affects of both the mountain's ecology and the mind. As I develop below, vacancy takes up the nascent posthumanism and materiality inherent in de Man, better describing it as affect that occurs within both the nonhuman aspects of language as well as the sinuous, real materialities of the world that transgress bodies, things, and figures. Figures of vacancy turn from the material-figurative, gendered, and human-posthuman binaries inherent to both deconstruction and new materialism to imagine a mutating form of affect that is at once the trace, the entanglement, and the movement of all of these.

One of the most important consequences of such materiality occurs when poets of vacancy move beyond and underneath gender categories, as they are created through both the sensing body and the reflecting mind. Vacancy is akin to affect without binary gender, or aside from gender tied to the binary sexed body, in women and men writers. Although most similar to David Collings's notion of "primary affect" as the ground of figuration and being, vacancy is not, as Collings's account suggests, predicated on the loss of the mother—a psychoanalytic lack that could serve to reify gender difference.[25] Distanced from sexed bodies and minds, vacancy becomes a form of nonbinary difference that produces and multiplies other differences, which are themselves fluid and liable to change. Vacancy offers a clear pattern of figural responses to sensibility's gendered emotional terrain, revealing how Romantic poets sought a way out of emotion's cagey and gendered ideological categories. Romantic vacancy offers an affect that is not interpretive, as Terada suggests "nonsubjective" emotion is, but rather dwells in suspended possibilities that lie without gender or interpretation—though not completely without meaning either.

"Come and behold the nothingness of all": Athwart the Vacancy of Romantic Methodology

While vacancy resides in poetry, its figuration necessitates certain methodologies, in particular a turn away from new historicism, so dominant in studies of Romantic-era writers, which can take for granted ideas about gender and impose them onto women and their poetry. Vacancy elicits forms of literary history that distort the empirical past to imagine new futures for women and other poets. To envision these more complex historical vistas, poets' late verse often enlarges its vehicles of vacancy to depict hollowed-out landscapes, which extend vacancy's disruptions of the individual body and the subject to the national and imperial grounds that constitute history. Turning from the problems of the empirical body, these poems broach the problems of empiricist history, so that history, rather than based on facts, anecdotes of lived experience, and linear causality, is provisionally tendered as one of many spaces auguring speculative relations. Smith's stark cliffs of Beachy Head—what she calls the "vast concussion"—Robinson's "Caves of Ice," Hemans's New World forest sanctuary, and Jewsbury's oceanic drift all suggest a hulling out or unsettling of English historicist narratives through the contemplation of shifting national borders, transatlantic realms, and the worlds beyond the European theatre.

When Smith contemplates Beachy Head as a pastoral prospect and as a continental divide, for example, she figures its history as anything but a sedimented past revealing a linear or teleological series of changes from then to now. Instead, she examines the layers of a cliff that have repeatedly erased the visible, unmistakable history forming England's coast:

> Hither, Ambition, come!
> Come and behold the nothingness of all
> For which you carry thro' the oppressed Earth,
> War, and its train of horrors—see where tread
> The innumerous hoofs of flocks above the works
> By which the warrior sought to register
> His glory, and immortalize his name—(419–425)

The treads of "innumerous hoofs" signify the many invaders—Danes, Normans, Romans—and their chattel who have made their mark on England's shores, yet even these stamps of imperial power are laid to waste by the cliff-side erosion that buries them as fossils of another time. Smith, however, does not unpack this history linearly by moving through the layered sediments chronologically, but mentions the invaders out of sequence, veering toward a cyclical or recursive notion of historicity. Among the important implications for Smith's model of vacancy, history becomes incommensurate with determinate material, empirical events, or evidence that might posit clear, sequential cause and effect.

Part of what exacerbates this effect is Smith's tinge of personification in the imperative, "Hither, Ambition, come!" As I have argued elsewhere, Smith's anthropomorphism of Ambition develops a technique both she and Robinson use in their sonnets—a tendency to create a posthuman force that entangles the imperial human agency treading the Downs with the tectonic and local movements of landscape and climate.[26] This posthuman agentialism masses a shared affect not simply through human emotion, the teleologies of human power, or the landscape's own contingent motions and rests. Rather, the ambition is for the entwinement of all of these motives into figural movements that become more than the sum of their parts and more than the accounting of their histories.

Such antagonism to empiricism has important consequences for what methodologies vacancy necessitates—as well as how vacancy might alter Romanticist uses of new historicism, deconstruction, and new materiality to read literary texts. Vacancy offers an important model to help Romanticists grapple with the cold war between theorists and new historicists still very much plaguing Romantic studies, especially as it relates to gender, by offering us the ability to question and then to construct alternate literary histories. While poets may attend to the historical, philosophical interplay that surrounds them, their broader, Romantic desire to move past the limiting philosophies of the day means that we cannot thoroughly explain vacancy by the historical understanding of sensibility and empiricism that has most often investigated questions of gender or revolutionary feminism. Seeking to find the contexts that then shape women's thoughts about their bodies, such historical materialism often begins with observations about the physical and social limitations to women's writing and their education, bound by the very empiricist epistemologies that vacancy challenges. *Romantic Vacancy*, therefore, does not retrospectively recover women, or their concrete erudition, to bring them into historical proximity with their philosophical fellow travelers. Instead, it teases out engagement with larger questions surrounding the gendered forms of knowledge that have been, and still are, a major preoccupation of speculative thought.

Romantic Vacancy allows history, for women and for Romanticism, to become once again a figure, putting into motion not empirical cause and effect but weirder kinds of time: counterfactual histories, a fierce suspension in an ever-changing present, and fantastic futures-to-come. Rather than the French Revolution's event of rupture or the recurrence of wartime losses that return a series of presences, vacancy poses repeated disturbances, a series of ruptures, and reverberations of revolution.[27] Language's disruptions, ever at the ready, leverage Romanticism's affective temporalities to unman the past, its contexts, its causal chains of cultural, bodily, and ideological expectation. Rather than manifesting only the negative affects of trauma, paranoia, or melancholy—Thomas Pfau's histories of shock, anxiety, and disappointment in the period—these Romantic poets turn to affect as the site of a past already tense with indeterminacy and potentiality, which has the virtue of upending presentist constraints and imagining seemingly impossible salubrious futures. Hemans's Spaniard, freed from the shackles of imperial militarism and its ideological aims, resides in the New World before rampant Western settlement has happened, thus offering a retroactive futurity unmoored from European colonial history. Jewsbury's anticipation of arrival in India in *The Oceanides* is similarly figured as an infant whose vacancy of history suggests a purposeful blindness to ideological ways of seeing the other, a futurity that consists of denuding the visual bias so potent in colonial contexts.

Vacancy, like deconstruction, undermines ideological categories and, at the same time, like new materialism, circulates a type of materiality without gendered embodiment. This book's methodology examines figural play to show how deconstructive language thwarts historicist, static notions of materiality—strict subjects and objects that function as discrete units within a regime of clear causal and bodily expectation. Following Terada's exploration of poststructuralist emotion, this study examines how poststructuralist theories about the instabilities of language can even more radically construct dispersed and self-altering forms of affect, which move at once materially and figurally. Disruptive, rampant figuration is a powerful ally for women seeking to undermine the supposedly stable epistemology of empirical sensation.[28] Despite vacancy's seeming proximity to de Man's automaticity of language as "a-referential, a-phenomenal, a-pathetic" (*Aesthetic Ideology* 128) and his notion of materiality discussed above, Romantic vacancy traces another sort of "materiality" within language. Here the figural finds its counterpart in affect studies and new materialism when it seeks to chart the dynamism of certain forms of matter as one and the same movement as language. Matter becomes materiality when it is, unlike de Man's, both real and incorporeal yet is untethered to a stable reference. Tropology and dynamic materiality are co-conspirators within the turning of figures, and together they intimate an affect based on movement itself.

Among the numerous, recent attempts to articulate de Man's notoriously elliptical notion of materiality, it is Derrida's reading that perhaps comes closest to vacancy's alternative account of language's interplay with affect and materiality. In "Typewriter Ribbon: Limited Ink (2) ('within such limits')," Derrida describes a materiality without matter as a "force of resistance" that conjoins language and materiality without resorting to the immediacy of bodies and letters.[29] He opens up materiality here in ways that, perhaps unrecognized by him, lead the way toward affect: "This force of resistance without material substance derives from the dissociative, dismembering, fracturing, disarticulating, and even dissociative power that de Man attributes to the letter. To a letter whose dissociative and inorganic, disorganizing, disarticulating force *affects* not only nature but the body itself—as organic and organized totality" (351; my emphasis). Derrida turns de Man's materiality, notoriously defined in the negative, into a disruptive force. Poets of vacancy, however, show us how we might understand this force as the unrecognized affective movements within Derrida's inscription. Not simply demonstrating the disruptive powers of the "letter," they furnish a means to conceive of constructive—not simply resistant—uses of the figural; rather than leveraging deconstruction's view of language's force to fracture, disrupt, or break down both meaning and knowledge, vacancy figures language on the move, on the make, roving in ever-new iterations. This agential movement of figuration's alleged gaps and blanks propels the turns of affect into making productive experiments in language, materiality, and difference to compose real, consequential, and ever-new forms of relationality.

In fact we can even read Derrida's own language, his surplus of creative writing, as such a material force that enacts the impossibly hopeful and promissory qualities of linguistic play. The colliding references, the repetitions, word play, paradoxes, and rhythms that defy patterning all evince those movements arising both from the nonhuman nature of language and from the struggling, if erstwhile, agencies of the poet. Derrida intimates what vacancy comes to write—a linguistic activity that plays outside the human by disrupting, energizing, and moving the material world. As Pheng Cheah argues in *New Materialisms*, Derrida's materiality might be understand as materiality without matter, a dynamism that does not leave matter behind. Karen Barad, in her essay on Derrida, similarly suggests how his writing invokes ghostly discontinuities and indeterminacies that might be surprisingly more material than we think, what she calls "ontological hauntological indeterminacy" (251)—and what might be more haunting, slippery, yet real than affect?[30] Figures of vacancy consider the ways that matter and language together offer dynamic movements among humans and the world around them. It enjoins de Manian materiality with a dynamic materiality of matter along the lines Barad suggests; only a combined discursive-material theoretical vantage can explain vacancy, as a tropology with material implications. In doing so, Romantic vacancy allows us to explore in more depth the posthuman, porous relations between material and language in ways that open up accounts of the power of Romantic language to alter ontologies, and to posit posthuman affect as the nebulous force of Revolutionary change.[31] The poetics of vacancy demonstrates poets' bold and spirited attempt to rethink how supposedly definitive new historicist Romantic contexts may be like Smith's cliffs—stark and powerful landmarks but also, particularly in the poet's hands, a dynamic materiality always slipping into the tide of a world remade by lyric breaks, interruptions, stutters, and paradoxes.

Tracing the Bounds of Vacancy

Although the chapters in this book proceed in a rough chronological order, and although claims can be made for a modicum of direct influence in some cases, these chapters are arranged based on a set of strategies to obviate the epistemological problems with embodied sensation, arising from sensibility's complicated genesis in empiricist philosophy, medical science, and literary discourse.[32] Smith questions eighteenth-century culture's addiction to luxury commodities and their sensory overstimulation; Robinson diagnoses sensibility's tendency to become monologic and monomaniacal; Wordsworth and Shelley worry over the contagious nature of sensibility; Hemans depicts sensibility's paralysis of body, mind, and will; and Jewsbury, finally, portrays sensibility's ability to haunt the body even when removed from its physical stimulus. Their poetic responses to those problems likewise differ. Whereas Smith looks to vacancy as an abstraction of affect's ur-movements of absorption and receptivity, Robinson alternatively seeks forms of intensity that resemble sensation but that move outside the body, only perceptible in their change from one sensory register to the next. Wordsworth and Shelley attempt to find a transmission of affect among bodies without overwhelming them, while Hemans and Jewsbury in different ways combine these concerns to think about affective histories that move beyond both body and nation into the global, post-Napoleonic world.

Although this study wants to theorize gender rather than simply "women's writing," it necessarily includes more women writers because they were most invested in such a project. Wordsworth and Shelley, perhaps due to their closer proximity to a number of important women writers, also devote considerable lines to critique the effects of gender on speculative thinking, feeling, and expression. Other male writers also responded to sensibility's problems in ways that have rarely been synthesized yet do not quite reach the pervasive, posthuman pitch of vacancy's affective registers. Samuel Taylor Coleridge, William Blake, Lord Byron, John Keats, and various women writers offer different alternatives to sensibility, or they sketch figures that hint at vacancy but to a lesser degree.

Coleridge seeks those breathy intimations that "Fill up the interspersed vacancies / And momentary pauses of thought" (46–47). Similarly, "The Eolian Harp" might seem to offer a new materiality when McGann describes it as "a non-conscious tool for revealing the vital correspondences that pour through the material world" (21).[33] This sense of nature, however, quickly gives way to Coleridge's rejection of materialism for a transcendental philosophy underwritten by German philosophy and Christianity. Blake's self-annihilation and energy transcend the boundaries of the individual, yet such dynamics still emanate from within the body. Steven Goldsmith describes Blake's version of affect as "the whole realm of dynamic transformation (across geographical, physiological, and mental spaces) made possible by embodied parts set in motion" (33). Blake's notorious attachment to what Tristanne Connolly terms his favorite image of the gendered body limits the gendered critique that might turn embodied sensibility into a more dispersed, material affect beyond the sexed body.[34] Keats perhaps unsurprisingly comes closest to vacancy's play with sensory depletion due to his storied depictions of sensory pleasure and gender ambiguity.[35] Early feminist scholars characterized negative capability as a feminine voiding of the self and, more recently, Jacques Khalip has described it as an ungendered, anonymous, clouded mysterium.[36] However self-voiding Keats's selves, they still rely on both sensation, however virtual, and embodiment, however shifting.[37] The Byronic hero's apathy oppositely anchors the masculine subject through an apotheosis of the vacant mind. Childe Harold's ennui reverberates with a pleasure taken in the vacant stasis that, for writers such as Robinson and Shelley, would oppose vacancy's proactive creation of new forms of affect.[38] The Byronic avatar's wandering charts a running escape from Manfred's insufferable woe into Don Juan's heteroglossic burlesque of emotions.

Much like Byron, Letitia Landon depicts the belated sentimental women whose glut of experience has rendered her vacant, or at a loss. Her incessant replay of the tragic romances of the lovelorn ironizes emotion without much recourse to affect because of the way emotion places women in structural positions of inequality. There is good reason for many women writers to continue to represent the political, economic, and emotional injustices of the female subject legally and ideologically harnessed to the Enlightenment yoke of submission. Similarly, both Landon and Mary Tighe, as preoccupied as they are with the contours of feminine desire, wrap their poetry within myth and romance to grapple with commodity culture's unending production of sensations and desires.[39] While it cannot be underestimated how much Mary Wollstonecraft influenced Robinson, Shelley, and Jewsbury, her attention was more consistently oriented toward the realities of the feminine subject imprisoned by social custom, English law, and political discourse. *The Vindication* largely critiques sensibility's excesses, and though there are passages in the *Letters*, particularly when describing the landscape, that hint at affect that touches the nonhuman trees and costal tides, the book's project largely explores permutations of the sentimental, national subject.[40]

Initial taxonomies of vacancy posed by Smith and Robinson in the 1790s set in motion later figures of vacancy by Shelley, Hemans, and Jewsbury. Smith and Robinson both work through eighteenth-century Enlightenment figures of oblivion, and then arrive at alternative and divergent models of speculation that unhand bodily sensation—Smith's, which works through abstraction of the empirical, and Robinson's, which delves into sensation outside the body. Both deal with two seemingly intransigent discourses from empiricism—taste and custom—but Smith's work also helps to explain, at the outset of this study, why Kantian reason is not a helpful alternative model for women. Moreover, because she constructs vacancy with linguistic aporia, she clearly articulates the difference between sensibility and vacancy, and her radical use of language's nonsignifying turns in relation to affect sets the stage for the other writers' figural experiments to come. While Smith's poetry, particularly her *Elegiac Sonnets* (1784–1797), is still seen to be the vanguard of high sensibility, it repeatedly voices a taste for sleep, oblivion, and nepenthe that would irrevocably block the tempests of sensibility and sensation. Chapter 1 explores how Smith's speakers repeatedly long to taste oblivion, an impossibility that critiques bourgeois, empiricist ideas of taste tied to sensibility's roots in embodied sensation. This aporetic act of ingestion excoriates knowledge gleaned from sensory perception and, in the wake of feeling, suggests an alternative to Derrida's Kantian conceptual free play of beauty. Vacancy's movement of absorption without its empirical materials enables a play of affects among poet, figure, and world. Smith's long poem "Beachy Head" (1807), beginning as it does with the "vast concussion" of England's coast, extends the possibilities of aporia to larger questions of imperial acquisitiveness. With the figure of a hermit whose imperative is to save all mariners lost at sea, Smith figures a form of acceptance, which unlike Derrida's unconditional hospitality that combats the strictures of law's abstractions, staves off the creep of the empirical through abstracted motions that cross the boundaries of human and nonhuman.

Mary Robinson likewise employs the trope of oblivion in early poems, but rather than a proto-Kantian critique, she attempts to find a more radical form of empirical sensation that is resolutely material yet unconfined to the body. Such a poetic experiment moves from Smith's repeated constructions of aporetic impossibility to vacancy's generation of *euporia*, a plethora of movements, relations, and affects. Chapter 2 examines an essential and important model for vacancy, the mind deprived of those habituated sensations and reflections that form the proving grounds of Locke and Hume. Robinson's sonnet sequence *Sappho & Phaon* (1796) diagnoses Sappho's problem with "tyrant passion" to be the sonnet of sensibility, which can offer only poetic mimicry dumb to anything but decades-old emotional and intellectual custom. The sole solution to such idiocy becomes Sappho's leap into the Leucadian deep. By the end of her career, however, Robinson turns to the ballad's repetitive articulacy to find repetition with differences, or another form of sensation, those Deleuzean intensities and rhythms beyond or before sensory perception. Through the ballad's refrain and its tendency to proliferate textual variants, this popular poetic form transforms empty repetition into chromatic, minute variations, which come to figure a flexible materiality through human and nonhuman worlds instigated by the turning of tropes and refrains.

Wordsworth, who serves as an important interlocutor for both Smith and Robinson, reciprocally considers the pressures of feminine sensibility on poetic expression. Acknowledging the propensity for sensibility to overwhelm the body, empty the mind, and infect others with stultifying force, the poet of the "Mad Mother" and "The Solitary Reaper" eventually turns to a more anodyne model for feeling chastened by Burkean custom, domestic regulation of sentiment, and metrical restraint. Chapter 3 explores how Wordsworth's singing women anticipate Shelley's own exploration of sensibility's tendency to spread like a disease from one embodied subject to another. The veiled maid of "Alastor" figures the fast and overwhelming transfer of contagious feeling, suggesting that what was thought to be revolutionary in the 1790s really only made men's and women's minds feverish, finally burning out into the emptiness of the poet's vacant brain. In response, Shelley exchanges "silence and solitude" for "vacancy," a trope that unearths the slower, more variegated human and nonhuman materialities shared by mind and world in Mont Blanc's affective, vibrant ecology that "flows through all things." Rewriting what we have come to see as a skeptical power, Shelley's vacancy does not so much denude thought through an iterative, deconstructive poetics, but rather, its material, dynamic ebbs and flows posit a nebulous new materiality moving in and among bodies, well beyond the empiricist, idealist, and medical discourses of his time.

Sensibility's contagion provides the basis for Hemans and Jewsbury to take the affective politics of nation and gender more resolutely into the realm of the transnational and colonial. Hemans reconsiders and combines Smith's more transcendental-leaning abstraction and Robinson's depictions of empirical overwhelm when she describes hysteria as the moment when idealist and empirical mindsets clash and eventuate in brain ruination. By interpreting "The Widow of Crescentius" (1819) and *The Forest Sanctuary* (1825) through contemporaneous brain science as well as continental theories of consciousness, the chapter views moments of hysteria as cognitive paralysis stemming from the consciousness overloading with perceptual data, which in turn shatters long-held concepts or beliefs—including sensibility's supposed hold over the feminine psyche. Intervening in cognitive models solely limited to the perceiving mind, Hemans formulates cognitive events as indeterminate, speculative, and continuously circulating between mind and world. Less interested than cognitivists in how emotions become codified, she delineates how to suspend sentimental categories to elude the re-imposition of ideological, nationalistic imaginaries, or emotions. In the *Forest Sanctuary*, the Spaniard's journey from Old World to New before it had been entirely colonized unleashes perceptual data about the sixteenth-century that has not yet been consolidated into imperial narratives. Hemans thus activates retroactive, counterfactual histories of the Americas before the Spanish and English occupations had done their worst.

Jewsbury ends the book because she ties together many of the different ways of composing vacancy's new forms of speculative affect. She inverts Smith's model of abstracted absorption into a form of cinematic projection while taking into account Robinson's sensation and the problems of monologic nostalgia, Wordsworth's and Shelley's problems with affective contagion, and Hemans's troubling of sentimental settler colonialism. Jewsbury's ambitious poetic sequence *The Oceanides* (1832–1833), written while traveling from England to India, concocts moving images, including phantasmagoric double visions of cocoa trees and images of "infants everywhere" along the screens of sky and sea. Jewsbury transforms the logic of exchange and the phantasmic nature of commodity into a proactive, incessant turning of tropes themselves, a rampant unresting motion. She employs the language of phantoms to speak to the sentimental nostalgia haunting the gaze of the British imperial subject, offering instead a figure of kinesis, a future of unending iteration of trope, affect, and materiality.

Of course, vacancy has dangers all its own, particularly the possibility of emptying the mind only to paralyze it permanently or to refill it with imperfect ideologies. Nevertheless, this study aims to show that these dangers are worth the risk. Romantic poets attempted important speculative work through remarkable play with poetics and affect beyond the guise of embodied, sentimental, empiricist epistemologies. *Romantic Vacancy* uncovers a range of women's individual contemplations about theories of knowledge in serious conversation with poetic and philosophical peers. All the while they attended to concerns of early cosmopolitan, transnational, and imperial politics as well as to the tensions between transcendental critique and understandings of materiality beyond subjectivity, embodied sensation, or lived experience. Romantic poetry read through the trope of vacancy shows us other ways to think about history and the body without completely obviating material concerns. Vacancy provides a necessary vantage for seeing the critique of gender through intense play with figuration that enables these writers to get out from under the requisites of empirical sensation that overcharged their bodies and to imagine language and reality well beyond what might have seemed possible. In turn, this poetic freedom opens the Romantic doors of perception to a repressed speculative poetic history that underwrites Romanticism's own figurations of itself, and more importantly, the material affective possibilities that might continue to change poetry and politics, if not the relations between mind and world.

CHAPTER 1

Charlotte Smith and the Taste of Aporia

Again and again, the speakers in Charlotte Smith's poems find themselves poised on the brink of the South Downs, seemingly saturated with sensibility as the Channel winds and waters rave below them. In her well-known sonnet "Written in the Churchyard at Middleton in Sussex," for example, the speaker in turmoil begins to envy the bones of the dead lying uncovered in a seaside graveyard:

> Lo! their bones whiten in the frequent waves;
> But vain to them the winds and waters rave;
> *They* hear the warring elements no more;
> While I am doom'd—by life's long storm opprest,
> To gaze with envy on their gloomy rest. (44.10–14)

Smith's speaker imagines the possibility of becoming deaf to the warring elements and blind to the restless waves when she compares herself to the whitening, quiescent bones—who can "hear the warring elements no more." Though the frequent, roaring waves recall the speaker's stormy life and the responsiveness of her body and voice, the white bones leached of nerves, flesh, and even color have shirked the female body and its physiological sensation. Metonymic of the gigantic white cliffs featured in both the *Elegiac Sonnets* and "Beachy Head," the bones figure an absolute absence of the sensation and sensory knowledge at the heart of empiricist reason, feeling, and embodiment. The speaker again returns to remember her own embodied oppression by "life's long storm" and seems to seal her doomed fate. Yet in the final line, the sonnet moves past either her sensibility or its longed-for absence, and turns to another figural motion, the act of gazing "on their gloomy rest," on the chiaroscuro of the bones, both still and in motion. Here the bones substitute human physiological sensation, or the sensory perception of the bones, for a movement that appears untenable to humans—movement amid rest, motion despite death.

As the sounds of raving waters fade and finally vanish, what Smith's speaker repeatedly longs for is more than a release from sensibility's excessive stimulation; she looks to her own poetic act of gazing to release her from the entire economy of sensibility's excessive feeling and its absence figured by the bones. Rather than the speaker attempting to gain solace by imaginatively mimicking the bones and becoming apathetic, the speaker gazes "on their gloomy rest," taking in this form of absence. To gaze on the whitening bones is to view a thing fading from sight; to look on their "gloomy rest" is paradoxically to watch rest, stillness, and the disappearance of their materiality. If the act of gazing in the prospect poem is a quintessential Romantic trope of internalization and even visual consumption that forms the feeling self, then what Smith traces in the final turn of the sonnet is the internalization of almost nothing. In tracing bone's gloomy rest, like the repeated turn in the *Sonnets* to drinking the cup of Lethe, the speaker attempts, impossibly, to ingest a well-known figure, which now no longer bolsters the self and its consuming sensations but marks another figural movement altogether.

Through this complicated figural gesture, Smith composes her version of vacancy: an impossible aesthetic act, a movement of absorbing something that eviscerates bodily sense. This catachresis sets in motion the mind as it moves repeatedly through a figuration that makes no rational or emotive sense. The human mind does not simply contemplate language's aporia but becomes part of a joint, ongoing figural movement, the motion of light on the bones, one that is not entirely human. These iterative acts of impossible consumption concoct something akin to affect: movements and rests not enacted by bodily sensation or perception but initiated through figuration's paradoxes. More than an encounter with a sublime landscape or even a critique of sensibility, vacancy moves beyond empirical sensation to seek shared tropic movements through (and past) bodies and the landscapes. Rather than simply discovering a new figure for disruption or belated coherence, vacancy slips the knot of that binary altogether by moving through and then beyond those categories.

Smith's *Elegiac Sonnets* in part gained their claim to contemporary fame as a landmark poetics of complaint that voices feminine self-expression and self-representation. Dozens of sonnets were said to repeat and amplify the excruciating sensations of women's woes, even when they threaten melancholy, hysteria, addiction, lunacy, and suicide.[1] Indeed, Erinç Özdemir highlights the "intrinsic negativity of the sentimental" in Smith's *Sonnets*, a negativity that leads to a sublime transcendence from the social world (466–467).[2] While Smith scholarship has clearly not ignored this painful, dark side of emotional and physical sensitivity, it has most often worked through Enlightenment categories of intense feeling and sensation on the one hand and transcendence on the other. Vacancy's figurative movements, however, require another critical vocabulary to describe something more significant than Stuart Curran's passing reference to "the void at the center of sensibility" (205) and something other than what Adela Pinch in *Strange Fits of Passion* calls "a kind of unconsciousness" (60).[3] When we examine Smith's figural practices, we can begin to see an affective, philosophical project that parts ways with the empirical subject feminized by her emotive sensitivities and tastes.[4] Instead, Smith's movements become closer to what Jane Bennett in vibrant matter describes as Spinozist impersonal affect, "which refers broadly to the capacity of any body for activity and responsiveness" (xii). Such an affect coincides and flows through moving materiality itself—human bodies, the landscape, and for Smith, poetry's formal and figural turns.

This chapter looks at the works that bookend Smith's career—her great commercial success *Elegiac Sonnets* (1784–1797) and her final, posthumously published "Beachy Head" (1807). In the *Sonnets* she devises vacancy through impossible acts of consumption that vitiate the bourgeois discourse of taste—a mainstay of empiricism and its gendering of women as consuming, feeling subjects. She begins by drawing upon John Locke's and David Hume's use of sleep, forgetting, and other bouts of unconsciousness to belay the sensory perception that forms the basis of taste. She eventually finds figures that move past these types of oblivion that still rely on sensory perception and on the imagination's ability to cohere accounts of self and world. The moments of impossible consumption Smith comes to, where the speaker takes in the whitened bones, have striking affinities with Immanuel Kant's own critique of empiricism and subjective taste through the free play of beauty offered in his *Critique of Judgment* (1790). Smith, however, resists the triumph of the rational, contemplating mind, or the coherent subject, and, rather than Kant's intellectual impasse and play with paradoxical concepts, Smith looks to create new forms of affect with repeated figural movements that thread together mind, body, and world.

Expanding the problems with the individual to the national body, "Beachy Head" rebuffs the larger courses of the sensory world—the pastoral landscape, the luxuries of market culture, and the larger imperialist narratives that mark the borderlands of the South Downs—in favor of a hermit who receives all aliens ashore, alive or dead. Like the impossibility inherent in consumption without taste, the hermit becomes a figure for impossible receptivity, limning but diverging from Kant's versions of cosmopolitan hospitality. For it is the cliff face that offers acceptance to the hermit and his mariners at the very moment when all their national identifications and indeed a portion of their humanity becomes washed away, as they become part of the coast's figural ecology.

Smith therefore begins this study because her resistances to empiricism and idealism eventually light upon affect to chart new directions in epistemology beyond the feeling, thinking subject. Concomitantly, she redraws Romanticism's long history of reading through deconstructive notions of aporia, as rational impossibility, when she offers vacancy as a technique of writing and reading that impossibly intertwines affect and language, the material and the figural. Intricately involved in the period's speculative discussions of epistemology, Smith reshapes the history of absence and affect—and not merely the history of emotional loss. Such affect unbinds itself from taste and empire to move between human bodies and nonhuman land, bones, and figures of oblivion, donning figures with material heft that transgress the limits of the human mind, the subject, and its empirical histories.

Elegiac Sonnets and the Impossibility of Taste

Most accounts of Smith's wildly successful commercial venture agree that the *Elegiac Sonnets* sold the language of sensibility for some sorely needed cash. A destitute mother of numerous children, whose husband had recently been thrown in debtor's prison, Smith marketed the autobiographical sonnets hoping that chivalrous customers would pay to help end her tales of woe. The volume seemingly became a call for feeling readers to extend the bourgeois values of kindness, sympathy, and real-world charity to those in pitiable personal and political straits.[5] The *Sonnets* now stand as a representative work of female subjectivity at the heart of Romantic and sentimental poetry. As a collection, repackaged and edited from 1784 to 1797, the poems have often been viewed as representations of late eighteenth-century actual, if embattled, female experience, whether Jacqueline Labbe's playful, performative femininity, Christopher Stokes's "incomplete, alienated, fragmented, de- or unconstituted" subject (144), or Samuel Rowe's negative turn into "subjectivity as an unarticulated space" (par. 1). Looking closely at the way Smith links the discourses of sensation and taste in these poems, however, reveals that she questions the very grounds on which such a subject is constituted—the empirical means through which the speaker, by way of sensation, comes to both emotions and aesthetic tastes.

Through the numerous sonnets that make up a continually expanding volume, the speaker recursively longs for the pastoral retreats of her childhood, as she describes them, those "scenes could charm that now I taste no more!" (31.14). More than nostalgia for rural comfort or for a pastoral relief that might reconstitute the feminine subject, these sonnets link the degraded position of women to debates about taste and aesthetics at the end of the eighteenth century. At a time when writers like William Cowper and, later, William Wordsworth capitalized on rejecting urban luxury and consumer culture for the rural beauties of nature, Smith likewise contemplates attitudes toward consumption, sensory experience, and judgments of beauty. She redresses those philosophical concepts and their consequences as they fix women's embodied position in British culture. Rather than representing women as good consuming subjects forming proper bourgeois taste, as many subsequent women novelists did, Smith's speakers never easily consume tasteful pastorals. Their difficulty advances an acute critique of fashionable, evanescent pleasures (akin to Wordsworth's "gross and violent stimulants" from the *Preface* to *Lyrical Ballads*) that both form and restrict the feminine body in all its metonymic associations with nature. Their articulations of the trope of inconsumable consumption push us, at the very start of the Romantic period, toward models for affect and knowledge based in figuration, well beyond a subject whose sensations sentimentalize and gender her.

In the first edition, references to "taste" begin with sonnet 11, "To Sleep," which is situated amid other sonnets that reject sensation and memory for a kind of numbness. In later poems, including sonnets 19, 31, 54, 60, 62, and 73, "taste" appears more frequently, a repetition that may suggest Smith's savvy editorial practices, as well as her intensifying philosophical speculations. The original 1784 volume went through at least nine different editions during her lifetime, and in the process she added a large number of sonnets, eventually including an entire second volume in 1797. The Preface to her first and second volumes straightforwardly addresses such readers of sensibility and taste: "I can hope for readers only among the few, who, to sensibility of heart, join simplicity of taste" (Curran 3).[6] The Preface to the second volume, however, complicates Smith's relations to taste, and by 1797, she must strenuously defend herself against charges of "*feigning* sorrow" and those critics who have, or who would accuse her of having, "theatrical taste" (Curran 11). Rather than assuming that Smith's sonnets mechanistically or neurotically repeat the conventional woes of sensibility, however, we can track the ways the poet-editor repeatedly reframes poems that call for an eradication of sensation through an increasingly sophisticated aesthetic project revolving around the rejection of empiricist taste. Because empiricist thinkers such as Hume explicitly tied together notions of taste, sensibility, luxury, and consumerism, Smith's critique of taste and sensibility leads the way to aesthetic judgments that release women from the demands of experiential knowledge, consumer sensation, excessive feeling, and feminine embodiment.

Smith intimates a tension between embodied taste and nonembodied aesthetics even in early sonnets that do not cite "taste" but rather imagine the act of drinking a cup of Lethe. In sonnet five, "To the South Downs," for example, the speaker implores the pastoral countryside for a healing drink to act as a sedative for sensibility's throbbing pains:

> Ah! hills belov'd—where once a happy child,
> Your beechen shades, "your turf, your flowers among,"
> I wove your blue-bells into garlands wild,
> And woke your echoes with my artless song.
> Ah! hills belov'd—your turf your flowers remain;
> But can they peace to this sad breast restore;
> For one poor moment soothe the sense of pain,
> And teach a breaking heart to throb no more?
> And you, Aruna!—in the vale below,
> As to the sea your limpid waves you bear,
> Can you one kind Lethean cup bestow,
> To drink a long oblivion to my care?
> Ah! no!—when all, e'en Hope's last ray is gone,
> There's no oblivion—but in death alone! (5.1–14)

Tutored as Romanticists are within a Wordsworthian framework that itself contemplates the efficacy of returning sensations to recompose a care-worn sense of self ("Tintern Abbey"'s "the picture of the mind revives again," for instance), we might be apt to read Smith's sonnet in those terms, that old sensations revivified by "hills belov'd" either can or cannot work to stop the pain that fractures the self. Yet, Smith's figuration of impossible taste—the cup of Lethe that cannot be drunk—rejects the entire apparatus through which we enter into sensation in the first place.

Since the South Downs represent Smith's childhood home and aristocratic upbringing, her memories of this place should soothe and comfort her now, stuck as she is in a troubled marriage with the son of a West Indies planter and merchant, writing sonnets by his side in debtor's prison. Smith's visions of her childhood, Edenic pastoral should offer visual memories replete with familiar, sensible qualities, what Locke describes as "the ability in the mind, when it will, to revive them again; and as it were paint them anew on itself" (II.x.148). Indeed, the first five lines of the poem attempt to do just that with their address to flowers and wild garlands, sensory recollections that might enable the mind to reenter the mental if not physiological experience of her childhood. The restoration of hills and turf, flowers, and song would then reinforce women's supposed ability to imbibe and then to recall easy pleasure or sensation. Such revivified sensations, however, cannot fully absorb the speaker or convey with enough force these earlier sensations and associated feelings.

Smith's formulations here resemble Hume's comment that a person's identity is really "a bundle or collection of different perceptions . . . in a perpetual flux and movement" that overwhelm any clear sense of self (*A Treatise* 300). However fluctuating, Hume insists on the mind's imaginative ability to cohere this bundle, aided especially by memory, which "discover[s] personal identity, by shewing us the relation of cause and effect among our different perceptions" (310). Smith's visions, the imaginative memories that might unify these impressions, neither "soothe the sense of pain" nor do they "restore" peace to her sad breast. The speaker's unhappiness has alienated her from this pastoral bower and its "artless song," and has compelled her to write a sonnet that is self-reflexive about the problems with sensational memory—without solving them. Much as in "Tintern Abbey," memory's mediation bars direct access to childish, embodied sensations, but unlike Wordsworth, Smith does not resort to the imagination or poetry to preserve the images of unpolluted pleasure or a clear sense of self based on her memories. What she desires is to "teach a breaking heart to throb no more"—not a Wordsworthian revivification of a youthful subjectivity nor a Kantian sublime transcendence through an amazing landscape—but rather a way of being that would stop the throbbing heart, and teach it to move differently. Such an education would permanently put to bed the feeling and sensory perception that make both experience and memory possible. As Hume writes, "were all my perceptions remov'd by death" he would become "a perfect non-entity"; bodily perception, however much we may need the imagination to make sense of it, remains for Hume the basis of understanding (300). Smith certainly works from empiricist skepticism about perceptions' ability to undo the self as well as the contingency of the speculative imagination to account fully for the excess of bodily perception. Yet, rather than pressing for constancy and coherence of sense data, as Hume does, she exacerbates imagination's inability to cohere subjects and objects. More importantly, rather than simply muting sensation, she questions its efficacy as the building block of experiential, abstract, or emotional knowledge.

Denied access to the delights of childhood recollection and plagued by present-day pain, the poet turns in the sestet from a vision of such stirring hills to two figures that offer alternatives to sense and the discourse of sensibility: the river Arun's "limpid waves" and the Lethean cup of oblivion. Here the volta that ushers in the waves suggests not just a mere negation of empiricist memory but a complete turn or movement from sensibility into affect itself, a meta-figure for motion not contained by the human body. Though the fluid motion and embodiment of the water might suggest a common metonymy for the tearful gush of sensibility, the waves here are figured as "limpid," clear liquid unmixed with particulate matter. This description begins to mute their sensory qualities that would make them perceptible and bring the sensing subject into being even as it emphasizes their motion and figurality. Smith then intensifies this figural turn when she exchanges the waves for the cup of Lethe, a figurative dose of liquid forgetfulness. This substitution purges the waves of their association with the nervous flows of sensibility and sensation and replaces them with a rolling movement beyond empirical experience.[7] Their figuration plots a fluid, clarifying motion as it contrasts with the embodied gloom of the speaker's breaking heart and saddened breast.

Rather than nourishing her sensing mind and body, the waves, as a draught she might consume, offer a mythical potion that would seem to erase her memory and numb her completely. As the speaker admits in the poem's final lines, the only irrevocable and undeniable form of such oblivion would be death. What Rowe terms the sonnet's "negative turn" clearly concedes the nihilism of such a solution, even in the textual death or *petite mort* that follows the effusive moan of the final couplet. It may seem as though the subject is overwhelmed with sensation to the point of dissolution in a model much like Hume's, or the poem may seem to preserve the deliquescent subject as a site of negativity, withdrawn from a world hostile to it, as Rowe claims. Yet Smith, I want to argue, figures something more complicated than the refusal of an unjust world, where subjectivity becomes a "contentless void" (Rowe par. 19). Such a view can only recapitulate the feminine emptiness and separation from the public world that constituted the very mainstays of Romantic-era gender ideology. The end of the sonnet imagines that the resignation of sensation would always return the subject, even if as a "fiction" or as an empty, apathetic one channeling anhedonia (Hume 303). However, the Arun's limpid waves denuded of their materiality and the speaker's untenable consumption of them as Lethe together mark a form of movement other than subjective, sensory perception, and they irrevocably alter the empirical status of speaker and waves. This second volta does not simply punctuate or terminate the sonnet argument, but rather suggests the iteration of repeated turns, in the form of seemingly unending figural and stanzaic motion throughout Smith's expanding editions of sonnets, which trope motion through language and different forms of matter.

Lethe's heady cocktail figures a form of consumption—poetic limpid waves to be swallowed figuratively as a Lethean cup—that is impossible. The speaker may be able to drink from the river, but she cannot drink a mythological figure except through some figural gymnastics. The figure of drinking oblivion fulminates a response to the pastoral that generates and eviscerates charming, sensory effects, even as it replaces them both with a shadow form of abstract material movement. Unable to easily ingest the previously experienced Downs, Smith's speakers can only engage in an act of consumption that bars consumption altogether, and it is this impossibility—not to mention the ingestion of oblivion without actually dying—that inaugurates Smith's vacancy. The motion of internalization is stripped of its content and sensation, tracing movements other than the physiological. Speaker and draught are both put in motion under the guise of consumption but without any of the sensing or reflecting that constitute the movements of the empirical subject. Smith simultaneously overturns the act of empirical taste and activates a paradoxical motion of aporia. The mind becomes suspended in the motions of this circular logic; because nothing is consumed, the act may begin again, in a figural perseveration of trope and matter at once. The more vacancy repeats throughout the *Sonnets*, the more it revokes the references of taste and instead substitutes a figural turn that invokes no knowledge except for impossibility made possible by figural movement.

This figural movement, neither simply embodied nor disembodied, offers a broad challenge to the discourse of taste and its underlying empirical epistemology—to both sensory consumption and the formulation of the sensing subject. In place of the empty or merely disfigured subject, Smith poses a nonsubject who cannot taste an unpotable beverage. Rather than forming the subject, even through the perception of oblivion's lack, Smith instead offers an untenable empirical or sensory interaction between the speaker and the waves that nevertheless binds them through a shared movement of the figural. Such a movement consequently questions the easy separation of subject and external sense object, a distinction that remains clear for Hume even when he doubts his ability to cohere their individual identities. When readers consume the poem's figures, they too enact the very figural movement of the poem itself, since the act of reading is an act of inconsumable consumption that depends on figural movement of a shared affect between nonhuman poem and the reader, in an interaction that supersedes any sensory thrill that reifies the reading subject. Vacancy spins a loop of iterative motion through the speaker's address, the Aruna's waves, and the cup of Lethe, the sonnet's turns, and the multiple occasions of the poem and volume's internalization. All are transformed into a figure that produces nonknowledge but also an abstract materiality: the repeated movement of consuming that which cannot be drunk, internalized, or ingested. Such impossible figural movement echoes in a large number of other figural cruxes throughout the *Sonnets*: dying without dying, ingestion without embodiment, repetition without cliché, figuration without representation, and perhaps most pointedly, taste without empiricism.

Unlike Frances Greville, Hannah More, Helen Maria Williams, or Ann Yearsley, Smith does not use the term "indifference" to label vacancy, nor does she merely repeat conventional aesthetic figures such as Helen's nepenthe, Werther's suicide, or Prospero's sleep. Her refusal to mimic feminine objections of "indifference" marks her project as a critique of the confessional mode of poetry when it seeks to represent actual feminine experience and its empirical foundations. Moreover, Smith's reworking, and often refusal, of empiricist tropes signals that she does not summon oblivion merely to deaden sensation, which would underwrite sensibility's extremes of excessive stimulation or its absence, but rather seeks another form of affect outside sensation and sensibility. The vacancy crafted by drinking oblivion suggests that Smith works through figures that resist the supposed accuracy of representation to depict experience. Although scholars have often probed Smith's representations of sensibility, gender, and revolutionary duress to read her works, she in fact favors a tropology that vexes empirical representation from the start.[8]

When Smith turns to use the actual word "taste" in her poems, the critique of sensibility enters the register of aesthetic judgment and generates her most direct response to empirical discourses and their gendering of the feminine, emotive subject. As she revisits the Downs' pastoral landscape in poems such as sonnet 31, "Written in Farm Wood, South Downs, in May 1784," she again attempts to recreate a visual memory of the Downs that might serve as a balm, an attempt that ultimately fails. Her critique of "taste" in this poem reveals an acute problem not only with the subjective and fleetingly empirical nature of aesthetic judgments, but also with empiricism's particular deterministic, teleological habits of mind:

> Spring's dewy hand on this fair summit weaves
> The downy grass with tufts of Alpine flowers.
> And shades the beechen slopes with tender leaves,
> And leads the shepherd to his upland bowers,
> Strewn with wild thyme; while slow-descending showers
> Feed the green ear, and nurse the future sheaves!
> —Ah! blest the hind—whom no sad thought bereaves
> Of the gay season's pleasures!—All his hours
> To wholesome labour given, or thoughtless mirth;
> No pangs of sorrow past, or coming dread,
> Bend his unconscious spirit down to earth,
> Or chase calm slumbers from his careless head!
> Ah! what to me can those dear days restore,
> When scenes could charm that now I taste no more! (31.1–14)

After proffering a brief description of the Downs, the poem presents a happy shepherd sustained and nourished by the pastoral landscape. There he finds "wholesome labour" and "thoughtless mirth" (9) while the spring showers "Feed the green ear, and nurse the future sheaves!" (6). Existing in a perpetual present of the rejuvenating spring, the shepherd, "unconscious" of suffering and "thoughtless" in his joy, is not altogether insensible, but rather feels the easy immediacy of the "gay season's pleasures." This heartfelt, sensory consumption is also characterized by the undemanding charms of the pastoral—both pleasure and repose. In the final lines, the speaker introduces herself into the sonnet by excluding herself from the very setting she has just described: "Ah! what to me those dear days restore, / When scenes could charm that now I taste no more!" (13–14). By denying the speaker such tastes, the poem reveals itself to be neither about the shepherd, nor about the poet's inability to partake of the natural scenery of her childhood, but rather a larger meditation on the impossibility of bourgeois taste for the thinking woman. Though corn can be nourished by the rain, the speaker cannot feed off this land—the landscape cannot act as nursemaid to *her* woes. The couplet offers the possibility of restoration in the first line, seemingly asking how to create a pastoral retreat through the imagination's use of a sensory memory revivified, but instead of an answer, the last line relinquishes that fantasy and the poem cruelly comes to a close. When the speaker can "taste no more," she no longer has access to the restorative "dear days" or the "scenes could charm," as if she cannot live in a land where time and space have empirical resonance. The poet refuses to regain Eden (and its Latitudinarian humanity) by consuming the pastoral.

As in "To Sleep" and "The Sleeping Woodman," the notion of taste in "Written in Farm Wood" appears at the end of the sonnet to reveal how the exigencies of the speaker's sensibility make taste an untenable disciplinary strategy for women's aesthetics. G. J. Barker-Benfield has explored how eighteenth-century culture and sentimental fiction especially were bent on denouncing, or at the very least controlling, the twin dangers of sensibility and female consumer pleasures. Such a reform movement was waged through the concept of taste, which "represented one attempt to spiritualize or moralize" women's appetite for urban commodities, something that had become a fact of life for many by the end of the eighteenth century (205). In periodical culture primarily aimed at women readers, Joseph Addison and Richard Steele's earlier program for taste still held sway even at the end of the eighteenth century. Women in *The Tatler* and *The Spectator* often served as natural models of self-disciplining taste, particularly when they were shopping or talking about dress, in a discourse that often circulated around the female body.[9] In its journey from Shaftesbury through Hume to Addison and beyond, the concept of taste is often credited with consolidating a middle-class public sphere by inculcating readers with the ability to make appropriate consumer or aesthetic choices in a burgeoning free market. Such choices would signify women's class interests and positions, while at the same time educating them in those values that reinforce a liberal, modern state.[10]

Taste, nonetheless, often placed women in a double bind because they were assumed to have special sensitivities even as their intense feelings required more vigilant discipline.[11] Both Pinch and Barker-Benfield have noted Hume's attention to what he terms the "considerable connection" between passion and taste in women in his essay "On the Delicacy of Taste and Passion," where he endorses the widely held maxim that women have both "more delicate passions than men" and "also more delicate taste of the ornaments of life" (*Selected* 345). For women, taste was less a thoughtful act of judgment than an act of consumption that always threatens to enliven the bodily passions: "Any excellency in these [ornaments of life] hits their taste much sooner than ours; and when you please their taste, you soon engage their affections" (*Selected* 345). From the prospect of Hume's psychology, taste "improves our sensibility for all the tender and agreeable passions; at the same time that it renders the mind incapable of the rougher and more boisterous emotions" (12). For Hume, the solution to Smith's overtaxed sensibility would be the careful and selective consumption of sensory input, a common-sense, Aristotelian approach to moderation using the controlled filter of taste.

Smith's figure of the woodsman and his relationship to the discourse of taste resembles Hume's figure of the "hardy hunter" in his essay "The Stoic," providing another clue to Smith's figural reworking of empiricist terms, figures, and characters. When Hume's hunter exerts "in the chase every passion of the mind, and every member of the body, he then finds the charms of repose" (*Selected* 86). Smith's speaker may be envious of the hunter or woodsman's ability to burn out bodily labor and passion to find repose, but she rejects such a method of simply purging sensation or its passions in her more pointed reply to the linked empiricist discourses of taste, epistemology, aesthetic judgment, and gender. What Labbe terms the "distressed speaker" of the sonnets can no longer partake in the pastoral's "charm," not simply because, as Hume writes, judgments of taste cannot be given when people "labour under some defect, or are vitiated by some disorder," such as melancholy or hysteria (*Selected* 147). Rather, Smith distances herself from value judgments born of sensibility because, these "charms" signify those pleasures that remain superficial because they are whims based on the body's temporary sensations and, therefore, on individual predilections. When she eschews taste and feeling, Smith looks to aesthetic judgments that might be true for all subjects—and indeed beyond the subject—regardless of the shape and responses of the body, or the demands made upon it.

In ways that have important implications for her unfolding epistemology, Smith's thinking sidles close to Kant's own critique of subjective taste when he writes, "Any taste remains barbaric if its liking requires that *charms* and *emotions* be mingled in, let alone if it makes these the standard of its approval" (69; emphasis in original). While there is no evidence that Smith read Kant, and she does not use his philosophical terms within her poetry, she does mount a critique of empiricism that is strikingly resonant with his ideas of form, though she develops a mode of affect different from his dependence on transcendence underwritten by sensibility. Kant's famous philosophical repudiation of empiricism, though not coincident with Smith's, can help us gain purchase on her unique transformation of empirical taste into an affect that moves beyond both embodiment and conceptual structures. He attempts to locate a type of aesthetic pleasure that admits neither physical sensation (what defines the agreeable) nor determinate concepts (which define the good), and his examples in *Critique of Judgment* notoriously trouble artistic representation.[12] Kant gives the following examples of the sort of free beauty that enables universal aesthetic judgments: "Flowers, free designs, lines aimlessly intertwined in each other under the name of foliage, signify nothing, do not depend on any determinate concept" (*Critique of Judgment* 93). These designs offer no referential meaning or ideas with preconceived ends, such as the tasteful woman reproducing British society and mercantile culture. Rather, they insinuate a beauty based on patterns and motions resistant to either concepts or individual tastes born from sensory pleasure.

When Smith declares that these "scenes could charm that now I taste no more," she leads us to read—and reread—the landscape description as divorced from consolatory, sensory mimesis (14). Upon rereading, we begin to see those free designs and lines: "summit weaves / The dewy grass"; "tufts of . . . flowers"; "beechen slopes"; and "bowers, / Strewn with wild thyme" (1–2, 2, 3, 4–5). The slopes, tufts, and wildness of the landscape slowly resist sensory stimulation; yet, more than simply avoiding any clear, replicable concept of beauty, they "signify nothing." While the speaker cannot taste embodied charms of Farm Wood or the South Downs, she does offer another form of consumption in the designs that move through the poem and her natural description. The repetition of movement within the descriptions, as well as the quick succession of different designs and lines, mute their sensory, physical content in favor of motion that does not signify. It is these figural movements that I read as a form of affect, the movements and rests of figuration that likewise thread through those of the poet and her nonhuman landscape. Smith presents an impossible act of tracing movement, of consuming abstractions, of moving the mind and the materiality around it despite the death of the sensing subject.

Kant, when he terms his version of this experience "free beauty," presents an aesthetics available to the subject, yet not through subjective taste based merely on individual instances of sensation. To understand how Smith diverges from Kant, it is helpful here to consider Derrida's own reading of "free beauty" as an aporia about concepts, which he terms as a cut or edging, something that garners both finality and interruption. In *The Truth in Painting*, Derrida sees such figural moments as revealing an impossible form of thought that would avoid the problems of Enlightenment rationality and neoclassical notions of beauty. For Derrida, free beauty is a form of intellectual play that, unlike "adherent beauty," is only "free" if and when it does not succumb to a concept's determined, teleological ends. The aporia of free beauty presents a form of wildness that orients itself toward an end, but cuts itself off before that end is achieved. Revealingly, Smith's landscapes, and the numerous dispossessed, wandering exiles in the *Sonnets*, offer the very resistance to *telos* that Derrida champions. Although her speakers move through the flora and fauna of the Downs or other pastorals for the purpose of finding a sensory succor, Smith's vacancy pointedly cuts off this very goal. The impossibility of consuming a figure resists the *telos* of either sensory satiation or negation.

However, Smith's aporias are, in fact, oriented less around the dangers arising from philosophical abstractions, with conceptual rules endangered by specific ends, and more around the normative teleologies emerging from the easy resurgence of empiricist feeling and experience, particularly for the supposedly feeling, tasteful woman. These dangers are particularly visible in a later sonnet of taste, the winter scene of sonnet 62, which returns us to Smith's aporia of consumption. Originally published as a sonnet written by the character Orlando in *The Old Manor House* (1793), Smith incorporated it into Volume II of the *Elegiac Sonnets*, published in 1797. Using an ambiguously gendered, wandering speaker, Smith depicts a pastoral landscape that has become a space almost completely devoid of sensory stimuli. As physical taste becomes increasingly impossible, the poem constructs a figural, formal beauty by way of poetic divestment:

> While thus I wander, cheerless and unblest,
> And find in change of place but change of pain;
> In tranquil sleep the village laborers rest,
> And taste that quiet I pursue in vain!
> Hush'd is the hamlet now, and faintly gleam
> The dying embers, from the casement low
> Of the thatch'd cottage; while the Moon's wan beam
> Lends a new lustre to the dazzling snow.
> O'er the cold waste, amid the freezing night,
> Scarce heeding whither, desolate I stray;
> For me, pale Eye of Evening, thy soft light
> Leads to no happy home; *my* weary way
> Ends but in sad vicissitudes of care;
> I only fly from doubt—to meet despair! (62.1–14)

At the very start of the wintery scene, the speaker is on the run—"While thus I wander"—speaking of emotion in the negative, "cheerless and unblest," as if craving the sensory stimulation and comforting cheer that the winter scene negates. It is this conjunction of the dampening of sensory stimulus and the pursuit of aimless movement that characterizes the poem's vacancy—"the cold waste, amid the freezing night" (11). The winter scene—the "hush'd hamlet" and the snow "dazzling" in the moonlight—paradoxically offers materiality in motion—hushing sound and dazzling snow—by way of its lack of sound and eventual absence of color. The subject, too, might be frozen by the wintry weather—the freezing night and the dazzling power of the cold—as its intense physical sensation could paralyze the body. In fact, the speaker constantly moves in paradoxical fashion, auguring movement or internalization without the sensations of joy, sound, or spatial sensitivity: "I wander, cheerless" and "taste that quiet" and "Scarce heeding whither, desolate I stray." The play on winter and whither doubles down on the aporia of movement without sensation, a meandery trajectory without the teleologies of the empirical body. Despite winter's absence of sensation—or because of it—the speaker hies through the poem offering an alternative account of figural movement. The speaker, working again in the negative, reiterates, when "thy soft light / Leads to no happy home," the failure of sensory perception of the landscape leads to undiscovered country.

The speaker's movement does not merely enunciate her melancholy flight out of town, but rather jointly figures the landscape's own emerging lines and shapes, in effect, overwriting the increasing absence of bodily feeling with new forms and wandering movements shared by speaker, landscape, and poem. Indeed, the speaker's "straying" through the "waste" suggests a form composed by her movements, her line "aimlessly intertwined," as Kant says, in a landscape that itself becomes an abstract shape not easily consumed. The speaker's "weary way" can sketch only a vague line through parts of a pastoral hardly seen through the soft light. The faint gleam, the last vestige of dying embers, the low casement, the cottage roof are all outlined by the "Moon's wan beam," until they finally merge into "the cold waste," a vague space traced, in the end, by the speaker's desolate straying. In Smith's frozen landscape, the speaker travels beyond the body to establish a line of movement through an abstract retreat and an inverted pastoral. It is a space that neither represents the idealized Edenic or heavenly landscape nor plays on the senses (as the descriptions of the Downs do). This sonnet traces formal shapes to outline an increasingly abstract form of beauty. In part, we can see this abstraction in Smith choosing to drain the landscape of color, since in eighteenth-century aesthetic theory color was often subservient to line.[13] As Jeffrey Robinson argues, line was analogous to the highest form of imagination in poetry: "The outline corresponds to traditional abstract form in poetry and a focus on the precision of identity expressed by the lyrical subject" (6). Painting the landscape as white and devoid of color, Smith emphasizes the line of her drawing, or the figure the poem makes, but one that moves through the speaker and the landscape, disrupting the identity of the lyrical subject. The speaker essentially traces a path from passionate childhood pastoral to adult numbness, until all that remains is the shape of a landscape outlined in snow and her flight through it, which are nearly one and the same.

As the poem offers a figural form divested of its sensory materiality akin to the "limpid waves" and "cup of Lethe" in "To the South Downs," here as well the speaker engages in a form of impossible consumption of a figure devoid of sensory content. As opposed to the wish to consume the sensory plenitude of a springtime pastoral in her earlier poems, here what the speaker wants to taste is the stillness and silence of the village at night. This vacancy once again represents an impossible form of consumption in two ways. First, the speaker desires to taste sensations that are increasingly unavailable in a sensory wasteland. Second, like the earlier attempt to drink the Lethean cup, the speaker attempts to consume a figure—the "quiet." "The quiet" can represent the absence of sound or activity, but it likewise figures the freedom from sensation. Here Smith adds an additional layer to the paradox, that tasting quiet would be to engage the quiet within a motion, an act of ingestion, that might, paradoxically, undo its coveted stillness and tranquility. Smith continues to knot the conundrum about how to engage in a type of intellectual consumption, an affective movement unburdened by sensation, consumerism, or individual wants. As the consumption of such a silent, frozen, and quiet pastoral allegorizes the difficulties surrounding bourgeois notions of taste, it dramatically installs an aporia of affect—the continual motion surrounding stillness—as the response to superficial pleasure so endemic to conceptions of women. It is no coincidence that this sonnet, originally voiced by Orlando when published in Smith's novel, then by the feminine speaker when published in the *Sonnets*, becomes one of her "androgynous sonnets," as such affective movement wends its weary way past binary gender.[14]

Smith's particular attention to the landscape's figural qualities attenuates the embodied charm of the pastoral landscape and opposes her landscapes to what Kant calls "mere form" (66).[15] In such a hollowed-out landscape, the speaker can no longer easily "taste" its sensory qualities, but instead must take in a different sort of line by intuiting its form—and its formal movements—without recourse to bodily sensation. We could easily read this as Kantian free play, where the imagination and the understanding wrestle with a conceptual problem (how to consume a figure) and resolve it in what Robert Kaufman, in his Adornian reading of Kant, calls "the generative impasse of aesthetic experience" ("Red Kant" 716). A Kantian reading might then see Smith circling around another form of sensation, the Kantian feeling of the mind's faculties at play. Magdalena Ostas, specifically addressing Kant's terminology of feeling in the third *Critique*, argues that the feeling associated with judgments of the beautiful is characteristically not rooted in embodied emotion. Rather, feeling is the state of self-reflection that the subject has for itself, its unity, and the harmony of cognitive functions. These sensations engender a feeling of reflection that keeps the subject in a repetitive loop whereby the imagination works on the understanding, rather than suspended in mental impasse. According to Rei Terada's account of Kantian "apatheia," even a "freedom from emotion would nevertheless constitute its own emotion," like Keats's "the feel of not to feel it" (Terada 52), which occurs within language. For Terada, emotions act deconstructively, positing interiority and subjectivity, breaking them down, then building them anew in a linguistic and emotive circle that bears resemblance to Ostas's description of Kantian sensation.

Smith's form of affect, however, created through both an impossible logic and an iterative figural movement, demands additional, repeated figural turns that avoid the sensations of self-reflexive intellection, referential emotion, or physiological experience. Her nonsignifying turns provoke the speaker's and landscape's contingency as they move together beyond both physical embodiments and feelings of mind's conceptual free play. Vacancy creates abstract movements that transgress the feeling and thinking gendered subject and the seemingly still landscape. This movement bars all perception but the figuration of that motion, carrying a "knowledge" or meaning that is not so much referential (or pleasurable) but relational and propulsive, and in that sense intensely material. Smith's "mere form" becomes a tracing of figural movement that travels outside the subject's play of faculties and outside referential language into a realm of mutual, worldmaking activity. Such motion lies before and beyond sensation, and one that marks the transgression of human consumption and the nonhuman, inconsumable quiet.

The poetic consumption of the churchyard bones, of oblivion, of the snowy, quiet landscape, and, later, of the chalky white cliffs of Beachy Head inaugurates a movement that resists tasteful subjectivity in favor of a confrontation with the indelibly thoughtless nonhuman. Smith's poems therefore anticipate and critique the history of Romantic subject-object relations as a phenomenological proposition to be rejected by women too often made the object of such subjective incorporation.[16] These aporetic figures abstract the empirical even as they are generated by empirical wandering and whims that more easily lead to intellectual movement across seemingly opposing things. Not quite Pheng Cheah's force without substance, the figural moves as abstract, figural, and material at once. Smith constructs vacancy as a confrontation that entangles the speaking, figuring subject and the nonhuman world of language and matter into movements that supersede both.

Vacancy written this way, through the denuding of the empirical, however, is always in danger of being subsumed back into the human proclivity for embodied experience. The implausibility of oblivion, death, or restful sleep even within a largely figural mental landscape, for example, underlines the resurgent demands of the body, which will eventually need to breathe, perceive, and consume something truly nourishing once more.[17] Indeed, the Orlando sonnet demonstrates how easy it is for the *Sonnets*' speaker to "fly from doubt—to meet despair!" falling back into the known comforts of overwhelming feeling in the poem's last line. Because of this problem, Smith iteratively presents and refigures vacancy for her reader in an ever-proliferating bulk of sonnets. This is a form of knowledge that can occur only as a string of moments of nonknowledge, an ongoing repetition endued by the mind fleeing from its own tendency to re-inscribe its understanding within regular expression and lived experience. Such flight, however, also repeatedly offers the path away from codified emotions and ideologies of sensitive feminine bodies back into affect's abstract material movements that have the ability to undermine gender and discrete embodiment liable to the disciplinarity of ideology. Where Smith's sonnets reject sensibility and empirical taste in favor of an impossible consumption wrought through this kind of aporia, Smith's final epic work, "Beachy Head," maps the impossibility of ridding bodily concerns from aesthetics onto the broader plane of a national landscape. Through this wider prospect, Smith rejects the individual, greedy sensations of imperial acquisition, transmuting the speaker's impossible consumption into the hermit's paradoxical receptivity to all who may come ashore, a vacancy that intertwines Napoleonic subjects within the landscape's beachy remains.

"Beachy Head" and the Hermit's Impossible Receptivity

In "Beachy Head," Smith turns her focus to the broader implications of empiricist thought unearthed in the nationalist and imperialist narratives that envelop the Channel cliff. By meditating on war and international trade, she contemplates their effects on the possibilities for universal freedom and ethical living during the Napoleonic age. The Lethean cup hollowed of its taste sets the scene for the two figures of vacancy in this poem that replace empiricist representations of the landscape rife with imperial consumerism. Beachy Head's great continental rift figures a tectonic break and the great cliff's shifting materiality, which buries invaders and enables the erasure of imperial history in Beachy Head's fossilized rock. It also houses a hermit who saves all mariners that come ashore. His hospitality exceeds the exigencies of embodied, empirical, imperial experience demanded by British trade prowess, as well as the idealizations of the pastoral and the alien laws built on cosmopolitan principles.[18] Smith depicts his acts as being conditioned and invited not only by the tumultuous, indeterminate channel climate but also by the many strangers who arrive there. In effect, both Beachy Head and the hermit become figures for receptivity at the very moment that both the hermit and mariners are stripped of all empirical status—their nationality, gender, class, life, and language. This impossible flouting of national and alien laws, not to mention empirical geological science, marks Smith's reworking of several empirical discourses: mercantile consumption, histories driven by empirical evidence, and individual acts of embodied sympathy. As her final figure for vacancy, the hermit's movements and those of the sedimented channel and its climate compose an abstraction of a material motion, a receptivity that intertwines the cliff and the variety of subjects eradicated by it.

We are first confronted with Beachy Head's poetics of vacancy when Smith calls attention to the landscape's features, beginning with that stupendous and steep rock face, what she calls its "vast concussion." The word "concussion" during its time could mean both an action of violent shaking such as an earthquake or rending of the heavens and also a heavy blow to the body, especially the brain. Alan Richardson, in his discussion of Jane Austen's *Persuasion*, suggests how brain injury reveals a cognitive unconscious, what he later terms in *The Neural Sublime* "sensory or emotional or conceptual overload" when "the mind blanks out and seems to undergo a physical collapse or meltdown" (31). Smith refigures such a "concussion" not to plot the tragic breakdown of the individual mind or national body. Instead, she leverages such trauma as a posthuman force that upsets land and body, individual and national ideologies, laying bare more native and fertile movement among different materialities, which, rather than simply paralyzing national subjects, has the potential to open up discourses and materialities to new configurations, new movements.

Set on a Brighton cliff overlooking the English Channel, "Beachy Head" is often seen as a feminine version of the Romantic pastoral, a lush, botanical antithesis to Wordsworth's transcendent nature. The poem allegedly routes the mountain's sublime status through the minute fossils and sedimentary materials that make up England's dramatic Southern coastline. By so doing, Theresa M. Kelley argues, it juxtaposes grand, national narratives with smaller, local histories. Judith Pascoe and other scholars have also shown how Smith delves into the empirical, material realities of the natural world—from the catalogues of local botany to laments about how the shepherd might make an honest living in an increasingly consumer culture.[19] For these reasons Labbe suggests that in "Beachy Head" Smith reaches the height of female erudition at the turn of the nineteenth century (*Charlotte Smith* 144). Unlike the stranger-poet's inset lyrics at the end of the poem, which only voice sentimental laments for lost loves and pastoral landscapes, the poem proper deals in the more heady subjects of geology, botany, and local historiography.

Rather than investing in such empirical knowledge, Smith's depiction of Beachy Head, in fact, challenges the stable material world beyond the bounds of gendered intellectual pursuits. Though her use of such aesthetic discourses as the sublime, the beautiful, the picturesque, and the pastoral has now been widely discussed,[20] she does not, as critics have argued, simply revise these received aesthetic terms. Instead, her figures of vacancy, like the opening "vast concussion," undermine the habits of language that associate women's bodies with the invaded, natural landscape and then provide a more porous and complicated alternative. The poem begins by rendering the violent geological and international forces that have created England's coastline, but not to stage a real, empirical encounter with nature. As Smith describes the cliff in the poem's first lines:

> Fancy should go forth,
> And represent the strange and awful hour
> Of vast concussion; [. . .   ]
>   [that] from the continent
> Eternally divided this green isle. (4–6, 9–10)

Beachy Head does not stand for the accumulation and aggregation of positivistic understandings about the land, English history, or the role of the poet, but instead "eternally" "represents" this first vast divide that echoes throughout all the other subsequent breaks in the poem. This concussive moment of division, this gap, comes to figure the rift of possibility when material reality and its history—and the very language used to articulate both—are thrown into question. Although, as Christoph Bode asserts, "sedimentation . . . is . . . the master trope of *Beachy Head*," it does not merely represent the "irreducible alterity of the self" or the modern subject available in trace elements (66). The chalky cliff more broadly becomes an epistemological and ontological figure for the permeability of all bodies. Such transgressive movement occurs in "the impetuous main flood rush between / The rifted shores," but even more grandly in the description of the scene that follows: its "rippling tide of flood," the cliff "sides precipitous," and even the "glancing" wings and "clamour" of the "restless" sea birds, the "chiding hounds," and the shepherd's "bleating flock" (8–9, 19, 21, 22, 26, 25, 26, 28). All this movement echoes and emerges from that first crumbling of material rock into the immaterial continental void. This process that "rent the solid hills" is anything but immobile or stolid, and it will later echo in the poem's dissolution of national and foreign subjects within its shifting sediments and waters (7).

Before Smith can fully offer the cliffside seascape as a figure for motion, she must first evade a past whose imperial and natural history would seem as staunch as the Channel cliffs, based as they are on empirical accounts of military invasions or newly found geological evidence. The first model of history the speaker gives us is one that resembles a palimpsest, a "scroll voluminous" that encourages memory to "retrace / The period" (373, 379–380, 120–121). Like manuscript scrolls, historical memory will be written, scraped away, and written again on the same sheet of parchment. Here, memory confabulates history and poetry into epic stories written on the scrolls, which, unlike positivistic, empiricist history, is repetitively retold, reworked, and refigured.[21] The manuscript of English history Smith goes on to write consists of those eras composed of the Danish, Roman, and Norman invasions of England. If "Beachy Head" had set out to supply a linear or an Enlightenment progressive history of the English, then Smith would have narrated the Roman invasion first, then the Danish, and ended with the Norman. Instead, she begins with the Norman invasion and its resonances with the contemporary conflict between the English and French, then moves back to the Roman invasion during the last century BC, and finally ends with a reference to the pirate Danes (eighth to tenth centuries AD). This plot of earth holds the histories of the native Britons, the Danes, and the Romans, who all lay buried in the layers of sediment on Beachy Head's shores. The historical narratives Smith unearths here resemble the strata that early geologists were beginning to uncover, strata that are less discrete than shifting over time and through interpretation.

Meditating on her own version of geologic history, Smith then moves to examine the various layers of historical sediments that make up the cliff wall, from sea to cliff top, yet "vain Science!" is no match for the dynamic materiality and the hand of the poet who can reveal empirical data as mere "conjecture" (390, 393). In a now well-known passage about geological science, Smith approaches "the strange and foreign forms / Of sea-shells" and their relation to the "fantastic shapes / Of bivalves" (379–380). Although Anne D. Wallace points out that Smith may not have been partial to any one geological theory floated during her time, Kevis Goodman suggests that the poem's "energies are too riveted . . . by the imaginative possibilities of geological science" (995). Goodman describes the well-cited fossil passage as offering us "movements that have conspired to produce the aggregate forms of the ground of the present" (992), yet empirical geology likewise becomes part of Smith's larger critique of empirical history. Smith's scroll passage already implies that history is built from layers of sediment and discourses not only intermixing with but also radically erasing one another, as they all become one and the same dirt, a shared and often indistinguishable materiality.

Later lines about Roman fossils offer even more radical statements about how retracing various levels of sedimentary history erases as much as creates it, here evoking complicated versions of nonhuman time and history. Looking upon elephant fossils from the Roman invasion of Claudius, Smith rebukes all past and future invaders of English land, because their grand ambitions to colonize and to possess the soil vanish as the topsoil erodes over time, and leaves no material trace of their humanity:

> Hither, Ambition come!
> Come and behold the nothingness of all
> For which you carry thro' the oppressed Earth,
> War, and its train of horrors—see where tread
> The innumerous hoofs of flocks above the works
> By which the warrior sought to register
> His glory, and immortalize his name—[. . .]
> All, with the lapse of Time, have passed away,
> Even as the clouds, with dark and dragon shapes,
> Or like vast promontories crown'd with towers,
> Cast their broad shadows on the downs; then sail
> Far to the northward, and their transient gloom
> Is soon forgotten. (419–425, 434–439)

The irony of the passage, that all three are "unremembered," emphasizes how their histories (represented by the fossil records and archeological sediments that are both literally and figuratively buried in the cliff face) have been leveled by the "pathless" surface of the earth atop the cliff (427, 430). Moreover, despite the purported goal of these invasions—to colonize the native inhabitants in order to rob the land of its natural resources—the conquerors end up buried under the land as fossilized ruins of their imperialist projects.

Here Smith verges on satire, mocking the imperial claims of the Romans, their "unwieldy" elephants, and their Virgilian epic mode with its linear, teleological historical narrative. The poem recounts national history and its material origins in order to rearrange and refigure them.[22] The hoof prints, signs of the Roman Empire's gigantic ambition, also turn out to be the signs of its inevitable fall when they vanish from the surface of the landscape, not so much sedimented as erased and forgotten.[23] As if emphasizing the power of figural movements to alter matter, Smith transforms these vanishing hoof prints via metaphor into clouds, which first cast shadows upon the earth, then they too dissipate and are forgotten. As one trace disappears or converts into the next, Smith's land and sky appear to accept even as they disintegrate human forms and representations into meta-figures for particulate, moving matter. The passing shadows of medieval nonhuman creatures and castles efface each other, forgotten except for their cloudy materiality with its tendency to move and alter its own shapes.

In the process, the speaker posits the very writing of history as a kind of perpetual erasure of one figure for another.[24] Yet, rather than simply signaling the absence of meaning or historical surety, Beachy Head's ecology tracks the movement between figures. Such underlying motion manifests an elemental affect parallel to the continuous, if more slowly, shifting of the beachy earth and its inhabitants—invaders, mariners, migrants, and the dying. The original colonial violence that the Romans and Danes inflicted on the native Saxons has been repaid by death's own brutal hospitality, the most universal equalizer. Stripped of their imperial quest for foreign resources or nationalistic expansion, these invaders are accepted into the earth by dint of the nearly vanished remains of their conquering claims. Beachy Head levels those colonial plots spurred on by material desires and the fantasies of European hegemony. The invaders scatter, as corporeal remains now disintegrated in the soil and as immaterial illusions, like those dragons and towers that once composed England's medieval imaginary but now have sailed on.

This moment foreshadows Smith's largest exploration of vacancy when she ends the poem with the hermit who saves and, more often, buries those mariners swept up in the Channel's waters. As the hermit's actions within the Channel figure his hospitality to all travelers, British and foreign, the shifting ground conveys Smith's thinking about the changing territory of tribal or national possession. In his 1795 manifesto on cosmopolitan right, *Perpetual Peace: A Philosophical Sketch*, Kant associates such hospitality with "the common ownership of the earth's surface," a principle that leads to "the idea of cosmopolitan right . . . an amendment to the unwritten code of national and international rights" (118). In contrast, when Smith endows sedimentary status upon England's former invaders, it is not due to "the common ownership of the earth" or to a cosmopolitan right, but thanks to a final resting place that buries and then washes away human and nonhuman remains alike. When the invaders are transformed into the beachy silt of the cliff, Smith—as a poet culling figures in the landscape— finds them a place within the coastline and portrays a grave that holds in abeyance both the invaders' marks and the possibility of any sublime transcendence of their remains. She suggests that only the hand of the poet can resist empirical abuse from invaders, traders, and smugglers through poetic figures that simultaneously disrupt, destabilize, and intertwine the coast's materiality and all sorts of human bodies.

In this poetic rendition, nature becomes potentially open to hosting even antagonistic invaders and their ruined imperial or material desires precisely at the point that they become figures of absence. The poem's version of vacancy can be more broadly understood as this impossible notion of receptivity. Rather than offering a type of hospitality based on the playful evocation of a Kantian universal code of human rights, the poet instead makes the landscape of Beachy Head accessible to all by dint of the unaccountable movements produced by its beachy metaphors. For Smith, this coastal history does not create a concrete, traceable fossilized record of invaders, smugglers, mariners, and shepherds so much as it bespeaks a future in which those identities and histories disappear into the eroding sedimentary rock of the coastline and its figural turns. No longer simply the buried and dead remains of England's imperial past and Napoleonic present, they come to figure a potential receptivity to all humans, but only as their empirical humanity becomes stripped away by the tide and the cliffside reception. This material intermixture of a variety of humans figures a hospitality that arrives only as they also become nonhuman, without gender, and without any sense that would take comfort in tectonic generosity. This affect—"Beachy Head"'s radically shifting acceptance—occurs as a series of interlocking figures for the transformations of the human into the nonhuman, which cannot be felt but only intimated by the repeated troping of burying and unearthing.

The salvific hermit—who initially appears to be the apotheosis of compassion and embodied sentiment—advances Smith's final figure of vacancy. Living inside the rift, burrowing within the cliff face, he constructs a life not only outside material luxuries, but also nearly outside the legalistic bounds of English jurisdiction:

> Just beneath the rock
> Where Beachy overpowers the channel wave,
> Within a cavern mined by wintry tides
> Dwelt one, who long disgusted with the world
> And all its ways, appear'd to suffer life
> Rather than live . . . (672–676)

The hermit lives between the sea and land, in a cavern that is less the womb that biographer Loraine Fletcher has suggested, and more a site of vacancy itself, with the "wintry tides" forever mining and chipping away at the hermit and his home. As a chink in Beachy Head's "vast concussion," the hermit's cave represents a figure of vacancy that anticipates and redraws the Romantic use of spaces, sanctuaries, valleys, and caves as allegories of the mind. The cave's erosion, and its partial shelter, signals the dissolution of the circumscribed mind or subjectivity created through clearly felt sensation. Just as the ocean erodes the cliff's materiality and creates the stunning white rock face for which the southern coast is known, so the hermit lives within a changing, contingent circumstance, cognizant of but not bound to material needs and sympathetic demands. He arrives at the end of the poem not only as a figure of displacement but rather of unforetold movements, of the simultaneous material and linguistic contingency that compose vacancy's affect.

If the poem's opening vast concussion seems to promise one set of social, political, and material transformations, then those transformations have resulted in the failures of empire, imperial economics, and nationalism. The hermit's situation bears witness to these repeated catastrophes:

> for his heart
> Was feelingly alive to all that breath'd;
> And outraged as he was, in sanguine youth,
> By human crimes, he still acutely felt
> For human misery. (687–691)

Once a man of society, he rejected those "human crimes" of luxury, corruption, and perhaps the ensanguined history of the Revolution haunting the Channel. As Smith elaborates in an endnote, the hermit is loosely based on a man named Darby who was believed to have lived in a cave for many years, eating only shellfish for sustenance. These details suggest that the hermit may have chosen his home by the sea to find a different relation to fluctuating materiality than the exigencies of a mercantile culture.

Structurally, the hermit culminates, but inverts, a sequence of acquisitive male figures from the poem, including the coastal smugglers, the traders, and invaders skirting the channel. Unlike their greedy approach to the material fecundity and international luxury augured by the coastal landscape, the hermit might at first appear to be a cipher of a different sort of sensational reality—the sensibility and sympathy that would encourage him to save any and all humans stranded in the channel waters. As Kari E. Lokke suggests, Smith might be playing into the trope of the compassionate hermit popularized during the end of the eighteenth century, and it is tempting to read him as a generic cipher for sympathy.[25] He devotes his "generous cares" to "unhappy" men, descriptions which might presuppose that he acts in accordance with Adam Smith's dictate to wield the impressions of his own senses in order to imagine another's suffering, "to enter as it were into his body" (I.I.2). This brand of sympathy, the author of *The Theory of Moral Sentiments* argues, is particularly palpable in the presence of imagined pain. However, there is, in fact, little interaction between hermit and those he saves and, furthermore, there is not much real or imagined emotional substitution that would put the hermit in the mariners' boat and allow him to sympathize with his charges. Most importantly, the hermit's repeated actions exceed mere personal responsibility, and they occur precisely within the absence of those material or imagined identifications that would enable embodied feeling.

Perhaps a response to Samuel T. Coleridge's adventuring mariner and Robinson's avaricious one, the hermit's cosmopolitan stance—welcoming and rescuing all sorts of international travelers—posits another movement within the world at large beyond its embodied alliances of nation or gender. Though the hermit does watch the tumultuous waves, he acts immune to their inducement to reify either personal grief or nationalistic nostalgia. Instead, he becomes famous for wading through them and saving whomever might become stranded by their caprice.

> Wandering on the beach,
> He learn'd to augur from the clouds of heaven,

> And from the changing colours of the sea,
> And sullen murmurs of the hollow cliffs,
> Or the dark porpoises, that near the shore
> Gambol'd and sported on the level brine
> When tempests were approaching: then at night
> He listen'd to the wind; and as it drove
> The billows with o'erwhelming vehemence
> He, starting from his rugged couch, went forth
> And hazarding a life, too valueless,
> He waded thro' the waves, with plank or pole
> Towards where the mariner in conflict dread
> Was buffeting for life the roaring surge;
> And now just seen, now lost in foaming gulphs,
> The dismal gleaming of the clouded moon
> Shew'd the dire peril. (692–707)

Patrolling the shores, the hermit develops great skill in reading nature. He learns how to "augur" storms and, in effect, becomes a master of understanding the various forms of motion the cliff's climate tends to develop. His first feat is learning to live within the constant change, permeability, and instability Beachy Head figures. The hermit positions himself as someone who understands large tempests—emotional and political—yet is not subject to them. Rather, he unwaveringly rescues those who would be drowned. As someone ostensibly exiled from the system, he acts as a countercurrent, pulling mariners—participants in the system—from its deadly grasp.

As an ethical engagement born through more than idiosyncratic, individual instances of aid, the hermit's mission resonates with Kant's scheme of universal hospitality formed as part of his plan for international peace (and Enlightenment freedom) in *Perpetual Peace*. Notions of universality are already circulating from the poem's outset since the channel's oceanic waters are associated with the Old Testament God of Genesis, who "Omnipotent / Stretch'd forth his arm, and rent the solid hills" of Beachy Head (6–7). The channel thus invokes a creative space for new notions of justice, equality, and universality. The hermit evokes Smith's own argument with the 1793 Alien Act, which required refugees from the French Revolution to register with a justice of the peace or have their habeas corpus rights rescinded.[26] Kant rejects this empirical regulation of nationalistic bodies by advocating for a "cosmopolitan right" that requires "the right of an alien not to be treated as an enemy upon his arrival in another's country" (118).

Further, he "may request the *right* to be a *permanent visitor* . . . but the *right to visit*, to associate, belongs to all men by virtue of their common ownership of the earth's surface" (118; emphasis in original). In discussing these views of hospitality and cosmopolitan right, Peter Melville argues that Kant's work reveals how a "foreigner's arrival plays itself out . . . as the nation's troubling recognition of its own internal strangeness" (74). The hermit's repetitive acts of unconditional salvation appear almost to be guided by an invisible "categorical imperative of hospitality" (Derrida, *Of Hospitality* 76), and his mission raises the possibility that he operates under an intuitively grasped concept of hospitality, one that might recapitulate the basis for a proper alien law.

"Beachy Head," however, expands vacancy not by defining a categorical universality that would come to replace embodied acts of Smithian sympathy, but by denuding embodied identity wrought by the gendered body, material acquisitions, imperial culture, or the happenstance of birth. In effect, Smith overwrites subjectivity, empirical or categorical, with a coastal, figural fluidity. Similar to the smuggler-shepherd who appears earlier in the poem and abandons his flocks for illegal trade, the hermit has jettisoned his place within society to troll the shores of the channel and participate in more abstract international relations. There he picks up not exchangeable goods but mariners—those stranded by wars and commerce gone awry.

> Often he had snatched
> From the wild billows, some unhappy man
> Who liv'd to bless the hermit of the rocks.
> But if his generous cares were all in vain,
> And with slow swell the tide of morning bore
> Some blue swol'n cor'se to land; the pale recluse
> Dug in the chalk a sepulcher—above
> Where the dank sea-wrack mark'd the utmost tide,
> And with his prayers perform'd the obsequies
> For the poor helpless stranger. (707–716)

With a large dose of poetic justice, Smith has the hermit rescue sailors from the sea only after they have been separated from their ship and cargo. In other words, he saves these transnational souls once the sea has freed them from—or taken revenge on them for—their roles in the trade economy or in a European war based in large part on imperial economies. Unlike either the penetrating imperial invasions or the blockades imposed by both England and France during the Fourth Coalition, the hermit stands as a figure of receptivity who, rather than inseminating the world with trade, ideology, or empirical identity, sits poised on the border, ready to receive what comes ashore.

As if baptized by the Channel waves, the "mariner" becomes the "unhappy man" and finally a "stranger" buried anonymously within the cliff face, not unlike the hermit who, in the following lines, will also come to rest in a grave unmarked but for the "chalk" of the Down cliffs. Death, however, is not the only equalizer here; both the hermit and the sailors have been bereft of their social identities and have become strangers to each other and the nations from which they came. Monica Smith Hart in her essay on Smith describes the "exilic person" as one whose "public identity as exile constitutes a lack of public identity" (317).[27] The hermit and the mariner alike have been stripped of various social identities and ideological claims, and they all become figures in transit. Much as empiricist taste is overturned for an aporia of consumption (or the ingestion of nothing) in the *Sonnets*, what would be the hermit's personal sympathy or categorical hospitality transforms into a receptivity, an acceptance that does not depend on sensate subjectivity.

The hermit once again returns us to the nebulous waters that muddy empiricist or idealist forms of knowledge, suggesting an alternative that not only skirts the embodied sensation at the heart of empiricist feeling, but also shirks a rule-bound law of hospitality or alien rescue. The hermit might at first appear to be akin to what Derrida, revising Kant, concludes is an aporia of unconditional hospitality, a "lawfulness outside the law" that seeks to circumvent the conceptual determinism of Enlightened reason, but that can never, as Derrida says, be fully realized.[28] As a figure of exile, Smith's hermit suggests that the promise of Enlightenment freedom might be redeemed only through pledging oneself to something beyond nationalism and strictly gendered identification. The hermit certainly eschews determinative identifications but not, however, through a Derridean "infinite idea [that] should resist law itself" (71). While Smith raises the possibility of an intuitive concept of hospitality, she engages the sways of figural abstraction to fend off the dangers of embodiment that install identity in the first place. Her contingency tracks the movements not only of language but also of matter through a form of affect that builds and constructs movements among and between different types of things (human, language, world). The trace structure of affect is its pervasive movement enabled by language, which moves even through absence. Not a resurrection of the presence of matter, vacancy pursues the continuous turning of all things. The hermit accepts, and in some ways materially receives, everything that is possible and impossible, including absence itself. In this way, Smith's hospitality suggests that the host must be subject not so much to a radical self-abnegation, as Derrida suggests, but a transformation into the poem's lyrical tide. Poem, oceanic climate, and human are indelibly bound together into a posthuman, dynamic figural materiality.

At the final precipice of the poem, the various structures of aporia come to a head with two successive disappearances—the pastoral poet who leaves his lovelorn ballads on trees and the hermit who leaves behind an absent epitaph that was to be written in the cliff walls. The poem enunciates this final moment of vacancy as a meta-poetic one. While the romancing stranger-poet resurrects the history of gender-bound verse, the unwritten epitaph offers a view of posthuman poetics in the offing. Before vanishing from Beachy Head, the wandering poet leaves behind a trail of his romantic ballads near old trees. In his "visionary, nursing dreams" (655), these poems about lost love represent a rustic poet who affixes his idealized views of the landscape to an idealized love for an unavailable maid. If the poet looks for freedom from urban luxury and corruption in the bower of the pastoral, then his lyric poetry futilely continues to look to the past for this freedom, rather than to the possibility of a different kind of future. His *telos*, like those of the Romans and the Danish pirates, has proven to be misguided. Though his hope is to be envied, his disappearance from the landscape would seem to comment on just how useless his poetic model has become. The rift he creates offers the possibility to reimagine the role of the poet and his linguistic propensities beyond the gendered, sensing body.

This future culminates in the poem's final lines, in the troping out of the hermit's representable existence and gendered subjectivity:

> Those who read
> Chisel'd within the rock, these mournful lines
> Memorials of his sufferings, did not grieve,
> That dying in the cause of charity
> His spirit, from its earthly bondage freed,
> Had to some better region fled for ever. (724–731)

As the poet explains, before the hermit died, he had chiseled on the rocks of his cave "these mournful lines." Critics have speculated on whether Smith never had the chance to write the hermit's epitaph, whether she deliberately left the poem an unfinished fragment without the inscription, or whether the poem itself stands in for his final words.[29] However we might read it, perhaps the lacuna is Smith's own final act of charity, freeing her readers from any kind of definitive meaning about Beachy Head itself. Unlike Wordsworth's peddler or shepherd figures from *The Excursion*, Smith's hermit disappears without preaching his words of wisdom. His sermon is his silence, and he finally remains outside any definitively human language, ever about to write his epitaph. Rather than actually chiseling his last words in stone, in language that will become monumentalized and hardened, the hermit seems forever poised in the moment just before the act of writing, or perhaps within a form of writing illegible except as beachy matter itself.

The venture begun in the hermit's cave ends not with cosmopolitan surety but instead with a moment of prelinguistic vacancy, where aesthetics and ethics remain poised on the brink of an anticipatory, future articulation—at once through the figures of the hermit and the shifting sediments themselves. In his ethereal flight to "some better region," the hermit has achieved Smith's longed for state figured in her earlier sonnets as the insensibility of death, sleep, and oblivion. Unencumbered by earthly bondage, his spirit is set free, as if death through charity has enabled him to evade earth, region, and body. He might represent the quiescence in a distant land that the mariners experience, but his missing epitaph signals that his death marks a figure for the possibility of a language beyond the demands of gender, subjectivity, and sensibility, of the pastoral, of international sentiment, and of empirical inscription, a possibility that can be marked only by vacancy. Within the blank epitaph, we encounter a place where the subject is already dissolved, received by both the cliffside and the movements of vacancy. Beachy Head finally figures inscription without an epitaph; the poem marks the motions of remembrance and response without any true memorialization. In the poem's final moment, sensation, consumption, and identification are all suspended within the aporetic stilling of the empirical that gives way to affect's doubly material and figural shifting sands of time.

In this recurrent motion of receptivity signaled by the hermit's absence, Smith marks an anticipated futurity always on the rise. For her, any future-to-come predicated on a radical hospitality is an unthinkable idea built not around an unconditional event as Derrida's is,[30] but through the exchange of individual, positivistic events for affect's continuous movement. These happenings still, however, leave traces of their history in the margins—margins such as Beachy Head's "vast concussion"—whose respective geological and biographical contexts are pointedly left to the textual events of the poem's copious endnotes. Unlike typically Romantic attempts to flee from history into the imagination, Smith ironically escapes out of the very history of imperialism she then sets as the vista of her final vantage point, as the text breaks into the historical endnotes that frame the poem.[31]

As a case in point, the endnote about the hermit mentions that the Parson Darby tradition might be thirty years old, a fact that would pointedly set the legend's origin around 1776. Rather than an unhistoricized figure, the hermit spans the beginning of the American Revolutionary War and events of the Napoleonic Wars contemporaneous with "Beachy Head"'s composition, especially the Battle of Trafalgar in 1805 and the beginning of Napoleon's blockade of English ports on the Continent with the Berlin Decree of 1806. What the hermit looks out upon from Beachy Head is some extremely contested naval space, fraught with imperial wars and blockades that encompass Continental Europe and beyond—as well as that nonhuman, oceanic expanse that moves regardless of such human signification.[32] This historicity of the endnotes leads not to specific, referential historical events, or contextual readings of them, but to a horizon of historicity. Like the chalky expanse of Beachy Head or its troubled waters, the toggling of the endnotes intimates the movement between the poem's future-to-come and the gestures of history within the notes. The poem, in effect, ends twice, as the historical footnotes become the poem's future anterior. The hermit signals Smith's need to keep history in her vista but let its experiences and laws slip through her grasp to imagine a different possible future that might reshape its contingencies altogether. Perhaps nearer to something like the circular scrolls gestured to during the poem's initial passages or the Channel's "utmost tide," the hermit's oblique story veers toward a figural account that would repeatedly ingest, circulate, and move beyond supposed sociohistorical truths. The poet reminds us that imperial and literary histories are constructed through a repetition of tropes that, like Romanticism itself, can best be forged not through empirical representation with its dependency on narrative, linked association, cause and effect, historical reference, or historical facticity, but through the impossible and recursive motions of the figural.

In tracing the vibrant aspect of Beachy Head's cliffs and the hermit's movements among them, what we trace is not the historical or literary movement of a body within a landscape but a figure extending from the human mind to the nonhuman cliffs to the sea below, from future to past and back again. The vacancy of Beachy Head reveals history to be a trope on an improbable rescue mission to disrupt the empirical. It only succeeds as a figure and a form of boundary crossing, including the boundary between the figural and material. This, Smith tells us, is what vacancy is and what it is good for: not so much to deconstruct categories (empirical/ideal, past/present/future), or to reveal creative mental impasse, but rather to uncover affect's interminable, figural movement through categories, materials, and temporalities always active in their disappearance and transformation. She definitively shows us the stark difference between the empirical poetry of representation—especially the discourse of sensibility—and the figural poetics of speculation that extends past the limits of the human into the more nebulous material world.

The danger in this method of figural antinomy lies with the potential that the mind will become suspended within a moment of impossibility—in an aporia that leaves us permanently out of thought and mind. There is the added actuality that the method for moving beyond both individual sensations and universal concepts must be repeatedly instigated because it is too easy to feel or reason once again. Smith's own shifting figuration and repetition is testament to such a problem, and it is one that Mary Robinson and Maria Jane Jewsbury will confront directly when they look to intensify affect's interminable movement. Rather than aporia's repeated single movement of impossibility, Robinson multiplies the affective movements through repetition with difference, varying them to outrun sensation through diversity, moving from an aporia to euporia. Smith, however, remains committed throughout her career to a type of figural antagonism that leaves us moving out of mind and body and into the vast concussion. When we impossibly drink the cup of Lethe or let the prospect receive us, we stand on the precipice of remaking knowledge and life, of uttering and doing something revolutionary.

CHAPTER 2

Mary Robinson's Intensities

Sensation after Oblivion

Mary Robinson's Sappho might appear to narrate the quintessential history of the poetess of sensibility who, gutted by the repetitive expression of her longing for Phaon, dies to memorialize her emotions and their mode of understanding. Unlike the "varying cadence" and "rival flow'rets" that tune Sappho's lyre at the start of the sequence, the famed poet is struck dumb and dull by a passion that repeatedly returns, left only able "to chant *one* name in ceaseless lays / To hear no words other tongues say" (1.4, 3.12, 6.5–6). Sappho's incessant chant certainly speaks a critique to sensibility's excesses, here the excess of feeling expression, but it even more trenchantly diagnoses a form of monomania. Her fixation on Phaon occurs through the vocalization of the same name, a repetition of a single sensation without any difference. Resembling empiricist accounts of idiocy, where the mind cannot construct new or clear thoughts, Sappho's stammering marks passion's tendency to make the female mind, so desirous of romance's banal sensations, into a mere container for unthinking, deranged, monotonous habit. Yet the poet's suicidal jump into the "Leucadian deep" signals not a capitulation to silence, death, oblivion, or simply the shutting down of her mind. Rather, Robinson charts a figurative leap into "loftier passions" that, in later poems, will move outside sensation or the sensing body. Where Smith works through the empirical discourse of taste, Robinson speaks back to another common strand of empiricism and its gendering of women's minds and bodies, the discourse on habit, custom, and prejudice. Robinson's version of vacancy, in contemplating empirical habit, marks another technique for auguring affect, not through aporia, but through repetition with difference.¹

Robinson needs additional poems to spell out her notion of these "loftier passions," where the repetitive stutters of supposedly raving idiots produce new affects through their unique forms of articulation. "The Savage of Aveyron" and "To the Poet Coleridge" figure emptied minds and open spaces that house vibrating matter not bound by physiological movement or its perception. While the eponymous savage repeatedly shouts the word, "Alone!" the poem's speaker instigates a ballad refrain with incremental variations of "I sigh'd to be—a traveller alone" (39). The idiocy of both boy and empathetic speaker reverberate aural modulations in speed, rhythm, and duration by adding pauses, words, and rhymes. These shifts do not foment minute perceptions to remedy idiocy with the sympathy of fellow feeling; rather, they promote nonsignifying, self-altering motions through language. The ballad's refrain spools out repetition through time, through iterative movement contingent to the stanza's meaning. Its floating variations are expressly not synthesized by the imagination nor do they cohere in bodies or specific genders; instead, they incrementally produce a new form of sensation outside mind and body.

It should be obvious to say that Robinson's poems are a crucial place for Romanticists to think about the problems of sensation, but, with the exception of Jerome McGann's reading of *Sappho and Phaon*, Robinson's work has rarely been seen as mounting a serious, philosophical inquiry into the nature of sensation as it relates to the imagination and its Enlightenment underpinnings.² Even Daniel Robinson, who shows us an extremely versatile, formally ambitious poet, nonetheless agrees with other scholars who make "no great claim for the profundity or the sophistication" of her poems (*The Poetry* 10). In contrast to empiricists David Hume and Edmund Burke, Robinson's poetry draws attention to the problem that repetitive sensations solidified into customs can diminish and degrade women's potential for knowledge. Empiricism decays into monomania when it turns into a gender ideology about the habits of the ever-loving female mind. Eventually, Robinson's work shows that the body too, as a conduit for sensation and for all knowledge, must be surpassed if detrimental behaviors are to be changed.

Although Robinson certainly works from Hume's ideas about custom and John Locke's discussions of power and liberty to take the leap into the Leucadian deep of affect, she questions bodily sensation as the building block of knowledge and the dialogic structure of empirical knowledge—sensation translated into reflection.³ The problem she identifies within the discourses of empiricism and sensibility, this oscillation between the fullness of sensation and its dearth, likewise cements other intellectual habits later reified into ideological customs, especially those revolving around binary gender. Robinson's exploration of idiocy and linguistic repetition, as a solution to such a binary, neither simply empties out the mind nor depends on a repetition caused by melancholy's embodied feeling that repeatedly recalls a lost love object. By returning the reflecting, measuring, empiricist, gendered mind back to the realm of pure sensation, Robinson's poetic idiocy provides another sort of movement through categories, subjects, objects, and bodily states via repeating, differential sounds and pauses.

This pursuit might be termed a radical empiricism that reforms sensation as a movement not dependent on the empiricist body. Such a project places Robinson in paratactic conversation with Gilles Deleuze's similar critique or rethinking of sensation, which he calls "a vital power that exceeds every domain and traverses them all" (*Francis Bacon* 37). He variously terms this power "Rhythm" and "intensity," a varying movement among faculties and bodies unbound by isolated sensory perceptions. While both Romantic poet and modern philosopher carefully receive and reshape the Humean empiricist inheritance, unlike Deleuze, Robinson constructs an intensity through tropic play, which initiates the fullest production of vacancy, and its movements of affect, beyond empiricism.[4] Such a solution can help us advance recent conversations influenced by Deleuze about empirical affect that have tended to see affect and language as antagonistic; Robinson helps to reveal another form of affect found within poetry's special attunements to tropes, repetitions, and formal structures.[5] When vacancy's repetition with differences generate iterative movements through multiple bodies and landscapes, it paves the way for us to think of figures that traverse and co-create a posthuman realm composed of a plethora of iterating intensities that cannot be codified or silenced by the songs of sensibility.

Vacant Repetition and the Leap Past Oblivion

Sappho's leap into the "cool concave" at the end of *Sappho and Phaon* may be the most well-known moment from Robinson's *oeuvre* dramatizing oblivion (43.8), but her early poem "Sight" (1793) affords perhaps her most bald exploration of traditional Enlightenment epistemology. This irregular ode clearly sets out to tout the "Transcendent gift" of the "SENSE DIVINE" (11, 23), since sensation enables the perception and reflection that lead to ideas, and eventually fulsome knowledge. Locke accordingly figures knowledge as light let into the dark room of the mind. Yet, on Robinson's account, such Enlightenment illumination during the age of the revolutionary terror seems appropriately always on the verge of total failure. In contrast to sight's coveted radiance, Robinson repeatedly turns to what she variously terms the "Oblivion horrible," "a melancholy blank," "ONE unenlighten'd void," and "the cold vacuum of the sightless eye" whose "cold Oblivion hovers o'er the mind" and "plunges Reason in its WORST ABYSS!" (26, 32, 47, 50, 68, 91, 119). Such linked figures frame oblivion as a vacuum, void, or abyss that bars the highest form of reason, perception and reflection, by blocking out the light altogether. Oblivion amounts to an absence of sensation that might lead to understanding. Ashley Cross has recently shown that Robinson's critique of the Della Cruscan terminology of excess and emptiness begins as soon as the poet engages in dialogue with Hannah Crowley and Robert Merry, with clear echoes of Charlotte Smith: already at this point in her career, Robinson sees no "sweet converse" in sensibility's highs and lows, but in a dialogue that only culminates in a dead-end for revolutionary knowledge (Cross, *Mary Robinson* 22). Whether Robinson seeks to join the Della Cruscan poetic scene or later reject it for something more like Romantic lyricism, her early poems, in ways we have not fully explored, are heavily invested in a philosophical consideration of empiricism. She identifies a major problem with empiricism: sensation's tendency to form a subject structured around the dialectic of sensory fullness and dearth. For feminine subjects especially, intense sensitivity to sensation, their sensibility, all too often leads toward oblivion and prevents new sensations that could form new thoughts and ideas. This epistemological binary is one that Robinson struggles with in the 1790s—to articulate and then trope beyond.

Robinson's periodic return to the "dread gloom opake" throughout the course of "Sight" suggests that light can enter the picture only when it has a void to fill. The image of a mind devoid of thought and feeling, barren because it is no longer receiving sensory input, expresses well the Lockean dictum that knowledge comes from sensations, which, when reflected upon, become ideas. The mind may begin as a tabula rasa but also at times appears as a "dark room," whose darkness figures the dearth of sensory knowledge, a chamber waiting to let the light in. In *An Essay Concerning Human Understanding*, Locke writes, "the understanding is not much unlike a closet wholly shut from light, with only some little openings left, to let in external visible resemblances, or ideas of things" (II.xi.17).[6] Oblivion presents a similar absence of sensory knowledge, and as a spatial void, it comes to resemble Locke's "dark room."[7] The "dread gloom opake" summons "The longing for that SOMETHING unknown, / Whose pow'r he feels, diffusing its warm touch / O'er every sensate nerve! that POW'R which marks / The varying seasons in their varying forms" (77, 78–81). These moments of oblivion strategically instigate "The longing for that SOMETHING unknown" to creep into the mind and spark new, blissful sensations, seasons, and forms.

Those very sensations, however, already intimate the possibility that sensory perception is not quite enough to fill the void. The dynamic "POW'R" Robinson describes certainly resembles a liberatory force, but here sensation is still very much bounded by vision, hearing, and touch. Such embodied experiences can vary only so much, so Robinson must paradoxically rely on oblivion to renew the action of the mind. That figure for the loss of sensation significantly gestures toward Locke's definition of power: the ability of the mind to make or receive a change, the prime demonstration of such power being "to begin or forbear, continue or end several actions of our minds, and motions of our bodies" (II.xxi.5). While the rhetorical surface of Robinson's poem concerns itself with a trajectory toward Enlightenment "sight" and understanding, the resort to vacuity leverages an implicit alternative that activates liberty—that power to think or not to think, continue or forbear.

Although "Sight" appears to present the Miltonic darkness of oblivion as an inevitable and unwanted state of mind, nevertheless, the poem actually demonstrates that the possibility of not thinking secures liberty as the potential to occasionally suspend—and then redirect—thought. The antidote to repetitive sensations and associations, which harden into customary feelings or ideas, becomes the cessation of thought altogether. The poem's repeated alternation between "Oblivion Horrible! to know no change" and "The varying seasons in their varying forms" suggests that to foment true knowledge within an empirical epistemology, sensation must deploy "no change" to set in motion further variation and movement. If, as Susan Stewart has argued, *poeisis* arises to "counter the oblivion of darkness" (2), then Robinson creates Miltonic darkness to emerge from it, to be filled with new sensations and thus the potential for new ideas.

Yet this alternation of emptiness and fullness nevertheless exerts quite a bit of tyranny on the feeling subject, who ricochets between sensory, emotional floods and droughts. When this empirical pattern of knowledge gets adumbrated within the discourse of sensibility, in the depiction of lovelorn Sappho, the sensible poet becomes either addicted to love, and its lays, or mute. It is this binary of sensory, embodied knowledge that Robinson strives to write herself beyond.

Both Cross and Daniel Robinson, in their monographs on Robinson, duly demonstrate *Sappho and Phaon*'s critique of the cult of high feeling.[8] But Mary Robinson's case against sensibility, I would argue, rests in the way the sequence spends a good deal of time engaged with a few particular, detrimental tendencies that arise when empirical sensation (and oblivion), rendered within the discourse of sensibility, comes to trap women in repetitive sensations and ideas. Robinson diagnoses Sappho's lovesickness as so repetitive and consistent that it necessarily leads to mental oblivion and, eventually, death. She indicts the tyranny of sensibility to suggest how feeling, or women's ideas about that feeling, becomes so strong as to overwhelm any other thoughts, leaving Sappho merely able to reiterate her despair. It capitulates in the famed poet repeating the same songs over and over again—"to chant one name in ceaseless lays" (6.5). Her mind synthesizes the repetition of sensations into one oft-repeated association or idea rather than allowing a variation of differences to abound.

Perhaps working from Mary Wollstonecraft's critique of sensibility in *The Vindication of the Rights of Woman*, Robinson suggests that because empiricism relies on sensation, women are forced to rely on their bodies for their information about the world, which can have the effect of always filtering sensation through a sexed body from the start. Even more problematic, when women use customary connection to make sense of empirical observations, their translation of that sense data into ideas is endued, through sensibility's prevalent ideology, with an indoctrination into very narrow customs of thought and very little diversity in their ideas about the (largely domestic) world. These habits of sensibility work, for Deleuze, as "a contraction . . . the fusion of that repetition in the contemplating mind" (*Repetition* 74). Sappho's mind contracts to a dull, mindless repetition, and her only recourse to end the cycle of extremes is to exit the tropology of oblivion, and take the leap into a vacancy, the oceanic "Leucadian deep." Its baptismal, rolling waves begin to draw a figure other than the dominant epistemologies offered to Sappho—the light of reason and the frenzy of sensibility—in order to wash away the source of reified sensations and ideas (including gender difference).

While oblivion has up until this point in Robinson's career operated as a figure for mental blankness, in *Sappho and Phaon* the eradication of sensation that frees the mind must be followed by a suicide that kills the body. Sappho's epistemological cliff-diving becomes a figure of vacancy's emancipatory promise: she refuses to continue to be made an idiot (in the empiricist sense) by empiricism's demands upon women that leave them vacant creatures at the mercy of romantic sensation. The sequence's final sonnet, written after the lyricist's voluntary demise, prophesizes the birth of a new poetics that will "more than mortal raptures claim" (44.13). Sappho's death pointedly spells the end of Robinson's poetics of embodied sensation and marks her commitment to a project whose cultivation of vacancy reenvisions rapture outside the body and the bounds of Enlightenment subjectivity.

The sonnet sequence begins with a description characterizing Sappho's well-functioning, creative mind as it operates through sensory plenitude. She achieves a "bliss supreme" through "varying cadence" that resists passion "By mem'ry goaded and frenzy driven" (1.2, 1.12). Such sensory variation is pointedly not found in the second sonnet's Temple of Chastity but rather in sonnet three's the "bow'r of Pleasure," where "Small tinkling rills bid rival flow'rets bloom!" and "tyrant passion finds a glorious tomb!" (3.4, 3.12, 3.14). These sonnets amplify alternating sounds that instigate a varying aural signal built not simply from repetition but one that contains repetition and difference. What we hear in only the briefest of murmurs in Sappho's verse will be explored more thoroughly in Robinson's late poems, once she has put sensibility's sway over sensation to bed. Only then can iterative sound—those tinkling of bells—fully ring in sensational variation and rivalry.

All too soon this "varying cadence" is blotted out by Sappho's monomaniacal passion, a single but feeble vein of sensation and perception. Beginning with sonnet four, where, as the title indicates, "Sappho discovers her Passion," she self-consciously documents a slow slide into cognitive decline:

WHY when I gaze on Phaon's beauteous eyes,
Why does each thought in wild disorder stray?
Why does each fainting faculty decay,
And my chill'd breast in throbbing tumults rise? (1–4)

In Robinson's sonnet, Sappho appears to move, within the space of the first four lines, from madness into a form of idiocy. Although Sappho's thoughts, when gazing on Phaon, first become disordered and wild like a madman's, the excess of sensation quickly leads to a form of idiocy—the "decay" of Sappho's "fainting faculty." Locke's mutual definitions of idiots, or "naturals," and madmen can help to unravel this self-diagnosis. While idiots "proceed from want of quickness, activity, and motion, in the intellectual faculties, whereby they are deprived of reason," madmen "have lost the faculty of reasoning" when they incorrectly join ideas (II.xi.13). Sappho's "throbbing tumults rise" in a now "fainting faculty" and "chill'd breast," slowed motions that point to this want of mental quickness and emotional malaise, as the overwrought motion of the body burns out into a cessation of thought and activity. Sensation's ability to vary and move the mind soon decays into the unhelpful repetition of a monotonous mental drift.

Soon after, Sappho is irrevocably struck dumb, paralyzed, and "stung by hopeless passion": "Mute, on the ground my Lyre neglected lies, / The Muse forgot, and lost the melting lay" (4.5–6). The famed poet must summon her "tuneful maids" to sing and soothe her—and complete her poem (5, 8, 10). Even at its initial moments of discovery in the sonnet sequence, Sappho's passion inevitably leads to the idiocy that eventuates in Sappho's empty mind. She can no longer make propositions, reason, or put together those numbers necessary for song. Unable to sing, her thought has been completely stymied. Her mind falls into that "want of quickness, activity, and motion" that characterizes empiricist idiocy (Locke II.xi.13), that mental void that anticipates the Leucadian deep into which Sappho will eventually leap.

Sonnet six most fully articulates the monomania of repetitive feeling: "to fix the tender gaze" or "to chant *one* name in ceaseless lays / To hear no words that other tongues can say" (1, 5–6). As the poem's title suggests, Sappho aims to describe "the characteristics of Love," but in doing so she reveals her penchant for inveterate thought that instigates emotional and intellectual tunnel vision. Again, in empiricist terms, because love will allow her to perceive only one set of sensory stimuli, her ideas cannot develop. Such monomania is certainly not true for all empirical experience, but it is particularly true for women of sensibility taught to think only of their love object or to perceive passion's sensations. For example, one might think of *Sense and Sensibility*'s Marianne Dashwood, who can only think of Willoughby regardless of other evidence that points to his negligence, or Mary Wollstonecraft's childish women whose habitual attentions are self-absorbed and bound to the fleeting sensuality of their beauty, their dress, and their charming suitors.

Both Robinson and Wollstonecraft clearly attend to the social habits indoctrinated into young women, but Robinson attends less to the superficiality, transience, or brute nature of sensation than its slavish repetition. Deleuze calls the mind's aggregation of repetition into a seemingly single sensation a passive synthesis, "our expectation that 'it' will continue . . . the fusion of that repetition in the contemplating mind" (*Difference* 74). It is the habit of the mind to contract a succession of instances, even the iambic tick-tock of alternation into a single moment, idea, or unity of sameness (74). Conversely, it is the perverse role of the imagination "to draw something new from repetition, to draw difference from it," as repetition once again appears as separate elements or cases (76). When Sappho contemplates her views of Phaon and her ensuing songs, she can only fuse them into the single song of sensibility and dooms herself to repeat that selfsame tune over and over again.

Similar problems occur across the sonnets as Sappho collects a bevy of reiterated terms that consolidate sensation into "tyrant passion." In sonnet 11, for example, where once and for all Sappho "Rejects the Influence of Reason," "Frenzy darts forth in mightiest ills array'd; / Around thy throne destructive tumults rise" (10–11). If repetition abounds in *Sappho and Phaon*, it is because the monomania of Sappho's feminine passion revokes her liberty and her status as a diverse thinker; she contracts her mind, again, into a habit of throbbing tumults. Her self-diagnosis is particularly distressing because it reveals how easily the vibrating potentiality of sensation can be subsumed into a static, customary sensibility.

Such an intellectual crux helps to illuminate the problem Robinson has with Charlotte Smith's "illegitimate" sonnets.[9] Robinson does not mention Smith by name in the poem's Preface but does cite her in a note on living authors' opinions regarding the legitimate sonnet. She quotes Smith's preface to *Elegiac Sonnets*, where Smith admits that she has not followed the Petrarchan model because of its formal difficulty in the English language and instead writes her sonnets "to consist of fourteen lines, and appear to me no improper vehicle for a single sentiment" (*Works* I:321). As critics now recognize, Smith's sonnets almost singlehandedly revived the sonnet through their ability to convey "a single sentiment" to their readers,[10] and it may be this perceived deterministic sentiment that Robinson rails against with her alternate vision of "rival flow'rets." Indeed, Robinson begins her Preface with a stark objection to the Shakespearean sonnet's formal tendency to conclude with a couplet, precisely because "winding up the sentiment of the whole, [it] confines the poet's fancy" (*Works* I:320). As a summary gesture, the heroic couplet with its immediate rhyme, unlike the Petrarchan sestet with its woven or alternating rhyme, literally enforces sonic repetition even as it risks unifying the sonnet's complex argument into a single theme, feeling, or sensation.

In addition to various other objections Robinson might have to the "heterogeneous mass of insipid and laboured efforts" that composed the sonnet craze of the late 1780s and early 1790s, she appears to critique the sonnet of sensibility specifically for its tendency to foreclose sensory variety and the fancy that stimulates new thought. This problem surfaces most acutely in sonnet 30, when Sappho hears "love-lorn minstrels" and a "Syren band / With tongues aerial to repeat my pain!" (6, 7–8). Unlike her tuneful maids who could sing the manifold cadences of bliss even when Sappho herself could not, now Sappho hears only minstrels like herself, who sing identical songs of impassioned pain. Her vocal and aural landscape has diminished even further, or as she puts it in sonnet 36: "now goaded frenzy grasps my shrinking brain" (9). Robinson ironically uses Sappho's anachronistic sonnet to lodge a referendum on the sonnet of sensibility as a genre that too often produces the shrinking, dull empiricist brain.

Part of the problem for Robinson is the way that representational language exacerbates the mind's tendency to synthesize repetition or sensation into abstracted experience reiterated by dead language—such as "tyrant passion," a term that Robinson repeats from Smith's own sonnets. As an endemic part of the discourses of sensibility and empiricism, poetic accounts of sensory stimulation too easily congeal into embodied sensation and its representations repeated through and across works. Deleuze, speaking directly to empiricist notions of habit, association, and representation in *Difference and Repetition*, targets empirical sensibility as something quite different from the faculty of sensibility that can initiate sensations leading to difference (and new knowledge). He pointedly argues that true variation cannot arise from "figures already mediated and related to representation" (144). Difference, or what Deleuze describes as "intensity," is a special form of sensation that violently rips through the faculties as it erupts with new knowledge. Such an element is not perceptible by "empirical sensibility which grasps intensity only already covered or mediated by the quality to which it gives rise, and which at the same time can only be perceived from the point of view of a transcendental sensibility which apprehends it immediately in the encounter" (144). For Deleuze, empirical sensation has already been mediated or covered by those secondary sensory qualities that it produces; true difference occurs through the immediate receptivity of immanent intensity prior to that embodied sensation that appears so elemental to Locke and Hume.

Whatever genuine movement exists in *Sappho and Phaon* becomes elided into those repetitious "throbbing tumults" of "tyrant passion." The body becomes an echo chamber for expected feeling that the mind cannot break itself free from rehearsing—or feeling otherwise. As much as the first few sonnets might envision an organic landscape materially lush and fertile, the overdetermined nature of the language of sensibility meets the body's echo-chamber to disastrous effects. It is impossible at this point for Robinson to envision an original encounter, what Deleuze calls "the 'pathic' (non-representative) moment of *the sensation*" that could provide difference through an immanent, pure, or free element of sensation such as intensity (*Francis Bacon* 37). Sappho, the woman poet of feeling, therefore chooses to close down sensory perception altogether, moving eventually into a vacancy that avoids the selfsame thoughts and that opens to more creative, differential sensation.

As she becomes incontrovertibly enslaved to what she calls the "thralldom" or the "tyranny of passion," she increasingly seeks out the "gorgeous shade" or, more drastically, the oblivion of "mental night" (11.14, 7.14). Without an easy cure, the stultifying nature of maniacal passion finally results in total, empty-minded oblivion—figured by darkened minds and landscapes recurring throughout the sonnet sequence. In sonnet 20, Sappho decries her separation from Phaon: "one long night o'er frozen Seythia reigns" (5), while in sonnet 25 she transforms the night into an eternally dark season at the poem's end: "No Sun-beams glitter, and no altars burn! / The mind's dark winter of eternal gloom / Shews 'midst the waste of a solitary urn, / A blighted laurel, and a mould'ring tomb" (11–14). The night, winter, and eternal gloom each summon a temporal waste, while the urn and tomb signify spatial metaphors for oblivion that, once again, evacuate sensory knowledge and the subjective world along with it.

In the penultimate sonnet of the sequence, Sappho "Welcome[s] returning Reason's placid beam" (9), yet reason cannot, in the end, combat her passion for Phaon. She must invite the Lethean waves "To calm rebellious Fancy's fev'rish dream," and only then will her "Lyre distain love's dread control" and end the tyranny over reason (11–12, 13). The recurring "fev'rish dream" of Phaon haunts reason with the specter of "love's dread control," revivifying sensibility through self-stimulating, repetitious sensations and visions that come unbidden to mind and body. Rather than touting the rational faculty, the oceanic void proffers suicide as a freedom from Sappho's enslavement to any empiricist understanding of her own sensitive body. Such a decisive act at once voids the mind's addiction to habituated sensibility and the body's nearly automatic receptivity toward the very sensations that create feelings and thoughts about Phaon in the first place.

Given these echoes, Sappho's final leap into the Leucadian deep allegorizes both social and epistemological freedom. In this poem, at least, freedom can be engineered only by leaping out of the empirical sensorium and the language of sensation altogether. Robinson may be referencing

Locke once again, as the example of the leap from a cliff appears in Locke's discussion of liberty as the choice to think or not to think:

> A man standing on a cliff, is at liberty to leap twenty yards downwards into the sea, not because he has a power to do the contrary action, which is to leap twenty yards upwards, for that he cannot do: but he is therefore free, because he has a power to leap, or not to leap. But if a greater force than his, either holds him fast, or tumbles him down, he is no longer free in that case. (II.xxi.27)

Freedom depends, then, not only on thoughtful choice but also on the ability to leap or not to leap; for Robinson, the ability to leap figures the palpable choice to eradicate subjectivity by killing at once the sensing body and the language of sensation that limits it.[11] This conscious decision characterizes Sappho's plunge into the Leucadian deep, marking the shift from oblivion as a figure for an unwanted void to vacancy. The Leucadian deep, with its "Lethean waves" of forgetting, figures the volitional negation of mental and physical activity. The poet's suicide thus does not mark the tragic collapse into the inevitable, hysterical death of the woman of sensibility, but instead offers an alternative figure for movement that indexes epistemological and ontological emancipation.[12] Women's minds and bodies take flight into waves that do not merely repeat, as Sappho's body is interred and dispersed within a sea both Classical and mythical, now doubly figural. As the "cool concave" of oblivion becomes vacancy's "Leucadian deep," with its "Lethean waves," Robinson uses the figural turns of the continuously rolling waves to move beyond the ideological form of woman and into a merging of Sappho and Lethe, a refiguration of them into a pool of waves, a well of unbecoming. The Lethean waves do not simply produce material movements by referencing a dissolution of the human body into oceanic turbulence. The repetition of the trope—"concave," "deep," "waves"—as well as the motion of the waves themselves figure a form of matter that exists within language's repetitive movements as well as within the world beyond the confines of the human body or its representations in the mind. Vacancy, with all its suicidal tendencies, marks the Romantic rejection of gender and subjectivity, but its deep gulf also intimates a series of spaces where bodies intermingle and slash through sensation and subjectivity to form other kinds of material, ontological alliances.[13]

Robinson presents Sappho's leap into vacancy as an exit from empiricist sensibility altogether into an epistemological and ontological great-beyond where the grounds of knowledge and modes of existence—especially our understanding of the feeling body—might be forged anew. Like Keats's *Hyperion*, Sappho becomes a storied figure of willful self-destruction for the sake of a revolution in systems of knowledge. Only through the Sapphic suicide of the feeling subject can the female body be reborn into new figures for sensation and knowing. In the sequence's final sonnet, written after Sappho's death, the speaker gestures toward this potentiality, looking to a host of "loftier passions" and "loftier themes" with a repetition intimating the troping of repetition with difference that will become Robinson's hallmark poetic technique (44.14). Robinson finally takes the plunge into a gulf that promises futurity in a wider, more fraught poetics, one that circles back to the sequence's initial endorsement of multiplicity and diversity, yet not tied to the human, sensing human body. Her particular verdict on repetition anticipates her later solution—to find a habit of language that initiates difference in repetition. Such a vacancy would open possibility of imperceptible movements and intensities to obviate the easy listening of the unchanging, feminine song.

Tracing the "Circling Bounds" of Robinson's Intensity

Toward the end of her career, Robinson develops vacancy as a figure for the simultaneous eradication of sensibility and the production of nonempirical sensation that moves through language into various forms of materiality. Poems after *Sappho and Phaon* present savants whose supposedly vacant brains provoke them into stuttering utterances that create new, differential sensations resounding with others and amid the landscapes that surround them. Robinson can help us to refract the Romantic fascination with idiocy as one about the rejection of normative subject positions (most particularly those feminized by overwhelming sensation or feeling, however ecstatic it may be), in search of forms for affect's material and figural movements manifested by and kept nebulous by iterative articulations. Through the repetitive refrains of *Lyrical Tales* and her newspaper poems at the turn of the decade, Robinson envisions repetition as perversely productive, rather than stunting. We might think of this verbosity as something akin to a reparative, alternative model of continuous cognitive, linguistic, and material movement rather than the vacant subject disabled by the dull emptiness of Enlightenment idiocy. She accomplishes this mental feat by jettisoning the classical forms of the ode and the sonnet and by tying her ideas about radical empiricism to formal experimentation with that other poetic vogue of the 1790s, the ballad. In particular, the structure of the balladic refrain helps Robinson focus her attention on the contrast between the repetitive associations found in Sappho's static sonnets and a lyric that becomes a site for a cascade of incremental variation and intellectual heterogeneity.

In the wake of the antiquarian revival, the ballad in the eighteenth century was thought to preserve cultural memory and literary bardic heritage at the same time it was the site for rampant if accidental variation in the form of oral variants.[14] The refrain offers a Janus-faced function: it signals the oral refrains, songs, and stories that reinforce memory and habit even as it generates minute linguistic differences that, in Robinson's poems, have the power to alter ontological and epistemological terrain. Rather than erasing habit altogether, Robinson now explores the possibility of pushing past habit's monotony—and the tendency of the mind to contract iteration into repetition—through verbal overproduction. The ballad's figural and aural repetition, in turn, describes and enacts disparate threads of matter that disrupt a poem's stanzaic spaces and that are unallied to the distinctly feminine or human body.

Deleuze and Felix Guattari point to the dual function of the refrain in *A Thousand Plateaus*, and their model has interesting implications for Robinson's politics at the end of the 1790s as well as for her ultimate vantage on epistemological alternatives to some of the pitfalls of empirical custom and experience. The child singing to himself, the folksong refrain, or even the national song all bring order to chaos, "to draw a circle around that uncertain and fragile center, to organize a limited space" (Deleuze and Guattari 311). The refrain's expression secures the territory of a nation, a village, or a domestic sanctuary. Yet, the inevitably imperfect repetition and its altering rhythm divulge differences already present: "A mistake in speed, rhythm, or harmony would be catastrophic because it would bring back the forces of chaos, destroying both creator and creation" (311). Robinson leverages these sorts of differential movements in her refrain—including speed or timing, the silence of caesuras, and the confusion of speaker and subject (melody and harmony)—to disrupt the customary epistemologies of the nation, the village, the sentimental home, the feeling feminine body, and, what is more, the woman writer as the overly sensible subject.

We do not see Robinson experimenting with the ballad refrains much before her stint as poetry correspondent and then editor for the *Morning Post*.[15] While her experiments with the form predate her literary conversation with Wordsworth and Coleridge's *Lyrical Ballads* in *Lyrical Tales*, they certainly play with poetic discourse as she repeats some of their poems—with differences.[16] Robinson's model for the productive repetition of the ballad refrain comes to fruition in a poem that most directly deals with the Enlightenment discourse of idiocy, "The Savage of Aveyron" (1801). Published in the year after her death, "The Savage of Aveyron" is a companion poem to "All Alone" from *Lyrical Tales*, which itself is a rewriting of Wordsworth's "We are Seven." This poem in particular presents Robinson's consideration of the productively vacant minds found in "The Idiot Boy" and, later, in "There was a boy" from the 1800 edition of *Lyrical Ballads*. Robinson's verbose boy presents not the fainting, decayed faculty of Sappho; instead, his brain becomes a creative motor for the articulacy of preempirical sensation.[17]

Both Robinson's savage, whose mind has been stunted by an early childhood trauma, and the speaker, after coming into contact with the boy, seemingly idiotically repeat themselves through the poem's pattern of refrains. The speaker of "The Savage" is itinerant and wandering in "the mazes of a wood" (1) when she meets a savage boy, who can only communicate by shrieking, drawing notches in a blasted tree, and crying, "Alone!" At first, the boy exhibits the signs of lyric repetition and affective intensity that characterize Wordsworth's Johnny from "The Idiot Boy." The savage can count the three beats needed to put together any kind of metrical foot ("And now he pointed one, two, three" [76]), he can shriek as if in final, ecstatic revelation, and he can say "alone," a verbal sign of lyric solitude. The boy's recitation of "alone" enacts the theme of a lyric even as it defines the lyric as a poem with only the pretense of solitude, written to be overheard.[18] These poetic gestures nevertheless trap the boy in his stultified state, but Robinson refuses to let the mimicry remain empty.

The poem supplies two interlocking tactics for rescuing the boy from his idle repetition: an Enlightenment explanatory narrative and the paratactic minute variations of the refrain, disconnected from the narrative or its emotional bent. The ballad's tale supplies a causal chain for the boy's nonsense, transmuting the utterances into a sign of his idiocy and his potential to be reincorporated into a sympathetic community that reasons away his difference. As Cairns Craig argues in *Romantic Empiricism*, "the associationist conception of the imagination's working is essentially narrative," constructing events, relations, and affective ties from "successive memories" that string together causal relationships (55).[19] Succumbing to the ballad's story, Robinson's speaker appears to participate in the Enlightenment tendency to engage in hypothetical histories of idiots.[20] From this perspective, the refrain varies to enable the narrative's associationist progression from one set of ideas and circumstances to the next. The poem's stanzas are each composed of three quatrains (*abbacccdeffe*), with the entire final quatrain serving as the refrain. The most stable form of the repetition begins in the second stanza, after the speaker meets the boy:

> Then, mazy woods of AVEYRON!
> Then, wilds of dreary solitude!
> Amid the thorny alleys rude
> I sigh'd to be—a traveller alone. (36–39)

During the first half of the poem, the refrain generally keeps the final rhymes and in the same order: Aveyron, solitude, rude, alone. Just after the midpoint of the poem, the refrains begin to vary along with the narrative the speaker is trying to invent, as she gives the boy a backstory to justify his primitive mind. For instance, after she relates how the boy's mother was accosted and killed by forest ruffians, she offers this refrain:

> When in the woods of Aveyron
> Deep in their deepest solitude
> *Three* barb'rous ruffians shed their blood,
> And mock'd, with cruel taunts, her dying groan. (132–135)

Most of these later quatrains preserve the rhymes "Aveyron" and "solitude," varying the final couplet with other rhymes. This variant incorporates the boy's tale into the poem, inviting both explanation and sympathy for the murder of the boy's mother, the originary act that is ultimately responsible for his savage state.[21]

Yet, at the same time, the refrain's minute variants transform the Enlightenment idiot into another sort of being, a producer of rampant difference itself. Both the repetitions and the slight differences in the refrain cannot help but call into question those causal tales when they highlight the involuntary contingency of such articulation. The repetition provides an even greater space for forming difference rather than either explaining it away or sympathizing with the destitute boy. These differences, however, do not simply separate out the multiple, if violent, sensations, but increasingly emphasize the lines' multiple forms of movement, their near-constant shifts in expression, context, and temporality.

The refrain's linguistic force becomes more dramatic and variable the longer it repeats, adding a secondary, dissonant harmony that pulls away from the poem's narration. The savage compels a wild redundant yet revolving contemplation in the mind of the speaker, as the last line of the larger refrain echoes continually but ever so slightly. After hearing the boy's first shriek, the speaker states, "I thought myself alone!" (12), but after deciphering the boy's yell as "Alone! alone!" (20), she changes her stance to "I wish'd myself—a traveller alone" (27). Watching him rush freely around the woods, the speaker responds: "I sigh'd to be—a traveller alone," (39), but after realizing the boy cannot speak, she decides: "And wish'd to be—a traveller alone" (50). The remainder of the poem piles on more variations: "I thought myself a traveller—alone" (63) and again "I wish'd to be—a traveller alone" (87). The speaker's changing ideas about herself are plotted through her shifting articulations of the refrain's main verb: "wish'd," "sigh'd," "thought," and "Waiting to seize." At times, this successive catalogue of sensations does build on the narrative trajectory of the poem, using the additive situations that occur in each of the narrative stanzas to provoke an array of subtle affective responses.

Even more substantially, the speaker's repeated articulations resist codifying a specific emotion or even an emotional range. The refrain alters through the duration of time, such that any seemingly identical return to a primal, savage state nevertheless changes with each passing iteration. Almost all the versions of the refrain include the lines "[. . .] mazy woods of AVEYRON! / [. . .] wilds of dreary solitude!" Their introductory words include "O!," "Then," "Yet," "When," or "While" as they alter both the temporality and the syntactical context of the description, tipping the reader off to slight changes to intonation, address, positionality, and temporality. The many changes are seemingly small, yet they prevent any synthesis into some sort of gothic narrative, singular and identifiable feeling, or conceptual difference. Perhaps the most pointed, continuous change occurs through the moving placement of the caesuras via the dash within the middle of the line ("—a traveller alone"), delayed until the end ("—alone"), or its removal altogether in the tetrameter line ("I thought myself alone"). These shiftings alter the speed and intensity of the refrain so as to change the poem into a potential field of alterations or relations actuated by the additive repetition of the refrain through time and space. The emphasis on the speaker's subjunctive mood (wished/sighed/thought), on the duration of her traveling, or on her various stages of loneliness all decrescendo into the moving dash of tonal and temporal motion that subsume more subjective meaning into the traveling movements of the caesuras' and the refrains' intensities. Although the speaker's redundancy mirrors the boy's, her habitual utterances draw something new into the minds of boy, speaker, and reader—incremental, chromatic differences— or more precisely differences in the act of being made.

As a result, the speaker no longer can be said to view the boy simply as an object of sympathy or pity, with whom she seeks to identify as a similar being, "a traveller alone." Robinson is pointedly looking beyond the discourse and moral logic of sympathy (and its use of nervous sensibility), beyond what Daniel Robinson calls the "typical humanitarian poem of Sensibility," or even the "darker atmosphere of alterity that resists sentimentality" (*The Poetry* 211). The boy stimulates the speaker's subjective dissolution through the mutual contingent generation of intensity, or sensation that moves beyond a series of felt or perceived bodily changes. The more she speaks, the more the speaker loses the solid bounds of her subjectivity, and the more she produces a rash of raging rhythms, speeds, and stutters, moments that do not become subsumed into clear sensation, a general rule of sympathy, or into a rational concept such as solitude. These differences render a field of possibilities too dispersed and minute to be collated, abstracted, or reflected upon into emotional states. This potentiality pointedly leverages the dullness of perception—Locke's inability to affix necessary connections—alongside a perversely productive lack of identification, passive synthesis, or clear sentiment.

Change rests in the power of these shifts to manifest an intersubjective dynamics of movement among savage and speaker. Vacancy's affect here resembles the preconscious quality of Brian Massumi's redrawing of Deleuzean "intensity," an affect that he describes as "a pressing crowd of incipiencies and tendencies," which remain merely potential until consciousness or language qualify them into emotion (30). Yet Robinson does not develop an anticipatory affect that is later codified or selected into something conventional, linguistic, narrative, meaningful, and social. Like other poets of vacancy, language becomes the motor for such nonreferential, uncaptured intensity. She accelerates language's repetitions to accentuate the movements from one tendency to the next—the "pressing" itself that can be instigated through shifts in figuration and rhythm without yet solidifying into what readers identify only later as retroactive "incipiencies."

The aesthetic tactic of the refrain—its construction of revolving, indeterminate differences—leads Robinson into a different political vein from the politics of sympathy or even Wordsworth's second nature of habitual feeling.[22] Robinson's late ballads and tales, with their destitute infants, animals, idiots, and madmen who nevertheless speak their minds, confront political and existential inequality with an alternative to the 1790s radical options: Godwinian rational deliberation or necessitarian benevolence,[23] the radical communitarian politics of the Corresponding Society, the

Painite egalitarianism she supports in her prose, or even the type of ecstatic transcendence of the *polis* or *demos* that we see in Wordsworth's idiot figures.[24] In the wake of the Corresponding Acts Society of 1799, which effectively sent leveling groups underground until after Waterloo,[25] Robinson's savage disputes any communitarian solution to political, social, and intellectual inequality. The group violence that leads to the murder of the savage's mother intimates the male brutality unleashed by the French Revolution and the start of the Napoleonic age. In "The Savage of Aveyron," the communitarian thinking of the Corresponding Societies is analogous to other instances of groupthink turned totalitarian, for example, France's "democratic" warmongering under Napoleon or the Terror's mass paranoia.[26] The gothic gore in many of Robinson's later poems often comes not from a single patriarchal threat but from allegedly reasonable group action. The refrains vocalized by the speaker of "The Savage" likewise bar the reincorporation of the savage or his witness into any normative community or political body. Exiled on the margins of life—and often on the edges of the nation—Robinson's characters, with their nonrational articulacy, cannot participate in a vision of a feminist or radical counterpublic sphere.

Both the savage and the observing narrator present examples of political exceptions who are neither part of minority blocs (such as the bourgeois, educated women of *A Letter to the Women of England*) nor rational individuals entitled to equality or to the identity that sympathy demands. The inhabitants of Robinson's world exist as a collection of chromatic variations whose unaccountable utterances move outside the territorializing abodes of house, village, state, or human subject. The spectrum Robinson presents in *Lyrical Tales* comes close to what Elizabeth Grosz in *Volatile Bodies* has described as Deleuzian Feminism: "a radical antihumanism that renders animals, nature, atoms, even quasars as modes of radical alterity" (179). Rather than the binary distinctions between woman and man, civilized or savage, man and animal, the savage of Aveyron helps Robinson eschew discourses that would install otherness, and she instead promotes a potential menagerie of differences that often cannot be categorized by language or perception. These figures sit without subjectivity as a collection of repetitions, movements of difference on the make, localized and placed in relation by dint of their shared affective and linguistic exchange not directed or codified by the observing body or by the rational mind.

Thus, the poem works through at least three different tactics to rearticulate difference: refrains that change as they recur through time; refrains that lodge a resistance to identity and universality secretly underwritten by the binaries of identity and difference, inclusion and exclusion; and finally, refrains that obscure the semiotic content in human language. With enough repetition, we eventually fail to hear the content or meaning of the refrain. Rather than emitting sounds stripped of their humanity that can still be perceived as aural sensation, the savage's music turns our attention to the sheer movements of the line. We stop being interested in the speaker's conceptual formulation of what it means to be "a traveller alone," but instead begin to listen only for the shifts in time, tone, and rhythm beyond even the lyric's sonorous differences. As Deleuze writes, the "imbrication of semiotic and material" eventuates in a situation where "music materializes matter," eschewing sound and form for "duration and intensity" (337, 343), what we might see in Robinson as a new type of sensation unmarried to identity, territory, or the empirically sensing subject.

This nonsonic sensory richness is most immediate in the traveling caesuras found in the last line of the refrain: for example, "And wish'd to be—a traveller alone!" or "I thought myself a traveller—alone" (51, 63). The optative mood of such declarations gives way to a caesura denoted by a dash that likewise connotes a momentary suspension of cognition—thoughts or feeling. The gap or void of the drawn-out lineal pause, dramatized by the dash, might seem to figure the thoughtless mental blank of Wordsworth's Johnny or the dull associations of the idiot boy, even as they celebrate the pleasures of such emptiness. Avital Ronell in *Stupidity* describes this lyricism as "vacantly glacializing ecstasy," adrift in the "suspension of occurrence: a caesura or syncope" that is at once pleasurable and delightfully beyond understanding (277, 276).[27] Such existential joy might likewise be akin to either Wordsworthian passive receptivity to nature's immanence or to those elementary feelings so endemic of rustic life.[28] In such case, the pauses would figure an enjoyable loneliness or a refusal of Enlightenment reason (or nonunderstanding) and the more primary, if codified, emotions about nation, home, and self that arise in the abeyance of logical association or abstraction. In contrast to either Wordsworthian passivity or ecstasy, however, Robinson repeatedly attempts to forestall both the complete void of syncope on the one hand and recognizable feeling on the other.

The caesuras not only interrupt and turn from the speaker's subjective thoughts and feelings but they also offer extended marks within the line that are at once material (as repetitive yet moving black streaks on the page) and figurative (signs for affective movement from one thought or feeling to another). The space and time marked by the dash anticipates the figure of the cave in Robinson's later poem "To the Poet Coleridge," where undefined affects circulate outside bodies before being codified into particular emotions or feelings. To put this another way, the poem's lineal pauses intimate a brief instance of nonunderstanding from which the speaker recovers only by articulating her position anew through the course of a subsequent stanza. This cessation of sensation, however, is not a mental silence so much as it is the motion of turning from one sensation to another—an intensity or shifting. By insistently returning to these moments of dashed intensity, the refrain discharges or routes "fancy-fraught" sensation, through language's force, mustered here not so much, as Richard Sha suggests, through the metonymy and substitution that offer the ends of movement, but within, in the middle of, that movement itself.[29] Caesuras show us that sensational variation beyond the senses comes not simply through the powerful force of articulation or a violence of sensation that slashes through the figural. What initiates our ability to break down the habitual synthesis of repetition into difference may be in part incremental variations, but it is also instigated by seeming gaps in cognition that signal the motion from one difference to another. The poem's caesuras therefore do not simply represent the vacant mind of the idiot but rather a continuous mark that materializes the movement of rhythm itself, a figure for affect that propels itself in and through various minds, bodies, and texts. Here caesuras represent not the absence of all embodied sensation but the disparate presence of matter as it moves outside the speaker's singular body. They enact the moving potential of intensity to put the mind in motion in a wide variety of ways. This link between absence and plenitude, the vacuum and the plenum, will become the major preoccupation of Robinson's "To the Poet Coleridge," where she most fully demonstrates how the poetics of vacancy paradoxically employs what appear to be figures of absence in order to create rich, nonempirical intensities.

Where "The Savage of Aveyron" reveals how an automatic articulacy might launch the mind of the idiot beyond empiricist sensation into a bevy of differential variation, "To the Poet Coleridge" most fully moves past the figure of the mind into the "circling bounds" of a wider landscape completely outside mind and body. Perhaps more important for our investigation of vacancy, this poem discloses how seeming figures of absence manifest the material dimensions of language's movement as they inaugurate affect's new form of sensation. Robinson effectively suggests why the poem's "circling bounds," caves of ice, and sunny domes do not return us to allegories of mental or dwelling spaces—the realm of representation, synthesis, and abstraction that might reify empirical sensation and gendered bodies. Instead, vacancy's tropes impel us even further into a new tempo of sensation beyond body, history, and the representations that solidify both. Though it may seem as though gender might be imported back into the picture of the vaginal caves of ice and sunny domes, in fact Robinson ironically gestures toward such spaces as new locales of nongendered materiality, satirizing, as we shall see, Coleridge's own gendered invocation of the damsel with the dulcimer, whose overly sensible wail he needs to make his own song reappear.

Much has been written about this poem as part of Robinson's and Coleridge's poetic conversation, and scholarly discussion has most often focused on the power dynamics and the conversation about forms between the younger male writer and the older poetess.[30] "To the Poet Coleridge" responds to a copy of "Kubla Khan" Coleridge had shown Robinson, and the woman poet certainly mimics some of the male poet's language in what Cross, following Daniel Robinson, terms a "self-authorizing rivalry" (Cross, "Coleridge and Robinson" 42).[31] Their competing versions of "passive responsiveness" (55) appear symptomatic of empiricist epistemology's focus on the passive, receptive mind.[32] The last in a longer series of their poetic exchanges, however, "To the Poet Coleridge" should be understood as Robinson's final repartee to explode the bounds of the empirical mind and feminine, sensible body once and for all. While Coleridge pointedly laments, at his poem's end, his loss of the "vision" of the damsel with the dulcimer and his inability to "revive" within himself "Her symphony and her song" (38, 42, 43), Robinson's reply heralds her attempt to map out a poetics and epistemology where the damsel with the dulcimer is not stuck playing the customary songs of sensation, emotion, and sensibility—as seductive as they may be. Even more drastically, her poem evinces a poetics constructed by nature's idiocy—a set of nongendered material relations. The poetic voice, rather than being actuated by sensibility wrought along feminine, sensitive nerves, becomes a manifestation of a movement of dispersed vibrations only the last in a series of eddies, torrents, rivers, and winds.

In this poem, Robinson unravels form and meter using a four-lined refrain that functions less like a stanza than as a paratactic boundary appearing and reappearing throughout the poem. Its performative repetition works to "trace the circling bounds," extensions of an ever-shifting space that then invites a prism of chromatic sensations, what Robinson describes in the poem's last lines as "*Minstrelsy*, SUBLIMELY WILD!" (70). The following refrain circulates four times through the poem:

> With thee I'll trace the circling bounds
> Of thy NEW PARADISE extended;

And listen to the varying sounds
Of winds, and foamy torrents blended. (5–9)

Such spaces, not unlike the hermit's cave in "Beachy Head," may at first appear to foreground the conscious and unconscious mental landscapes that might build new conceptual terrain. Their figuration, however, works to destabilize notions of a static subject or mind by repeatedly furnishing new ground for iterative intensities, whose main property is their immediacy and their movement. Only after the "circling bounds" have been temporarily apportioned can wind and water rush into the rocks, hills, and streambeds, creating the varying rhythms and constant motion of this world. As with "The Savage of Aveyron," the refrain alters ever so slightly, as the first line repeats: "With thee I'll trace the circling bounds," "Then will I climb the breezy bounds," "There will I trace the circling bounds," "I'll raptured trace the circling bounds" while the "sounds" in the third line of the refrain receive different modifiers: "varying," "distant," "awful," and "varying" once again (5, 22, 40, 55, 7, 24, 42, 57). The refrain then materially enacts the repetition that might instigate a synthesis of the refrains into an idea but instead veers, however slightly, from such linguistic and mental habits.

The seriality and repetition in "The Savage of Aveyron" reaches an even wilder pitch in this poem because the refrain is completely paratactic, arriving at unexpected moments among stanzas composed of differing numbers of quatrains and rhyming couplets. The poem continues until it cycles through twenty-six separate rhymes, ending with the picture of Coleridge's phantasmic, visionary maid:

She sings of THEE, O favor'd child
Of *Minstrelsy*, SUBLIMELY WILD!
Of thee, whose soul can feel the tone
Which gives to airy dreams *a magic* ALL THY OWN! (69–72)

Robinson may be speaking directly to Coleridge here, but she does not simply echo his hyper-aural, formally experimental "Kubla Khan."[33] This moment signals a repetition of her own poetic project, as she revisits her articulation of a poetry that archives but does not organize a collection of sensations and differences. The poet blatantly resists the customs of ready-made forms and instead uses the refrain's quatrain to trace an array of rhyming couplets, their structure itself an encapsulation of material repetition with difference. With such music, the refrain creates a "prism," "various vibrations or decompositions," a Deleuzean "Rhythm" built from "augmentations and diminutions, additions and withdrawals, amplifications and eliminations" (Deleuze and Guattari, *A Thousand Plateaus* 348). The world of distinct objects and emotions has been overthrown for matter in flux, luring readers to pay less attention to formal measures or tropes than to the paratactic shiftings between quatrains and couplets as movements that change the speed and density of the poem without reference to determinate cause and effect. This experience promotes neither a focus on the body nor its representations but rather on what Dorothea Olkowski describes in "Deleuze's aesthetics of sensation" as "the action of invisible forces on the body producing, not feelings nor representations of violent feelings but affects . . . spasms, contraction, dilation" (282).

We could easily cite the difference between the first stanza's "blue, wavy, lucid stream / 'Mid forest gloom, shall slow meander" and the "foamy torrents" or "The mystic fountain, bubbling, panting" just a few lines later (2–3, 8, 10). These descriptions of water, which evince a change in the liquid's speed from slow to fast, occur on either side of the first iteration of the four-line refrain. Without a patently linear causality here, the scene evokes an emergent force of materials—both variable sound and nonsonic intensity—moving without instrumentality: the lucid stream, foamy torrents, and the bubbling fountain. Here we have a system of differential relations with heterogeneous components that offer an open field of material movement. Robinson's notion of affect here as a kind of shared materiality resembles Jane Bennett's "impersonal affect," where matter is shared among bodies, placing them in relation, as bodies that affect one another. Robinson's poetics, however, unlike Bennett's new materiality, advance aural *and* tropic repetitions that inaugurate imperceptible material movements. In and among the circling bounds, we are, finally, beyond or before the thinking subject, perhaps in a state of constant contraction and relaxation that adduces repetition and difference through the varying relations among components whose connected rates of change continuously alter. These relations perhaps materialize a more layered version of what Robert Mitchell calls the "irregular rhythm" that composes a Deleuzean immanence apparent in Shelley's poems.[34] Sensation finally has become perpetually variable movement through the altering material densities of the lines, and perhaps more strikingly through the water's different figural repetitions.

Robinson pointedly waits until the end of the poem's last stanza to evoke the act of empirical hearing—the act of listening to and for the damsel with the dulcimer, saying, "I hear her voice!" (65). This deferral of aural, embodied sensation suggests at least two provocative aspects of Robinson's vacancy. First, that the sensation of hearing, or of hearing a particular voice, comes only after intensities have been manifested and then labeled by sensory experience and its attendant, gendered language. That the voice only a few lines later again becomes "vibrations sweet" suggests the reversibility of empirical sound, that the feminine voice can once again become a stew of intensities beyond aural perception by dint of another figural turn. Second, Robinson suggests that the attempt to hear voices—the attempt to ascribe certain sensory or formal characteristics to women's writing—itself is a fallacy of embodied sensation and empirical thinking. Here is the full force of what the speaker says she hears: "I hear her voice! thy *sunny dome*, / Thy *caves of ice*, loud repeat, / Vibrations, madd'ning sweet" (65–67). "Hearing" quickly becomes the sensing not of sound but the vibrations repeated by the domes and caves, themselves repeatedly articulated by the speaker, the damsel, Coleridge, and also the "SPIRIT DIVINE!" (60). That ambiguous spirit is evoked in the poem's second line: "SPIRIT DIVINE! With THEE I'll wander" and later "SPIRIT DIVINE! With THEE I'll trace / Imagination's boundless space!" (2, 26–27). Robinson suggests that what the speaker finally "hears" is not the damsel's subjective voice or even Coleridge's but the maddening vibrations of the spirit divine. This spirit of poetry is material potentiality itself when it comes to actualize itself temporarily in Robinson, Coleridge, the damsel, and others. For Robinson, while the spirit can momentarily be translated into sensory perception, the spirit itself—the potentiality of poetry—cannot be seen, felt, or heard but only intimated through the force, intensity, and momentary figural shifts in that field of potentiality.

This formulation finally brings us to the crux of Robinson's vacancy: those sunny domes, caves of ice, Imagination's boundless space, and the circling bounds that evoke the poem's vibrating rhythms and intensities. These bounds reveal and reiterate the figural turning of vacancy, as it posits voids that produce rampant materiality prior or aside from the empirical. If the "circling bounds" create the space for the potentiality of variously changing vibrations, those bounds nevertheless present a series of figural abstractions that interfuse mind and landscape. Such a trope at first might seem to violate the notion articulated by those interested in fluid, transmaterial affects or sensations, beginning with Deleuze, that figural representation obstructs true sensation. As Deleuze explains in *Difference and Repetition*, pure sensation is a material catastrophic force that rips through both the harmony of the faculties (empirical understanding, conceptual reason, synthetic imagination) as well as the abstractions those faculties have created. We can see this violence too in *Francis Bacon*, when Deleuze describes the artist painting a figure that he then slashes through with a sensation's worth of paint, eradicating representation and sending us down a path of vibration. Once there, various bits of resonating materiality eventually and momentarily emerge from the potentiality of sensations into a localized arrangement of relations before dispersing again.

Yet unlike Deleuze's attempt to reformulate sensation, when Robinson's vacancy speaks to both intensity's catastrophe and its emergence, it ultimately shows us how the figural can in fact engage new materialities when it becomes itself a floating boundary, at once material and speculative. Rather than seeing tropes as merely references to ideas created by the mind's refraction of the world, Robinson suggests that the constant movement of a trope such as vacancy, with its turning from one figure to the next, from one material-rhetorical tension to the next, and from one refrain to the next, realizes localized fields of potentiality that draw relations among things, including the material, the rhetorical, and the metaphorical. This ever-shifting nature of the figural's articulation alongside its constantly altering field of meanings together belie its e-motion, its intensely affective material status.[35] The "boundless space" and the "glittering entrance" to caverns no longer correlate to the "mental blank" of "Sight," that empirical dearth of all sensation so reminiscent of Locke's "dark room." Rather than the static trope of empty space, whether in the mind or in the landscape, these figures enact fluctuating boundaries of knowledge that repeatedly circle around a changing set of variable affective movements, either those not yet codified into empiricist reflection or those able to reverse habitual experience through repetitive articulation. This marking-off produces—and, with the next refrain, reproduces—a temporary field, or "thy NEW PARADISE extended" (6).[36] It is the repeated, performative tracing of the circling bounds—the turning of tropology—that paradoxically inaugurates a localized field of actual sensations even as it calls to the virtual field of potentiality—all those intensities and movements possible now, in the future, and in the past.

Unlike Smith's abstracted and suspended movement available through the aporias of consumption, Robinson's vacancy both stands *opposed* to the figural, which for Robinson can become an abstraction through Sappho's passive synthesis of repetitive figural acts, and *apposed* to it, as a moving boundary that repeatedly transforms the field of potential relations or tensions: between materiality and language, between language's materiality (rhyme, rhythm, for example) and its metaphoric figuration, and most especially between the world and the figure, whose fluctuating boundaries tells us which relations temporarily apply and which has the possibility of moving into being, as vital movement itself. Robinson's circling bounds become a trope of tropes: to trace a moving boundary means to redraw repetitively the field of difference, by shifting not only from one material metaphorical "vehicle" to another but also from one localized field of meanings to another. Her final poem presents systems of differential relations that shirk representation and entail the figural as one of these relations whose inevitable changes make the poem move. The upshot of Robinson's epistemological-ontological model suggests that Robinson harnesses words in motion, which form a conduit between being and a world. Vacancy opens the perforated forms of body and landscape to the vibrant, turning matter of the poetic spirit. That spirit achieves a kind of feminism that is not aporetic, like Smith's, but prolifically relational, with impossibility only one of many associations. Its differences do not synthesize new genders; rather, they subsume gender into a field of changing relations and boundaries like the figural itself.

Like Sappho's turn toward "loftier passions" and "loftier themes," Robinson's poetics emphasizes experiments that evince transformative sets of relations. Excess in Robinson's hands does not conjure a tyrannical Kubla Khan dreaming of the wailing woman or damsel with a dulcimer, who can only recapitulate the song of sensibility.[37] Instead, her vacancy necessarily entails the breakdown of the feminine subject and the formation, however temporary, of open spaces that might reveal a bevy of materialities, variously defined: "Thy *caves of ice*, loud repeat / Vibrations, madd'ning sweet," vibrations that help to manufacture a poetics "ALL THY OWN" (66–67, 72). We could say that Robinson, in her final poems, turns from sensibility's banal customs to vacancy's simultaneous tropic and affective dispersal, which moves amid bodies, landscapes, and the mind's flux.

Robinson's poetics of vacancy accentuates not only her use of empiricist tropes to repeal the epistemological errors of empirical habit and the customs of sensibility but also the extent to which she attempted to enact a poetics that might redraw sensation, if it could be rid of its inhibiting epistemological and poetic baggage. Her late poems liberate materiality from gendered bodies through a gender critique of sensibility's stultifying ways. Romanticism's upheaval of the Enlightenment subject moves by way of figures that shift the boundaries of actual and potential materialities. Shelley even further multiplies the spirit of poetry's ability to furnish a virtuality of affect, when he considers how the capaciousness of abstraction and synesthesia can house an even wider range of figural movements. Closer to Shelley's radical politics than Wordsworth's natural piety, Robinson's idea of linguistic production does not attempt to rescue or reincorporate those real people excluded from society but instead moves us all beyond feminized and individual bodies through forms of repetition that subtend human and nonhuman boundaries and that allow all manner of things to find a vibratory, ontological great-beyond.

CHAPTER 3

Reaping Songs and Ineffable Tales

William Wordsworth and Percy Shelley's Singing Women and the Rave of Affect

For some time we have become accustomed to the narrative that male poets represented singing women as witchy, foreign lures. In this account, women's monstrous excess is a symptomatic projection of male anxieties about poetic prowess onto women writers, who infiltrated the public sphere especially through the culture of sensibility.[1] In William Wordsworth and Percy Shelley, at least, we can find figures for women poets that both evince the excesses of sensibility but also voice a concern about the fate of women's poetics entrapped by it. A number of Wordsworth's women sing powerful tunes: the mad mother croons a woeful lullaby with a "fire" in her "brain," and the solitary reaper intones a siren song that the poet cannot translate yet cannot forget. The veiled maid from Shelley's "Alastor" presents another seductress: "Herself a poet," her "tremulous sobs" and "eloquent blood told an ineffable tale," so much so that her "intermitted song" eventually infects the poet "with excess / Of love" (161, 164, 68, 172, 181–182). These visions of the singing woman, who weeps tremulous tears and whose body quivers with emotion, evoke the poetess of sensibility. She overwhelms the poet with the material force of her sensation, and both poet and maid become so aroused by the language of sensibility that she disappears and leaves him with nothing but a "vacant brain." Although such an allegory can be read as a critique of sensibility's feminizing excess, Wordsworth's poems intimate what Shelley's verse more fully illustrates—the ideology that identifies "women's writing" as a poetics bound by the seductions and failures of the discourse of sensibility. Both Wordsworth and Shelley portray feminine figures who vibrate so excessively that they infect their listeners with poisonous songs. Rather than underwriting this gendered poetics, both poets question sensibility's propensity to incur mental paralysis in those feminized and trapped by its gendered roles.

In Wordsworth's poems about singing women such as "The Thorn," "Joanna," or "The Solitary Reaper," the male speakers turn from sensibility by domesticating the rush of sensation that all too often deadens the minds of singers and listeners alike. Scholars as diverse as James Chandler, Susan Lanser, and Mary Favret have shown that Wordsworth primarily turns to habit, the restraint of meter, and the palliative domestic affections to stem feeling. Yet his poems pointedly address sensibility's contagious nature—the tendency of overwhelming sensations to travel from body to body—and they start in small ways to figure vacancy's alternative affective turns. In "The Solitary Reaper," for example, we can see the beginnings of a productive cognitive opacity, when the reaper's song continually compels the speaker to ask, "Will no one tell me what she sings?" until all he retains is the "music in my heart" (17, 31). With this ineffable music, the reaper purveys mobile, indeterminate affect, as it undermines the speaker's ability to translate her song or, as a consequence, to categorize her lyricism as clearly gendered or foreign. Although Wordsworth certainly figures mental and cognitive emptiness at other places in his work, he only hints at figures of vacancy that offer new affects moving beyond gendered emotion and thought in his poems about women singers.

This problem becomes much more central to Shelley, as he amalgamates Wordsworth's influence with Charlotte Smith's troping of oblivion and Mary Wollstonecraft's trenchant diagnosis of sensibility's crippling gender ideology. Like Wollstonecraft, he envisions a more radical reform of gendered writing than Wordsworth, a literary practice that seeks to eradicate the ideologies that separate feminine from masculine poetics as a means to ameliorate the dangerous aesthetics of sensation for all poetry. Shelley scholarship has certainly been sensitive to his investigations of radical sympathy, revolutionary sensibility, and even his intimation of Deleuzean approaches to sensation.[2] Yet his attention to feeling and affect has yet to be synthesized with his critique of the revolutionary project of sensibility, his interest in feminist poetics, and, above all, his unique version of the trope of vacancy. Where almost all male writers of Shelley's ilk questioned the poetics of sensibility, it is Wordsworth and Shelley whose responses to sensibility find the trope of vacancy—a series of figures that may be wielded by women's voices but, in Shelley most prominently, ultimately undo the constraints of gender.

Much like Mary Robinson and Felicia Hemans, Shelley dwells on the tendency for the language of sensibility to purvey physiological vibrations of raw sensation that overwhelm and, subsequently, empty the mind completely, grinding its functions to a standstill. Unlike Burke's sublime, which depends on novelty or obscurity to overpower the mind with feeling, Shelley suggests that the dead metaphors of sensibility and the ideology that feminizes such language together exacerbate the flow of sensation even as they mute meaning. His poetry focuses on the particular quandaries surrounding the transmission of affect as a dynamic form of materiality, and he reorients us from the problems with individual minds and bodies to the movement of affect from one body to another, human and nonhuman. When material vibrations cross bodily boundaries, through even mountains and river valleys, they compose vacancy's more variegated circulations of affect that have the power to undermine sensibility's gendering as well as modulate its excesses.

Shelley's well-known comment from his late prose fragment "On Love" would seem to underwrite a continued attachment to human-to-human transmission of affect, when he writes "if we feel, we would that another's nerves should vibrate to our own" (*SPP* 503). Yet this reading overlooks Shelley's pivot at the end of the fragment to incorporate, pointedly, nonhuman, transcorporeal affect: "the tongueless wind and a melody in the flowing brooks," whose "motion" forms "a secret correspondence with our own heart" (504). Depicting a reciprocity that amalgamates streams of matter and spirit's immaterial motions, Shelley's later poetry finds an underlying affect that flows among all things, staunches the contagion of nervy sensation sped along by empty language, and disrupts the cycle of excess and emptiness. Beginning with "Mont Blanc," he exchanges the mountain's snowy "silence and solitude," the dead language of both the sublime and sensibility, for "vacancy." This trope does not simply articulate human cognition of the sublime mountain but uncovers the invisible circulation of particulate materiality that creates the posthuman affects moving among human and nonhuman bodies. "Mont Blanc"'s "unremitting interchange" of the "universe that flows through all things" channels a variegated circulation of affect through the human mind and the nonhuman landscape.

In what follows in this chapter, I build on longstanding narratives about Shelley's materiality alongside attention to his characteristic abstraction and philosophical ambitions. Julie Carlson has recently helped us place figure and affect together in Shelley, suggesting that his analogical style allows humans to try on different ontologies in the process of loving them. Amanda Jo Goldstein similarly brings language and materiality together when she suggests that Shelley's Lucretian poetics allows for figures to descend as parts of objects, or simulacra with material heft. Yet, syncretic thinker that he was, Shelley was undoubtedly influenced by his combined readings of Lucretian particulate materiality, Spinozan responsive activity, and Hartleyean vibration, among other accounts of materialism and affect. By bringing these threads together, we can understand his vacancy as composing not synecdochal instances or parts selected from a universal materiality, but rather contiguous, fluid movements within and through bodies. The chaotic materialities of the affects—both the mind's motions and the Arve's raving, bursting flows—swirl through the poem, revealing an affect figured as shared, underlying reciprocal material activity among humans and nonhuman nature.[3] "Mont Blanc"'s superimposition of mind and world literalizes the transmission of affect between individual and environment, later echoed in "Epipsychidion" and "Ode to the West Wind." These movements and rests, however, are composed not only by material transmissions but also by figural abstraction that admits an even wider range of all the affective movements we might imagine. Once it dispenses with sensation's fits and the human mind's imaginings of silence and stillness, Shelley's vacancy discloses a nebulous, and at times incorporeal, materiality that recomposes our relation to both bodies and the world at large.

Wordsworthian Intimations

Although Shelley certainly gleaned the problems of sensibility from many sources, he may have found in Wordsworth the basis for strange fits of passion tied to feminine lyricism.[4] In 1812 Shelley read a heady olio of David Hartley's *Observations on Man*, Wollstonecraft's *Vindication of the Rights of Woman*, and Wordsworth's *Lyrical Ballads*, which together pointed to the material problems of excessive sensibility for women and their intellectual lives. As Adela Pinch writes glossing William Hazlitt's observation, "it was Wordsworth's access to feminine feeling that gave the *Lyrical Ballads* their characteristic power" (106).[5] Shelley clearly sharpened his critique of sensibility through the many women in Wordsworth's *Lyrical Ballads* whose lyrical self-expression all too often veers toward madness, death, and infectious transmission.[6]

Wordsworth was certainly tutored under the sensibility of Helen Maria Williams and Charlotte Smith (among others), yet even when he turned away from its gothic excesses, he contemplated the problem of how its embodied epistemology gendered women and the lyric. The mad mother, the forsaken Indian woman, Goody Blake, and "The Thorn"'s Martha all croon from bodies and brains overheated by excessive sensibility.[7] Noel Jackson has discussed how entangled Wordsworth's project was in the "language of sense" as an historical and political aesthetics, and while he shrewdly suggests that a "poet's sensory acuity might just as plausibly jeopardize the communicative function of poetry itself," he does not connect such poetic and mental stultification to gender (42).[8] Susan J. Wolfson alerts us to the presence in *Lyrical Ballads* of male sensibility that is consistently "disrupted by the transgressive power of feminine passion," as female voices infect masculine narrators with passion that both destabilizes and contains gender difference (34, 52).[9] Seen as allegories of not merely female passion but the discourse of sensibility's empowerments and liabilities, women's songs become detrimental because their affective force overwhelms the body and must be domesticated by a more anodyne language of sentiment. Yet the "referential opacity and pure expressiveness" that Wolfson describes also offers a glimpse into how women's voices anticipate vacancy.[10] These songs begin to articulate a mobile affect whose travel among bodies undermines the sensational feeling or lyricism tied to gendered bodies.

In "The Mad Mother," voluptuous hysteria finds a therapeutic route when the babe becomes a proper receptacle for affection, one that acts to staunch the overflow of feeling and feminine song. The eponymous speaker admits that she is viewed as mad—"They say that I am mad" (11)—and that she was once so: "A fire was once within my brain" (21). Wolfson writes that the poem recapitulates the chivalric ethics of the masculine rescue of women from distress when "the boy born of her body rescues her from her body" (38). It may be, more specifically, that her laborious participation in affective exchange cures her: her singing and her baby's nursing. She says, "And I am happy when I sing / full many a sad and doleful thing," and in the next stanza: "Suck, little babe, oh suck again! / It cools my blood; it cools my brain; / Thy lips I feel them, baby! they / Draw from my heart the pain away" (31–34). As affective acts, singing and nursing are parallel and inverse actions. Both reiterate sensibility's liquid economy, akin to Smith's in *Elegiac Sonnets*, in which the emitting of sound or bodily fluid serves to remedy the madness by drawing off the excess of feminine gush. In the end, her love for the boy "saves" her from the excess of feeling, and she is able to resist oblivion's pull to palliate affective intensities. Perhaps finally finding what Jackson describes as the "experiences of powerful sensation [that] can guide the poetic mind to truths unavailable to sensuous apprehension" (72), the mother eventually locates a more reflective course that leads to domestic contemplation: "And I will always be thy guide, / Through hollow snows and rivers wide. / I'll build an Indian bower" (53–55). Even if they go through the highs and lows of affective swells, mother and child refuse to die into a new life beyond embodied feeling and sensation, as Robinson's Sappho and Smith's speaker do. The mother's newly imagined scene reinforces a less virulent, more protected strain of feminine sentiment controlled by the imagination's conversion of bodily exchange into customs of domestic feeling. "The Mad Mother" represents Wordsworth leaning toward both Burkean habit and Hume's cautionary advice to use muted empiricist passions—here found in the restful pastoral and the restraint of meter—to constrain wilder feelings.

Such feminine lyricism evokes songs whose frenzy initiates not simply hysteria, as Alan Bewell and Wolfson have suggested, but more pointedly Lockean madness and delirium. Like Robinson's Sappho, this extreme cognitive and linguistic opacity speaks to both the deadening tendency of excessive sensation, but here Wordsworth likewise intimates an awareness of men's lack of knowledge about women and their minds. In "The Thorn," the speaker tells us "A cruel, cruel fire . . . almost turn'd her brain to tinder" (128, 32). A dumbfounded Martha is left barren to bawl, "Oh misery! oh misery" several times throughout the poem. This repetition does not simply transmit Martha's pain and suffering but culminates into a refrain signifying a lack of knowledge, as it induces the speaker to disclose his ignorance of her complete tale: "No more I know, I wish I did" (155). Her song blocks the speaker's knowledge and our own ability to ascribe clear meaning to her story. The overly rational narrator becomes inane as he attempts to find evidence, plot a narrative, and attest to what "all do still aver" about the woman, whose vocalization presents a thorn in the side of what might be knowable about the emotional lives of women, or about emotional lives more generally (240). Certainly, the unreliable narration causes a healthy dose of skepticism in the reader, yet the tale of excessive sensibility also links the cipher-like woman to the eradication of concrete, local knowledge. Like Robinson's play with ballad refrains, Martha's repetitive moaning attains a skeptical force that undermines clear emotional categories and that critiques what male readers assume about women's sensibility and their supposedly excessive lyrical expression.

Joanna's laughter in "Poems on the Naming of Places" likewise emits a ravishing voice that stands in contrast with the Wordsworthian speaker's natural piety, and similarly begins to offer a model for affect more like vacancy. Her laughter cuts through the hills and dells, until the cavern of the mountains—and the ancient Woman—amplifies it to "a loud roar," a kind of pure aural noise that shirks referential meaning. The speaker's subsequent act of chiseling Joanna's name in stone ironically memorializes such a material, cutting force that can reverberate through the body and the landscape.[11] The resort to habitual rhythms and the logic of naming ultimately reveals how the poet of *Lyrical Ballads* capitulates to trying to shape, if not control, affect with human categories of understanding. In the language of habitual feeling, Wordsworth finds codified emotions as a means of mediating affect's transmissive force. The language of sympathy enables the poet to reject Joanna's harsher, inhuman guffaw for the experience of calmer sentiment and fellow feeling controlled by the imagination. In this fashion, Wordsworth contains the spontaneous overflows of emotion and their tendency to overwhelm all sorts of bodies through the recollection and reflective habit inherent in meter, domesticity, and piety.

Wordsworth revisits the *Lyrical Ballad*'s use of feminine song in his later "The Solitary Reaper," a poem that figures an affect that cannot be accurately translated yet nonetheless reproduces itself in the heart of its (male) listener. The Wordsworthian speaker remains attracted to a feminine lyricism that he literally and figuratively does not understand, even as he privileges such difference. The "Solitary Reaper" has long been read, starting with Geoffrey Hartman, as an allegory about the lyric, as the male speaker comes upon the "solitary Highland Lass" "reaping and singing by herself," filling the Vale with "overflowing . . . sound" (2, 3, 8). Yet, more crucially, she figures sensibility's transmission from one body to another. Her "voice so thrilling," "melancholy strain," "plaintive numbers" all emphasize aspects of sensibility (13, 6, 18).[12] Her complaint travels to her listeners even as her numbers move in tune with her body's swinging of the scythe. Although such measurement reinforces her own bodily and poetic labor, her thrilling and melancholy strain invite the listener alternately to become affectively overwhelmed by "overflowing" sound that circulates within the Vale, but more potently through the body and from one body to another (8).

Perhaps the poet seeks to possess the lass's song, as Alan Richardson suggests, colonizing the feminine speech he envies.[13] The Wordsworthian speaker would then appropriate her air because of its easy lyricism— the song is all tune. The speaker momentarily identifies such thrills as melancholy, binding its affect to a certain emotional structure of feminine woe and paralysis—or perhaps colonial sorrow.[14] But her voice does something irreparable to him too—she is, after all, a reaper. In the exact middle of the poem, at the beginning of the third stanza, the speaker asks, "Will no one tell me what she sings?—" (17). The Norton editors tell us that she is probably singing in Erse, but in fact we don't know, and this uncertainty changes the power dynamic, and the affective transmission, of the poem. In the end, we are left with only the song itself: "The music in my heart I bore / Long after it was heard no more" (31–32). This music has been transmuted from the song of habitual emotion into something more unidentifiable, as the intensely affective song razes clear meaning, including its secure status as a feminine or Scottish tune. The song resists the shell of the melancholy lyric that the poet creates around it, as its thrilling strain rises beyond the iambic doldrums of the male speaker—a strain he cannot aurally translate into his poem or fully convey to the reader—doubly forging a poetics of mobile yet undeciphered affect.[15]

The poem's final rhyme, "bore" and "no more," does not so much promise the clear and "abundant recompense" of the Wordsworthian poem. Rather, it ironically suggests that the lass's power consists of her ability to transmit stunning affect, to daze the feeling mind and to negate clear understanding of the lass herself except for a desire for the affective force of her song. The poem presents an incipient sense of vacancy that theorizes moving songs as separate from sensation and feeling. The speaker is left constantly revisiting what David Collings terms Wordsworth's notion of "primary affect," a loss of clear feeling, thought, or form, which he cannot articulate or comprehend. Yet this version of primary affect, for both Collings and Wordsworth, is nevertheless caught in the pursuit and gratifying loss of the feminine.[16] In this sense, Wordsworthian vacancy is always nostalgic for a gendered embodiment however productive its loss. The reaper, therefore, at least in part, represents a lyrical voice whose mysterious and untranslatable presence gives the speaker the pleasure of contemplating affects because they remain gendered and foreign. Her exotic, untouchable lyric instigates pleasure in feminine loss that also recapitulates sensibility's sway between excessive sensations and their absence. Wordsworth thus approaches vacancy's eradicating force and its affect with a song that seems to but cannot quite undermine ideological categories such as gender.[17] This oblique lyrical pleasure, wrought both by and at the cost of the feminine singer, incites Shelley's preoccupation with the veiled maid's ineffable tale as a poetic transmission of lyrical gender difference.

Entrainment in "Alastor": Eloquent Blood and Vacant Brain

Shelley's "Alastor" offers an allegorical narrative of a pioneering figure who—when he cannot recover from the loss of the veiled maiden's paralyzing voice—tends toward the abyss. The structure of poet's journey framed with a final commentary by a Wordsworthian narrator may be in part modeled upon the Wordsworthian speaker who revisits his earlier poetic quandary about the lure and difference of feminine lyricism.[18] Scholars as disparate as Timothy Clark, Teddi Chichester Bonca, Tilar Mazzeo, and Nahoko Miyamoto Alvey have recognized the connections between the veiled maiden and the discourse of sensibility, but these accounts have yet to attend to the tropic tension between sensibility and the vacant mind that together account more fully for the figural drama of the poem.[19] If, as Timothy Clark has argued, the "Alastor" poet presents a man of feeling, then his counterpart in the veiled maid figures a singer of sensibility.[20] Appearing in a dream vision just after the "Alastor" poet has brushed aside the silent Arab maiden, the veiled maid has most often been read as the idealistic poet's solipsistic fantasy of unattainable nature or a "wet dream" of his feminine ideal (Brown 1).[21] Much can be said for the Eastern aspect of the maid's passion not to mention the reflective and seductive qualities of her song.[22] The narrator clearly announces that the veiled maid is "Herself a poet" (161), which, as Jessica Quillin argues, "supports [the maid's] agency as a poet in her own right with her own enthralling voice" (65). That fact should encourage us to consider seriously the possibility that Shelley, if not the Alastor poet, is confronting a model of gendered poetics whose promise and failure infected male and female writers alike.

It is fairly surprising, given Shelley's consistently growing circle of writing women, that we have not adequately considered the veiled maid as a poet or, more subtly, as an allegory for feminine poetics confined to sensibility's promises of revolutionary reform in the 1790s and its failures.[23] "Alastor," after all, is a poem Shelley wrote while squirreled away to live the domestic life of the mind with Mary Shelley at Bishopsgate. The Shelley circle was filled with sisters of sympathy, even if at times electrified in a multidirectional web of sexual cathexis.[24] The ensuing psychodrama sometimes overshadows the fact that at any given time multiple women living with Shelley were occupied with their own intellectual writing lives.[25] His attitude toward women's writing was especially supportive—one might go so far as to say that, for Shelley, liberation from tyranny required both women's freedom and the leadership of their literary, political, and philosophical voices. Yet, as Nora Crook writes, "Shelley's promotion of women as published writers through patronage, encouragement, and collaboration awaits a contextualized reassessment" (79).

Despite, or perhaps because of, his play with ventriloquizing women's voices, his advocacy for women's writing entailed a pointed critique of the ideology of gendered voices, songs, or poetics. Shelley's feminism, ambivalent though it may seem to some critics, has not yet fully been extended to his thoughts about women's writing. Accounts of his revolutionary plan for poetics have similarly not fully addressed his thoughts about gender ideology and its roots in the discourses of empiricism, materialism, and affect—discourses whose interlocking elements Shelley used to revise both notions of gender difference and the poetics that promote them. The figure of the veiled maid queries whether the culture of sensibility—a reform movement dispensed through the pages of novels and poems—offered the best language for a radical project that included those of all genders and persuasions. Rather than offering sensibility's reforming feeling, her voice produces only a poet whose mind has been deadened by deranged, feminine sensibility and whose poetry can only repeat the cycle of overwhelming affect and cognitive paralysis.

The maid's voice is first described in reflexive terms: "Her voice was like the voice of his own soul," an expression that may signal the very infectiousness of her song, which the male poet covets for his own (153). If she mystically seems to sing the tones of his soul, such a radical dream of intersubjective poetic sympathy stems from its nearly automatic interpersonal exchange of affect that is, momentarily, not confined by the gendered body. Her song and its affect at first moves as if it were something nonhuman altogether: her "woven sounds of streams and breezes, held / His inmost sense suspended" (155–156). The shift into a naturalistic register for song's transmission of affect hints at the thrilling, wavy vibrations endemic to the poetics of sensibility, even as it redacts gendered bodies for nonhuman ones, where affect travels regardless of human gender, nationality, or embodiment. The body, when it moves as rivers and winds, actually indicates a ubiquitous transmission of matter among all sorts of bodies, despite morphology. The hint of this resolutely nongendered approach to bodily and affective transmission, however, quickly becomes overturned, first by sensibility's tendency to excess and then by its function as an ideological discourse that solidifies gender and bodily difference.

The flows of the maid's voice effectively, if momentarily, halt the poet's mind—"His inmost sense suspended." This material transmission leaves sensitive bodies, like those with excessive sensibility, liable to overwhelming sensory stimulation. The passage famously ends with a more permanent expiration: "His strong heart sunk and sickened with excess / Of love" (181–182). Tracing the pulse of blood in Blake, Steven Goldsmith writes that the notion of impulse sketches "a figure swept by emotion into inaction" (229). As William Keach has noted, "Shelley here evokes an emotional intensity so extreme that it checks or inhibits the verbal outpouring it inspires" (83). Held in the grip of their sensory transmission that is "woven" as if by the continuous sounds of wind and water, the poet receives these material vibrations even while his perception of them is halted or his understanding becomes entirely caught up in the perceptual act.

The more she sings, the more intense and overpowering becomes her rush of affect, only eloquent in the blood:

> Soon the solemn mood
> Of her pure mind kindled through all her frame
> A permeating fire: wild numbers then
> She raised, with voice stifled in tremulous sobs
> Subdued by its own pathos her fair hands
> Were bare alone, sweeping from some strange harp
> Strange symphony, and in their branching veins
> The eloquent blood told an ineffable tale. (161–168)

There are few clues as to what ignites the maiden's "solemn mood," exciting her to "wild numbers" that infect her audience as well as her own body. A type of autopoiesis may arise from sensation's masturbatory feedback loop where an increase in vibrations repeatedly sent along the nerves tends to multiply to the point of overwhelming stimulation—even to madness or delusion.[26] This paradox of motion and insensibility suits the maiden and the poet, particularly when the maiden's voice is "stifled in tremulous sobs" and "subdued by its own pathos." Even as she is stimulated into a higher, more moving emotional register, her sobs are stifling and the pathos subduing. The emotion that allows her to speak to the poet—rather than remain silent and yearning like the Arab maid—simultaneously imprisons her in the very sensations that give rise to her voice.

To exacerbate this sensory transfer further, the veiled maid's song becomes increasingly less discursive, as if the longer it continues the more sensation it conveys, unmitigated by meaning, logic, or form. Her "strange" harp plays an even stranger symphony, rushing through her "branching veins" and "eloquent blood" until it becomes "ineffable." Both Shelley's earlier use of waves and wind as well as the permeating fire of the blood here evoke nervy emotion reminiscent of those thrilling, wavy vibrations endemic to Newtonian physics, Hartleyan vibrations and association, and above all the medical discourse of sensibility (155–156).[27] Ann Wroe reminds us that Shelley "had a special love for quivering things" from his early readings of Hartley throughout his career (38). Hartley anticipates not only a "modern and comprehensive neurophysiology on the basis of Newtonian physics," as historian Richard C. Allen argues, but his doctrine of vibrations also intimates a physical chemistry where infinitesimal particles can compose or emit "'free' forms of matter, which exist as fluids expanding through space" (85, 94). Hartley's science thus affords a model for wide-ranging affective transference, especially when he discusses the myriad ways that different minute particles "communicate" within and without the body, for example: "There can be direct vibration of light rays onto the optic nerve odoriferous particles that communicate directly to the gustatory and olfactory nerves as well as to the aether, which would serve a supporting and regulatory role in passing along the vibrations, but not producing them" (14). External objects can impress small vibrations (or vibrunticles) traveling through the aether, through vibrations of the aether, which excite infinitesimal particles in the nerves.[28] These vibrations themselves are composed of particles in repulsion and attraction, and may provide the basis for Shelley's understanding of both the chemical transmission of affect among bodies as well as the occult sympathies created through unseen material transmission.

It may at first seem as though Shelley uses a series of analogies that liken sensibility's vibrations along the nerves to the communication within the blood, and eventually to those affects circulating through aether both within and outside the body. That is, nerves, blood, and aether do not directly communicate but circulate affects in similar ways. As Richard Sha writes, "since so much was understood about the mechanics of blood circulation, nerves were imagined as circulating nervous fluid or force so that science could analogize force from circulation" (22). However much Shelley may have disputed Hartley's mechanistic approach to matter and the ensuing additive form of association it promoted, he very much took to heart the notion of vibrations that travel through the agitations of small, infinitesimal particles—and within multiple kinds of matter.[29] These vibrations in Shelley no longer simply mark an analogy or correspondence but literal, material flows in and among human and nonhuman bodies.

Shelley's eloquent blood suggests that the physiological body, whether through nerves or blood, exudes chemicals or particulate materials that transfer affect not unlike Teresa Brennan's contemporary accounts of "entrainment." Her concept delineates a physical transmission of affect through hormones and pheromones, first circulating in the blood, then exuded into the air before being absorbed by other bodies or incorporated into the atmosphere at large (9). Entrainment often occurs through the circulation of pheromones, but it can also transpire through images, sound, and especially through "bodily movements and gestures, particularly through the imitation of rhythms (effected by sight, touch, and hearing)" (70). Such rhythms "can lead either way—to well being or anxiety" (70). In Shelley's syncretic theory, the veiled maid's "eloquent blood" speaks much the way hormones and pheromones transmit chemical affect, directly from her body to the poet's. As Sharon Ruston writes of Shelley's plant poems, "Shelley seems to imagine here a life force that can be felt and communicated from one body to another" (137).

This "fleshly code," as Brennan calls it, moves more quickly than human language or awareness: "the body is there before the slower ego consciousness gets it" (157). While for Brennan, the body's codes signify the unseen intelligence of physiology, for Shelley, the magical swiftness of affect's transmission is encouraged by the repetitive, naturalistic language of sensibility: "The beating of her heart was heard to fill / The pauses of her music, and her breath / Tumultuously accorded with those fits / Of intermitted song" (169–172). Body and mind tire with vibrations and rousing words long before their messages can be meaningfully investigated: "He reared his shuddering limbs and quelled / His gasping breath, and spread his arms to meet / Her panting bosom" (182–184). This interplay between sumptuous torrents of material and the abrupt cessation of the receptive mind becomes a hallmark of the maid and poet's interactions. The maid's song of sensibility traps the poet when it begins to exceed the cultivated, selective perception that, according to Clark, distinguishes Shelley's refined sensibility. The veiled maid's music overwhelms any other impressions—its tale is ineffable. We might describe this living death as a mind so swamped with material input that, like the state of the brain in Alan Richardson's neural sublime, it is unable to begin the process of reflection, perception, and articulation. Alternatively, the cognition of such material may become so overwrought that the mind fails to make meaning from the web of voluptuousness. The fiery, blood-boiling symphony supercharges the listening poet with a glut of overpowering rhythmic vibrations. This transmission of sensation, in all its haptic force, helps to explain why her song grows "tumultuous" and "bursting" until the poet becomes "sickened with excess," and the maid dissolves into thin air (171, 174, 181).

Where Wordsworth seeks to contain sublime sensibility's excessive and deleterious effects, Shelley frames the veiled maiden's explosive poetics within a critique not only about its evasion of rational thought but more pointedly about the gendered nature of her song—the ideological purview of a seemingly naturally gendered poetics of sensibility. Her music notably promises to convey pure knowledge in service to a liberatory project: "Knowledge and truth and virtue were her theme / And lofty hopes of divine liberty" (158–159).[30] In this view, the language of sensibility purveys a seemingly transparent, easy transport of revolutionary energy. Although both pleasurable and transforming, this contagion, when written as a feminine, ineffable force, becomes the very reason for the poetic failure of the veiled maid's song. As a result, the poet loses his imaginative ability to dream her up, and her disappearance from the poem marks a devastating absence of poetry and song. After she yields to his "irresistible joy," the poet "Folded his frame in her dissolving arms. / Now blackness veiled his dizzy eyes, and night / Involved and swallowed up his vision" (185, 187–189). The poet places his body into her dissolving form, as if tendering his own embodiment to her poetics of sensibility that can only disappoint him.

More dramatically, his loss of vision startlingly refracts the entire allegory about gendered and embodied poetics as also about an ideological illusion. It is her eyes—her way of seeing and suffusing the world with affective energy—that chase and repel the poet for the remainder of the poem. Both the veiled maiden and the poet's vision reveal themselves as just that: mystified dreams of poet and poetess structured by the inspiring but haunting feminine agent of sensibility who infuses men with a contagious, impassioned, but ultimately damning revolutionary poetics. Such a dream of the effusive poet, Shelley tells us, is always mediated by the constraints of sensibility itself, its tendency to become overwrought. As Ruston and John Mullan remind us, medical science deemed "excessive sensibility" a "specific illness" that came as "the result of experiencing and communicating social feelings and sentiment" (Ruston 135).

The figure of the dream vision and its collapse alerts us to the possibility that we must read it as a symptom of the poet's own ideological beliefs. The discourse of sensibility's entrapment in gender ideology assumes women to be naturally "identifiable with greater suffering, with weakness, and a susceptibility to disorder" (Barker-Benfield 9). This ideology of sensibility restricts the possibility of seeing women writers through anything but the lens of sensibility. Male and female poets alike imbibed the discourse through novels, poems, and revolutionary prose that they helped to create and perpetuate. In "Alastor," the poet's dream resounds with an acute literary disappointment of men and women poets during the revolutionary era—their dream of emancipatory voices and radically embodied intersubjective sympathy felled by the sickening qualities of an overtly gendered, and hence imprisoning, sensibility.

The maiden thus figures a major symptom of post-Revolutionary trauma—the extent to which sensibility was so frequently co-opted as an explanatory gender politics by various political and gendered factions, especially in the 1790s.[31] The dream, then, is endemic of the structure of ideological fantasy that surrounds the understanding of the women of sensibility as a democratizing force. As Slavoj Žižek explains, people "know that, in their activity, they are following an illusion, but still, they are doing it" (*Sublime Object* 30). The maiden becomes a fixation, a self-conscious illusion of the woman of sensibility allegedly destined to reform men and elevate women. The point to be made here is not simply that Shelley critiqued sensibility's complicity in the promises and tragic failures of revolutionary rhetoric, as Barbara Judson has duly claimed.[32] Women poets' entrapment in sensibility—through their own devices and through the fantasies of their male counterparts—was already well understood. By 1815, if not already in the 1790s, sensibility's liberatory force was considered to be an ideological illusion, yet men and women writers nevertheless continued to rehearse it as *the* prime model of revolutionary feminine poetics. Like the fervid monomania of revolutionary reason, sensibility's explanatory power was so pervasive and so pleasurable that it obviated alternative conceptions of revolutionary feminine poetics.

So seductive is the fantasy that neither poet nor narrator can stop chasing it throughout the rest of the poem. Speaking to the swan on the Chorasmian shore, the poet writes the bird into his own human narrative: a mate's return is answered by lustrous eyes, like those the poet still chases:

> thou voyagest to thine home,
> Where thy sweet mate will twine her downy neck
> With thine, and welcome thy return with eyes
> Bright in the lustre of their own fond joy. (280–284)

Even watching twilight fall, he personifies the dusk as a feminine, veiling "her braided locks / O'er the fair front and radiant eyes of day" (338–339), and in the "darkest glen," he feels the presence of a Spirit with "two eyes, / Two starry eyes, hung in the gloom of thought, / And seemed with their serene and azure smiles / To beckon him" (449, 489–492). Displacing his own ideological illusion onto her vision of the world, it seems as though feminine figures beckon him wherever he roams. The vision of the veiled maid therefore presents both an allegory about the failure of sensibility and also an allegory describing the shared failure of the dream of women's poetry as being primarily a poetics of sensibility. Rather than simply marking the poet's visionary yearnings as an absence that propels further projection and desire,[33] "Alastor" signals that the empty dream of revolutionary poetry is inextricably tied to the lost cause of gendered poetics.

At the core of Shelley's critique is sensibility's deadening legacy to human affect—both its uncontrollable excess and the mind-numbing emptiness such surfeit leaves in its wake. In "Alastor," the rough entrainment of affect leaves the poet in a void of static emptiness; the second error in the poet's education, inevitable though it may be, is his fall into the void absent of sensation.

> Now blackness veiled his dizzy eyes, and night
> Involved and swallowed up the vision; sleep,
> Like a dark flood suspended in its course,
> Rolled back its impulse on his vacant brain. (188–191)

After the veiled maid vanishes, the poet can see nothing but "vacant woods": "His wan eyes / Gaze on the empty scene as vacantly / As ocean's moon looks on the moon in heaven" (200–202). As the poet travels aimlessly, despairing and bereft, he wends his way through a metaphorical terrain replete with figures of sleep and voids of sensation: the "beautiful shape" of the maiden is "Lost, lost, for ever lost / In the wide pathless desert of dim sleep"; the rain and mountains "Lead only to a black and watery depth"; "at night when the passion came" it "led him forth / Into the darkness"; the Chorasmian shore becomes a "melancholy waste" as the poet's impulse leads him to "meet lone Death on the drear ocean's waste" (211, 209–210, 215, 224, 226–227, 273, 305). The dizzy poet descends into a blackness that blocks out vision and leaves the "dark flood" of sensation or perception suspended entirely. As Neil Fraistat argues, the poet's mind "is generally becoming a vacuum," an emptiness that confirms the poet's solipsism: he has "refine[d] the mind out of existence" (166, 168). Yet we might see the poet's vacant brain as a result of the overwhelming flood of sensory stimulation that produces a kind of rolling blackout in the poet's mind.[34] The unadulterated transmission of sensibility is no mere women's hysteria but the collective fantasy that raw affect, as the pure song of knowledge, is so rich that women poets must "dump" it on men, even while it remains too potent for anyone to absorb.

As the first two chapters of this book suggest, the figure for mental blackout already has a long literary history, including figures for oblivion in both Charlotte Smith's and Mary Robinson's sonnets.[35] In their poems, oblivion often indicates the active desire to numb feeling or to evacuate sensation, and like Burke's sublime, its tropology proffers a more or less temporary escape from empiricist thought or embodied feeling. Similar to Robinson's early notions of oblivion that "knows no change," such a flood eventuates in a paralyzing stasis. In Shelley, we again see these antipodes dramatized when the poet becomes addicted to the alternation between full sensation and the complete absence of it—and the gendered narratives such a cycle produces.

In this intoxicating cycle of feast or famine, Shelley's passage about the vacant brain even more directly echoes Mary Wollstonecraft's *Mary, A Fiction* (1788). Read along with Mary Shelley and Claire Clairmont during their 1814 European tour (Holmes 239), the novella has stunning resemblances to "Alastor." Like the "Alastor" poet, Mary is driven by her repeated attempts to find an earthly object of feeling—first through her relationship with her impoverished companion Ann, then through her forbidden love for consumptive Henry, and finally through acts of benevolence and emotional sympathy with a variety of poor villagers and vagrant mothers whom she meets in her travels. Each of these quests, in the end, leaves Mary vacuous, completely without sense. When the eponymous heroine finds that her parents have arranged a marriage for her to secure the family property, she completely freezes up: "Overwhelmed by this intelligence, Mary rolled her eyes about, then, with a vacant stare, fixed them on her father's face; but they were no longer a sense; they conveyed no ideas to her brain" (14). Her longing almost always results in too much sensation, followed by the language of the void or the vacant mind. Much like Wollstonecraft, Shelley concerns himself with the mental despair and emptiness that so often results from powerful sensibility and the transmission of affect. The recursive loop between complete affective exchange and the desert waste of oblivion demonstrates the inevitability of sensibility's either-or affective extremes. Shelley's poet lusts after the poetess of sensibility and her stimulating charge, which stunt his own growth as a poet. The avenging spirit may be the poet's inability to rid himself of the desire not for the maiden but for his ideological dependence on her specific brand of overwrought lyricism and the feminine embodiment it entails.

We can reframe the rest of "Alastor" as a struggle with this double vision: the nostalgia for the starry, enflamed eyes of the veiled maid's impassioned poetics and the reflexive, if reactive, sleepy, deathlike calmness that figures the failures, or tranquil defeat, of gendered lyricism. The figurative surface of the landscape in the last part of the poem acts like the maiden's "fits

/ Of intermitted song," fluctuating between the dizzying force of water, such as the beating of the heart or blood, and those pauses signified by glassy pools, verges, the abyss, and the gulph (171–172). As the whirlwind pushes along the poet's boat, he descends into a "black flood on whirlpool driven / With dark obliterating course" and the "multitudinous streams / Of ocean's mountainous waste to mutual war / Rushed in dark tumult thundering" (328–329, 341–343), until the poet lands at the cavern whose eddying waters "With alternating dash" give way to "A pool of treacherous and tremendous calm," "a smooth spot / Of glassy quiet" threatens to drown the boat "Down the abyss" (382, 386, 392–393, 395). It is no wonder that even after he arrives at the narcissus-filled bower, he seeks not celebratory union with those "yellow flowers," but rather "Nature's dearest haunt, some bank, / Her cradle, and his sepulcher" (429–430). The intense color of the flowers, suggesting as they do funeral colors, can only meet with demise, as the poet can only see a narrative where the glut of their stimulation ends with sensory absence. "Alastor" cannot but end in death, the final figure in a tropic ligature of empty minds and spaces.

So engrained is this cycle of sensational affect that even during the frame narrator's final comment on the poet's death, he cannot help but summon Medea, another feminine figure whose intoxicating potions would resurrect the poet from the "voiceless and vacant air" (622).

> O, for Medea's wondrous alchemy,
> Which wheresoe'er it fell made the earth gleam
> With bright flowers, and the wintry boughs exhale
> From vernal blooms fresh fragrance! O, that God,
> Profuse of poisons, would concede the chalice
> Which but one living man has drained . . . (672–677)

Even the Wordsworthian narrator, in his critique of his youthful indiscretions—like Wordsworth's own recursive return to women's reaping tunes in his 1798, 1800, and 1807 volumes—cannot see the persistence of his gendered visions of lyricism. In this sense, as Tilottama Rajan has argued, poet and narrator "are essentially similar beings, like Wordsworth and his younger sibling in 'Tintern Abbey'" (*Dark Interpreter* 76). All of these figures, I would add, are intoxicated in varying degrees by a fantasy about who has access to and can purvey the language of sense.[36] The narrator acknowledges the draught might create yet another Wandering Jew, but he cannot help but wish for this woman's poison, to be once again the "living man" who has drained the chalice, even if it leads him to death.

The opposite of both the drink of forgetting and the leap into oblivion that figure in Smith's and Robinson's work, Medea's alchemic mixture would revivify the "wintry boughs" with "vernal blooms" and all manner of sensation, particularly that fragrant entrainment imparted by feminine poesies. Here the narrator neglects or fails to read the allegory of the veiled maiden's hectic song, just as Wordsworth replicates his own repudiation of and addiction to the gendered poetics of sensibility from *Lyrical Ballads* within "The Solitary Reaper." For the narrator, the repose the poet had craved amounts to "pale despair and cold tranquility" (718). When he asks for another application of mythical, feminine overstimulation, he marks a preference for chasing the maiden who proffers the transmission of sensory stimulation, despite its blight on his understanding.

The permanent disappearance of the poet in the poem's finale, in defiance of the narrator's wish, amounts to a lamentable absence of all poetry, thought, and feeling. The deaths of the poet and the maid together, however, represent the necessary, wholehearted erasure of sensibility's poetics, and this death eventually allows for more free-flowing materiality in "Mont Blanc" to escape the bindings of gender ideology. More importantly, it obviates the sequestering of women within the poetics of sensibility and of men within its fantasies of siren women and gendered lyricism. The poet's death, in particular, critiques the poetry that infects writers with a wrong-headed fantasy of feminine writing and its speedy entrainment of chaotic affect. With such a penchant for this ideological cycle of the boom and bust of sensation, neither the narrator nor the poet has a notion of vacancy that might rescue and use such emptiness to create a new poetics. As with Robinson's Sapphic suicide, the disappearance of both poet figures, however, marks the emergence of Shelley's trope of vacancy—the absence that frees both male and female poets from the legacies of sensibility and prepares the way for new forms of affective poetics in the future.

From Vacant Minds to Vacancy

While narratives of women's song in "Alastor" furnish allegories about the vacant stasis that results when excessive sensibility plagues human bodies, "Mont Blanc" begins to map the mental space whereby the vacant mind might be converted into vacancy, a trope that uncovers another form of affect, the affective, material moving underneath and through all bodies, human and nonhuman. "Mont Blanc"—particularly with respect to the formulation of "vacancy" in its final lines—has most often been read as an analogy for the mind as it comes to knowledge, how it is that "the everlasting universe of things / Flows through the mind" (1–2). For some time scholars have tended to view this poem as a magisterial illustration of a transcendental subject who asserts the priority of mind over mountain,[37] a view that Cian Duffy and Hugo Donnelly have reversed by understanding this "flow" as Shelley's attention to the mind as an empirical sensorium.[38] Rajan, on the other hand, argues that the changing relations between mountain, ravine, and river speak to the dialectics of skepticism and idealism running throughout the poem (*Dark Interpreter* 87). Turning to think more materially about the landscape, the mountain for Karen Weisman represents a resistance to the deconstructionist accounts of Shelley that reject "the presence of an extra-textual absolute" and ignore the quotidian "materials and objects of poetry" that the inefficacy of language uncovers (9). To solidify that material sense of the world, the Arve's fluctuating materiality has lent credence to Lucretian readings of the dance of the atoms[39] and, more recently, to the encounter of the mind and an object-oriented world not beholden to it.[40] Looking past Mont Blanc itself to the "the unremitting interchange" that surrounds it, Anne C. McCarthy has recently pointed our attention to the Arve's contingency as the poem's central drama, which speaks to "Shelley's willingness to suspend binary thinking and enter fully into a relation with a contingent, unconditioned 'universe of things'" (360).

This contingency, I argue, operates at the behest of a material affect that "flows through the mind" but also, more vibrantly, through the Vale of Chamouni's affective ecology that includes "The fields, the lakes, the forests, and the streams" of stanza four but even more directly the pines, winds, rainbows, and waterfalls intervolved in stanza two's lovely scene of affective entrainment. "Mont Blanc" converts the veiled maid's exceptionally poisonous waves into the tremendous rushing Arve, as Shelley enlarges his notion of material affect. While he builds on Hartley's model of entrainment where vibrations are passed from one body to another, he does so by thinking in terms closer to Jane Bennett's notion of "impersonal affect" in *Vibrant Matter*, where affects are already shared among assemblages of things. Bennett attempts to "equate affect with materiality, rather than posit it as a separate force that can enter and animate a physical body" (xiii). Rather than a transmission of intensely felt sensation and physiological change, Shelley's shared, relational affect redresses contagious and maddening vibrations with "particle-forces delineating the impact of one body on another" (Bennett xiii). Both Shelley and Bennett, syncretic thinkers that they are, draw from Spinoza's notion of affect as responsive activity and Lucretian notions of invisible particulate matter traveling or shared among bodies. If characterizing nature's motions as flows or forces seems to anthropomorphize them in an effort to help signal their vibrancy, then Shelley, too, dehumanizes human flows of matter. This double articulation helps reveal how human emotions are already imbued with affects outside subjective human emotion, a tropic eradication of and alternative to the discourse of sensibility. The poem finally teaches the averting mind to turn from sensibility's human, sensational flows with a vacancy that figures another world of movement.

The motion of Mont Blanc's entire ecology—all the force-bearing bodies within it—reveals how a more varied affective ecology can help to stem the tide of sensation without silencing or stopping affective transmission and exchange. If we look more closely at the repeated "flows" throughout the poem, we see an affect that even more acutely signals not empirical sensation but the prior movements of an often invisible, and at times abstract, materiality shared and dispersed among human and nonhuman bodies regardless of gender. Paradoxically, affect flows by dint of language's own figuration. What Hogle terms Shelley's "preconscious process" not only "is first perceivable" in the poem's figural transformations (*Shelley's Process* 4), but Shelley, as I show, gives us a new materialist literary methodology that intertwines relational, moving matter with language's own dynamism, inefficacy, and the capaciousness of its abstraction.[41]

The poem begins with two stanzas that both figure and mimic affective force, first through the rolling rapid waves of the River Arve, which "ceaselessly bursts and raves" and then again in the second stanza when it comes "Bursting through these dark mountains like the flame / of lightening" (11, 18–19). This rash of movement figured by the raving river pulses with nervous energy, the waves of affect so fast and forceful they burn up in flame. These intense vibrations seem to correlate with the mind's empirical sensorium, as if nature's raving is a latent personification, an anthropomorphic analogy explaining how the river's movements are like the mind's.

Yet "Mont Blanc" circulates "the everlasting universe of things" that flow both through the mind and throughout the larger ecological terrain. This swerve of "things," as both Lucretian *rerum* and affects not bound by a subject, begins to intimate something more than an allegorical overlay of mind and world, but rather the possibility of nebulous material movement literally among them. Stanza two mitigates the bursts and raves when it evokes synesthesia as a means of managing impersonal affect that exists and circulates in relationships between multiple kinds of bodies. While the pines cling to the banks of the Arve, "The chainless winds still come and ever came / to drink their odours, and their mighty swinging to hear," winds that eventually participate in creating "Thine earthly rainbows stretch'd across the sweep / Of the aethereal waterfall" (22–23, 24–25). If entrainment occurs through aural vibrations, it also, and for Brennan more provocatively, issues when pheromones are secreted into the air, communicating between bodies over distances. The winds come to imbibe—like the intoxication in "Alastor"—the tree's odors even as they hear themselves influenced and altered by the material qualities of the trees. This model of transmission travels through a tree-wind-water-light assemblage of bodies in relation to each other by dint of their shared material affect. Such a "pulsation," what Goldsmith terms Blake's impulse of blood, "describes a primary, autonomous rhythm before and beyond integrated life" (238). Shelley's bursts and raves travel even more literally among and between bodies. In this communal sharing, the mountain becomes only one actual manifestation in an affective ecology.

The second stanza expands this affect so that we see how Mont Blanc—its ravine and its river—"renders and receives fast influencings" (38). With this phrase, Shelley suggests that, in fact, the mountain does not merely serve as an allegory for the mind but literally shares affect with it. Carlson has offered a compelling model of affective transfer, when she argues that Shelleyan love operates by "perpetually un-building the object world . . . by showing objects to be as ethereal and ever-changing as subjects" (75). Simile works, she writes, "to *mobilize* subjects by allowing otherwise disparate energies to cohere for a time" and reveals "Shelley's conception of the world [as] analogical" (75). Using her model, the mind might give equal ontological credence to the river and the mountain, yet they would nonetheless function as correlates for human subjectivity. The affective ecology Shelley amasses in *Mont Blanc* certainly reveals this flexible, ever-changing materiality of both objects and subjects, but the poem, even more radically, offers a world that is not analogical but rather a set of bodies whose dispersed yet shared affect brings them together in literal exchange and mutual conversation.

If the mind receives the manifold movements of the river and its winds, then the world likewise receives the speaker's affects in the form of those "legion of wild thoughts," which rise to populate the cave of Poesy with the "Ghosts of all things that are" (41, 46). Jane E. Phillips notes that this figure marks Shelley's use of Lucretian simulacra, where atoms arise from objects, then coalesce into images that are both materials and representations. Yet these simulacra form the other part of an exchange already begun with the winds and waters. Human thoughts are not so much a synecdoche for "things," but rather the choric transmissions of affect loosed into the world alongside the flow of winds and water. The mind's energy imparts its residue into the aether, sending ghostly imprints "of all things" into the world, things that are nearly invisible and unidentifiable except through their haunting motions, as they fly beyond brain or body to communicate with the environment. Human physiological movements become only one type of vibrating matter, however, and overcome the boundaries of the body—and the ideological excesses of sensibility's gendered poetics—when they converse with particulate vibrations in the environment. Mont Blanc, then, asks us to ponder not what the mountain says but how it moves regardless of gender amid the landscape, the mind, and its figures.

When "Mont Blanc appears—still, snowy, and serene—" in stanza three, it at first seems to replicate the allegory we have seen in "Alastor," as the rush of affect rendered in stanza one, disregarding the more subtle affective exchange of stanza two, tumbles both mountain and mind, object and subject, into a void of sensation. Stanza three seemingly denudes the space of its materiality: without motion, the hush of sound, or the presence of human subjectivity, the poet appears to empty the great mountain more globally of organic, material vitality inherent to life itself. As Rajan recounts, the legion of ecstatic, visionary thought falls into the dead sleep of skepticism. Subsequently, the mountain's solid representation arises after stanza three's introduction of the figures of death and sleep. Yet to see Mont Blanc whole and still in the face of the raging materiality of the first two stanzas is to resurrect the figure of the vacant brain or empty, static space. Such a view of the mountain valley suggests the mind can only handle the repetitions of affect, which is always on the move, by countering it with its opposite, a snowy surface that is immobile, silent, and apart in its solitude.

However, vacancy is more complicated here. The poem's final lines seem to ask us how to make meaning from the chaotic rolling affect on the one hand and the absolute absence of affect on the other. But the lines' infamous irony suggests that is exactly the wrong question to ask of the mountain's affective ecology. In this last passage, Shelley tenders once again the lightning, the snow, and the vapors from earlier in the poem but now offers vacancy as an alternative to sensory perception that might "render" or embody the mountain's impersonal affective relations. His description now capitalizes on language's ability to construct sensory paradoxes or synesthesia revealing the affective movements that belie silence or solitude:

> Winds contend
> Silently there, and heap the snow with breath
> Rapid and strong, but silently! Its home
> The voiceless lightning in these solitudes
> Keeps innocently, and like vapour broods
> Over the snow. The secret Strength of things
> Which governs thought, and to the infinite dome
> Of Heaven is as a law, inhabits thee!
> And what were thou, and earth, and stars, and sea,
> If to the human mind's imaginings
> Silence and solitude were vacancy? (134–144)

The winds, which have already been contending with the raving river since the first stanza, now "heap the snow with breath." The snow becomes interspersed with moving air and, even more, with human respiration, as a form of dissipated materiality that trespasses human and nonhuman boundaries by locking them in a conspiracy of breathing together. Therefore, the repeated silence of the snow and wind can only obtain in the human mind's imaginings—when the mind renovates the picture of the mountain through mere visual sensation instead of inhabiting this nonhuman, material exchange. Similarly, while lightning may emit no sound, the light invokes the visual, and its lack of voice denotes not the failure to attain human agency but a material force beyond the mere human. Finally, "the vapour broods": it breeds by sitting and waiting. What might seem like a personification indebted to Milton and Wordsworth's own gestures to the fertile imagination, in the context of the other synesthetic moments, becomes a figural gesture that involutes mental perseveration with a nebulous, hovering materiality.

The landscape's dialectical descriptions—the interminable, unstoppable movement of winds and the still, snowy, serenity—are turned into paradoxical configurations of movement-within-suspension and particles-within-force. Rather than simply offering the absence of either aural or visual sensation, Shelley's description of the landscape negates sensation even as it evokes movement through synesthesia where a single sense impression is intimated, undercut, and then gives way to something beyond the sensing body. Synesthesia leads to what might seem like inefficacious or fuzzy abstractions of generalized movements evoked with the rhymes "heap," "keeps," "broods," and "inhabits." Instead, the involution of one sense in another belies not so much a "mystical unity," as Glenn O'Malley long ago suggested, but more specifically an underlying materiality moving as affect, only briefly captured through a series of sensory perceptions (68). The subtle action of the vapor reveals how vacancy constructs movements of shared materiality that are seemingly invisible in solitude and silence. Yet such affects actually accumulate more precociously in the poem's figural movements—the amassing inherent in heap, keep, brood, and inhabit, the subtly fricative near-rhyming of these verbs, and their intimation of affects that occur autonomously and incorporeally.

Shelley's play with different senses resembles Brian Massumi's notion of affect as "synesthesthetic, implying a participation of the senses in each other: the measure of a living thing's potential interactions is its ability to transform the effects of one sensory mode into those of another" (35). According to Massumi, synesthesia is a tactic to localize and actualize affect, which participates in a field of preconscious intensity before it is perceived as sensation or captured as distinct physiological states. Shelley's use of synesthesia intimates a state prior to specifically articulated sensations or emotions—and the alterability within them. It suggests that sensibility, with its vibrations felt through the human body, is only one method of capturing an affect much more capacious in the figural and material realm. Beyond subjective emotion, affect circulates among bodies through a materiality that underwrites but also exceeds specific sensory impressions. If, as Andrew Warren argues in his Lucretian reading of "Epipsychidion," Shelley's "[l]anguage creates an image where there is merely an unstable pattern" ("Unentangled Intermixture" 85), it also intimates a field of preconscious affect that "keeps," "heaps," and "broods" all the actual sensory patterns but also all the abstract, incorporeal moves affect might make outside its translation into sensation or words. Shelley's language here, even before he enunciates the figure of vacancy at the poem's end, deconstructs the alleged silence or stillness of the mountain, then foments the dissipated, shared materiality that inhabits mountain, snow, wind, light, and breath at once.

The poem's figuration therefore allows us to see how we might adequately feel, or make the voice of the mountain felt, but without invoking the language of feeling and sensation bequeathed by sensibility. When Shelley does invoke the word "vacancy," it is with a logic of testing, querying the reader to consider whether the poem's ultimate figure will be read as human triumph, stark negativity, or a much more subtle form of posthuman material and figural movement. Part of this jeopardy occurs through Shelley's practice of repeating many of his descriptive words through the poem, a technique that I would argue ironizes such concepts from sensibility, yet realistically runs the risk of rendering those words repetitive—in the way of Robinson's "tyrant passion," singing the selfsame song. Christopher Hitt characterizes the particular phrase "silence and solitude" as "an outdated idiom" of the sublime, "a prescriptive and formulaic mode of experiencing the wild landscape" taken from numerous popular novels (157). The descent into a vacant mind results, in part, from the reiteration of stock language. Resembling Smith's Petrarchan exclamations against feeling too much and Robinson's parroting of Ovid's and Pope's quandaries about passion, Shelley's silent serenity, by the poem's end, recirculates words and phrases that are definitely not "unapprehended relations" (*Defence*, *SPP* 512). Such sentimental poetry, Shelley says in *A Defence of Poetry*, eventuates from "the recurrence of impressions blunted by reiteration" and annihilates the universe of our minds (533). He shows us how, if readers can release themselves from the ideological language of sensibility, "Mont Blanc" might find figures for affect that do not immediately translate its presensory qualities into sensory, individual, or subjective instances of emotion.

The drama at the end of "Mont Blanc" arises precisely from the tropological substitution of "vacancy" for "silence and solitude," and it tasks us to read, retroactively, the sleep, silences, and ravines of the poem as in fact intimating the brooding vapors of affect. "Vacancy," though certainly not a neologism, presents a rarer figure than oblivion or negativity that displaces sensibility altogether. As Shelley explains in his fragment "On Life": "It [vacancy] reduces the mind to that freedom in which it would have acted, but for the misuse of words and signs, the instruments of its own creation. . . . Our whole life is thus an education of error" (*SPP* 507). Vacancy undermines the dead language of "silence and solitude" and along with it the either-or affective quandary of excess and absence or transcendence that characterizes Romantic sensibility and empiricist epistemology. As a pioneering philosophical-poetic process of linguistic or rhetorical reform, vacancy eradicates misused words and signs, through language that quite literally "marks the before unapprehended relations of things," the relations of impersonal affects within Mont Blanc's figural ecology (*Defence*, *SPP* 512).

Carlson defines vacancy as an "undifferentiated" state, "a lack of distinctness that characterizes the infant's 'unpracticed sense'" (83). Accordingly, vacancy feeds a process of self-making and self-destruction enacted through simile that enables the capacity of the self to inhabit other ontologies, even across species. Shelley's most encompassing version of vacancy, however, occurs when wielded in even more distinctly nonhuman terms outside a psychoanalytic model, as it is increasingly in "Mont Blanc," "Ode to the West Wind," and "Epipsychidion." Shelley intimates the intertwining of multiple entities that are fluid and not only confronting their differences. This mobility transpires through a continuously shared affect beyond or before codified feelings such as Carlson's notion of love. Although synesthesia appears to work as a cross-sense analogy similar to simile's own analogies, for Shelley it actually posits a form of affect that travels through human emotion and nonhuman materiality, revising the relation between the two as something more than mere correlation—something that is, to use Shelley's phrase in *Prometheus Unbound*, "involving and involved" (IV.241).

Other accounts of "materialist figuration," to use Monique Allewaert's term, describe the interplay between the material and the figural, as Goldstein does: "figures are fractions of the real estrange from their sources" (74).[42] Vacancy, however, does not estrange parts from the whole but rather through linguistic abstraction attempts a return to that whole, not as an origin but as a set of unstable relations and affective flows created by humans and nonhumans, material transmissions and figural ones. Because synesthesia's multiple sensory captures carry with them what Massumi calls "a living thing's potential interactions," vacancy's figuration returns us to the retroactive field of affect as a range of potential movements—both real and abstract, corporeal and incorporeal. In Shelley's poem, vacancy, in its use of synesthetic figuration, consistently refers sensation to an underlying material movement. Although such motion seems antithetical to language, the repeated figure of synesthesia enacts this movement that only language can evoke. Vacancy's disruptive energy, for Shelley, infuses seemingly singular bodies, sensations or feelings, with others that speak to affect's virtuality, which enables the reversibility and alterability of individual affective moments. Vacancy, then, answers the problems of overwhelming sensation and dead language by constructing a figural process that uncovers both a shared affective materiality and a reservoir of yet-to-be reified sensations. Language's inefficacy—its ability to link abstractions like "heaps" with tactile verbs like "keeps"—speaks to the capaciousness of words to voice what Massumi calls "bare activity" or "world stirring" among a field of connected things (*Politics of Affect* 52). Language not only transports the material rhythms of phonemes and morphemes but also offers a conduit to the incorporeal materiality impossible to feel except through language's movements. Vacancy allows for affect's diversified transmissibility through synesthesia's intervolving figuration.

"Epipsychidion" and the Gender of Spirit

By focusing on how the nonhuman can alter affective transmission more generally, Shelley seems to slip the knot of gender in "Mont Blanc." To say that the mountain ecology offers affect without gender may be facile, yet it does provide a model that Shelley revisits in "Epipsychidion" when he reconsiders the problem of how to add human relationships to the variegated transmission of affects circulating in Mont Blanc. "Epipsychidion" combines the inquiries of "Alastor" and "Mont Blanc" to consider how the poetics of vacancy can alter human relations, particularly the difficulties of gender, by opening them to a larger-scale affective materiality that flows through multiple bodies and things. This poem has classically been read as Shelley's contemplation about desire and the efficacies of metaphor to herald sexual and political difference and yet still place faith in the unfinished political and personal project of perfectability and love.[43] At the heart of these concerns, Shelley returns to the possibilities for feminine poetics and figuration—not simply metaphor—to compose new affective relations.

This solution comes with the poet's third and final vision of his soulmate, after the "electric poison" of the first "one" and the cold tranquility of the second. The first two potential figures for gendered poetics repeat the allegory traced so far in this chapter of intense sensation and vacant withdrawal, and the three figures together can be seen not only as the essences of Shelley's biographical or ideal lovers but also as allegorical figures for the extremities of feminine song.[44] The third "one" arises from the sensory absence of the Moon's affective chill: "Athwart that wintry wilderness of thorns / Flashed from her motion splendour like the Morn's, / And from her presence life was radiated" (323–325). These lines recall those in "Alastor" where the lone pine "stretched athwart the vacancy" as it girds itself against the repeated "inconstant blast" even as the river falls into an "immeasurable void" (562, 563, 569). This speaker arrives at a similar juncture, standing athwart another vacant space whose wintery thorns suggest the desolation of sensation and feeling altogether. Yet, rather than "dramatiz[ing] nature's inability to substitute for human relationships," as William A. Ulmer suggests of "Alastor," Shelley finds a middle position that echoes the dispersed materiality and synesthetic interplay of "Mont Blanc" (48). The extremities of heat, fire, and poison of the first "one" and the cold, distant moon, and ice of the second are undone by the third "one." Shelley's third option offers not Emily, a woman, or a particular sensory pattern. In the vacancy of particular emotional captures or narratives about feminine emotion, she figures a final synesthetic constellation that assembles a diffuse and gentle affect.[45]

The metaphorical vehicle for describing the feminine figure has shifted from one of heat and cold, storms and tranquility, to several intertwined figures, including radiating light and inspiring sound, which are penetrated by spirit.[46] Shelley's "spirit," when it enables multiple instances of synesthesia at once, offers a meta-poetics of vacancy as an ineffable and underlying movement that is at once figural and material. Unlike divine transcendent light or the reflection of enlightenment illumination, however, this synesthesia of light and sound presents an underlying permeable transmission of particulate matter:

> With flowers as soft as thoughts of budding love;
> And music from her respiration spread
> Like light,—all other sounds were penetrated
> By the small, still, sweet spirit of that sound,
> So that the savage winds hung mute around; (328–332)

Flowers and music signify different aspects of feminine poetics, stimulating at least three different senses—the visuality of flowers and light, the sounds of the sweet spirit of music that mutes the savage winds, and the less perceptible haptics of the flowers' softness and the music-like respiration. When, further down in the passage, Shelley asks us to comprehend "musical respiration" that acts "Like light," he translates sheer affect—material activity and receptivity—into three forms of sensory perception: aural, visual, touch. The one's flowers, her poetry, are soft and initiatory while her music spreads through periodic respiration of air. These expressive touches potentially circulate as both particles and waves.[47] Shelley's figural alternation undermines any one sensory perception of her voice so that she may inhabit several. Together, in their overlap and alternation, they finally mute those "savage winds" characteristic of the previous squalls of sensibility. Underneath and through the simile of a music like light, spirit—not savage winds—purveys a shared, material motion, the "sweet spirit of that sound" that penetrates nonhuman sounds, human music, floral budding, and ubiquitous light.

This affective spirit may harken back to "Ode to the West Wind"'s uncontrollable spirit as well as the wind's "azure sister Spring," whose "mildly feminine" figure, as the Norton editors say, inaugurates simultaneous embodied and social change. Affect "respires," has room to breathe, as it moves through various sense impressions and things. Unlike the measured circulation or pulsation that Wordsworth offers in the Preface to *Lyrical Ballads*, where, as Lanser has suggested, meter stems the tide of unwieldy speech and sensibility, Shelley increases the circulation of affective "spirit." The movement among the senses enacts what Shelley describes as adding "spirit to sense" in *A Defence of Poetry* (*SPP* 528). We have been accustomed to thinking of the spirit in Shelley as a form of transcendental knowledge, the magnetic force of vitality, or even repeated mental and linguistic transferences, but spirit is a more flexible, buoyant affect that pervades all things yet is not bound by any one sense or body.

Counter to de Man's argument in "Kant and Materialism," that the figural produces affect as inhuman automaticity, Shelley suggests that the figural marries human and nonhuman movements, including that of real matter, all of which can be found in, and actively motivated by, the capacious abstraction of "spirit." Rather than translating affect into feeling through language, spirit's language of vacancy reverses that instantiation by transforming feeling back into affect—an affect that is, in the end, not gendered. Shelley shows the aural expression that intertwines human and nonhuman sound—as opposed to voice—is likewise predicated on a nonhuman fluidity within language's own nonhuman sinews. Combining Smith's suspension with Robinson's constant movement, Shelley's vacancy offers synesthesia's cognitive involution and its retroactive remapping of one sense onto another that finally broods a slow attention to a pool of anticipatory affects.

Read together, these poems suggest that when Shelley thinks of a poetics of embodiment, he worries less over his legendary medical neuroses than the fate of sensibility's "paralyzing venom, through the affection into the very appetites" (*A Defence*, *SPP* 522) that empties the brain, as it does in many of Wordsworth's *Lyrical Ballads*. Both poets grapple with problems of affective entrainment—the fears about what the body forcefully communicates—and how the translation of infectious, excessive sensation becomes unfortunately coded as feminine. Shelley's solution comes through figuration and its ability to staunch the fits of embodied sensation while evoking other material movements—among humans, their nonhuman environment, and language itself. To rescue the vacant brain, he evinces "vacancy," a tropological process that bespeaks affective capaciousness. It moves us past empirical sensation and codified human-centered feelings into affects and material in shared movement among bodies. Vacancy's secret alchemy is, in part, born from Shelleyan synesthesia that does not so much heighten sensual feeling but rather intimates the thin thread of ungendered "spirit." Vacancy uncovers this virtual affect of all the moves all the bodies might make by enacting the piling up of synesthesia's metaphorical vehicles. For Jewsbury, inveterate exchange itself will become an emancipatory structure or spirit all its own. Shelley, however, teaches us how to widen the course of affect by attending to affects circulated by nerves, winds, and water, as well as by figurative language. Rather than simply leaving affect behind or suspending us in a cognitive state before and beyond feelings, he strives to intervolve the diverse flows of a dispersed, new materiality through vacancy's synesthetic ability to interfuse the energies of the world.

CHAPTER 4

Felicia Hemans's Ruined Minds

Cognitive Overload and the Soul of Freedom

Felicia Hemans's political and ideological affiliations have remained potently ambiguous for scholars,[1] an uncertainty that has invited probing research into her global politics and her portrayals of a geographically and ethnically diverse set of women in any number of roles—social, political, familial, and even multiply gendered.[2] Yet what has never been uncertain is her poetics of sentiment.[3] Our accounts of her poems still identify emotion—whether domestic sentiment, patriotic fervor, or revolutionary passion—as an essential quality of her verse. In "The Widow of Crescentius," during a classic scene of Hemans's tragic women in crisis, the eponymous character watches her husband's execution and the republic along with it. She seems to stand inundated with fear, anger, and passion: "With bloodless check and vacant glance, / Frozen and fix'd in horror's trance / Spell-bound, as every sense were fled, / And thought overwhelm'd" (I.260–263). Susan J. Wolfson reads the widow, and female revolutionaries like her, through Shelley's veiled maid from "Alastor," whose "passionate incandescence of the female body" and "radiant impassionata is the vengeful eponym of *The Widow of Crescentius*" (Lau, *Fellow Romantics* 102).[4] Such agential, puissant passion characterizes Romantic readings of Hemans's politically vexed but actively emoting women. Victorian scholars, by contrast, working from Isobel Armstrong's notion of how poetic form can help to restrain and control sensibility, argue that

Hemans attempted to filter her passion with a form of "reasoned feeling" (Rudy 545) or "reason and thought as well as emotion" (*Women Poets* Mason 26). Such balanced emotion often motivates passion toward building the state if not the nation (Kelly; Lootens). Yet, the widow's frozen and fixed stance belies a welter of cognitive activity, as she stands "spell-bound" and "thought overwhelm'd," a condition that cannot so easily be categorized by reason or emotion. In this trance state, the widow figures a mental crisis that reveals Hemans intent on exploring what lies beneath emotion, questioning its very basis.

The "spell-bound" widow, on the one hand, appears to exhibit a mental paralysis, which results from the brain's inability to process a rush of brain activity. On the other, the description of the widow alters considerably from earlier characterizations of her in the poem, when she appears as a figure of Apollonian prophesy: "With glances of impassion'd thought / As fancy sheds in visions bright, / O'er priestess of the God of Light" (I.145–147). In these lines, her mind is illuminated by a more intuitive or transcendental understanding of Italy, its empire, and the heavens at large. When crisis scenes occur in Hemans's poems, her most spectacularly suffering men and women figure moments where brain activity furnishes more cognitive activity than they can process into clear perceptions—or than they can understand with the mind's powers of abstraction. Taken together, these passages illustrate Hemans's vacancy: a brain overwhelmed by sensory data at the same time it shatters the mind's long-held transcendental means of understanding. This crisis makes the self, especially the self informed by concepts of gender, sentiment, and patriotic domesticity, unrecognizable.

In terms of the taxonomy of vacancy this book has traced so far, Hemans's poems renegotiate Smith's antagonism to empiricism and idealism through another version of Robinson's postempiricist multiplicity. Systems thinker that she is, Hemans coordinates at least two strands of epistemology: transcendental, innate knowledge underwritten by notions of God and materialist models of the brain that develop from empirical accounts of nerve theory, medicine, and phrenology,[5] and she explores crucial mind-brain problems that would occupy both early brain scientists and continental philosophers of the nineteenth century.[6] In Hemans's middle-period poems, vacancy ultimately occurs from the shock produced by the encounter between cognitive experience and abstract thinking—including the near automatic ability to categorize emotions.[7] This crux pits the immediacy of brain activity, both conscious and not, against abstraction, a collision within the ruined brain that figures what Žižek's has termed "the parallax view," "the confrontation between two closely linked perspectives between which no neutral common ground is possible" (4). The halting of the dialectical process that would synthesize them places into relief two disparate perspectives, so that they might destabilize perception and invoke not so much a gap in knowledge but affect's continual movement between models and explanatory theories about them.

Hemans's speculations about the mind and brain first come to a head with her 1819 volume *Tales and Historic Scenes*, when the aftermath of the Napoleonic Wars rehabilitated both the potential for democratic rebellion and the resumption of monarchial prowess. In "The Widow of Crescentius," her inquiry begins with the widow's paralysis at her husband's wrongful execution and ends when, transformed into a minstrel, she transmits her ruined mind to the tyrant Otho. Her act of soulful singing converts Shelley's concerns with the transmission of affect into a political allegory for the productive mental stymying of the patriarch and his regime. Hemans even more resolutely turns to examine the interplay between ruined minds and the effects of empire in her long poem "The Forest Sanctuary" (1825), after the Mediterranean and South American revolutions have taken place. The poem features vacancy through the newly opened mind of a Spanish Protestant who travels to the New World's forest sanctuary before colonial settlement has solidified. Hemans's rewriting of the Inquisition's hysteria into affect, similar to Smith's hospitality in the Napoleonic era, likewise disrupts causal history in favor of other possible futures. When the Spaniard finally settles in the embowered repose of the forest sanctuary, that space, most like Robinson's circling bounds, augurs free-floating, breezy whispers of unprocessed, partially unconscious material movements. Such a field of affect becomes shared among the Spaniard, the fire flies, the trees, and other spirits of the New World.

Hemans's vacancy of a purely embodied model for cognitive processing prevents her new-world denizens from resuming feminine emotions or gendered subjectivity. Following Shelley, Hemans refigures another way that raw affect might flow through brains and worlds, redrawing cognitive models to reveal how human cognitive flurry and the world's restive materiality circulate together—how they might form an interchangeable, posthuman affect. Rather than privileging the construction of self that preoccupies many cognitive theories of affect, she instigates the wealth of cognitive data and materiality, so that mental and geographical vacancies—together and at once—suspend the synthesis of new subjectivities, genders, and nationalities.

CHAPTER 4

The "thought overwhelm'd" Widow and Her Soulful Ruination

Set as the opening poem in *Tales, and Historic Scenes, in Verse*, "The Widow of Crescentius" was published several months before the Peterloo massacre, and the poem, as well as many others in the volume, has as its major preoccupation revolution by unlikely members of society.[8] The two-part poem tells the tale of the Roman consul Crescentius, who is overthrown and murdered by the Pope-backed tyrant, Otho. Occurring in the last four years of the tenth century, the events in the poem resonate with the formation of the Second Coalition against Napoleon, in 1798, which included Naples and the Papal states. After witnessing her husband's death, Crescentius's widow, Stefania, dresses as a boy minstrel in Otho's train and eventually poisons him before committing suicide herself. The narrative poem, however, spends a good deal of time describing the ruined Italian statuary dotting the countryside as a correlative for the destruction of Stefania's mind. Both parts of the narrative poem climax in lyrical moments dwelling on this damage: part one ends by detailing Stefania's paralysis while part two deals with Otho's ruination at her hands. Wolfson's editorial notes set into relief Hemans's unique form of domestic politics. She suggests that such a poem provides the first in a series on "the fate of female passion in political conflict" that forms a "macrotext" on the topic of "insurrection inspired by female domestic affection" (Hemans, *Selected* 70). The tropological brio that ties together revolution and the besieged mind enunciates far more than a feminine lament: the widow's insurrection serves to overthrow assumptions about women's passion and the domestic affections.[9] As a performative, intellectual experiment about how the mind itself works—and might be dramatically changed, she stands as a demonstration of Hemans's speculative prowess.

Although the poem does describe Crescentius's own "calm" bravery in enduring his bitter fate, the entire first part leads up to Stefania's reaction as she watches her husband's execution:

> Yes, in the wildness of despair,
> She, his devoted bride, is there.
> Pale, breathless, through the crowd she flies,
> The light of frenzy in her eyes:
> But ere her arms can clasp the form,
> Which life ere long must cease to warm;
> Ere on his agonizing breast

> Her heart can heave, her head can rest;
> Check'd in her course by ruthless hands,
> Mute, motionless, at once she stands;
> With bloodless cheek and vacant glance,
> Frozen and fix'd in horror's trance;
> Spell-bound, as every sense were fled,
> And *thought o'erwhelm'd*, and feeling dead.
> And the light waving of her hair,
> And veil, far floating on the air,
> Alone, in that dread moment, show
> She is no sculptured form of woe. (249–266; my emphasis)

Denied the comfort and stability of her husband's body, the widow is physically restrained from action by "ruthless hands." While her body is "check'd" by others, her own "wildness" and "frenzy" effectively paralyze her. The signs of her femininity—her hair and her veil—wave in the wind, their external motion contrasting with her internal, mental trance. If her hair and her veil show that "she is no sculptured form of woe," if she does not display a kind of melancholy or despair frozen in time, then the question becomes what state of mind does the "spell-bound" widow represent?

At first glance, the widow's trance might appear to resemble those that Franz Mesmer and his disciples used in public displays of hypnosis and phreno-mesmerism beginning in the mid–eighteenth century and repopularized in the 1820s with Johann Spurzheim and F. J. Gall's phrenology. The passage, however, does not suggest that either the martyred Crescentius or his nemesis Otho has induced Stefania into a hypnotic state, nor does it use language denoting the presence of animal magnetism or magnetic fluid.[10] Neither does the spell-bound widow seem to figure the kinds of gothic or fairy enchantment present in Keats, for example. If the widow has been evacuated of sensation "with bloodless cheek, and vacant glance," her brain paradoxically is still frenzied: "thought overwhelm'd." This language suggests that Hemans is describing something closer to contemporaneous accounts—from both early brain science and post-Kantian philosophy—of the brain or the mind caught in action.

Such a situation renders the mind as it attempts to navigate—or fail to navigate—between reflective, intuited concepts that turn out to be incorrect and crisis moments when the brain manufactures and then reveals to the conscious mind a barrage of physiological, sensory input. Though these mind and brain models are often seen as antithetical, as Alan Richardson points out in *Romanticism and the Science of the Mind*, both proponents of brain science as well as German idealist philosophers adamantly regarded the mind as active, opposed to empiricism's view of the mind as a passive recipient of the world's sensations (6). Both camps, moreover, touched on the propensity for the brain or mind to work itself into states of sensory or cognitive paralysis, whether the Kantian sublime, Hegel's "dark night of the soul," or what Richardson has more recently coined as the "neural sublime." Hemans's depiction of the widow places mind and brain in tension that can help to explain the poem's important interstitial moments, such as the widow's slack-jawed trance.

To take the materialist account of the brain first, in their historicist accounts of brain science, both Richardson and Jonathan Miller have brought to light nineteenth-century versions of a pre-Freudian unconscious, which was thought to be revealed by trance-like states. They argue that writers beginning with Coleridge drew on contemporaneous formulations of the unconscious, formulated by Erasmus Darwin, Pierre-Jean-George Cabanis, and Gall among others. Unlike the later Freudian model based on the repression of emotional content, the nondualistic, materialist notion of the brain posited the brain as generating "continuous activity" through its own unconscious internal impressions as well as sensory impressions channeled via the nervous system (Richardson 18). Cabanis's model was particularly similar to sensibility's nerve theory, shaping an understanding of the brain where cognitive processes like breathing as well as some perceptions and judgments occurred automatically and not necessarily with conscious awareness or volition. How this conversion from sense data to perception or ideas occurred was the subject of debate then as it is now. At issue, as well, was the existence or extent of a superintending ego, or a mind, that would, with corresponding political valence, govern chaotic and unconscious brain activity.[11] William Lawrence, both Richardson and Marilyn Butler remind us, became a household name due to the link between riotous brain activity and political upheaval. The brain did not act alone, however, and the method of communication from nerves to brain—whether through a vital force, a fluid, or a system of nerves—foregrounded a nebulous material system of communication. Hemans, through her figures of mental crisis, offers speculation on all these topics.

Her embodied depictions of women almost certainly have their roots in medical theories about sensibility,[12] but also the varied accounts of materialism that extended ideas about nerves circulating sensations through the body and brain. Hemans would certainly have gleaned these developing theories from her voracious reading in popular periodicals of her day. Phrenology and brain science were notorious in the press, Gall in particular due to his ideas about the correspondence between skull shape and personality traits. Yet Gall's theories were more extensive than craniology, as he thought concertedly about a cognitive unconscious. In Hemans's commonplace books, she records an anecdote about Gall taken from a footnote to an article in *Lacon, or Many Things in Few Words* (1826),[13] and in a letter to James Simpson in 1824 she notes that she has received the *Phrenological Journal*. This Edinburgh publication sought to defend the science of Gall, Spurzheim, Charles Bell, George Combe, and others by excerpting negative reviews of phrenology, exposing their unjust polemic, and then turning to offer other articles in support.

Alongside these overt references, passages from Hemans's works in this period seem specifically attuned to phrenology's attention to the relationship of mind, brain, and facial expression,[14] as do these lines from *The Vespers of Palermo* (1823), which pay particular interest to the shape of the skull:

> Now shall I read
> Each face with cold suspicion, which doth blot
> From man's high mien its native royalty,
> And seal his noble forehead with the impress
> Of its own vile imaginings! (IV.i.78–82)

Here rebellion leader Procida deems he can determine whether his son Raimond is guilty of treason based on his "mien" and "forehead." Hemans would no doubt have gleaned some of her information from contentious debates about materialism in the pages of the literary reviews,[15] just as she likely imbibed materialist principles through her reading of her contemporaries, particularly Shelley's "Alastor," Coleridge's *Remorse*, and perhaps "Kubla Khan."[16] Such popular science circulated widely in intellectual circles—especially among those thinkers considering the means to radical political action—and there is every reason to believe that Hemans's voracious reading afforded her opinions and theories of her own, which she formulates through her figures of trance states.

Particularly after Mesmer so publically demonstrated the unwilled, automatic actions that could be coaxed from his subjects, the unconscious became a notoriously powerful, if dangerous, force. As Miller suggests, in the nineteenth century "the hypnotic trance . . . exposed the action of these unconscious processes" (par. 39). Many activities associated with consciousness happen in part unconsciously not so much because latent content is repressed but because brain activity occurs more quickly and effectively without conscious supervision. The trance state, such as those

Hemans's characters depict, places this process on display, tendering an explicit view of the materialist brain. As Miller continues: "By artificially paralyzing the will, a broad layer of automatic action was now made conveniently visible" (par. 39). While he documents ideas of cognition as they develop from mesmerism and phrenology into less supernatural and more physiological brain science, Richardson argues that Romantic writers "were aware of the 'alternate' unconscious outlined by Miller, more productive than repressive, working to a large extent independently of the conscious subject, rendering the mind a theater of instinct, emotion, and desires as well as of reason, perception, and ideas" (58). Both Gall and Cabanis mention sleep and dreaming as one state in which the brain's hidden activity might be revealed, as it was in mesmeric experiments: "In artificial somnambulism the soul is disengaged from the trammels of the body, so as to cause it to exercise its faculties with greater freedom" (Gall 53).[17] Such states as Coleridge's hallucinations, De Quincey's reveries, or Hemans's trances reveal the machinations of a consciousness not always self-apparent to the thinking subject.[18]

Rather than the intersubjective sexual and political dynamics operating through mesmeric hypnotism, Hemans's trances represent a single mind erupting into cognitive activity during moments that are emotionally and intellectually difficult to process. Much as Shelley refracts stillness and silence into vacancy's underlying affective motion, Hemans redraws paralysis not as suspension but as a movement from clearly labeled emotion experienced in the mind into affect's unseen brain activity. Although the widow may "feel dead" to her mind's powers of abstraction and emotional capture, while she is "fix'd in horror's trance," her brain nevertheless has become potently "overwhelm'd." Affect theorist Brian Massumi, working from neuroscience models, calls what lies within such seeming cognitive gaps the field of "pressing crowd of incipiencies" that occur before language and even consciousness (30). Within these gaps in perception, the body may be fielding stimuli or producing autonomic reactions without awareness; intensity constitutes an array of "motion, vibratory motion, resonation" before body or mind has selected a chosen response by perceiving or enunciating it in language (26). Brain activity becomes more than only those cognitive sensations not yet sensed but also those movements that have not yet happened, but might. What belies Hemans's figures of "frenzy" and "vacant glance" is a bevy of indeterminate, unforeseen, and virtual mental movements.

Displaying such "unconscious cerebration," a later nineteenth-century term used to describe this bottom-up, nonvolitional cognition,[19] Stefania's mind becomes "ruined" precisely at the moment when the host of unconscious incipiencies are revealed to her consciousness—before such nervous impulses might be easily labeled as passion or reflection, or individual emotions for that matter. Hemans will employ more mimetic descriptions of this affective flood in "The Forest Sanctuary," yet it is clear that she does not want readers to assume that the widow has been captured by despair when she warns, "She is no sculptured form of woe." Vacancy identifies the widow's ruined mind as part of the larger operation that critiques the tendency for cognitive events to be mistakenly translated into clearly defined emotions, such as despair. With a line written in the negative, Hemans refuses to allow Stefania's emotion to be identified. She anticipates readers' assumptions that the widow—with her hair and veil waving in the wind—represents an embodiment of tragic femininity, a form of woman, and a paralyzed femininity, so classic that it could be the subject of Roman sculpture. Hemans tells readers, "no," do not reify the widow's body within the emotion of despair or sorrow; look to the conjunction of frozen mind and active brain in fruitful tension.

With the refusal to label Stefania's emotion, Hemans formulates a model of affective distancing that explores a dichotomy found in neuroscience, psychology, and affect theory, what Steven Goldsmith describes as "the traditional distinction between higher order *emotions* involving sophisticated judgments and primitive, precognitive, or autonomic *affects*" (23). Emotions often come into being only as we cognize physical effects or nebulous affects into specific feelings, particularly through descriptive language, which can begin to create a reflective self.[20] Massumi conceptualizes emotions as individual "captures" of the larger field of affect, and it is affect that accounts for the missing "half-second lapse between the beginning of a bodily event and its completion in an outwardly directed, active expression" (29). This gap can help us see Hemans's intimation of unconscious cognitive activity during narrative hinge moments. The shock and awe exhibited in "The Widow" and other poems display affect's chaos before it is identified as distinct emotions—such as the cocktail of anger, woe, and sadness, or even the sensibility we might use to characterize the widow. This vacancy that figures her state pointedly undermines any clear naming of her crisis, and instead reveals it to be frenzied brain activity that suspends any easy processing of neural or worldly activity, by either mind or brain. Vacancy's intervention effectively aims to move beyond traditional feeling *and* thinking, whether coded as feminine or masculine. Here Hemans seems to argue against Gall, when she suggests that the universality of materialist model should undermine a gendered view of the brain.

When Crescentius's murder renders Stefania unable to act, her will is suspended, asking us to consider what has happened to the widow's self-determining mind or imperial soul. The Gordian knot of activity that has begun to overload her brain paralyzes self-conscious thought: "When consciousness again shall wake, / Hath now no refuge but to break" (273–274). The "wake"/"break" rhyme and the nod to "consciousness" signals that methods of self-consciousness and self-determination that the widow had previously used to assemble her mind will no longer work. In doing so, Hemans draws us to consider how Stefania had previously composed a whole enlightened and emotive mind—and with what epistemological tools. When we move back through the poem to look for such prior consciousness, she encourages us to consider—and ruin—a second model of thought, some form of transcendental abstraction, already at play.

Our first introduction to Stefania heralds not just the "hope and love" of the republic, but its signal light: "in her eye / Lives all the soul of Italy!" (I.141–142). Apollo's "thought impassion'd . . . priestess," she has direct access to the god of knowledge's light, ostensibly through Delphic prophesy and "visions bright" (I.148, I.147). This high-born soul intuits truths when she lights up from within, and she manifests the spirit of Italy through the vitality of her eyes and face: "a cheek, whose kindling dyes / Seem from the fire within to rise; / But deepen'd by the burning heaven / To her own land of sunbeams given" (I.151–154). The metaphors of light and fire secure Stefania's Roman privilege, and position her as a beacon of transcendent understanding in touch with the celestial sphere. Her light—the inner machinations of the mind that animate her with the visage of enlightenment—comes from within, even as it is deepened by that special access to the "burning heaven" given to Italy, that great crucible of republican freedom. Here we have an interesting depiction of transcendental truth: inner intuitions are deepened by that knowledge granted by the universal and heavenly, including perhaps those supposedly universal categories of emotion sensed by the impassioned priestess. To put this in terms of a soulful consciousness, Stefania inspires clear knowledge of the world when her intuitions connect to the world spirit, both made of the same light. Once the widow experiences her cognitive mental breakdown, however, Stefania's consciousness can no longer reach the stars; that light has gone out, replaced with another kind of fervor.

This shift in metaphors as the poem proceeds, from heavenly enlightenment to cognitive ruination, reveals Hemans's epistemological confrontation. Her deployment of cognitive overload ambiguously puts into antagonistic relation the deluge of sensory information about an event and those explanatory concepts of nation, gender, and power that appear innate or intuited by the self-determining, heaven-inspired consciousness. Vacancy in "The Widow of Crescentius" and later in "The Forest Sanctuary" enunciates the problem of knowledge as an irresolvable parallax between overwhelming cognitive activity and those intuited concepts that can and will compose consciousness. This doubling of epistemologies questions the supposedly naturalistic basis of sensibility's gendered account of physiology, assumptions about how that physiology operates, as well as the ideological tendency to see feminine emotional understanding as heaven-born—such as Edmund Burke's depiction of Marie Antoinette as the maternal yet heaven-sent morning star. Although for Steven Goldsmith the agitations of emotion "discomfit" with a "political valence to the notion of subjective disturbance," Hemans questions the hegemonic sways of emotion's moral judgment and the categorization that necessarily secure the gendered subject, however disturbed (23).

Žižek spells out this problem in the reverse, arguing that it is abstraction or conceptualization that resists the unseemly barrage of cognitive incipience that Hemans portrays: "This is where Hegel comes in, with his praise of the infinite negative power of abstraction that pertains to understanding: consciousness is possible only through this loss, this delay with regard to the fullness of immediate experience—a 'direct consciousness' would be a kind of claustrophobic horror, like being buried alive with no breathing space" (*Parallax View* 241). Yet, from Hemans's point of view, Hegel's abstraction leaves out the wealth of affective activity that might interfere with conscious decisions and disrupt abstraction's hegemonic tendencies. In "The Widow of Crescentius," Hemans's moments of paralysis enact the "claustrophobic horror" of "direct consciousness," deploying cognitive overabundance precisely to undo the negative power of abstraction or intuition. Žižek points out that "the function of *blocking* is an elementary function of consciousness," but for Hemans, the fullness of affective response induces a reverse blockage, creating so much brain activity as to scramble the soul and to hinder the mind feeling its way to an idea (240). Hemans's mental disruption halts abstract thought, and then, with added provocation, forces the mind to reconcile its own ways and means.

This important aspect of vacancy revolves around the positive or productive consequences of the ruined mind. The perversity of the widow comes from the violence that she wreaks on reigning mental concepts and eventually unleashes on the new tyrant, as her brain dysfunction offers an allegory for bottom-up revolution. Richardson reminds us of the connection between political allegories and brain science: "an association between brain-based psychology and radical ideologies could be taken for granted in the mind of the common reader" (*British Romanticism and the Science of the Mind* 25). Stefania is highborn, yet the myriad cognitive affects clogging her mind might be read as a figure for the masses, such as those at Peterloo, who attempted to wrest control from an aristocratic oligarchy. The material unconscious likewise becomes a somewhat apt figure for women's lopsided role in the public sphere because it represents untapped power. As Miller writes, "if the situation calls for a high-level managerial decision, the Unconscious will freely deliver the necessary information to awareness" (par. 56). Following Miller, high-level wives like Stefania could be seen as stealthy providers of secret information or uncommon potentialities to a husband and public executive. In terms of a gendered division of labor in the brain, after the masculine will has been stymied by the failure of its imperial plots, the feminine material archivist of movements is able to infiltrate the ideological superstructure and change it from the inside out. Hemans is able to rally what Mary Fairclough identifies as "the disruptive implications of sympathetic communication," but in even more radical service of simultaneous mental and social unrest (21). The widow, as a secret informant by dint of her gender difference, figures the potential disruption of the very system by which gender subjects come into being. When the trance state suspends the impetus to act, the widow, as a high-level wife, is able to inject unconscious incipiencies into the consciousness, altering even how we conceptualize historical events, if not the very terms of that history.

This project of revolution waged by a bottom-up cognitive model of thought might at first lure us into redrawing these trance moments through the aesthetics of the empirical sublime.[21] Richardson suggests a similar state of mind in his descriptions of the neural sublime: "as conscious thought reaches its limit and flickers out, the brain is left conceptually bare, momentarily impoverished and bereft of ideas" (30). Patricia Yaeger might help as well when she defines the feminine sublime as "a vocabulary of ecstasy and empowerment" (192), while Barbara Claire Freeman sees it as a mode of experience, a confrontation with the other that is "excessive and unrepresentable" (2).[22] Stefania's mental breakdown might then be read as a politicized neural sublime, aimed at overthrowing tyrants and their ideologies through revolution from below.

Yet in most accounts of the sublime, especially those of Burke and Kant, one element within an epistemology (Burkean sensation, Kantian apprehension) overwhelms the mind and temporarily stops it from functioning (and ends by reassuring the subject of his rational functioning, safe from danger). None of these formulations accurately describes what amounts to an epistemological clash between two systems of thought, in effect the movement of the mind itself. The widow's cessation of thought belies the mind grappling within the gap created by multiple perspectives or philosophies from divergent traditions. In epistemological terms, the widow becomes a crisis figure for the conflict between bottom-up bodily activity and top-down conceptual thought, intensity and emotion, used to interpret big events and their place within larger cultural narratives. Such a vacancy offers the opportunity to refigure the relationship between mind and brain as well as between mind and world.[23]

With "vacant glance" the silent widow of Crescentius stands saturated in unprocessed cognitive information, devoid of those signifiers that manifest codified ideas, and yet she is not completely without soul or volitional agency. This finer point about the emergent brain's relation to the executive mind is Hemans's final figurative gesture at the end of the first part of the poem, when she states that the widow's mind has been ruined both materially and figuratively:

> But in the glow of vernal pride,
> If each warm hope *at once* hath died,
> Then sinks the mind, a blighted flower,
> Dead to the sunbeam and the shower;
> A broken gem, whose inborn light
> Is scatter'd—ne'er to re-unite. (279–284)

After Stefania's husband dies, she is left destitute. The blown flower image here certainly evokes notions of ruined femininity such as hysterical deaths or ritual *sati* that had women following their husbands to the grave. Nanora Sweet has discussed Hemans's repeated use of the blown rose image as an emblem of feminized, historical evanescence and rebirth, but the passage emphasizes the extent to which the widow's tragic state occurs because her "mind" "sinks" "ne'er to re-unite." The second metaphor, the broken gem with its light imagery, transfers the tenor of the passage from an emphasis on the destruction of nature or natural femininity to the disruption of reason, or more broadly to Enlightenment ideologies. The cracked gem and scattered light figure not simply the loss of reason itself but the loss of reason's function to cohere the subject through the powers of abstraction. While from the point of view of the 1790s Revolutionary agenda, this scattering or immolation is a tragic figure for the failure of the Enlightenment, from the vantage of the post-Waterloo resurgence in liberal causes, the widow of Crescentius's ruination represents an inevitable eruption of revolution that will smash the ideological system itself into shards, or reconceptualize it altogether. Rei Terada calls such ruin a "submersion in an ongoing process," a damage "such as that which must occur when the system fills to capacity with damaging stimuli, but does not overflow," something she says resembles a queer life after ruin ("Living" 215). Vacancy engages such a process at a granular level, as its figures plot a confrontation between the ideological system, its stimuli, and the unbound flood of affect that cannot be fully experienced. It, moreover, initiates not only a deconstruction of these opposing epistemologies or categories but rather offers a movement between these doubled figures of mind and brain—and the possibility that such a motion might eventually provide new potential—and nonbinary—trajectories for affect.

In the second half of the poem, Stefania disguises herself as Guido, the boy-minstrel, and through her soulful music, the widow plots to transfer her mental disruption to the tyrant Otho, to destroy his mind as well, through the transmission of affect. The movement of chaotic, destructive affects or materials between the widow and her onlookers is first figured by her "vacant glance" and later more literally transmitted through her melancholy, infectious songs. If her cross-dressing serves to emphasize the queer nature of her brain and her body, her labile song transmits its dangerous affects across political factions and gendered bodies.

Before heading to the poem's murder-suicide denouement, Hemans pauses to describe Stefania as Guido, once again focusing on the state of woeful Guido's mind: "Oh! where can ruins awe mankind, / Dark as the ruins of the mind?" (153–154). Her thoughts and passions about current events remain "still, unexpress'd" and concealed, except when she emotes them musically: "In music's eloquence alone; / His soul's deep voice is only pour'd / Through his full song and swelling chord" (170–172). Music's eloquence, its "full song" and "swelling chord," can purvey "each wounded feeling's tone"—not feelings themselves but the tones of unconceptualized cognitive activity. This notion of expressive music evokes something like Hegel's "dark night" of subjectivity. In Hemans, as opposed to Hegel, the idea is not to return from the abyss of pure subjectivity back into the realm of the conceptual and symbolic. Instead, the widow willfully passes along her ruin, now directed to antagonize the concepts that Otho lives by. The soul's "deep voice" and Guido's "swelling chord" bundle and actively transmit this chaotic brain activity, as the widow's musical eloquence becomes a metonym for her second volitional act of destructive revolution—her poisoning of Otho.

In the final scene of the poem, Otho calls again for Guido's song at a feast and, in the same breath, raises his goblet, unaware that both song and wine contain his death.[24] Guido's liquid poison and music's mellifluous eloquence allow for the easy consumption and ingestion of a substance that has the power both to stimulate and destroy consciousness and the concepts of self and world they maintain. The draught of poison wine appears as a desperate but necessary material ploy that spreads such violence through the ranks of tyrants. Though Otho thinks that poetry (as well as drinking) should "banish all resembling woe" and lull his pain, they have the opposite effect when they enflame his brain (230). Stefania stuns him to death with a "hectic dye," as if she manages to transmit her affect into Otho's own mind. As she finally unmasks herself to the tyrant and his minions, Stefania has the last word in a final speech that includes these lines:

> Deem'st thou my mind of reason void?
> It is not phrensied,—but destroy'd!
> Aye! view the wreck with shuddering thought,—
> That work of ruin thou hast wrought! (269–272)

At the poem's finale, the widow finally articulates what has been going on in her head all along. She refuses to be seen as insane, out of control, or "phrensied" with violent emotion, if only by dint of her ability to enunciate and transmit her mental ruination, and its pool of affect's incipient potentialities. She calls on Otho to look on her face as a sign of her ruined mind and "view the wreck with shuddering thought," that is, to replicate this state of mind in his own brain. The accusation itself becomes a performative poetic act, and it overwhelms Otho—to death.

We might assume that the widowed woman lacks much agency, as if she passes along her diseased sorrow in an autonomous act of dumping the affects she can no longer manage. Yet, her cross-dressing and her "swelling" composition paradoxically endue such uncontrolled destruction with volition. What Guido will not articulate about the state of Rome through poetic language he can transmit through his soul's deep voice. It is here that the soul makes its return, indicating that Stefania-Guido has some driving aspect to her consciousness, an agential affective flow that paradoxically transmits the disabling mental ruination. Hemans's repeated use of "mind" and "soul" signals her preoccupation with up-ending top-down structures while preserving their intuition of force and agency within the bottom-up brain model. Richard Sha has recently contested the notion that Romantic forms of affect are solely autonomous, suggesting they can be "a space of automaticity but one that does not banish intent" (40). Like Robinson's and Shelley's notions of "spirit," Stefania's soul-deep song, and

Hemans's figuration of it, suggests that it is figural movement, necessarily outside subject, that intertwines agency and automaticity.

This soulful music signals that Hemans's goal is neither simply to destroy nor to restore the transcendental subject but to refigure a willful, conscious destruction that holds brain and mind in a functioning parallax. The ruined brain figures an impossible movement between two antagonistic systems, here not crossed through metaphor but forever separated and intertwined, forever moving back and forth with in the parallax's double figuration. This conflict, in turn, makes manifest how the cognitive upheaval in the widow's mind might erupt other similar material forces in others and in the world at large. Hemans's vacancy, rather than Smith's impossible consumption or Robinson's emersion into a nebulous material world, inverts Shelley's dangerous transmission in "Alastor" so that the destructive force of affect takes its toll upon the ideological frame, the emotional song underwritten by patriarchal desire and the feminine subjectivity that purveys it. Its figural tension challenges gender inequality while preserving difference as a means of questioning gender roles that commit their players to tragic narratives.

At the poem's end, the word "wrought"—not unlike the phrase "hectic dye"—creates a crucial pun. It both connotes the act of artfully making something yet also references an older use of the word, meaning made rough or agitated.[25] This paradox suitably describes the artful act of the brain purposively disquieting the mind, a conundrum that also describes Hemans's poetics of vacancy in "The Widow of Crescentius." The "thought"/"wrought" rhyme will strategically recur in "The Forest Sanctuary," its echo again heralding Hemans's preoccupation with tropes of mental ruination that nevertheless entail soulful speculation and hidden material insurgency. By giving agency to cognitive ruination and pre-sentimental, nebulous affects, Hemans unveils new ontological materialities that evoke and exceed the epistemological crisis of the empirical subject. It is not Stefania's mind, reconstituted, that returns but her choral figuration—a figure of affect that eschews wholeness or coherence of the emotional subject, a figure that creates movement between systems and bodies, auguring the transformation of both.

"The Forest Sanctuary" and the New World of the Mind

Where "The Widow of Crescentius" contemplates mind-brain problems to overthrow tyrannical mental conceptions, "The Forest Sanctuary" repeats the trope of brain ruination to think in even more complex ways about how the raw materials of Old World history might compose a New World mind and world. While the earlier poem was concerned with staging revolution, by 1825, Hemans is preoccupied with mapping new geopolitical and cognitive landscapes following the revolutions in the Mediterranean, Spain, and Latin America occurring in 1820–1824. The poem plots the conversion of a sixteenth-century Catholic Spanish conquistador, who, after watching his childhood friends killed in an *auto-da-fé*, converts to Protestantism and flees for the Americas.

Compared to "England and Spain" (1808) and "The Siege of Valencia" (1823), Hemans's earlier meditations on what Joselyn Almeida has termed the Anglo-Hispanic imaginary, "The Forest Sanctuary" concentrates less on the exigencies of Spanish politics than on the "mental conflicts" that frame the Spaniard's mind, a point that Hemans emphasizes in her Preface (*Selected* 269).[26] As Wolfson and Sweet point out, Hemans germinated the idea for the poem after reading José Maria Blanco White's 1822 *Letters from Spain*. Part of that volume was first published in the *Monthly Magazine* along with a review article he wrote on Michael J. Quin's *A Visit to Spain*, where he repeatedly calls Catholicism a "source of mental perversion" and the Protestant reformation a form of "mental emancipation" (241).[27] In the manuscript version of the poem's Advertisement, Hemans writes that it is "intended more as the *record of a Mind*, than as a tale abounding with romantic and extraordinary incident" (*Selected* 292n3; emphasis in original). As Anne Hartman comments, "in this it resonates with *Alastor*, which is described in its preface as being about 'one of the most interesting situations of the human mind'" (par. 26).[28] Hemans is very much absorbed with refiguring the mind as capable of asserting itself against—and undoing—the exigencies of imperial, religious, and intellectual history.

After having served time in Spain's South American military exploits, the Spaniard comes home, only to have a crisis of conscience—and his conscious mind—when he finds the ruthless law of the Inquisition turned upon a fellow conquistador and his family. After abandoning his Catholic beliefs for a more freethinking mindset, he emigrates to the New World. The Spaniard's mental ruination, however, does not easily resolve through his transformation into a Protestant American, a political and religious identity more in touch with the true Godhead. In "The Forest Sanctuary," Hemans posits vacancy as an open cognitive state, replete with a bank of unfiltered cognitive incipiencies that plot alternative histories of the New World. One of these new futures is the sanctuary where affect is shared among the Spaniard, his new world, and other creatures in a fluid epistemological and ontological landscape. The New World presents the lure of a space free from intellectual tyranny, but Hemans remains aware about the propensity for characters to end up in new ideological structures that would capitulate to the romance of the New World. The poem ultimately provides interstitial moments that manage and struggle against—not get beyond—both conceptual hegemony and the tendency to subsume new materials into subjective desires and political ideologies.

As a retrospective retelling of the Spaniard's mental conversion, the poem's narration heightens the supposition that speculation occurs when confrontations with the past furnish new future possibilities for both mind and nation, and their mutual histories. As the Spaniard stumbles upon the Inquisition scene where Alvar and his two sisters are being marched to the stake, Hemans again uses the "wrought"/"thought" rhyme to signal that he is describing a cognitive event: "They move'd before me but as pictures, wrought / Each to reveal some secret of man's thought" (194–195). This "sullen mass," with its procession of people that each figure some thought, recapitulates the figure for a collective hidden mass of unconscious activity lurking beneath society's structures. The procession foreshadows the cognitive catastrophe that will come crashing down onto the Spaniard when the narrator recognizes his childhood friends as Protestant victims of the Inquisition: "I gaz'd, I saw, / Dimly . . . In silent awe / I watch'd" (176–177, 177–178). Violence paralyzes his conscious mind when those he sees about to be burned at the stake become countrymen he can no longer recognize.

Activating a nested structure of altered consciousness, the striking scene of the *auto-da-fé* summons the memories of the Spaniard and Alvar's time fighting in the Andes, which then occasions a memory of a battle wound to the head. This blow not only disrupts the narrative but also breaks the secure frame of understanding and identity the memories should confirm or create. As soldiers, both men were clearly defined by their masculine heroics in service to the crown, but soon enough the Spaniard is felled by a lance during battle that disrupts his consciousness and serves as an allegory for his dislocation from the Spanish imaginary altogether.[29] The blast on the head ushers in a "rush of visions" that signal a cognitive deluge of visual data that incapacitates both body and mind (253):

> Till, in that rush of visions, I became
> As one that by the bands of slumber wound,
> Lies with a powerless, but all-thrilling frame,
> Intense in consciousness of sight and sound,

> Yet buried in a wildering dream which brings
> Lov'd faces round him, girt with fearful things!
> Troubled ev'n thus I stood, but chain'd and bound (253–268)

As the Spaniard recalls how he lost consciousness, the memory both evokes and mimics a moment of cognitive and sensory disorientation. The process of consolidating memory, an executive function that can help to define the self and which might provide the Spaniard with a template for reacting to Alvar's imminent death with a coherent emotional response, ironically ends up replicating an experience of insurgent mental chaos. The lance blow renders the narrator unconscious, and when he wakes, his mind produces a flow of fragmented sensations that he only retroactively identifies. The multiple phrases connected by dashes evince a paratactic series of disconnected but parallel movements: "—the shivery light, / Moonlight on broken shields—the plain of slaughter, / The fountain-side—the low sweet sound of water—" and so forth (I.256–258). Thus the widow-esque trauma of seeing Alvar's execution both literalizes and then figures another blow to the Spaniard's brain, bringing back into consciousness all these past sensations as if they had never been processed. The memory, and its shock, reopens his mind so that he begins to see landscapes as an asyndeton of visual motions of wind, water, and slaughter.

The sensory perceptions he finally does see gesture toward the mind's latent intensities—the affects that occur but are never felt as sensations or perceived as images. Massumi explains this retroactive sensation, "organized recursively before being linearized" as the body being stimulated and "absorbing impulses quicker than they can be perceived" (28). The entire event remains "unconscious, out of mind" until it is "smoothed out retrospectively to fit conscious requirements of continuity and linear causality" (28, 29). What Hemans preserves, however, is not simply the retroactive linearity of the event or its fragmentary remembering. The impulse of retroaction intimates both the unconscious affect that has been translated and that which has not, the other items not yet stacked, the uncodified affects that never will be a part of her list of the mind's and world's movements. The rush of "direct consciousness" leaves the Spaniard unable to process Alvar's death as anything but unthinkable. His subjectivity, like Robinson's savage of Aveyron, gives way to affective movement, from one image to another, figured by the line breaks and caesuras composing a dashed narration.

The Spaniard's personal history becomes a morass of cognitive activity, as if when replayed, the copious, varied materiality of the world has taken over his mind. This processual stutter leaves the Spaniard forever lost in a translation, within a vacancy between mind and world that provocatively disrupts any subjective, conceptual notions of Spanish masculinity or imperial prowess. At this moment the Spaniard is, as Žižek would say, "included out" of the Spanish imaginary, or to be more precise, a subject who is "included at the very point at which signification breaks down" (*Ticklish* 109). Rather than gaining self-awareness, the Spaniard's attempt to narrate his place in the world only initiates the shock of those raw events he must but cannot fully incorporate into Spain's symbolic order or his own self-relating.

The Spaniard's mind, however, does not remain merely destroyed. He is able to locate a figure for his own Hegelian "dark night of the soul" when he hears one of Alvar's sisters singing at the stake—and describes her voice much in the same terms as Guido's minstrelsy:

> But the dark hours wring forth the hidden might
> Which hath lain bedded in the silent soul,
> A treasure of all dreamt of;—as night
> Calls out the harmonies of streams that roll
> Unheard of by day" (I.307–311).

It is the dark hours that punningly ring/wring forth the hidden might within the soul, to eventually merge with the harmonic treasure of evening materiality. Into the daylight of enlightened, soul-directed, willful consciousness, the moving tones of the sisters' song bring with them the "unheard" "harmonies of streams that roll" into affect's cognitive unconscious. Once again, Hemans evokes an unsettled relationship between the emergent brain activity of unconscious intensities and the soul that should cohere it. The sisters' song figures the voluntary emission of cognitive disarray and mobile affect, just as Hemans's figuration enigmatically purveys it to her readers. To be soulful in Hemans's post-Waterloo poems is to give voice to, not proselytize, a brain overwhelmed with the "bedded," incipient materials of the world. Unlike Shelley's veiled maid in "Alastor" whose song imprisons the poet within feminized sensibility, Hemans's rolling affect, when it overwhelms the Spaniard's brain, frees him from embodied and ideological subjectivities.

The song's invitation to cognitive overload creates a transportable neuronal reservoir of material stimuli and cognitive activity that has the potential to rewrite personal and global counterfactual histories. New cognitive data, or latent incipiencies, supply unheard, unseen affects that might change the relations among factions or events that create world history. For Žižek, such retroaction ensures a repetitive Hegelian dialectic into and out of the realm of pure subjectivity, to forge new or updated subjectivities. As he suggests in *The Parallax View*, "it is via the detour through the past that our present experience itself is constituted" (212). This temporal act of self-consciousness first occurs "as a kind of negative; in its primordial dimension, the experience of some perturbation, in this spontaneous pattern or organization" (241). The disturbance and the subsequent self-awareness it spawns "is not of the free choice which grounds his character (his ethical 'nature')—that is to say, this act is radically unconscious. . . . Here again we encounter the subject as the Void of pure reflexivity" (246). One way to translate this idea would be to say that the subject's bank of neuronal activity, a plenitude of potential material relations, erupts to disturb the subject's stasis, a disruption unconsciously furnishing a host of cognitive alternative possibilities, whether or not they are made apparent to the conscious mind. These unconscious possibilities might then ground a dialectical return to the self, where self is reforged through its relation to the past. Hemans's Spaniard, however, and his latent affective activity that can never be recovered resist such a narrative enclosure back into subjectivity, leaving subjectivity itself perpetually undone and subject to new affects—both the mind's cognitive information and the world's uncategorized material fluxes. Here again, we see Hemans's vacancy at work. Its doubling parallax reveals these vibrations without sealing them off as particular thoughts or emotions of mind and body, or as merely the material movements of the world.

The disturbed Spaniard now decides to emigrate from his fatherland, and this transatlantic movement signals how a newly raised cognitive materiality might present the possibility for the Spaniard to initiate alternative movements through the New World. When the sixteenth-century Spaniard braves the great beyond of the Americas, he runs toward a landscape much less populated with European symbolic meaning than it would be in the nineteenth century, a continent not yet entirely incorporated by colonial settlements or inscribed by the manifest destiny beholden to land, labor, and capital. The Spaniard arrives only after nomadic travels first through his past killing fields of South America. Once he escapes from the haunting, sentimental "voices of home," he continues traveling northward—all the way, it would seem, to New England.[30] Hemans conspicuously does not state where in North America the Spaniard establishes his "bower of refuge." She does, however, use several footnotes to reference works about North America, and each of these alludes to particularities of the American landscape describing the forest sanctuary the Spaniard eventually inhabits:

the cane grass of Tennessee, the torrent waterfalls of New York, and the arcades of trees in New England.[31] It would be easy to argue that the geographic and historical ambiguities of the verse constitute an exceedingly romantic America—a homogeneous, blank space with the more material, regional contours of the country abjected to the poem's footnotes.[32] Yet the specificity of the references within the footnotes—culled, as Sweet and Simpson note,[33] from recent travelogues by Adam Hodgson, Washington Irving, Anne Grant, and Alexander von Humboldt—complicates Hemans's America. Any blandly occluded history becomes overwhelmed by the poem's final paratext, as it retroactively injects geographical specificity and history back into the body of the poem.

The Spaniard's landing so far north certainly makes sense when we consider Hemans's close correspondence with Andrew Norton and William Ellery Channing as well as her resounding popularity in America that developed in the wake of the poem's publication. Nonetheless, it is a rather odd bit of history that the Spaniard would end up in what seems to be northern forests that Spaniards were not known to frequent, even considering the vast swath of the South and Midwest explored by Hernando de Soto in his discovery of Florida during the mid-sixteenth century.[34] According to Blanco White's article on Protestantism during the Inquisition as well as the references in Hemans's poem to the conquistadors' battles in the Andes, the Spaniard most likely comes to North America at the end of the sixteenth century, before either Jamestown (1607) or Plymouth Rock (1620)—or if he does they are nowhere in sight.[35] The Spanish had already settled Florida, New Mexico, and Arizona, and the French had established Jacksonville as a haven for Huguenots, but the Spaniard does not flee to any of these settlements.

The Spaniard's unusual placement represents something of an anachronism, a strange narrative swerve that marks Hemans's retroactive history as peculiar and inventive. If his mere presence dismisses any easy narrative about English colonial claims to North America, the wandering Spaniard disinterested in either discovery or settlement suggests something of a virtual or counterfactual history, presenting the case of an immigration to North America that might have happened but did not.[36] This retroaction portends a counterfactual history of Spaniards in North America as well as a potential futurity for nineteenth-century English who might themselves ruin their own colonial and imperial minds. Such a future has become possible because Hemans—and Blanco White before her—dredges up the forgotten moments of fifteenth-century Spanish Protestantism and then uses such an event to reimagine a virtual sequence of historical events.

The Spaniard's forest sanctuary exists in a brief moment of latent possibility, a crevice between the tapering off of Catholic Spain's imperial vantage in North America and the beginnings of English experiments in a Puritan settler colonialism. It temporarily frees Spain from its imperial past, England from its colonial future, and America from its deracination of what the Spaniard calls "the red hunter's land" (II.646). Less a settler than a nameless wanderer, his trajectory plots one of many incipiencies that had previously not been selected by the mind, an incipiency that is not so much captured (as Massumi would say) but let out to move and play in the world.

This counterfactual speculation is instigated by the Spaniard's brain ruination and generates what Žižek calls a retroactive temporal loop of freedom: "it is not simply a free act which, out of nowhere, starts a new causal link, but a retroactive act of endorsing which link/sequence of necessities will determine mine" (204). Counterfactual history becomes a means of either turning back time or of reenvisioning potential effects in order to choose retroactively which sequence of causes could determine self and history in the future. Read as a retroactive temporal loop, the Spaniard's wayward journey figures a past impossibility now made possible by the resurgence of historical incipiencies made new. Rather than explaining well-known, deterministic historical narratives of colonization, or simply anticipating new effects, the Spaniard's journey opens up new possible futures for the global imaginary. Neither John Stuart Mill's notion of freedom as a "freedom from" nor Byron's Epicurean "freedom to," Hemans's notion of liberation does not encourage readers either to follow the institutional law as a guarantor of universal rights or to do whatever they want. The temporal loop that she envisions enables the freedom to light upon a future from an attention to a greater morass of germinal possibilities—historical and affective—than history has hitherto warranted.

Hemans thus constructs vacancy as that which does to history what it has already done to the subject—places its conceptual structures into impossible tension. This figural parallax creates the activity that—when suspended from ideological imposition, temporal linear movement, and perceptual assumptions—posits a material archive (even if unconsciously) available for the furnishing of retroactive futures and landscapes. Hemans's model of individual or historical agency posits an alternative to the self-made Romantic subject and to the determinism of a networked brain by opening both to a newfound reservoir of unconscious material activity. Hemans's footnotes and their references to events and her reading likewise sketch a textual unconscious, with all its potentiality to haunt the page, as well as the minds and bodies that read it.

The question then becomes what occurs in the wake of such possibility.[37] Hemans ultimately does not evoke the parallax of cognition and consciousness to find new, actualized subject positions or histories. Instead, she keeps the mind suspended before the act of self-definition can occur, to enlarge the space where affects' incipiencies might remain as flexible cognitive materialities—still offering the possibility of new pathways through the mind's hidden stores and the world's topographies. Despite the New World's promise that the Spaniard might become someone else—a veritable Protestant American—he, like Smith's hermit and Maria Jane Jewsbury's infant, resides inside a vacancy of personal and historical narratives at the end of the poem, itself an anticipatory incipiency. Our vagabond roams, small child in tow, as a Rousseauvian wanderer allergic to constitutional governments.[38] His fluidity explains why his sentimental wife—who does have a name—passes away on their transatlantic voyage. Similar to Robinson's Sappho and Shelley's veiled maid, Leonor poses the symbolic death of the sentimental woman who must die for the new-world mind to flourish. The Spaniard commits to no alliances and locates himself outside the modern liberal state even more strenuously than Robinson's marginal figures in *Lyrical Tales*.[39] He neither lays claim (by work or by deed) to what he calls the "wilds of the red hunter's land" (II.646), nor does he seek to ameliorate the "free solitude" of his "bower of refuge" (II.647, 652). He evokes but ultimately dissolves any identity that is either masculine or feminine (or both), that is rooted in any specific nation, region, or domestic home, or even that consolidates a cosmopolitan, global hybrid.[40] His itinerancy leads to the forest sanctuary—itself a paradoxical allegory for the mind that suspends self-consciousness from recognizable identifications. Both when he travels as a new-world nomad and when he settles within the forest sanctuary, our protagonist's anonymity and itinerancy suggest that he becomes an incipiency himself—no longer a Spaniard but a figure of displacement, postponement, and unforeclosed anticipation.

With sentimental subjectivity held in abeyance, the material world can finally come out to play. Much as Shelley's "Mont Blanc" interfuses "the everlasting universe of things" with the human mind, when our nomad becomes released from even his humanity, he mingles fully within the world's affects. Here Hemans complicates cognitive models to show how reversing that process can enable a communication among neuronal activity and the world's responsive materialities—both its perceptible movements and those still hidden in the landscape's "unconscious." Hemans's final descriptions of the Spaniard's new "home" figure isolated sensations and perceptions of the landscape as exposing one more bank of raw cognitive activity, now not in frenzy but in vibrant repose. Only quasi-embowered, the airy sanctuary ends the poem with a vacancy where mind and world collapse into an open, permeable site of cognitive freedom:

> At eve?—oh! through all hours!—From dark dreams oft
> Awakening, I look forth, and learn the might
> Of solitude, while thou art breathing soft,
> And low, my lov'd one! on the breast of night:
> I look forth on the stars—the shadowy sleep
> Of forests—and the lake, whose gloomy deep
> Sends up red sparkles to the fire flies' light.
> A lonely world!—ev'n fearful to man's thought,
> But for His presence felt, whom here my soul hath sought. (II.692–700)

After the Spaniard wakes from those uncanny dreams that cloud his view—not only at night but during "all hours"—he can "look" and "learn" with some modicum of direct sight. What he finally sees is the dark wastes of the "breast of night," the "shadowy sleep / Of forests" and the "gloomy deep" of the lake, whose darkness represents not repressed memories but the cognitive unconscious of affect summoned by a soul no longer in crisis. At rest, the mind is sprinkled with materials like the stars or the light of fireflies, as sensory observations that do not unify or abstract the open cognitive terrain. Rather than completely vanquishing thought with absolute silence, the sanctuary constructs experiences of partial sensations, allusive of a cognitive semiotic or an affective chora. Rebekah Sheldon refigures the Platonic chora, or womb, as a generative space of dynamic materiality that collapses form and brings new things into life. Here, I would suggest that the widow's song and the Spaniard's sanctuary are less character expressions or settings than figures that offer these pools of material flux, where different materialities form, permeate, and collapse. This reservoir, in its openness and its partial inaccessibility, resists being subsumed into symbolic meaning or clearly felt subjective emotions that might once again lead the way to the hysterical woman of sensibility. The mind can now collect and encircle isolated sensations, rhythms, or tones—the coming to perception—even while it defers symbolic meaning-making or embodied feeling, knowing there are always more incipient movements. In effect, the meditative Spaniard sees and lets them pass him by. The sanctuary becomes not so much the airy home of a disfigured subject but more radically what Massumi calls a "highly differentiated field" (*Parables* 34). It is a space that contains various regions: the Spaniard as "preindividual," night, world.

Characterized by "actions at a distance between elements," the sanctuary and the Spaniard resonate so that "a shape or structure begins to form, but no sooner dissolves as its region shifts in relation to others with which it is in tension" (Massumi, *Parables* 34). Although the special features of the land generate encounters that might be integrated into a new, localized prospect of America, the Spaniard's disinterest in processing or fully conceptualizing these moments allows him and the sanctuary together to remain free from being determined by emergent cognitive events. Without capturing particular emotions or a fully drawn perception of the scene, the bower facilitates a comfortable movement suspended within moments beyond or before understanding. The forest sanctuary is no second Eden, but an open field of posthuman affect.

Hemans emphasizes this dangling consciousness by once again deploying material, rampant lineal pauses. The description of terrain loosely aggregates a paratactic asyndeton of stars, the deep, the red sparkles of light through the sequence of a dash, an enjambment, another dash that anticipates the caesura, and two line endings before the exclamation, "A lonely world!" If we were to read Hemans as a sentimental poet, we would assume the caesuras to be a measure of the speaker's overwhelming feeling. Michael O'Neill, for example, argues that this formal technique creates "verse full of expressive and strong caesurae, underscoring the dramatic power of the speaker's outpouring" ("'A Deeper'" 11). More than mere placeholders for the speaker's emphatic, pulsating moments of the feminine gush, however, Hemans's repeated technical breaks emphasize the paratactic suspension of cognitive material outside conceptual or self-conscious incorporation into an intuited idea, a clear feeling, or a plastic subjectivity.[41] Sensory data from starlight or fireflies, which could light up the sky or lake's "gloomy deep" with meaning, remain hanging in the air, unconceptualized and partially unfelt as lonely, dashed movements.

If this luminosity represents the failed resurgence of Enlightenment reason or feeling, then it more certainly signifies Hemans's Protestant God—who very well might have the ability to imbue with transcendent or sentimental meaning the light's perceptual *qualia*. For Hemans, the world is lonely and fearful to thought but for the presence of God. The resuscitation of meaning through patriarchal religiosity might initially appear to wrap America (not to mention Protestant England and Germany) in a veil of syncretic surety and Hegelian synthesis.[42] Hemans ends the poem, however, by qualifying the nature of her Protestant God, a presence "whom here my soul hath sought." The final "thought"/"sought" rhyme overturns any definitive meaning that God might secure and instead becomes that kind of thought always sought after yet never achieved, at least in this life of the body. The sanctuary has space enough for "varying creeds, / With all that send up holy thoughts on high!" proffered by the "most secret tone / Drawn from each tree, for each hath whispers all its own" (II.663–664, 685–686). The scattered breezes carrying such sensations, not unlike Shelley's airy imagery in "Epipsychidion"'s mental bower, signify material receptivity even as they represent freedom of speech and religion in the New World.[43] As each reader might attach different meaning to perceptions of starlight, so she might add her own affective movements and intensities to the "secret tone," conceptualizing God as highly charged by these individual affects and, in the end, largely unaccountable.

If the bower's cognitive sanctuary routes representations of God—or clear theological doctrine—so Hemans's upended, suspended consciousness may, at the same time, proffer her impression of the transcendental soul. The field of mind and sanctuary gently supports an array of cognitive relations within the world without incorporating them into a self or a settlement that identifies in one way or another. This state of being, in effect, preserves a reservoir of material affect as means to shirk the creation of reason or feeling—or the Enlightenment subjectivity responsible for both—as well as a means of maintaining a connection to the spiritual realm or the world spirit. To put this another way, Hemans's trope of vacancy reveals that cognitive potentiality entails a means of intuiting the incomprehensible universe—and vice versa. The sanctuary, her poetic construction of figural space, acts much like Guido and Alvar's sister's voices, all of them soulful containers for and conduits to an unseen, unheard world of moving, cognitive possibilities.

Ending with the forest sanctuary, Hemans poises the poem on the brink of the future as a larger set of possible worlds retroactively fashioned. These narrative possibilities, previously unrecognized, are only brought to contemporary consciousness by a blow to the historical mind—ushered in by the force of the soul's own *poeisis* and released through the excess of dashed narration that surrounds the history of modern empires. Yet the final lines of the poem remind us that utopian futures are really nowhere but a repeatedly suspended present that continuously remains "fearful to man's thought." Hemans locates epistemological freedom where directed ruination of the mind and intuitive mindfulness of the world meet. The forest sanctuary recalls the widow's soulful song of brain ruination, where manifestations of cognitive suspension do not simply stymie the brain. Rather than instituting a centralized, decision-making self or historical consciousness, Hemans's soul becomes the permeable but agential resource of unexecuted cognitive incipience, the swiftly tilting worlds of and within affect itself.

Hemans helps us to see vacancy as neither a passive repetition (as in Robinson) nor an aporia (as in Smith) but as a détente of the two, a figure that collects a plenitude of emergent cognitive and worldly material it should not be able to hold or to move. She reconstitutes the mind's relation to the world through the troping of a relation between a suspended subjectivity that denies any calcified humanistic view and the world's unidentified, immanent movements; she lets the world come into its own only when it can be intuited by language's affects that leave the mind mostly undone. Much as Shelley, Hemans strikes a balance between abstraction and the rushing flows of affect, but her poems seek an even more stark undoing of history's own unconscious events. Ultimately, poetry's music, like the living pillars of the forest sanctuary, compels her readers to delay the ideologies of sensibility and reason and to live in a present suspended from determination, with a glimpse of an only partially realized future.

CHAPTER 5

Maria Jane Jewsbury and the Phantom Feelings of the Moving Image

In the inaugural piece for her *Athenaeum* series "Literary Sketches" (1831), Maria Jane Jewsbury stops to assess the type of feelings that are too often abused in poetry: "PASSION is a poetical watchword of the day;— unfortunately it is also something worse—a species of literary Goule that preys upon good sense, good feeling, and good taste" (Waters 168). Jewsbury's observation is one salvo in a much larger campaign throughout both her prose essays and her poems "to manage female intellect in connexion to female sensibility" ("On Modern Female Cultivation, No. 4" 521). For Jewsbury, passion haunts women as a particular type of ghoulish pyrotechnics that—like William Wordsworth's "gross and violent stimulants," Mary Wollstonecraft's masturbatory sensation, or Percy Shelley's "electric poison"—addictively provide cheap pleasure and dramatic, visual effect at great cost to the developing mind.[1] Ghoulish passion repeatedly reappears in Jewsbury's works when she conjures the ghosts of absent family and pastoral scenes in *The Oceanides* (1832–1833), written as Jewsbury sailed to India. When the speaker's sea cabin transforms into a "tomb" filled with reminders of home, she turns to the sky, only to see a succession of images of her sister and father, which rather than provide an antidote, "regret they heighten" (6.20, 27). The speaker, "grown sick with pining / After things that *were*," is stuck seeing, and longing for, the faces of her family, a situation that results in a deeper contemplation about the nature of vision itself (6.38–639). These visions revivify images of past visual sensations and cannot help but instigate a blinding onslaught of unwilled emotional response. The nostalgia of friendly memories, for women whose emotional lives are thought to depend on notions of home, unleashes the ghouls of sensibility, which then enervate and trap them within feminized minds and bodies. Although ghostly memories can return past sensations, the immaterial aspect of these visions nevertheless implicates how the blockage of sight might invite vacancy. Figured first as a series of revolving images and then as the kinesis beneath and through those images, vacancy moves past empirical, clear sights, homebound feeling, and embodied sensations.

Choosing an avenue of sensory perception different from, and perhaps more complex than, Charlotte Smith's critique of taste and consumption, Jewsbury focuses on the problems inherent in the sensory, cognitive, and aesthetic facets of embodied vision during an imperial age. Though she begins her query as early as her first publication, a miscellany entitled *Phantasmagoria* (1825), it is her ambitious poem tracing the sights and sites of the voyage from England to India that most fully investigates the phantoms of sensibility following the woman traveler into new imperial vistas. Writing a sequence of twelve poems as she traverses multiple oceans, Jewsbury's itinerant speaker of *The Oceanides* undermines received notions of homebound, embodied, feminine feeling only to find those sensations return within haunting pictures of domestic objects and people left ashore. It has been typical of Romantic scholars writing of women and the landscape to concentrate on material examples tied to the female body, its sensations, and its embodied feelings.[2] Recent scholarship on women and travel assumes women to be writing in the genre of the "purely picturesque or literary travelogue," where women observe foreign landscapes in empirical detail only to place them in proximity to the British viewer's nostalgic memories of England, Scotland, and Wales; Indian scenes are framed, distanced, and controlled for the British reading public (Leask, *Curiosity* 220).[3] In *The Oceanides*, however, Jewsbury repeatedly summons pictures to undermine securely anchored, embodied acts of seeing: family and friends become ghosts projected on the screens of sky and sea. She does so not simply to disrupt the naturalized stability of colonial bodies but to show another problem, that these images carry with them transportable sentiments that can revivify past sensations and project the entire mechanism of gendered, domesticating feeling abroad.

Yet the phantom also becomes an extremely useful structure for beginning to critique and find substitutes for such haunting feminine sensibility tied to England's imperial project. Upon her arrival at Ceylon, the poet constructs a phantasmagoria of the landscape, with a double vision of cocoa trees, as a "column, and its crown a star!" and "[s]ome vision of a desert grave!" (52, 56). Described in turns as aesthetic object and commodity, the trees gives rise to phantom images that circulate and critique

Britain's imperial past and future. Any clear sight of British India has already been obscured by affective allegiances to English domesticity, even as these images raise the specter of those similarly phantasmagoric commodities that the English covet for luxury consumption.

Specters offer what Derrida calls a "hauntology," or a structure of both summoning and exorcism whose dual nature is both material and immaterial, characterized by an emancipatory yet continually deferred future-to-come. The ghosts of the past chase the speaker of *The Oceanides*, troubling her ability to envision present and future vistas, her place in British India, and the sentimental nostalgia for sensations of the past she carries with her.[4] The logic of the phantom likewise helps to place into relation a number of visual technologies running throughout Jewsbury's work, all structured around this crux of absent but haunting sensation. These include her critique of Lockean picture memory culled from her careful reading of Wordsworth, the protocinematic technologies of nineteenth-century moving-picture shows, and the commodity culture that turns cocoa trees into British fetishes of the subcontinent. Yet, for Jewsbury, such a hauntology figures the trace of movement beyond mere visual sensation, an affect born of the kinesthetic form of the phantasmagoria. Its structure of substitution and inveterate movement later in the poem offers the hope of eventually fabricating other, ethical ways of viewing the world and other forms of affect untethered to imperial experiences of the body.

Jewsbury's version of vacancy is therefore best sketched through her use of and subsequent turn from the phantoms of sensation and sentiment to the floating image of a tireless infant disconnected from a nostalgic past—a figure for affect's continuous movement unbound by haunting embodiment. The penultimate poem in the sequence describes a technique to "Image infants everywhere" (11.33), which suspends the nostalgia always looking, sentimentally, backwards. As a figure for vision emptied of its empiricist ghouls, the infant presents an allegory for the infinite motions of affect made possible by the movement of tropes. Rather than Smith's vacancy based on what cannot be ingested or taken into the body, here its motion finally tropes that which cannot be projected upon the embodied, sensing, imperial subject. The ineffable infant becomes a figure for visual knowledge that iteratively eludes empirical sight through its continuous transit. This kinesis within and through figuration offers women caught within a domestic, imperial economy a form of being not determined by sight or feeling—a form of affect born by living through the sways of fluid figuration.

CHAPTER 5

"No more, no more": The Haunting of Nostalgic Picture Memory

The Oceanides begins as we might expect, with a speaker pining away for the English homeland and its domestic charms. Even at the outset, though, the visual memories and poetic representations of familiar faces, objects, and landscapes undermine what reassurance the speaker might find in her last direct, immediate sights of England. The very first poem, "The Outward Bound Ship," begins with the contrast between the oceanic drift and the Devon landscape slowly passing from view: "She is on her way, a goodly ship, / With her tacklings loosed, her pilot gone" (1.1–2). The movement forward propels the speaker to look "Behind, beneath, around, the deep" even as it instigates nostalgia for a land "Fading / fast fading" (1.3, 5). To embark upon the ocean is to be haunted by a homeland quickly become a thing of the past, made present only through visions of England and its people freighted with emotion. In the third stanza, "the sounds of land will break / The spell" of the sea, with a bird's cry, a sailor's call, the lowing of animals in steerage, and the ship's band "send[ing] their spirits home" (19–20, 19). These material sounds are eventually figured in visual terms: "often precious, often dear / As waking dreams of—Far away" (31–32). The speaker cannot help but convert the material or acoustic qualities of sound into precious dreams that cost the speaker the real England. Already fading, even the ship band's music reminiscent of England cannot evoke domestic charms except through their return in dreams—in tenuous visual imagery recalled by the imagination.

Here we see Jewsbury begin to confront an empiricist inheritance, no doubt derived from Wordsworth, where sensory experiences create material pictures in the mind, which in turn produce both memories and also verifiable empirical representations of the outer world. After dedicating her first book, *Phantasmagoria*, to Wordsworth, she eventually befriended his daughter Dora and visited Rydall Mount, and despite the fact that he suggested Jewsbury leave off writing poetry for other genres, she sustained a serious parlay with Wordsworth's visual poetics throughout her writings.[5] Jewsbury, who announced her favorite poem to be "Tintern Abbey," surely contemplates its line, "The picture of the mind revives again" (62), and the epistemological quandary that ensues when sense-bearing images are revivified by reflection. For Laura Quinney, Wordsworth's own techniques are indebted to Locke's formulation that the mind can "revive" perceptions and ideas, "and as it were paint them anew on itself, though some with more, some with less difficulty" (Locke II.x.148). Wordsworth's picture memories are "'haunting' because they are both vital and elusive at the same time—substantial and immaterial, interior and foreign" (Quinney 75). Reconsidering the vital but elusive nature of memory, Jewsbury attends to the evasive automaticity of sensation that arrives without our will to return us to domestic scenes.

As soon as the pilot is gone—if not even before that moment—the speaker's sights become unmoored from actual, material England and imbricated with "waking dreams." The very start of the poem enunciates just how completely past sensations and experiences beleaguer the speaker's mental landscape. As Derrida writes of the nature of the specter, "One cannot control its comings and goings because it *begins by coming back*," always already preceding itself and thus scrambling linear time and any space's relation to Enlightenment chronology (17). Past and present, memories and projections, confound the phantom image and the notion of a stable landscape or securely embodied thing. Sights can never simply supply material engagement with the sensory world; the specter of the past, immaterial and invisible, already haunts the speaker. With England out of view, such images are increasingly severed from their physical referents, to the point that it is almost the "waking dreams" that allow England to appear in the poem at all.

When these images recur, they reproduce former sensations and domestic sentiments abroad. By this poem's end, the speaker proclaims her desire to move away from this attachment to the English coast, finishing with a stanza that vehemently eschews nostalgia: "No more, no more: we are on our way: / The tropics are gained, and who would pine / For the pallid sun of an English day?" (1.41–143). The repetition of the phrase "no more"— which will recur later in the sequence—serves to void her own tendency to "pine" nostalgically for an English climate that only brings a sickly sort of "pallid" health. Nostalgic picture memory becomes irrevocably associated with mental and physical decline, a phantom menace of sensory insipidity. The speaker's "waking dreams" of England disrupt the more quaint terrain of the travelogue, as the scene of departure compels her to conjure comforting visions of the past. This impulse threatens the speaker with the possibility that, adrift on the sea without anything else to stimulate her senses, her mind will furnish past sensations—which can dangerously recapitulate English domesticity and gendered sensibilities abroad.

By poem number six, "The Voyager's Regret," the speaker reveals how such haunting images hold the potential to lock the speaker in a sea-bound prison of her own sentimental memories. She has been traveling for long enough that she not only calls up visions of her family but also forecasts what distant kin imagine of the travelers:

> THEY are thinking far away
> Of their loved ones on the water;
> The mother of her son,
> The father of his daughter (6.1–4).

Though the son and daughter, like the speaker, sail "on the water," it is the parents who, ostensibly in England, envision their progeny. This type of reproduction entails a forward-looking projection of the son and daughter, which is the obverse of the speaker's backward-looking nostalgia. As nostalgia becomes its own emotion, both types of longing soon become confining as the speaker describes herself as "A prisoner on the ocean" whose "cabin-room / On this wilderness of motion / Reminds me of a tomb!" (6.17, 18–20). The voyager's regret is double—the speaker misses her family, and at the same time rues her remembrance of them as an uncanny haunting that entombs her in a cabin populated by apparitions.

These images occupy the speaker's body and mind when they revamp the sensations of familial relations and simultaneously transport miniatures of domestic comfort upon the water. Such a visual mental landscape eventually crowds out other images from view and distracts the speaker from the potential to gain new knowledge from the landscape before her eyes.

> Strange birds the blue air cleaving
> Attract the wanderer's sight,
> And strange creatures weaving
> Their path, through waves as bright;—
> But I, grown sick with pining
> After the things that *were*,
> Over the deep reclining
> But see 'mid strange or fair,
> My sister's sweet face shining!—
> My father's thin grey hair! (6.33–642)

The poet acknowledges that it is because she has "grown sick with pining / After the things that *were*" that she can only see the faces of her family members. The exclamatory tone of need and exasperation emphasizes just how these emotions and the ghosts they engender together hinder her ability to interpret, internalize, or perceive the vague, cleaving and weaving "strange birds" and "strange creatures." All the while, the sea and sky act as two different yet sequential backdrops for nostalgic images moving through them. Although nostalgia tends to disperse sensations across time and space, such sensation always travels as reified, bodily perceptions rather than the "strange creatures" who anticipate the potential for an affect not circulated by defined bodies through the movement of dispersal itself. Although the speaker wants to recollect friends and family, her pining for these faces—her sensible desire for loss and recovery—restricts any new knowledge to be gleaned from the tropical seascape set before her. The recompense that memory provides masks other types of vision, and in doing so, makes the speaker excessively aware of how sensation and sentiment affect visibility. Upon the ocean, affect and associations already transform landscapes into mediated images, and the views she projects are colored by her uncontrollable feelings.

These lines echo a letter from Jewsbury to Felicia Hemans after the two had spent time together in Wales, a letter in which Jewsbury "pines" for images that evoke her friend's presence:

> I would I could shake myself free from my associations [. . .] I pine after the flowers, and that sky of earth, the green meadow-land, and your sister's music and your imagination. The sun seems shining to waste, when he only shines up on streets of houses and bustle. This *is* morbid, but I do pine on my sofa here. (qtd. in Gillett xliv–xlv)

This passage, on first reading, appears to be what we might expect from two poets trained under the aegis of sensibility. Jewsbury conjures the absence of her female companion through a parallel loss of the rural landscape, which has been badly substituted by Manchester's "houses and bustle." Afterward, Jewsbury paints a melancholy picture of herself: "I do pine on my sofa here," laying on a couch, nostalgically mustering flimsy, second-rate pictures of Hemans, her musical sister, and the Wales countryside.

This line subtly evokes some others from both writers' favorite poet, Wordsworth—particularly the end of his "I wandered lonely as a cloud." Where Wordsworth lies vacant upon his couch, summoning the images of daffodils that "flash upon that inward eye" (21), Jewsbury pines on her sofa, grasping after images of the flowers, "that sky of earth," and the green meadow. As Jewsbury's letter to Hemans testifies, this pining after England "*is* morbid," and it deadens the poet and her imagination. The Wordsworthian use of renovating memory attached to particularities of the landscape in "Tintern Abbey" does not work here.[6] She cannot recapitulate her former self, England, nature, or the imagination in a way that would allow her to transcend depressing Manchester or the lonely ship. She seems to acknowledge as much in the way that she frames the letter's reverie with the declaration, "I would I could shake myself free from my associations." As a preface to her performance of affect and nostalgia, Jewsbury already wonders whether emotional visualizations don't do her more harm than good. Channeling yet resisting Wordsworth, the poet goes so far as to imagine a way of thinking that would dispense with feeling associations altogether. Unable to "shake myself free," the poet cannot but see images that are inaccessible and that obstruct other kinds of vision. Grown insightful to her own blindness, she admits that she is too homesick with nostalgia to take in any new perceptions. This vacancy of the representations of sensibility—and their associations with an embodied politics of the languorous, couch-ridden woman—will, later in the sequence, parallel her refusal of stable, static images to describe the foreign landscape. Here Jewsbury, like Robinson and Shelley before her, evokes the mere absence of sensation or vision alongside its fullness as an empiricist quandary she seeks to ameliorate with other types of figuration.

So far, *The Oceanides* signals the double nature of the specters of England upon the transoceanic journey. Travelers may conjure these phantoms to remind them of past people and places, but those images can trap them into pining for the real faces, people, and things they no longer have access to—except through the sentimental sensations that such images supply. This problem is especially palpable for women who have been conditioned as subjects of sensation by the "goules" of passion. Already dependent on using and viewing their bodies as a site of sensory stimulation, English women cannot open their eyes to imperial terrain without pining for a sentimental, visual fix on England. Thus Jewsbury's "hauntology," that revenant of an affective past, presents both a curse and a blessing. For women writers in particular, nostalgic images laden with affect all too easily trap the mind as a haunted room full of past ghosts—which the mind both covets and cannot exorcize. The danger of ghostly images lies in their summoning of sensory stimulation that threatens to trap women writers and readers in old feelings. Jewsbury's phantoms are troubling, if helpful, figures that materialize the severe legacies of sensibility; she shows us that specters are horrifying because they are forms of knowledge that develop lives of their own, those which can never be rid of sensation.

At the same time, such specters draw attention to their own haunting presence, and in so doing the phantom calls attention to the damaging nature of sentimental picture memory—as well as to the possibility of evading it. To put vacancy's figural effect another way, recurring pictures of the past eradicate the notion that the woman traveler can see either direct, material views or even accurate representations anchored to empirical reality. As a paradoxical figure, feeling's phantom status also suggests that its inability to rematerialize fully England abroad could present a potentially productive gap in vision. What Derrida calls the revenant's "bodiless body" or "the silhouette of the sensuous body that it nevertheless lacks" makes body and image partially inaccessible to the viewer (150). For Jewsbury, the phantom's ability to produce and then transport invisibility paradoxically engenders a means of revealing the ideology of sensational sight. It likewise affords travelers the opportunity to watch for other visions, however partial they might be. Jewsbury's specters of home, when placed in contrast with the oceanic "strange birds" and "strange creatures," conjure vacancy as the ethical impossibility of fully seeing British India throughout the rest of the sequence.

Phantasmagoric Vision and Vacancy's Ethical Blind Spots

The poet's contemplation of a visual-verbal aesthetics not surprisingly coalesces in a poem written after Jewsbury had arrived in Ceylon (modern-day Sri Lanka). The ninth poem, "The Eden of the Sea," marks the speaker's first poetic encounter with South Asian landscapes. As with the first part of the sequence, although the speaker sets out to describe the scene as she experiences it, such representations give rise to phantom images that haunt her. Once in Ceylon, she begins to describe a pleasant and pastoral view of the land—finally a respite from the wearying sea—only to invoke the phantoms of commodity culture. Rather than the speaker's haunting personal history, Jewsbury now evokes a global material history that cannot be ignored. This foreign landscape calls forth a second problem with sentimental visuality: if nostalgic sensations of home occlude visions of present or future vistas, the sense-driven luxuries of imperial trade have already shaped her view of the tropics. To shift the grounds of such visual practices, Jewsbury begins to exploit the phantom's double vision to impair any one view of a colonial landscape. Such a kaleidoscopic perspective means that European viewers cannot impose their sights as definitive, posing the landscape not as a stable object but as a moving figure of visual and linguistic viewing practices. Moreover, thanks to the conflicting nature of these images, vacancy can show us an ethical blind spot in our vision—the inability to see the foreign pastoral with sweeping clarity, particularly when imperial viewers project it as a metonym for the wider colonial landscape.

The ensuing Edenic scene—including a partially glimpsed squirrel moving through tree leaves and cocoa trees seen amid the changing light—highlights the shaky perspective of the speaker, as if she cannot rid herself of the oceanic motion she has spent many months watching and feeling. Finally on solid ground in Ceylon, the speaker has "exchanged" "narrow walks" on the ship for "roaming" on land; however, it is the surveyed objects that most appear to move (8–9). These variable physical forms, as metonyms for other, hidden bodies populating the tropics, repeatedly evince not naturalistic motion or biological oddity but changeable perceptions that alter depending on the viewer's perspective and her ideological baggage. The speaker describes "The air alive with glancing wings / Tame creatures pecking at my seat," and then more closely watches a squirrel "Racing along the cocoa leaf / You see him through its ribs of green / . . . / Anon, the little mime and thief / Expanded on the trunk is seen" (42–43, 45–48). The moving animal is hidden and then seen, a picture that itself gives way to a more murky vision of cocoa trees.

In "The Eden of the Sea," the poet again bases her visual epistemology on Wordsworth's visual poetics, rewriting his image of the tree in "The Intimations Ode." It may be no coincidence that Jewsbury's stay in this colony was framed by a heady conversation about Wordsworth with her host, Reverend Benjamin Bailey, as she reports in letters to Dora.[7] Wordsworth's lines appear just before his famous questions about the disappearance of visionary gleam ending the first draft of the poem in 1802.

> —But there's a tree, of many, one,
> A single field which I have look'd upon,
> Both of them speak of something that is gone (52–54)

As commentators have duly explored, Wordsworth feels his loss acutely on a spring morning during the season of rebirth or renovation, which only makes him feel all the worse.[8] As recompense, the tree helps Wordsworth rebuild a visionary sight, when many trees combine into one, or into a single field.[9]

Jewsbury had already done some important thinking about this poem in her essay from volume 2 of *Phantasmagoria*, "Why Is the Spirit of Poetry Anti-Cheerful?" where she describes the shadowy associations gathered in the absence of direct sight: "a withered leaf, a flower, a shadow, can exert over him a mighty and a subduing influence; calling up by the magic of association, things 'to dream of—not to see'—early impressions, lost ideas, and shadowy recollections—all that has been described by a master spirit in Wordsworth's well known line, as—'Thoughts that do often lie too deep for tears'" (163). Beyond the pale of tears, deep thoughts evoke "the magic of association" reminiscent of the double vision of that famous gothic disrobing in "Christabel" of Geraldine's maternal and sexualized bosom: "A sight to dream of, not to tell!" (253). For Jewsbury, the great ode summons competing images of an object, based on what we have come to understand as the inextricable, dialogic tie between Wordsworthian visionary Romanticism and its Coleridgean gothic phantom.[10]

In "The Eden of the Sea," she almost directly responds to his passage about a unified vision of trees from the "Intimations Ode" by transforming it into a phantasmagoria of cocoa trees—the circulation of both Wordsworth's and Jewsbury's phantom trees. Such emphasis on exchange and movement signals that Jewsbury's tropes of visuality in this poem begin to formulate a kind of substitution predicated on commodity exchange. Within earlier poems in the sequence, the speaker tries to watch the oncoming seascape only to summon phantoms of English people and landscapes. By the time the speaker turns her gaze to Ceylon, the materially embodied pastoral eventually gives rise to gothic phantoms that trail an English imperial residue. Jewsbury's poem evokes not a Wordsworthian Platonic image (an ideal form of forms) but a double vision of both the pastoral cocoa tree and its commodity use, which might be hiding within the tree's supposedly aesthetic leaves and flowers.

> These cocoa-trees—not fair in woods,
>   But singly seen and seen afar,
> When sunset pours his yellow floods
>   A column, and its crown a star!
> Yet, dowered with wealth of uses rare,
>   Whene'er its plumy branches wave,
> Some sorrow seems to haunt the air;
>   Some vision of a desert grave! (9.49–56)

This series of views of the tree begins with a field of "singly seen" trees separated from the many. Contrasted with an English forest of "glorious oaks" (14) mentioned earlier in this poem, which compose the grand, rolling English countryside, cocoa trees are not grouped in woods but "singly seen" from a distance. The trees are singular, as if they cannot be conceptualized or generalized like English oaks.

To construct the double vision, as the light changes, so does the image. The setting shifts from the squirrel at "morning sport" to the sunset pouring his "yellow floods" to the more shadowy and perhaps nighttime "vision of a desert grave." Here Jewsbury may be drawing from a moving-picture technology even more recent than the phantasmagoria, the new and widely acclaimed diorama, originally pioneered by Louis Daguerre. In later versions of the diorama, called the "double-effect technique," pictures were composed from at least two layers of screens colored with varying degrees of translucent paints, and shades would move behind the scenes to change the lighting and thus the picture. When night falls in this scene, the tree first becomes a column—a stately edifice—and then a crown with a star in it, as if it were a proleptic sign of South Asia as a jewel in Queen Victoria's crown. The silhouetted image of natural beauty at night belies monarchical rule. The picture turns once more, in the second half of the stanza, to reflect back the tree's instrumentality to Western eyes, those "uses rare" that convert the tree's beauty into wealth, or commodified chocolate.

Thus the tree, when put into conversation with Western ideas and desires, unleashes sorrow and death that "haunt" the landscape. This collocation of English imagery evokes similarities that might make the Indian trees readable; at the same time, the attempt to perceive cocoa trees within a Western context provokes an apparition of absence and woe, the "vision of a desert grave." By raising the specter of commodified chocolate, Jewsbury's cocoa tree transforms the scene into a phantasmagoria where commodity haunts the colonial gaze even as it likewise gifts imperial eyes with a critical view of their own ways of seeing. Such optics essentially reveal the ideological circuits—and fetishes—of their visual technologies. In other words, Jewsbury conjures the phantasmagoria as a mode of critique that seeks to represent if not rid the gaze of its inevitable commodified desires.

It is worth touching on Jewsbury's early thinking about the multiple moving-picture shows that lit up popular imagination concerning the mind because, for her, both shows and pop ideas function to instigate sensory stimulation in ways that invite an epistemological suspicion of the empirical. Jewsbury employs the phantasmagoria as a trope for disclosing the ideological nature of seemingly embodied, empirical, emotive experience. In discussions of pre-cinematic and urban entertainment, both Terry Castle and Richard Altick have attested to how thoroughly the moving-picture shows became absorbed by literati as a colloquial figure for the mind's own spectral haunting. In her article "Spectral Technology and the

Metaphorics of Modern Reverie," Castle explains that the phantasmagoria had begun "to figure imaginative activity itself, paradoxically, as a kind of ghost-seeing" (29). In a footnote later in the article, she identifies the tendency for authors to compile miscellaneous collections as a formal representation of shifting scenes, locations, and voices much like the magic lantern shows—and cites Jewsbury's *Phantasmagoria* as an example.[11] Both the genre and the optical illusion present figures for the imagination as a dreamy collage of visual chimeras. Jewsbury's own miscellany convenes a collection of ventriloquized poetic and critical voices—everything from the annoyingly precocious Oxford literary critic to the ingénue writing gossipy letters from boarding school.

One selection stands out as a template for the literary genre of the phantasmagoria itself. The speaker, somewhat tongue-in-cheek, romantically riffs on dreaming in a meta-poetic piece entitled "A Vision of Poets." She muses: "Authors are your only accomplished dreamers;—they can dream when and what they please—by day as well as night;—awake as easily as when asleep. Indeed it might in many cases be said with truth, that authors dream to live, and live to dream" (*Phantasmagoria* I, 55). In this particular piece, the author falls asleep, dreams up a colloquy of Britain's famous poets, and attends to their conversations about the current state of literature and its canons. This fantasy of a grand British writers' conference illustrates Jewsbury's idea of the imagination as a magic lantern beaming the specters of British poets across the mind.[12] Pointedly, the speaker hints at but refuses to name those assembled. While we might assume from several clues that Wordsworth, Milton, and Pope are probably at the table, their shadowy presence not only alludes to a canon of British authors still very much in the making but also occludes any cult of personality in favor of a debate about values. Their spectral presence may likewise question how assumptions about embodied presence and empirical sensation get tied to gender when literary histories are written. Representing a synchronic collocation of British literary history, the literati do not replace each other successively in history but, collectively summoned, haunt the pages of literary history. And because they function as revenants—they begin by coming back—they evoke a past that is always already also present and future.

The erudite ghosts in "A Vision of Poets" nonetheless suggest the gothic atmosphere for the actual phantasmagoria shows. As described by Sir David Brewster in an 1832 book entitled *Letters on Natural Magic*, this optical illusion was like a magic lantern show but with slides that would project the figures of "ghosts, skeletons, and known individuals, whose eyes and mouths were made to move by the shifting of combined sliders

[. . .] In this manner, the head of Dr. Franklin was transformed into a skull" (qtd. in Altick 218). These "spectre-raising shows," like Jewsbury's Ceylon landscape, might appear in the freshness of life and then suddenly decay before the spectators' eyes. *The Oceanides*'s putrefied "vision of a desert grave" similarly conjures the haunting, gothic phantasmagoria of multiple visions whose reality is questionable. This type of gothic visuality, as Sophie Thomas has argued in *Romanticism and Visuality*, was not simply a nod to the prevalence of the gothic during the period but evidence of that genre's integral connection to the rise of pre-cinematic technologies.[13]

By the 1830s at least part of the British viewing public was quite self-aware of the illusory quality of the images generated by moving-picture shows. As Thomas and William Galperin elaborate, the dioramas, which successively displayed two pictures of the same scene, toyed with what might be seen and unseen, depending on the degree of light, the audience's position, and the manipulation of the performance. The first iterations of the diorama in London, mostly of landscapes—though seldom tropical ones—staged two pictures by rotating the viewing room from one aperture to another, with the pictures each at the end of a separate tunnel (Altick 166). By 1834, Daguerre began experimenting with the aforementioned "double-effect technique," where two pictures of a scene were superimposed on the same backdrop.

Even if the mechanics of such illusions were hidden, reviews in such magazines as the *Athenaeum* made clear the mediated nature of natural scenes, particularly the disordering of sight that occurred as one painting switched to another over a span of time. As Galperin writes, "if the Diorama can lend itself to the business of interpellating viewers [. . .], it's [sic] more important and commoner function is to demystify this work by exposing and disrupting the ideological circuit" (69). He goes on to explain, "it does this typically with the assistance of an audience, whose instability before the image [. . .] spells misfortune" for the pleasurable and nonthinking immersion amid illusory images (69). Similarly, Altick points out that both the phantasmagoria and the diorama created the illusion of reality and, at the same time, operated through the production of knowingly irrational illusions. This viewing practice pointedly distinguishes itself from the panoramas, with their sweeping views of faraway places including Europe, the Mediterranean, or even India (Altick 135). Those large-scale vistas tended to grant the viewer enough distance from landscapes to allow them to assume mastery over scenic views and, like the picturesque, to assert hegemony over foreign lands.

For Jewsbury, the viewer's self-awareness of a dioramic or phantasmagoric exchange of images offered the potential to uncover a picture's ideological stakes. As her poem traces the surface of trees, animals, flora, and eventually human forms, their images cannot help but exude their phantasmic nature, a double effect of pastoral nature and commodified sight. The gothic undertones project an anxiety and a suspicion about ways of seeing that first appear uncomplicatedly embodied, natural, and physically stable. Rather than mystifying the very real violence wreaked upon the "Eden of the Sea" and its inhabitants occluded from view, the gothic trappings of this poem—the phantom images that lurk behind the supposed direct sight of the tree—self-consciously conjure the brutality of imprisonment and mastery over both women and colonial subjects.[14] The "vision of a desert grave" may, for example, refer to Britain's bloody suppression of the indigenous rebellion in recently colonized Ceylon. Under British rule, commercial exports grew as agricultural, subsistence farming waned, at the cost of rampant rural poverty and famine well into the nineteenth century. Jewsbury describes a cocoa tree that would not be introduced to Ceylon as a cash crop in 1834–1835 but had already been brought to Madras, just a short distance away, in 1798. The cocoa imagery, with its haunting imperial vision, conjures the shady side of commercial agriculture (whether cinnamon, chocolate, or coffee), surely the gothic other of Ceylon's individual trees.[15] The haunting picture of the cocoa trees releases the commodity fetish that hides behind the Romantic depiction of native, untouched beauty. These secondary images ultimately insinuate the violence achieved in the name of capital, not to mention the resulting ideologies of colonial domination.

By espousing an epistemology based on moving images, the abutting of the two images of the cocoa tree—as a sign of untouched nature and as a pillar of the British economy—throw the entire representational system into an ethical mode that frees the tree of its capacity to be seen or marked as known. The double vision of colonial nature superimposes both intimate and destructive images of the tree, images that can never coincide and thus reveal a blind spot in the tree's visual semiotics. Because Westerners cannot yet see the tree without thinking of chocolate, they cannot yet know it. Unlike the oak tree, universally revered for its English purity, cocoa trees exist as a sight that provokes a comparison which, in turn, obscures codified images or any single, dominating gaze. If, as Mary Jacobus writes, Wordsworth figures vacancy "as a trope for negative seeing," Jewsbury's vacancy places her doubly "unseen things" into motion (130, 129). Rather than an empty void (blindness or paralysis), her kaleidoscopic vision at once bars sight even as it produces shifting movements from one image or figure to the next. Her route out of colonial sentimentalism relies on a way of seeing that is primarily about tracing movement—and movement's ability to interrupt subjective vision.

The double vision of the cocoa trees reveals the drag of property and commodity forever following the English traveler. These gothic effects and moving-picture technologies effectively disclose the tree's multifarious nature as a commodity, one that rises beyond material satisfaction and evokes what Karl Marx in *Capital* called the "mystical nature" or "phantasmagoria" of commodities. For Marx, once an object is put into exchange, it is no longer identified by its use value or purely physical attributes but reflects social relations among men. Commodities accrue exchange value based on how men put them into conversation with each other, a value that bespeaks social, ideological bearing. As Derrida writes in *Specters of Marx*, "For commodities [. . .] do not walk by themselves, they cannot go to market on their own in order to meet other commodities. This commerce among things stems from the phantasmagoria. The autonomy lent to commodities corresponds to an anthropomorphic projection" (137). Commodities are phantoms whose material nature is no longer completely accessible and whose value might appear natural but is constructed by social and economic relations, by anthropomorphic bodies in relationships with each other, relations which are themselves phantasmagoric.

According to Derrida, Marx's analysis attempts to exorcize this "mystical character" from the commodity and rescue the use value of an object from its contingent worth inscribed by its exchange on the market. Derrida characteristically argues that, in fact, there never was an originary use value of an object to begin with: "We are suggesting on the contrary that [. . .] the ghost had already made its apparition" (161). Derrida famously abjures nostalgia for the object or for human relations without the specters of capital; there is no rescuing real, material bodies. For Jewsbury, too, there is no authentic sensory experience of Ceylon that has not already been overlaid with the language of sensibility and empirical acquisition. The cocoa tree never was just a beatific landscape feature nor a nourishing source of chocolate, but rather the object only comes into view as a commodity constructed by the aesthetic and commodity desires of its consumers. As a double vision from the start, it already signals the complicated exigencies of colonial relations in British India. In epistemological and ontological terms, subjects and objects, commodified women's bodies and imperial goods, are already imbricated in relation to one another and to consumer desires.

When Jewsbury traces sensory and material residues etched into the gothic vision of English relatives and foreign trees, she does not seek to exorcise the commodity and to find once again the real, feeling body. Such a project would be a futile goal for the woman traveler already entangled within the oceanic sways of commodity trade and global displacement.[16] Like Smith's figures of impossible consumption, the phantom trees suggest viewers must find a way through commodity's substitutive movements, not without them. While Hemans finds vacancy in a parallax that produces a motion between two different ways of seeing the world, Jewsbury finds a means to rotate different historical and epistemological visions. Yet, as Jewsbury probes the contingency of the separation between subjects and objects, or between commodified women's bodies/imperial goods and those with less exploited use value, she suggests other relations on the rise. Following Karen Barad's reading of Derridean hauntology, because subjects and objects are always contingently and repeatedly constructed, different entities can be "cut" other ways to give rise to new relations. For Jewsbury, it is the kinesis of the moving image—in fact, the image that becomes movement itself—that offers those iterative "cuts" that define new things and alternative relations. This affect finally unleashes the collapse of the distinction of subject and objects altogether in favor of new human and nonhuman materialities.

For this reason, Jewsbury cannot live with the phantom's double form, which always threatens the return of embodied sentiment, however ghostly. The cocoa tree always remains partially mired in fetishistic desire just as the woman traveler remains liable to those fetishes for the female body and its images, further heightened when the Anglo-Indian woman is trafficked to British settler colonies. Jewsbury ultimately eschews the phantom and seeks to suspend, for however short a time, its sensory qualities by instigating another figure for affective movement. The commodity's logic of exchange becomes the phantom's remedy, but only as Jewsbury wrenches exchange and substitution from the grasp of embodied sensations and revenant emotions—in ways that bear striking similarities to Smith's denuding of empirical sensation from consumption. For the initial circulation of the tree presents a sign not only of phantasmagoric colonial horror but also that movement disclosed within the phantasmagoric. Not quite a structure, this affective movement allegorizes how the sway of linguistic exchange might come to release the speaker and other colonial bodies from their rooted reality and definitive forms of understanding. Vacancy unsettles secure sight in the tropics, and then eventually turns to offer another account of vision altogether—the playful action and moving spirit of infancy. More like Robinson's multiplicity of "circling bounds" that produce affective variation, the phantasmagoria will turn from the pre-cinematic cycling of images into a series of ceaseless movements.

Vacancy's Vision: The Image of the Infant, Kinesis, and Pure Interchange

Jewsbury's trope of vacancy eventually turns from the phantasmagoria's critique of sensationally and sentimentally bound vision and then looks to a figure for vision that would posit an alternative visual epistemology instigated by restless movements of affect that outrun sensation, embodiment, and exchangeable, commodified emotions. Jewsbury first highlights childhood as an important metaphor not coincidentally in the poem written from Ceylon, just before the passage on the squirrel and the cocoa trees. This childish approach to the world interferes with both prejudicial vision and the illusion of pure sight in the native tropics:

> No, in a world as childhood new,
> Is it not well to be a child?—
> As quick to ask, as quick to view,
> As promptly pleased, perchance as wild?
> Deride who will as childish wit,
> My scorn to-day of graver things;
> Let *them* be proud, but let me sit
> Enamoured of a beetle's wings. [. . .]
>
> I know that creatures strange and fierce
> Here lurk, and here make men afraid;
> But let the daring hunter pierce
> Their hidden lairs—in this bright shade,
> Let me forget save what I greet (9.17–24, 37–41)

Nearly reversing Coleridge's description in "Christabel" of the child "[t]hat always finds, and never seeks" (661), the speaker's childish state of mind makes her "[a]s quick to ask, as quick to view." As the poem's constant rhyming, repetitions, and questions suggest, she never definitively finds a single perspective. Although she sees Ceylon as the new, earthly Eden—with its intimations of primal innocence—the verse promptly forgets those haunting assumptions about "hidden lairs" of animals or natives who might be naturally atavistic or savage-like. In order to do so, the viewer's gaze becomes "perchance as wild" and imbued with possibility, as she exchanges adult pride and fear for childish greetings of beetles and other ludic bodies. In this way, these lines call forth what Linda Austin has labeled the infant's mnemonic vacancy of childhood, an absence of preconceived perceptions or memories that might color interpretations of foreign sights. This trope of childhood and infancy retains its characteristic receptivity of vision and vacancy, but one that has a greater chance of extending into the future—and representing futurity itself—by shedding the quality of stillness for a dalliance with play and movement.

In a poem entitled "The Eden of the Sea," we might assume that an English speaker would naturally describe an island colony as a post-lapsarian Eden that, by dint of its immunity to civilization, has preserved its innocence. The poem's speaker, however, appears to be imminently self-aware of her use of childhood as a liberating trope. First, the repetition of "as" four times in the first quatrain emphasizes that Ceylon is a world *as* new as childhood, not actually Eden itself. Instead, it acquires a figural status conferred by the English viewer. Such a constructed view is further highlighted when we return to the first line of the poem: "A dream! a dream!" (9.1).

One might likewise be tempted to discuss how, under the woman writer's gaze, the infant intimates a biological imperative to repopulate India as British India.[17] In another poem, the repeated image of the child might be read as a sign of naturalistic, feminine, embodied maternalism. Such a biographical reading would characterize Jewsbury as a memsahib-to-be, a woman with the prerogative of reproducing English culture and progeny abroad. According to Francis Espinasse, Jewsbury's India journal does document her attention to native youth: "She tried to win her way into their confidence, beginning with the children, who appreciated little gifts and kindnesses" (332).[18] Yet, in addition to her noted "customary dislike for communities or groups of Anglo-Indians" (Espinasse 333), which disqualifies her as a memsahib in the offing, the poem repeatedly figures childhood as a state of wonderment not coercion, one that releases the traveler from the constraints of English civil society and from the reproductive body. The infant—as an image attached to various representations of animals and inanimate objects—intimates visual, not necessarily biological, reproduction. As D. B. Ruderman has recently argued, the idea of infancy in nineteenth-century poetry offers "a radically new figure for poetic reproduction," which travels beyond historicist notions of actual children, uncivilized childishness, or reproductive biopolitics (12). The female speaker is neither unreasonable nor a weak-minded woman writer who has been infantilized by her marriage or by a craving for babies. Rather, the child itself becomes a meta-trope, a trope that figures the constant production of new images, and then new movements within them, in a poetic process that ultimately questions the limits of visual perception and its allegedly civilized preconceptions.

Consequently, the "childish" sights of Ceylon eventually give way to the exuberant figure of an infant two poems later in the penultimate number of the sequence, "To an Infant Afar." With this last figure of vacancy, Jewsbury's vision rolls along without becoming bogged down by past intimations or future impossibilities. Her poem begins with the speaker calling up an image of an English infant, perhaps of a friend or relative back home. Here any nostalgia for English domesticity is not converted into a haunting image of a specific loved one but a figure for tropic and affective movement. Jewsbury blatantly exemplifies these ideas poetically in a refrain that changes as it moves through the poem:

> THOU art sleeping or at play,
> Happy one! pretty one!
> Laughing, lisping, far away,
> Heedless of the salt-sea spray,
> Happy one! pretty one!
>
> When they ask thee, where am I?
> Little one! distant one!
> Thou dost neither smile nor sigh;
> All thy world is very nigh,
> Home-encircled little one!
>
> I am sailing on the sea,
> English one! city one!
> And long years must come and flee,
> Ere I look again on thee,
> Changing, growing little one! (11.1–15)

This infant who neither smiles nor sighs notably lacks feminine or melancholy affect, and we have no indication of its gender throughout the poem. "Laughing" and "lisping," the baby babbles in shifting, nonsignifying sounds. It is perhaps even more remarkable for its "changing" and "growing" than for its innocence or joy. Despite the fact that it is "home-encircled," the child still provokes movement in the viewing, speaking subject. Finally "heedless" of its surroundings and unmindful of affective associations, the child ignores—or cannot perceive—differences in space and time. Thus the child illustrates buoyancy—but not so far as transcendence. It figures for the speaker a type of continuous, if repetitive, motion, what Ruderman calls infancy's "recursive iterative structure" (4). Ruderman brings our attention to a new poetics of form and thought, through infancy's internalizations or introjections that return us to an inchoate processual self and its self-altering embodiment. Jewsbury's infancy limns this temporality, but her resistance to stable, gendered bodies encourages her poems to broach a kinetic materiality whose ubiquity moves beyond subject, body, or form, however turbulent. Similar to Robinson's use of the ballad repetition, Jewsbury's exact rhymes coupled with a varying refrain "Happy one! Pretty one!" "Little one! distant one!" "Home-encircled little one!" "English one! city one!" "Changing, growing little one!" "Gentle one! fragile one!" disperse any grappling poetic form into the affective aether of sky and sea, a projection of movement itself.

In the next stanza, the poet turns to glance at the ocean, only to find the image of the infant replicated everywhere. Not a figure for ghostly nostalgia or messianic procreation, the infant actually presents the nonbiological and aimless production of an image that is as malleable as it is conversant with the varieties of the landscape.

> Yet, how oft I see a thing,
>   Gentle one! fragile one!
> That, before mine eye can bring
> Thee, by Fancy's symbolling
>   Gentle one! fragile one! (11.16–20)

Though the view of the "thing" calls forth "Fancy's symbolling," it does not simply activate a memory of an actual infant afar. Although other objects in the landscape may evoke the association of the infant within the speaker, soon after it takes on a life of its own as an image on the water, an image that in turn impels the figuration of many other things. The next two stanzas produce a list of items conjured for the reader: pictures of "nautili that sail the deep," "tiny birds that over it sweep," "flying fish that upward leap," and "baby billows" (21, 23–25). All of these visions noticeably include modifying clauses that both mimic and figure motion inherent in the seascape (or they incorporate nouns that double as verbs such as "billows"). As a result, "Fancy's symbolling" does not so much mechanically reproduce the infant afar but assembles metonymic representations of the child based on the shared attribute of constant activity. The following stanza provides even more replicas of the babe in "many a cloud at morn and night," "many a moonbeam's quivering light," and glow-worms, both "making ocean's bosom bright" (26, 28–30). Here the sense of movement resides in the repeated "many" and the "-ing" ending connecting the participle "quivering" to the nearly allegorical "making [. . .] bright" of the verb.

The ocean's motility encourages aqueous instability, as if its active backdrop or moving screens provoke the fecundity of moving images. This motion once again intertwines with the poet's rendering of changing light, echoing the pattern found earlier in the double vision of cocoa trees as dusk falls. These elements of clouds, moonbeams, and the reflecting ocean all emit and eventually dim the amount of light in the seascape, as if the poet is constructing one final light show. Here, however, the tropic substitution does not blindly automate an equality among these images; the changing light reveals the hand of the poet making metonymic exchanges among things that are alike but not really the same, among images that can be interchanged but do not coincide.[19] Their constant movement presents not so much a continuous vision or complete sight but rather a series of images that preserve the gaps between them. These brief flickers, visual caesuras, figure and materialize the invisible motion from one to the next that the eye can never capture.

Reprising *The Oceanides*' associations with the "Intimations Ode," this ebullient, restless figure shares traits with Wordsworth's "young lambs [who] bound" (20, 174) or the "Child among [. . .] new-born blisses" (86), who is "profoundly resistant to narratives of development" (Ruderman 38). In a sequence with many dialogic parts, Jewsbury emphasizes the multiplicity of odic, childish figures as a means of concocting multiple poetic valleys and posies. Her view of childhood certainly uses the scenes of nature to resist both social construction and fixed, embodied landscapes, and she perhaps does only a bit to entwine the infant into a particular socioeconomic—not to mention colonial—fabric. Yet she opposes what Alan Richardson labels Wordsworth's "organic sensibility . . . frozen in a state of eternal innocence" (*Literature* 72) with a quality even beyond that found in painting, poetry, and especially the moving-picture shows—undirected movement.

In an apt closing of the poem, the speaker recycles the verb "to image" first seen in "The Eden of the Sea." Whereas Ceylon helped "to image forth far the far-famed tales," here the scenery promulgates images of the infant everywhere:

> All things that are weak and fair,
> > Rosy one! merry one!
> Image infants everywhere,
> Careless, amid cause for care (31–34)

The infant's repeated connection to "symbolling" and "imaging" mark it as a meta-image or meta-trope—a figure that stands for itself and as an allegory of how vision, and the ontic knowledge it elicits, might work. Jewsbury's unusual verb—"to image"—comments on childhood as a certain flexible, daring activity or action of the mind parallel to being "careless amid cause for care." This paradox gestures toward two others running throughout the poem. First, the child as a cipher or a representation of weak, feminine, unthinking domesticity, in this poem, becomes a figure for what Jewsbury, in a letter to Dora Wordsworth, calls "the life of a Gipsey," a wandering, tropic carelessness that pointedly shirks overly feminized feeling.[20] Second, as a figure for visual knowledge tied to nostalgia, the infant allegorizes something that moves beyond the visible and clear structures of feeling. Its image, composed of a series of views, cannot sit still or be pinned down. If the child possesses cheeks spread with color, it also typifies playing and laughing, not so much what Nancy Yousef in *Romantic Intimacy* details as the proximate, emotionally infused intimacies of "interest, withdrawal, responsiveness and abstention," but a figural form of sheer activity, an abstraction of continuous movement (21). In this way we might say that the poet attempts to push past the physical and representational limits of her medium and, at times, representation altogether.

At this point it seems necessary to revisit the question of ideology since such a trope or tropic structure might appear quite ideological itself. As with Smith's hermit in "Beachy Head" and his epitaph ever about to be written, Jewsbury's infant perhaps recycles another version of Wordsworth's "evermore about to be," what Jerome McGann in *The Romantic Ideology* calls the ideology of process in Romantic poetry. After all, as some recent commentators on childhood have argued, it is all too easy to impose utopian narratives on representations of children.[21] Perhaps more to the point in this poem, invisibility, taken in a colonial context, might all too easily augur ideological color-blindness. Yet this turn in *The Oceanides* again can be seen as a means of drawing out the problem of who will be viewed and how. While Jewsbury mostly conducts her experiments on the landscape, the absence of Indian subjects in the sequence may be, in part, a refusal to picture them for English audiences abroad. This mode of viewing preserves the other's resistance to Western visibility, eliciting the spirit of that which cannot be customarily seen by the English. As Simon Jarvis suggests in *Wordsworth's Philosophic Song*, the "Intimations Ode" similarly forestalls the "common light of day" that enables "custom" or customary seeing. Just as the childishness of the speaker obviates preconceived narratives of Ceylon, similarly the replicas of infants not only present a being before habituated language but one whose kinesthetic spirit suggests just how productive the inability to fix landscapes (or temporalities) might be.

Moving images summoned along Anglo-Indian trade routes propose the notion of visual movement as a liberatory, ameliorating substitute for the commerce responsible for the abuses of the imperial project, as well as the ebb and flow of sensibility. Jewsbury's poetic practice anticipates what Emerson, five years later in "The American Scholar," would call "That great principle of Undulation in nature" (62). Following Cornel West's well-known reading of Emerson, the use of undulating nature serves as a liberationist strategy that transports exchange from its domination of the material realm into a type of repeated tropic operation. Such poetic substitution allegorizes objects put in motion, past memories that conjure empirical sensation or even past our own secret fetishes for them.[22]

Rather than the specter's material affective histories of women and colonial others, the infant summons a particular sort of emancipatory spirit. Derrida calls the messianic spirit a structure that "upsets all calculations, interests, and capital" (136). The infant likewise appears as a tropic movement (and a trope of movement) that releases its viewers from even phantom feelings, their memories, and the history of empirical sensation. As an alternative to the phantom, it entails a vigorous figural-material conjunction that defers ideological calcification, and even the deferred return of affective histories. Not simply resistant to what upsets or shirks, it playfully moves on its own, an autonomous affect forged through the figural. As with the inveterate motions of Derrida's impossible messianism, the infant never arrives at adulthood yet never can fully shirk that telos, and so repeatedly calls forth additional spirited images. The poet, by assembling a series of tropes, attempts to speed forward into a present, even if it is an acceleration that can never fully outrun the ghostly demarcations of past sensations, sentiments, and histories.

Even more radically, Jewsbury's final model for revolutionary figuration suggests that if we cannot remove ourselves from the images and language of commodity, then, as Smith does with the discourse on taste, we might abstract its structure in order to find poetic language that has the power to recreate alternative movements among things and people. Although commodities speak to each other through exchanges that equalize things and essentialize their value, Jewsbury's vacancy, with its seeming unending string of metonymic exchanges, suggests how poetic surpluses might free both thing and commodity from any one value, as the next trope appears on the horizon. Rather than veering into a neoliberal mode of exchange, Jewsbury indicates how thinking via tropological movement temporarily frees figures from meaning by always already putting them into relation with an unending chain of other things, people, and landscapes. The spirit of the trope is its ability to place together a myriad of ever-changing relations, comparisons, and differences in a material field created not simply by the human mind and body but through incessant tropic movement among and between bodies. This technique marks deconstruction's secret obverse—the overabundance of figural articulation and material fecundity that anticipates rather than undoes meaning. By manufacturing an excess of figures, the structure of futurity, which can never fully finish the chain of substitutions, appears even when its meaning does not.

Jewsbury shows us how such a linguistic process does not simply amount to a textual disruption of the empirical but one whose iterative troping might reveal new ways of being for women and others beyond embodied sentiment. Rather than wandering as a memsahib, the poet lives the life of a roving figure. Although the haunting resurgence of the material bodies and feelings put into transit in the spaces between England and India may lend a structure to the phantasmagoric critique of imperial commodity and sentimental settler colonialism, it is only unending tropological movement that might provide a material process for the articulation of new vistas and relations among things, people, and landscapes. Rather than always returning to the body's perceptual change as a motor for understanding self and other, as it tracks the altering scenes along the rolling waters, the infant's buoyant kinesis suggests other forms of movement born of the figural, and its speculative, affective projections. By capitalizing on swaying, oceanic movements and the nondirectional play of the infant, the mental traveler needs no empirical, imperial trumpery but only the impetus to enact its own liveliness and the vitality shared among humans, sky, sea, land, and their figuration.

Coda

The Phantom Menace and the Spirit of Affect

Jewsbury's preoccupation with the phantom reminds us just how easy it is—and has been—for women to become haunted by the empirical, overly sensible, commodity culture that would make them phantoms themselves. Indeed, this has been the legacy of Romantic women writers who until very recently have been like ghosts, haunting the grave-like canons that mark their literary disappearances. The efforts of critics have, unsurprisingly, endeavored to build bulwarks against these past and future losses by evoking the experiential, emotive qualities of their verse and the empirical evidence of women's literary culture.[1] Jewsbury's own evocation of that very labile form, the phantom, helps us to see how such sensibility, with its nervous sensation, is haunting but not necessarily omnipresent. When we stop seeing women writers as already contextualized by the gender and embodiment that would either limit them or encourage their resistance, we can begin to understand all poets as establishing other, fluid forms of affect, figuration, and being in the world unbound by either conscription or rejection, burdensome sensibility or forbearing oblivion.

As I have endeavored to show, poets of vacancy provide some of the most interesting working through—and past—the crucial problems and infamous skepticism inherent to empiricism and sensibility: the continuous flux of sensory perception that provides humans with sense data about both the external world and themselves; the speculative nature of our translation of that sense data into reflection, ideas, and emotions; and the "fiction of the self" built from our shifting perceptions and our speculations about them. Even more resolutely, poets of vacancy supply a neglected critique of empirical philosophy that questions the gendered bias of knowledge derived from bodily sensation, particularly its translation into sensibility. Not only does sensation, particularly within the purview of sensibility, often lead women back to the sexed bodies and experiential difference of romance, but its translation into thought is also extremely susceptible to being shaped by gender ideology. Sensibility itself, in addition to its notorious excesses, raises questions about the contagious nature of emotional and affective transmission, its tendency to solidify monomaniacal thought (about luxury commodities and love objects) and to instigate paralysis (mental and political). As a discourse and a form of physiological response, its easy ability to be consumed superficially and to be projected onto others likewise encourages the consolidation of embodied differences (especially pertaining to gender but also those of race).

This book has attempted to elucidate poets' deep thinking about the problems of empiricism as they relate to epistemology—both how we understand the world and come to emotion. It simultaneously, and no less importantly, sheds light on how those inquiries are equally those of ontology—how forms of affect prior to sensation uncover material transmissions, exchanges, and movements among different sorts of bodies, entities, and spaces that alter what we know about matter and its relations. Above all, however, both of these inquiries occur through figuration in Romantic writing, as language's different kinds of movement posit something akin to affect through its own nonhuman motions, among all that matters in the world. Not simply a skeptical or deconstructive disfiguring of the self, poets of vacancy ask us to consider what other trajectories of thinking, feeling, and being might occur—might have already occurred—if we move aside from the subject and through vacancy's figural turns. (And not in ways that obviate politics, despite the tendency to associate politics with subjective choice.) This stepping away from all fiction of the subject includes, for Smith, a brief contemplation of an alternative aesthetics that resemble Kant's transcendental subject, which has for so long dominated Romantic thought. But Smith, like other poets of vacancy, is more interested in creating "mere form" through figures that imbricate and blur the boundaries of human "subject" and their nonhuman "objects." Vacancy transports us into a realm beyond selves, subjects, objects, and beyond the mere figures of language too. Rather than a return to deconstructive Romanticism, *Romantic Vacancy* aims to intermix it with some of the insights of speculative realism, new materialism, and affect theory, to arrive at other sorts of unstable, material movements that occur in language but also in and through more ineffable forms of matter.

Jewsbury culminates and thus reviews many of the techniques of other poets of vacancy, and not simply because she comes last in a linear literary history. Her figural assessment of visuality inverts Smith's impossible consumption into an impossible act of projection, while it simultaneously takes into account the fecundity of figural multiplicity available in Robinson's repetition and Hemans's parallax. Like Hemans, Jewsbury adumbrates Wordsworth's and Shelley's concerns with contagion, particularly through imperial sensibilities that infect tyrants, colonists, and the women domesticated by them, to target at once the habits of nostalgia as well as the hegemonic sways of imperial sentimentalism. Questions of travel—particularly the dispersed transmission of affects through particulate matter and through figuration—enunciate a final frontier for vacancy to boldly go beyond nation and empire into a figural transverse. Jewsbury again adumbrates the impossibility inherent in Smith's aporia and Hemans parallax, where figures bring together the empirical and ideal to create a constant tension of unending movement between them. Yet the infant's unending movements also accumulate the materiality of Robinson's varying post-empiricist sensation, Shelley's vibrations, and Hemans's pool of cognitive incipiencies, each of which intimate a virtuality of potential movements that multiple bodies might make together. This virtuality is unearthed through spaces that house the materialities of the human body, various sounds, and the flowing winds and waters of the landscape: Robinson's "circling bounds," Hemans's forest sanctuary, or Shelley's affective ecology of the universe of things. It is a virtuality, however, that occurs through language's incessant movement figured by repetition, parataxis, asyndeton, and synesthesia. These figural movements expose an affect that transcends human-centered sensation because it occurs in mind, body, language, and world at once and because it includes both actual and incorporeal activity (all the moves bodies and less bounded entities might make). Vacancy's figuration offers both those affects we can partially sense and those we can only intimate.

At the heart of this study, therefore, is a version of Romantic affect that is both figural and posthuman. These readings attempt to transform our perceptions of Romantic poetics, gender, and women's writing at once—demonstrating how Romantic poetry, when it acutely addresses affect and gender, can reshape our understanding of figuration as initiating affect that travels through both language and matter of all sorts. That vision disrupts what we have come to know as poets' thinking on gender, history, and subjectivity, especially women poets, and reveals their radical speculation on epistemology and ontology. What this means for writers, particularly those concerned with the ideological gendering of minds and bodies, is that bodies and genders do not always come first as a context that shapes writing as and before it is written. Instead, figures come into and are brought into being by writers who are not always thinking about their social contexts or who think those sociopolitical realities might be changed. However much gender might have been transferrable to different sorts of bodies in the period, as Claudia Johnson and Susan J. Wolfson have so engagingly shown, in the poetics of vacancy, writers attempt to use figures of gender critique to move past binary gender—or simply to exist in spaces and temporalities where such gendering does not manifest. In other words, just as vacancy strips certain figural acts like consumption or projection of their empirical content, so vacancy strips gender of its dimorphism (sexed bodies and minds). Gender then becomes dissolved into the many figural turns and fluid forms of matter—either as nonbinary affect or as loosely held collections of fluidities. Poets of vacancy do not always or only live the life of the downtrodden woman writer or the life of the Romantic mind; they live the life of figuration. An augmented reality perhaps—a life lived through and as figuration means sharing materiality without constantly returning to selfhood or bodily boundaries—but with corporate meaning and feeling not so much deferred as always on the wing.

If vacancy suggests that more historicist scholars—of women's writing and Romanticism—relax the grip of context, embodiment, and gender around texts, its notion of figuration likewise proposes we redraw Romanticism's entanglement with high theory. Romantic poetry's alleged deconstructive turn, which razes language of its signifying and referential power, turns out to have been all along a special kind of turning motion, an affect, the trace that moves both poetry, the dynamic, ever-shifting materiality of the world, and ourselves as composed, in turns, by both. Romantic poetry, when it concerns itself with figurations of and antagonistic to binary gender reveals how vacancy's linguistic aporias and repetitions are semblances of affect. Its movements and rests are those that are most impossible to consume and that flow through the universe of things. These are affects that might in some small way save us from our bodies and our*selves*—and certainly provided new ways of being women in the nineteenth century, by offering a less anthropocentric model of change that is mental, social, material all at once.

Vacancy does not merely make much of oblivion, blindness, stultification, and paralysis to uncover hidden mental depths or a sullen resource of inchoate sensation. It reveals the secret strength of things—not to deconstruct and critique what we think we do not know, but to create a form of change, the eternal revolution within one word calling for, following another, one form of reparative materiality threading through another (de Manian, new materialist, and affective). Vacancy reminds us of one thing everything shares—not impermanence or mutability—but movement as a virtual mansion of all its lovely forms of motion. Such an archive may offer a more kindly approach to the things, words, people, and places that seem to be not like us. What better care of the other could there be but to speak within a language whose very turning constitutes a movement through difference. Like Jewsbury's infant, vacancy, as a troping of tropes, figures the playful and brisk movement that can only hope to see its own unexpected actions and those of others.

Notes

Introduction

1. Notable exceptions include Adela Pinch's and Kevis Goodman's work on Charlotte Smith and Mary Favret's brief discussions of Smith, Robinson, and Hemans in *War at a Distance*.

2. Here I am working from Massumi's quotation of Baruch Spinoza in *Parables for the Virtual*: "Spinoza defined the body in terms of 'relations of movement and rest.' He wasn't referring to actual, extensive movements or stases. He was referring to a body *capacity* to enter into relations of movement and rest. This capacity he spoke of as a *power* (or potential) to affect or be affected" (16). For Massumi, this relation is a form of affective transition within the body, though later more broadly within fields and regions of affect. Here the term "affect" is meant to give a basic notion of motion that extends through the body, language, and other forms of matter, such as the Romantic landscape.

3. The seminal work tying together Romanticism and high theory is Orrin N. C. Wang's *Fantastic Modernity: Dialectical Readings in Romanticism and Theory*.

4. For the disparate foundations of sensibility, see especially Barker-Benfield, Ellis, and Csengei.

5. See also Jessica Riskin's *Science in the Age of Sensibility*, where she argues that science was crucial to theories of sensibility, and conversely, sensibility was also endemic to methods and ideas within science as well (7).

6. See Adam Smith's *Theory of Moral Sentiment*, for example, part I, chapter 5.

7. Important sources for sensibility's revolutionary aspects include Chris Jones, *Radical Sensibility: Literature and Ideas in the 1790s*; Janet Todd, *Sensibility*; Christopher Nagle, *Sexuality and the Culture of Sensibility in the British Romantic Era*; Robert Mitchell, *Sympathy and the State in the Romantic Era: Systems, State Finance, and the Shadows of Futurity*; James Chandler, "The Politics of Sentiment" and *An Archeology of Sympathy*; Susan Chaplin, *Law, Sensibility, and the Sublime in Eighteenth-Century Women's Fiction*; Lynn Festa, *Sentimental Figures of Empire in Eighteenth-Century Britain and France*; and Markman Ellis, *The Politics of Sensibility: Race, Gender, and Commerce in the Sentimental Novel*.

8. G. J. Barker-Benfield's *The Culture of Sensibility* and Claudia L. Johnson's *Equivocal Beings* most provocatively treat sensibility's role in the Revolutionary debates. This is not to say there were not valiant critiques of sensibility made by Mary Wollstonecraft, Jane Austen, and Maria Edgeworth, not to mention recent scholarship by Daniel Robinson and Ashley Cross on Mary Robinson's sallies against the cult of feeling. Until now, however, we have not really understood how such critiques actually led the way to other forms of affect, being, and thought beyond bodily sensation or, for that matter, eighteenth-century discourses of Enlightenment reason.

9. The first chapter of G. J. Barker-Benfield's *The Culture of Sensibility* duly delineates the connections among and between empiricism, nerve theory, and the discourse of sensibility that appeared later in literature. See also many of the works noted below.

10. Thomas Laqueur's seminal *Making Sex: Body and Gender from the Greeks to Freud* famously makes the claim that eighteenth-century thinkers transformed a single-sex into a two-sex model, solidifying gender inequality through sex difference.

11. Scholars have parsed these overlapping terms differently. In this study I try to reserve the term "affect" for more contemporary notions of various kinds of movements within and among bodies. This capacious notion describes physiological movements that are not sensed or have not yet occurred (including Giles Deleuze's intensity and Brian Massumi's notion of the virtual) as well as those material movements of what Jane Bennett calls "impersonal affect" that occur among and between different sorts of bodies, beyond the circumference of a self-conscious consolidated subjectivity. Women poets have actually, again surprisingly, not been considered through these more abstract ideas of affect, something that this book tries to remedy. Emotion refers to the labeling of human physiological states, which a subject will self-consciously identify upon consolidating and conceptualizing felt experience. "Feeling" is often used as a blanket term that combines emotion with other kinds of mental ideas or evaluations about the emotional life. While sympathy, following Adam Smith, often refers to a sort of imagined fellow feeling, sensibility denotes both the sociopolitical movement aimed at reforming manners and feelings as well as the particular sort of embodied, sensory experience heralded in poems such as Hannah More's "Sensibility: A Poetic Epistle to the Hon. Mrs. Boscawen" among others.

12. We might add to this list superb studies of women's writing that reiterate sensibility as the mainstay of poetics or aesthetics: Claire Knowles's *Sensibility and The Female Poetic Tradition, 1780–1860*, Elizabeth Dolan's *Seeing Suffering in Women's Literature of the Romantic Era*, as well as Susan J. Wolfson's important essays on Smith and the "female tradition."

13. See Michael O'Neill, *The Cambridge History of English Poetry*.

14. Of course, Jane Austen, Wollstonecraft, and Mary Shelley have been slowly included in theoretical scholarly ventures—for example, Tilottama Rajan's

Romantic Narrative: Shelley, Hays, Godwin, Wollstonecraft, Peter Knox-Shaw's *Jane Austen and the Enlightenment*, and a large body of work on Wollstonecraft, including Orrin N. C. Wang's *Fantastic Modernity* and Jacques Khalip's *Anonymous Life*. Likewise there has been excellent scholarship on women writers' use of Enlightenment philosophies, particularly surrounding the Revolutionary crisis. We should not turn a blind eye to Mary Wollstonecraft's, Mary Hays's, or Elizabeth Hamilton's attention to "modern philosophy" and the wars over reason waged during the 1790s. Helen Maria Williams, too, volunteered her own salvo about the political and philosophical efficaciousness of sensibility, not completely disparate from Anna Barbauld's visionary imagination or Madame de Staël's enthusiasm. See Adriana Craciun, *British Women Writers and the French Revolution: Citizens of the World* and Neil Fraistat and Susan S. Lanser's introduction to the Broadview edition of Helen Maria Williams's *Letters Written in France*. Philosophical thinking that exceeds the bounds of the historical, however, occurs even more pervasively through the tropic labor of poetic speculation.

15. For recent important studies that adumbrate this sense of a separate, gendered spheres of writing to conceptualize of "women's writing," see Paula Bacscheider's *Eighteenth-Century Women Poets and Their Poetry: Inventing Agency, Inventing Genre* and Stephen C. Behrendt's *British Women Poet and the Romantic Writing Community*. Even when feeling is read as a mode of thought, it often replicates sensation's prior and opposing relation to reflection by the very nature of empiricism's logic.

16. Important studies include Daniel P. Watkins, *Anna Letitia Barbauld and Eighteenth-Century Visionary Poetics*; Orianne Smith, *Romantic Women Writers, Revolution and Prophecy: Rebellious Daughters, 1786–1826*; and Penny Bradshaw, "Dystopian Futures: Time-Travel and Millenarian Visions in the Poetry of Anna Barbauld and Charlotte Smith."

17. An important line of scholarly criticism has established how poetry often breaks down the feeling subject or renders it an empty site of critique or recreation. See for example, the work of Jacqueline Labbe; Christoph Bode, "The Subject of *Beachy Head*"; and Yopie Prins and Virginia Jackson's "Lyrical Studies."

18. For a thorough examination of the problems of autonomy (including the destabilizing influences of affect) inherent in Enlightenment thought and its byways in Romantic literature, see Nancy Yousef's *Isolated Cases*.

19. Isobel Armstrong's Kristevan analysis has demonstrated how a variety of writers might think affectively by using techniques of negation, not to attempt to represent unrepresentable feelings (or use the semiotic to disrupt the symbolic) but to instigate the mind to thought and vice versa. See Armstrong's "The Gush of the Feminine: How Can We Read Women's Poetry of the Romantic Period?" and her book-length study *The Radical Aesthetic*. More recently, Ildiko Csengei in *Sympathy, Sensibility, and the Literature of Feeling in the Eighteenth Century* and Naomi Booth in "Feeling Too Much: The Swoon and the (In)Sensible Woman"

have separately historicized those psychological moments of insensibility when characters experience syncope, that novelistic penchant for "the swoon" in novels of sensibility. For Csengei, the temporary loss of consciousness launches an affective form of protest, in other words, "an available and socially acceptable form of *emotional expression*" (149; my emphasis).

20. In this pursuit, vacancy shares concerns with some lines of affect studies, particularly when Robinson, Hemans, and Shelley search for types of sensation outside the feeling body in figures that veer toward the nonrepresentational, though not necessarily prelinguistic. Nevertheless, Robinson and Hemans are less concerned with expressing felt experience than a kind of knowledge prior to sensory perception and certainly before such moments might be defined as emotional or experiential.

21. In *Anonymous Life: Romanticism and Dispossession*, Jacques Khalip delicately teases out the figure of the female melancholic evincing a subjectivity reticent of full engagement with the world. Her withdrawal also characterizes skepticism as an act of Enlightenment critique that nevertheless is attached to a rationality she cannot escape. Melancholy, like skepticism and the sublime, provides a valiant resistance to certain elements of Enlightenment understanding, yet, unlike Romantic vacancy, it cannot fully divorce itself from passionate or rational forms of reflection. See also earlier essays such as Kathryn Pratt, "Charlotte Smith's Melancholia on the Page and Stage," as well as Elizabeth Dolan's work.

22. See Favret, *War at a Distance* (79–82) and Goodman, *Georgic Modernity* (101–105).

23. For more on Shelley's dialectical propensity for destruction and creation, see Lloyd Robert Abbey, *Destroyer and Preserver: Shelley's Poetic Skepticism*, and Forest Pyle's essay, "Kindling and Ash: Radical Aestheticism in Keats and Shelley."

24. Alongside important work by Kevis Goodman, Noel Jackson, and Adela Pinch, Steven Goldsmith's introduction to *Blake's Agitation* patiently wades through contributions to Romantic notions of affect by James Chandler, Mary Favret, Thomas Pfau, and Jacques Khalip.

25. See Collings's essay, "Emotion without Content: Primary Affect and Pure Potentiality in Wordsworth" in *Romanticism and the Emotions* (183).

26. See "Surfing the Crimson Wave: Romantic New Materialisms and Speculative Feminisms" in *Romanticism and Speculative Realism*.

27. I would contrast vacancy with other accounts of affective history by Favret and Goodman. Favret's necessary anachronism, developed from Ian Baucaom's notion of melancholy historicism, suggests Romanticism's temporality as a wartime loss that is never put to rest but recurs as a perpetual present. Goodman's noise of history similarly limns an unsettled present with the "social experience 'in solution,' not yet or never quite precipitated out in the form of 'known relationships, institutions, formations, positions'" (2).

28. Paul de Man's "The Epistemology of Metaphor," famously demonstrates metaphor's propensity to critique the empirical.

29. See the essays in *Material Events*, which includes Derrida's "Typewriter Ribbon," the *Romantic Materialities* Praxis volume, and of course de Man's essays from *Aesthetic Ideology*, especially "Kant's Materialism."

30. See Karen Barad, "Quantum Entanglements and Hauntological Relations of Inheritance: Dis/continuities, SpaceTime Enfoldings, and Justice-to-Come."

31. For another recent account of the entanglement of science and poiesis, see Janina Wellmann's *The Form of Becoming*, where she discusses the imbrication of rhythm, physiology, and biology in the Romantic period. Specifically, she argues that "the living world, especially organic development, was rethought in terms of rhythmic patterns, rhythmic motion, and rhythmic representation," rhythm being both an abstract measure and a material force (21). Vacancy works through a similar adjunct of abstraction and material force, and certainly rhythm, as Teresa Brennan suggests in *The Transmission of Affect*, is a mechanism for transmitting affect, yet vacancy, I would argue encompasses a much broader material-figural conjunction that includes many other techniques.

32. Both Ellis (7–8) and Csengei (9) also make this argument.

33. Ashley Cross in her investigation of the dialogue between Coleridge and Mary Robinson likewise suggests a moment in his career where he is quite invested in a model for affective, material response that seems to develop sensibility past the bounds of the body or the individual Enlightenment subject.

34. G. S. Rousseau remarked long ago that "Blake reserves nervous sensibility for his men, as if to reverse, even in gender distinctions among mythological figures, the prevalent scientific traditions of his time" (232). See also Chris Bundock's more recent analysis of Blake's problems with but capitulation to the hysterical male, national body, as well as classic work on Blake and gender by Connolly and Helen Bruder. For an exciting new description of affective circulation and contagion, see Lily Gurton-Wachter's forthcoming essay, "Blake's Blush."

35. Marlon Ross and Wolfson have undeniably narrated Keats's resistance to sensibility's effeminizing force, which nevertheless haunted his reputation and gender transgressions. La belle dame and Lamia loom large as epochal demon lovers who arouse the male poet while sucking him dry of material energy, and have their repetition in the figures of woman chasing the poet round the urn in "Ode on Indolence." Rachel Schulkins corrects these views, drawing on Wolfson's accounts of Keats's ambivalence about gender, to suggest that Keats does not abject the feminine, but images of masturbation (sensory and imaginative stimulation) recapture womanhood and disturb the conservative sexual politics of repression. See also Najarian, Hoeveler, Homans, Henderson, Hofkosh.

36. See Wolfson ("Manhood" 18, n19) for this account of negative capability.

37. For Keats and affect, see Thomas Pfau's argument in *Romantic Moods* that Keats's melancholy mood ushers in a Romantic subjectivity that cannot account for the trauma of its own making, and Jonathan Mulrooney's response in "Keats's Avatar," which reads Keats's virtual selves as affectively traveling from one perceptual regime to the next.

38. McGann characterizes what Byron calls the "vacancy absorbing space" as an ironic pleasure "beyond the dialectics of good and evil" (154).

39. See Daniela Garofalo's chapter on Landon in *Women, Love, and Commodity Culture in British Romanticism* and Harriet Kramer Linkin on Landon and Tighe.

40. See for example, Deborah Weiss, "Suffering, Sentiment, and Civilization: Pain and Politics in Mary Wollstonecraft's 'Short Residence.'"

Chapter 1

1. Lauren Berlant's seminal *The Female Complaint: The Unfinished Business of Sentimentality in American Culture* has its precursors and reverberations in Smith scholarship, perhaps beginning with Judith Hawley's "Charlotte Smith's *Elegiac Sonnets*: Losses and Gains"; Elizabeth Dolan's *Seeing Suffering in Women's Literature of the Romantic Era* and "British Romantic Melancholia: Charlotte Smith's Elegiac Sonnets, Medical Discourse and the Problem of Sensibility"; Ildiko Csengei's *Sympathy, Sensibility and the Literature of Feeling in the Eighteenth Century*; and Stokes's "Lorn Subjects: Haunting, Fracture and Ascesis in Charlotte Smith's *Elegiac Sonnets*." We could also add the numerous studies that examine the association between sentiment, hysteria, and the gothic novel, prime examples being Claudia Johnson's *Equivocal Beings: Politics, Gender, and Sentimentality in the 1790s* and Steven Bruhm's *Gothic Bodies: The Politics of Pain in Romantic Fiction*.

2. See Erinç Özdemir, "Charlotte Smith's Poetry as Sentimental Discourse," as well as Behrendt's "Remapping the Landscape: The Romantic Literary Community Revisited"; both have categorized the negativity toward sentiment as a vestige of the sublime or even the aspiration to Romantic, other-worldly transcendence.

3. See Curran's seminal "Romantic Poetry: The I *Altered*."

4. Pinch locates the rhetorical and conventional tenor of sensibility in *Strange Fits of Passion*, while both Jacqueline Labbe in *Charlotte Smith and British Romanticism* and Christoph Bode's "The Subject of *Beachy Head*" reveal the performative and representational qualities of Smith's deconstructive poetics. Most recently, Özdemir highlights sensibility and sentiment as a Bakhtinian discourse in "Charlotte Smith's Poetry as Sentimental Discourse."

5. Perhaps the first essay to make such an influential claim is Jacqueline Labbe's "Selling One's Sorrows: Charlotte Smith, Mary Robinson, and the Marketing of Poetry."

6. Citations from the Prefaces are taken from Stuart Curran's *The Poems of Charlotte Smith*.

7. For a reading that more fully explores how the limpid waves interact with other kinds of materiality in the seascape, see my "Limpid Waves and Good Vibrations: Charlotte Smith's New Materialist Affect." This chapter attempts to consider how Smith leverages such a materiality—outside sensation and the body—not only by describing the contiguity between waves, winds, and human

voice, but through aporetic figures that intertwine the material and linguistic, the human and the nonhuman. So this chapter moves outward from the South Down's internal liquid, fluid ecological world to consider a poetic practice that forges a material relation between the speaker's figuration and the coastal seascape.

8. Goodman makes another claim about Smith's vexed representational practices in "Conjectures on Beachy Head: Charlotte Smith's Geological Poetics and the Grounds of the Present," arguing that the poet in that later poem has another version of form, which she calls "combinatory creativity" that eschews either mimesis or transcription. I would suggest that Smith's figural practices begin as early as the first edition of the *Sonnets* and are interested in figuration as much as form, a figuration that may be combinatory but is even more specifically paradoxical.

9. See Erin Mackie's excellent discussions of fashion, dress, and taste in both her study *Market à la Mode: Fashion, Commodity and Gender in* The Tatler *and* The Spectator and her collection of essays from *The Commerce of Everyday Life: The Tatler and The Spectator*.

10. See especially Timothy Dykstal, "The Politics of Taste in the *Spectator*" and Marc Redfield's introduction to *The Politics of Aesthetics*. Dykstal argues that Addison's ideas about taste helped to shift the main activity of the public sphere from action to "making," that is, the making or selection of consumer goods that would, in turn, signify a class. Redfield, in *The Politics of Aesthetics*, on the other end of the period, traces the political ends of aesthetic discourse through Matthew Arnold's insistence that liberal education would make better or even ideal citizens.

11. For a good discussion of the relative values of the senses, see Denise Gigante's introduction to *Taste*. Hume is used here as the commentator of note because Hume attends to the conjunction of taste, the passions, and women. While there is no external evidence that Smith read anything other than Hume's *History of England*, there are patent similarities between Smith's and Hume's figures of the woodsman or hunter and their discussions of the relationship between insensibility and philosophy. In "The Stoic," for example, Hume depicts him as a representative of that reasoned industry that naturally refines the passions and reaps repose: "See the hardy hunters rise from their downy couches, shake off the slumbers which still weigh down their heavy eyelids, and, ere *Aurora* has yet covered the heavens with her flaming mantle, hasten to the forest. . . . Having exerted in chase every passion of the mind, and every member of the body, he then finds the charms of repose" (*Selected* 86). Unlike Smith's hind, this rural laborer works, sleeps, and *can* taste the charms of nature after a well-deserved repose.

12. We might also think of Shaftesbury who, in his writing on taste, talks about the need to evacuate social concerns in order to arrive at disinterested judgments of taste. See Gigante's *Taste* for a good discussion of Shaftesbury's obsession with literally evacuating and emptying the body of taint to arrive at a personal disinterestedness "from which all idiosyncrasies of birth, habit or circumstance have been purged" (49).

13. Jeffrey Robinson similarly discusses how line and color relate to the categories of imagination and fancy in *Unfettering Poetry: Fancy in British Romanticism* (5–6).

14. For a reading of Smith's androgynous sonnets, see Anne Myers, "Charlotte Smith's Androgynous Sonnets."

15. See, for example, Rodolphe Gasché's *The Idea of Form: Rethinking Kant's Aesthetics* for a longer discussion of this idea.

16. From the standpoint of contemporary theory, Smith's figurative operation might be seen to pose an alternative to the claims by speculative realists or object-oriented ontologists who sue for the primacy of the object over and against the human subject's blindness to its own epistemological and ontological hegemonies. In effect, Smith slips the knot of subject and object by finding a form of figuration that retains materiality outside of the subject. In doing so, she might provide another critique of speculative realism and object-oriented ontologies by showing another way to undermine the tyranny of subjectivity without losing the tools of language, discourse, and figuration.

17. Smith herself used opium occasionally with her friend Henrietta O'Neill, who ended up dying from an opium overdose. Her friend's accidental achievement of quiescence further added to Smith's pain in the loss of a dear friend and a wealthy benefactor.

18. In response to the increasing influx of French émigrés from post-Revolutionary France, Britain enacted the 1793 Alien act, which did not prohibit immigration but required visitors to register with a local justice of the peace and enabled them to be held without bail and deported if deemed in violation of the act.

19. See especially Judith Pascoe, "Female Botanists and the Poetry of Charlotte Smith"; Donnell R. Ruwe, "Charlotte Smith's Sublime: Feminine Poetics, Botany, and *Beachy Head*"; Kandi Tayebi, "Undermining the Eighteenth-Century Pastoral: Rewriting the Poet's Relationship to Nature in Charlotte Smith's Poetry"; Anne D. Wallace, "Picturesque Fossils, Sublime Geology? The Crisis of Authority in Charlotte Smith's *Beachy Head*"; and Theresa Kelley, "Romantic Histories: Charlotte Smith and *Beachy Head*."

20. Ruwe has contended that the poem works to deconstruct both the sublime located in the stupendous cliff and also the beautiful or picturesque found in the poem's pastoral descriptions of the mountain's surface, and Tayebi has similarly argued that Smith unravels the idealized eighteenth-century pastoral by populating the landscape with real shepherd figures.

21. In *Romanticism, Lyricism and History*, Zimmerman argues that Smith's earlier use of memory in the *Sonnets* documents how the poet's growth in this poem becomes the historian's ability to recover past social history. For Zimmerman, the lyric practice associated with memory services Smith's larger historical project, defining memory as a straightforward process of recollection (65). I would instead suggest that Smith's use of repetitious memory involves a cyclical process of selectively remembering, forgetting, and rewriting.

22. I follow Brian Wilkie's account of the epic in *Romantic Poets and The Epic Tradition*. Rather than viewing it as a genre, Wilkie sees the epic as a shared tradition of literary characteristics. Its main attributes include the use of tradition that typically rejects the past (the "epic paradox"), a display of heroism, or a code of conduct, as well as the imitation of various conventions like the ordeal-journey or supernatural agencies. There has not yet been a thorough discussion of "Beachy Head" as an epic poem—or as a Romantic epic, where the journey is an internal one, and the hero Byronic or otherwise conflicted. Smith's poem does not, at first glance, appear to use any of the typical epic conventions she must have known about through reading Milton, Spencer, Ariosto, and others. It does attempt a history of Britain, and Smith's copious descriptions of flora and fauna might qualify as imitations of the listing or series of descriptions in other epic works.

23. Smith's view of the Romans would seem to oppose Edward Gibbon's arguments about the fall of the Roman Empire, which Smith read, according to biographer Loraine Fletcher in *Charlotte Smith: A Critical Biography* (80, 95). Though Smith might agree with Gibbon that, alongside the Romans, an effeminate, English aristocracy was already corrupting the foundation of English Empire, Smith here satirizes imperial, masculine ambition itself—the very drive to make history by conquering peoples and claiming a piece of land as property.

24. Paul de Man most famously proposed this version of history as narrative erasure in "Shelley Disfigured," in *The Rhetoric of Romanticism*.

25. See her book chapter, "Embodied Compassion: The Figure of the Hermit in Charlotte Smith's *Beachy Head*" as well as her article, "The Figure of the Hermit in Charlotte Smith's *Beachy Head*."

26. This law was a particular problem for Smith's daughter, who had married a French émigré, and is a topic of Smith's poem *The Emigrants*, as Amy Garnai discusses in *Revolutionary Imaginings in the 1790s: Charlotte Smith, Mary Robinson, and Elizabeth Inchbald*. My reading of "Beachy Head" as supporting the emancipatory rhetoric of the Revolution follows from Garnai's argument that Smith sustained her radical sympathies throughout her *oeuvre*. I want to suggest, however, that in addition to railing against the oppressive tyranny of the Pitt government and the 1793 Alien Act, Smith is thinking through the theoretical and philosophical underpinnings of "unconditional hospitality," one that moves well beyond a concept of the national alien. For a perspective on Smith's transatlanticism, see Jared Richman's essay on the specters of America within her novel *The Old Manor House*.

27. Monica Smith Hart, "Charlotte Smith's Exilic Persona." Michael Wily likewise writes on Smith's notions of displacement, replacement, and cosmopolitanism. For a more theorized approach, see Kristeva's *Nations without Nationalism*, where she argues, "the universalist breakthrough continued to make progress up to Locke, Shaftesbury, Montesquieu, and, in my opinion, did not die out but rather took on a new orientation with the Freudian discovery of our intrinsic difference; let us know ourselves as unconscious, altered, other in order better to approach the universal otherness of the strangers that we are" (21).

28. Derrida's writing produces the notion of universal hospitality that becomes the impossible condition for the acceptance of the Other, an open-ended cosmopolitan identity and, for Derrida, the promise of democracy. Derrida insists that hospitality occurs before any kind of interpellation that either excludes the visitor or names him a foreigner: "Let us say yes *to who or what turns up*, before any determination, before any anticipation, before any *identification*, whether or not the new arrival is the citizen of another country, a human, animal, or divine creature, a living or dead thing, male or female" (77; emphasis in original).

29. For a reading of "Beachy Head" as Romantic fragment poem, see John Anderson's "The Romantic Fragment Poem As Mosaic." Jacqueline Labbe reads these final moments as both the dissolution of the author and of any stable notion of subjectivity, both of which "disallow closure and resolution" (159). Loraine Fletcher writes that Smith sent "Beachy Head" to her publisher five months before her death, and though she might have been too sick to finish the poem, it is a possibility that she intentionally left the hermit's epitaph unwritten. See *Charlotte Smith: A Critical Biography* (335). Florence Hilbish's earlier biography of Smith may be helpful here as well.

30. For Derrida, the aporia of unconditional hospitality signals "*l'avenir*" or "the Enlightenment-to-come": "criticizing unconditionally all conditionalities" (*Rogues* 142). Here Derrida strives to find a reasonableness beyond the confines or failures of Enlightenment reason. For him, the future-to-come or the Enlightenment-to-come will arrive when the ideals of nationality, law, and eighteenth-century Enlightenment reason are surpassed and exceeded (*Rogues* 143).

31. Aside from Jerome McGann's *Romantic Ideology*, see Alan Liu's seminal *Wordsworth: The Sense of History* for the classic argument on that poet's ideological escape from history.

32. Matthew Bray argues that "Beachy Head" represents Smith's critique of Britain's nationalistic Anglo-Saxon exceptionalism. Rather than seeing the two nations as permanently severed and separate, Bray argues that Smith espouses a shared history between the two nations, encouraging Britain to incorporate French Revolutionary and even Napoleonic ideals. Though the Channel obviously connects France and Britain, the generic figures of the hermit and the mariners he saves, I would argue, seem to suggest the larger global framework of European conflict and cosmopolitanism during the Napoleonic Wars. See Bray, "Removing the Anglo-Saxon Yoke: The Francocentric Vision of Charlotte Smith's Later Works."

Chapter 2

1. Ashley Cross uses this term, "repetition with difference," in her monograph on Mary Robinson to indicate the poet's larger technique of dialogue and exchange (7). My account focuses more narrowly on Robinson's epistemological intervention into forms of habit and repetition, particularly those that involve

the translation of sensation into ideas, and my notion of repetition and difference is drawn specifically from Gilles Deleuze's own parsing of empiricist habits of mind.

2. In "The Myth of Sappho" McGann argues that Sappho's sensibility provides an alternate form of reason, a revolutionary project all its own. Robinson's urbanity and commercial bent has been the fruitful subject of many essays including Judith Pascoe's "The Spectacular Flâneuse: Mary Robinson and the City of London," Diego Saglia's "Commerce, Luxury, and Identity in Mary Robinson's *Memoirs*," and Timothy Webb's "Listing the Busy Sounds: Anna Seward, Mary Robinson, and the Poetic Challenge of the City." For scholarship more squarely on empiricist sensation, see Jeffrey C. Robinson's *Unfettering Poetry: The Fancy in British Romanticism* and Ashley Cross's long essay on Robinson and Coleridge's poetic conversation, which supplies a more empiricist account of their depictions of passive sensation via the Aeolian harp. This chapter not only argues for Robinson's critique of sensibility but also suggests that Robinson's investigation of sensation consists of an extremely thorough speculative, epistemological project that pervades her career.

3. It seems clear that Robinson was at least familiar with Lockean concepts of knowledge and education. Julie Shaffer, for example, points out in her Broadview edition of Robinson's novel *Walsingham* that Robinson draws on the epistemological and educational theories of Locke when she describes Walsingham's tenacious memories and impressions of his childhood home (47n1).

4. For precedents on Deleuze used for feminist critique of the empirical body and its gender implications, see Ian Buchanan and Claire Colebrook's *Deleuze and Feminist Theory*.

5. For an encapsulation of the antagonism between affect on the one hand and language, meaning, and intention on the other, see Ruth Leys, "The Turn to Affect: A Critique."

6. We might also consider Locke's broader discussion of interrupted consciousness, including the problems of forgetting, sleep, and drunkenness, in chapter XXVII, "Of Identity and Diversity," beginning especially with section 10, as part and parcel of this larger consideration about the mind's propensity for returning to a blank state.

7. For more on Locke and the void in a philosophical and historical context, see Edward Grant's *Much Ado about Nothing*.

8. Both D. Robinson's and Cross's readings overturn Jerome McGann's long-cited view that Sappho gloriously displays the "social, philosophical, and intellectual power of 'sensibility'" (126) to break through emotional and intellectual convention (130).

9. Daniel Robinson argues that Robinson has a feminine rivalry with other women poets, including Smith, and by refusing to mention them by name in her introduction to the sonnet sequence she effectively silences them in her drive to capture the poetic of laurel of fame for herself; see D. Robinson, *The Poetry of*

Mary Robinson (123). See also Cross chapter in *Mary Robinson and the Genius of Romanticism*, where she alters this reading by suggesting that Robinson formed a dialogue—however unwanted—with Smith on the nature of the sonnet.

10. Stuart Curran first heralded this estimation of Smith's poetics and her influence, beginning with his introduction to *The Poems of Charlotte Smith* in 1993 (xxvi). See also Sandro Jung, "Some Notes on the 'Single Sentiment' and Romanticism of Charlotte Smith," and Silvia Mergenthal, "Charlotte Smith and the Romantic Sonnet Revival."

11. Although a leap of twenty yards (sixty feet) may not cause certain death, it does potentially pose a mortal danger. By extension, Locke's example suggests that freedom entails the ability to commit potentially suicidal acts. For a much longer discussion on Robinson's portrayal of a Romantic suicide influenced by Locke as well as Mary Wollstonecraft and William Godwin, see Singer, "Mary Robinson and the Idiot's Guide to Suicide and Oblivion." For a broader revision of Romantic suicide, see Michelle Faubert, "A Family Affair: Ennobling Suicide in Mary Shelley's *Matilda*."

12. This liberatory gesture undoubtedly draws from Johann van Goethe's *Sorrows of Young Werther*.

13. This reading is indebted to Jane Bennett's *Vibrant Matter* and her notions of distributive agencies among and between human bodies and things, very much inspired by Deleuze's own work with sensation, materiality, and assemblages. Robinson, I want to suggest, begins to articulate ways to think of humans interacting with the material world that might put us in conversation with those theorists like Bennett who are interested in an intensely particulate, material world, beyond the rational, reflective, and sensory models of Enlightenment subjectivity that separate and privilege the mind from the world. As Brian Massumi and Romantic scholars such as Mary Favret have argued, affect very much can be seen as part of the material world, both within and without the body.

14. Ballad collecting gained steam in the mid-eighteenth century with *Reliques* (1765) by Thomas Percy, who notoriously attempted to produce originary and authorial versions of many traditional ballads. Other editors, such as Joseph Ritson, would critique Percy's editing methods, offering another model for ballad collecting with *Robin Hood: A Collection of All the Ancient Poems, Songs, and Ballads, now Extant* (1795). This volume gathered a number of ballad variants, helping to shape an understanding of any one ballad as a collection of tales and tunes circulating around a generalized plot or trope. Robinson often revised her ballads as they traveled from newspaper verse in the *Morning Post* to her volume *Lyrical Tales*, and one might go so far as to argue that Robinson was a part of the new vanguard who sought to highlight or exploit the ballad's instability as one of its most interesting characteristics. Nick Groom recounts Percy's editorial practices in *The Making of Percy's Reliques*. Stephanie Barczewski cites Ritson's revolutionary editing in *Myth and National Identity in Nineteenth-Century Britain: The Legends of King Arthur and Robin Hood* (99–100).

15. Daniel Robinson and Cross have both compellingly written about Robinson's forays into newspaper verse and the conversations such verse spurred between Robinson, Coleridge, and Southey. Cross most recently has renovated the newspaper poems as a particularly important genre for all writers and their experimentation in the limits of sensibility and humanity through the leitmotif of insects. See Robinson, "The Poets 'Perplext': Southey and Robinson at Work on the *Morning Post*," and Cross, "Robert Southey and Mary Robinson in Dialogue."

16. Cross's "From *Lyrical Ballads* to *Lyrical Tales*: Mary Robinson's Reputation and the Problem of Literary Debt" most strenuously argues for a realignment of our understanding of the literary debts that Robinson, Coleridge, and Wordsworth all owe to each other, reversing the standard narrative that Robinson in some sense was beholden to the earlier male poets' volume. For Cross's account of Robinson's dialogue with Robert Southey about the newspaper poem, including the ballad romance, see her chapter on the two poets in *Mary Robinson and the Genesis of Romanticism*.

17. In "Mary Robinson and the New Lyric," Curran has remarked on this poem's postmodern texture, what he calls "the vacuity in signification at the heart of modern culture" with a style of "no essence only representation" that attends to signification without stable or needful reference (13, 12). The argument to be made here entails the poem as not merely repeating signifiers to excess but jettisoning standard Enlightenment representations to arrive at a rich texture of materiality created through the repetitive articulacy of the idiot.

18. I take this idea about the lyric from Sarah Zimmerman in *Romanticism, Lyricism and History*, who, of course, derives the idea of overhearing from John Stuart Mill's essay on lyric poetry. Zimmerman argues that the lyric was a very public, social genre, written to be overheard and to employ its audiences in social and personal reflection. Robinson seems to argue something similar by having a boy cry "alone"—a gesture that both articulates his solitude and his wish to have an audience who will not only hear him but also participate in reconstructing his story.

19. See Craig's chapter, "'Kant Has Not Answered Hume'" in *Romantic Empiricism: Poetics and the Philosophy of Common Sense, 1780–1830*.

20. See Alan Bewell's discussion of hypothetical histories in *Wordsworth and the Enlightenment* (57–64).

21. For a reading of this plot as playing into notions of the gothic sentiments and violence, see Jacqueline Labbe's "Romance and Violence in Mary Robinson's *Lyrical Tales* and Other Gothic Poetry."

22. I am, of course, referencing James Chandler's influential chapter on Wordsworth's quiescent turn to Burke's customs and habitual feeling in *Wordsworth's Second Nature*, a stance Robinson's full-throttle rejection of empiricism routes.

23. In the mid-1790s Robinson met both Coleridge and Godwin, and, as we know from Godwin's diary, Robinson socialized with his radical set and would have been familiar with the empiricist underpinnings of their works. Biographer

Paula Byrne reminds us that Robinson met both men in February 1796 and published *Sappho and Phaon* in October of that same year (321–323).

24. Robinson's radical political affiliations have most astutely been tracked by Adriana Craciun in *Fatal Women of Romanticism* and *British Women Writers and the French Revolution*; Amy Garnai's *Revolutionary Imaginings of the 1790s: Charlotte Smith, Mary Robinson, Elizabeth Inchbald*; and Harried Guest, "Charlotte Smith, Mary Robinson, and the First Year of War with France."

25. See Edward Royle and James Walvin, *English Radicals and Reformers 1760–1848* (91–92) for an account of the government's attacks on the democratic societies.

26. Ashley Cross explores Robinson's thinking about the 1790s spy culture and paranoia in her brilliant monograph chapter on Robinson's rewriting of Godwin's *Caleb Williams* into a queer panic in her novel *Walsingham*.

27. See Ronell's book *Stupidity* for a thorough discussion of the Romantic idiot, particularly Wordsworth's idiot boys (246–277). Here Robinson's vacancy may bear some resemblance to Sianne Ngai's aesthetics of stuplimity, not in the way stuplimity holds opposing affects together, but in the way both stupefies and, at the same time, opposes sublimity's recuperation of the thinking, rational subject (267–271). Ngai's notion sounds even more like Robinson's tactics when Ngai describes it in terms of Deleuzean repetition: "a relationship to language founded on a not-yet-qualified or -conceptualized difference" (252).

28. For Alan Bewell, Johnny's vacant mind fosters a receptivity to a quasi-religious, prelinguistic nature, with its nonrational, amazing educative power (65). In an article about Wordsworth's vacancy, Joseph Viscomi likewise argues that Wordsworth uses "mental vacancy" in *Lyrical Ballads* to refer to "the tranquility induced by nature's sedating sounds, which vacates and prepares the mind to receive nature's impulse" (44). Both Chandler in *Wordsworth's Second Nature* and David Bromwich in *Disowned by Memory* argue that Wordsworth's grappling with associationist principles brings him to espouse a blind mechanism that leads to habits of feeling that make us human. William Ulmer likewise provides a recent narrative about Wordsworth's rejection of Godwinian association for Hartleyan feeling, elaborating on the hints of his more comprehensive rejection of empiricism in "Tintern Abbey." Even more recent accounts of Wordsworth's philosophy of association in the *Preface*, such as Rowan Boyson's *Wordsworth and the Enlightenment Idea of Pleasure*, suggest that whether or not Wordsworth resuscitates or rejects Burkean habit, his poetry attempts to address men through the pleasures of fellow feeling.

29. See Sha's discussion of force and metonymy in *Romanticism and the Emotions* (22), its ability to elide substance and movement (29), as well as his discussion of how emotion as force or transmission extends beyond the human (31).

30. The most generous commentators appraise the relationship between the two poets as "a confluence of aspiration," as Susan Luther described it more than twenty years ago (396). Recent criticism by Daniel Robinson and Ashley Cross has aimed at restoring the literary and textual networks surrounding the *Morning Post*

as the setting through which to understand the poetical exchanges of Coleridge, Southey, and Robinson, who all wrote regularly for the paper. Earlier essays have suggested other aspects of the relationship, attempting to decipher Coleridge's praise for Robinson's ear, his concern for her health, but also his criticism of her work, and his refusal to contribute to a tribute volume after her death. Eugene Stelzig argues that at the end of her life Robinson sought fame by linking her works to a younger generation of poets. Judith Hawley takes a more conservative position and views Coleridge as acting as Robinson's patron—supporting her poetic efforts, defending her reputation, but distancing himself from her after her death. Tim Fulford's "Mary Robinson and the Abyssinian Maid," in assessing the gender dynamics of their relationship, claims that Coleridge used Robinson as a muse, adopting her feminine voice and music even while desiring a position as the dominant poet. Ledbetter and Cross similarly both contend that it was Robinson's poems that provided inspiration (and material) for Coleridge, who had much to benefit from the older poet's celebrity and experience. My argument seeks to underline the philosophical component of their conversation.

31. There is no conclusive evidence to explain why Coleridge showed Robinson "Kubla Khan," a poem he was protective of, though Martin Levy has claimed it was because both used opium and had drug-induced poetic experiences. Paula Byrne suggests that the exchange actually may have begun earlier, with Robinson's poem "The Maniac," originally published as "Insanity" in the *Oracle* in 1791. Robinson's daughter alleged that this poem about "Mad Jemmy" was written during an opium-induced haze, a topic Daniel Robinson also explores when he argues that the two poets began and remained in a heady poetic conversation about the topic of dreams and the unconscious. Both Cross and D. Robinson have duly explored the larger conversation between the two poets through poems that, if not exchanged, were speaking to each other in the pages of popular newspapers. Moreover, as Byrne points out, the effects of drug use are compared to philosophy in Robinson's 1796 novel *Angelina* (272), and I would argue that if anything the exchange of these poems represents Robinson and Coleridge in a wider discussion not simply about opium but about the ways in which abnormal psychology might depict and explore empiricist epistemologies.

32. Coleridge, of course, garners his own rejection of empiricism. By this time he had already become familiar with Kant's alternative critical philosophy, as Monika Class has recently argued. While his trenchant rejection of associationism is traditionally dated from 1800–1801, it may be that "Kubla Khan"'s imaginative failure, marked by the loss of poetic voice as the poem becomes a fragment, signals the demise of Hartleyan mechanistic fancy in Coleridge's aesthetic epistemology. See David S. Hogsette's reading of "Kubla Khan" as Coleridge's early rejection of Hartleyan association for the Kantian "pure imagination" in "Eclipsed by the Pleasure Dome: Poetic Failure in Coleridge's 'Kubla Kahn.'" For the opposing view, placing Coleridge's repudiation later, see William Hatherell's "'Words and Things': Locke, Hartley and the Associationist Context for the Preface to *Lyrical Ballads*."

33. Daniel Robinson's essay, "From 'Mingled Measure' to 'Ecstatic Measures': Mary Robinson's Poetic Reading of 'Kubla Khan,'" explores the rhythmic variations that Robinson used to compose "To the Poet Coleridge," which Robinson argues was part of the female poet's ambition not to imitate the male poet's dexterity but to challenge it with her own metrical prowess and combinations.

34. See Mitchell's discussion of Shelley's rhyme in "The Transcendental: Deleuze, P. B. Shelley and the Freedom of Immobility" and David Collings's response, "Rhyming Sensations in 'Mont Blanc,'" where he specifically calls critics to find other poetic procedures of such Deleuzean intensity.

35. For more on the physics of emotion, see Richard Sha's "The Motion behind Romantic Emotion: Towards a Chemistry and Physics of Feeling" in *Romanticism and the Emotions*.

36. Various Deleuzean-inspired theorists have developed notions of the localized field. For Brian Massumi, "a shape or structure begins to form, but no sooner dissolves as its region shifts in relation to the others with which it is in tension" (34), while for Karen Barad matter aggregates into phenomena that "enact a *local* resolution *within* the phenomenon of the inherent ontological indeterminacy" (133). See Massumi's *Parables for the Virtual* and Barad's "Posthuman Performativity: Toward an Understanding of How Matter Comes to Matter."

37. See Fulford, "Mary Robinson and the Abyssinian Maid," for this reading of "Kubla Khan."

Chapter 3

1. In his discussion of male Romantics' depictions of motherese in *The Neural Sublime*, Alan Richardson argues that feminine moaning and presemantic sounds represent a male anxiety about women's claims to poetic language and to language acquisition. This wave of feminist criticism of high Romanticism might also include Richardson's "Romanticism and the Colonization of the Feminine"; Marlon Ross, *The Contours of Masculine Desire*; Sonia Hofkosh, "A Woman's Profession: Sexual Difference and the Romance of Authorship"; Mary Jacobus, *Romanticism, Writing, and Sexual Difference*; Adriana Craciun, *The Fatal Women of Romanticism*; Diane Long Hoeveler, *Romantic Androgyny: The Women Within*; Susan J. Wolfson, *Borderlines: The Shiftings of Gender in British Romanticism*, "'Something must be done': Shelley, Hemans, and the Flash of Revolutionary Female Violence," "Keats and the Manhood of the Poet," "*Lyrical Ballads* and the Language of (Men) Feeling: Wordsworth Writing Women's Voices," and "'Their She Condition': Cross-Dressing and the Politics of Gender in *Don Juan*"; Timothy Fulford, "Mary Robinson and the Abyssinian Maid: Coleridge's Muses and Feminist Criticism"; Elizabeth Fay, *Becoming Wordsworthian: A Performative Aesthetics*; and many of the essays in Anne K. Mellor's *Romanticism and Feminism*. Of course, more recent work, particularly on Wordsworth but also on other writers, has sought to bring

male and female writers into amicable conversation, perhaps first and foremost is Beth Lau's edited collection *Fellow Travelers* and Jacqueline Labbe's *Writing Romanticism: Charlotte Smith and William Wordsworth, 1784–1807*. See as well Ashley Cross's discussion of gender dynamics of the demon lover trope in *Mary Robinson and the Genesis of Romanticism: Literary Dialogues and Debts, 1784–1821* (209) and Rachel Schulkins's reevaluation of feminist Keats criticism in *Keats, Modesty and Masturbation* (5–6).

2. See, for example, Timothy Clark's *Embodying Revolution: The Figure of the Poet in Shelley*, Jennifer Lokash's "Shelley's Organic Sympathy: Natural Communitarianism and the Example of Alastor," Teddi Chichester Bonca's *Shelley's Mirrors of Love*, or Robert Mitchell's "The Transcendental: Deleuze, P. B. Shelley, and the Freedom of Immobility."

3. Jerrold E. Hogle's *Shelley's Process: Radical Transference and the Development of His Major Works* similarly characterizes the poem's fascination with "the motion that produces mind" but in rich psychoanalytic and deconstructive veins (75).

4. Christopher Nagel has most recently examined Wordsworth's debt to and use of (rather than resistance to) sensibility.

5. Duncan Wu, in "Wordsworth and Sensibility," likewise demonstrates how much Wordsworth learned from the feminine poetics of sensibility gleaned in his reading and response to Helen Maria Williams, Charlotte Smith, and gothic texts, particularly his attention and allergy to "emotional extremity" (477). Brent Raycroft retraces the genealogy of the Romantic sonnet of sensibility.

6. This form of insensibility likewise marks intriguing similarities to William Godwin's *Fleetwood* (56) and perhaps even Lord Byron's descriptions of the gluttonous but vacant Childe Harold in Cantos I and III.

7. For an alternative reading of the women in these poems as evincing a tension between medical hysteria and the imagination, see Alan Bewell's "'A Word Scarce Said': Hysteria and Witchcraft in Women's Poetry."

8. John Barrell's "The Uses of Dorothy" in *Language, Poetry, and Politics* is perhaps the seminal text that arrogates Wordsworth's "language of reflection" from Dorothy's "language of sense." Even more trenchant investigations of Wordsworth's women and their repetitive, disruptive voices include Adela Pinch's chapter on Wordsworth in *Strange Fits of Passion* and Susan J. Wolfson's "*Lyrical Ballads* and the Language of (Men) Feeling."

9. See also the debate within Wordsworth scholarship regarding Wordsworth and the sonnet of sensibility, helpfully summarized by Peter Spratley, who argues that ultimately Wordsworth manages his relation to gendered poetics with the "assumption and appropriation of the voice of sensibility in his sonnets" (98).

10. Both Joseph Viscomi, in his essay "Wordsworth, Gilpin and the Vacant Mind," and Mary Jacobus, in her chapter on Wordsworth's vacancy in *Romantic Things*, attend to the deconstructive nature of Wordsworth's aesthetics, what Jacobus describes as "both an unbalanced state of mind and a description of the mind's unplumbed depths" (129). My argument here is that Wordsworth anticipates,

even if he does not fully explore, a more radical figure that moves beyond the depth model of the mind to seek a more lateral, transmissive, and posthuman affect through figural movement among bodies, whose transgression is modeled on the citation and undermining of gender difference.

11. Certainly Wordsworthian emotion has garnered critical attention for its tendency to eschew strict gender boundaries and for its instigation of Romantic contingency. The preference in the poem for rational sympathy may be, as Wolfson suggests, "sympathy . . . with a masculine infusion" (*Lyrical Ballads* 33), his natural piety an emotion closer to Anne-Lise François's notion of "a kind of trust and openness to contingency" (François 63). Yet, I am arguing that Wordsworth's continual resort to gender nearly always returns us to the vale of binaristic sentiment gendered through sensibility and sensation.

12. Barker-Benfield reminds us that the word "thrill" was language endemic to sensibility: "[v]ibrations' more common synonym . . . was 'thrill.' . . . 'Thrill' was an old verb (a variant of 'drill') meaning to flow, trickle, or percolate" (20).

13. See Richardson, *The Neural Sublime* (136), and his "Romanticism and the Colonization of the Feminine" in *Romanticism and Feminism*. See also Peter J. Manning's reading of the poem in *Reading Romantics: Texts and Contexts*.

14. For an analysis of melancholy as an emotional structure of racial encounter, see Anne Anlin Cheng, *The Melancholy of Race*: *Psychoanalysis, Assimilation and Hidden Grief*.

15. For earlier treatments of Romanticism and doubt, see Laura Quinney, *The Poetics of Disappointment: Wordsworth to Ashbery*, and Andrew M. Cooper's *Doubt and Identity in Romantic Poetry*. See also Don H. Bialostosky's *Wordsworth, Dialogics and the Practice of Criticism* for a different approach to Wordsworth's penchant for critique.

16. Collings, writing of Wordsworth and affect, describes "primary affect" as "the utter loss of a world, in the erasure of any *specific* form, image, motive, thought, or feeling" (183). For Collings, such primary affect is predicated on loss of the mother-child relationship. Although, as "a space logically prior to any particular affective scenario" (184), it is not inherently gendered, this account—predicated as it is on the loss of the mother as the alibi for the loss of all reality and figuration—reinscribes affect, for Wordsworth, as a gendered lack. Woman becomes the perennial figure of loss—both the loss of control of her own feelings (sensibility's excess) and the loss eventuating in the infant's own lack of attachment and nourishment.

17. For another reading of such affective force, see Marjorie Levinson's article on Spinozan affect in "A Slumber Did My Spirit Seal." Levinson emphasizes how Lucy becomes part of a larger affective terrain of the rocks and trees at the end of the poem, and we could contrast and contemplate that reading here as perhaps offering an affect that dispenses with Lucy's gender at the same time it amplifies the loss of the feminine (or girlhood) as the foundation for affect, as Collings similarly argues. In other words, Wordsworth's "motion and spirit" that "rolls through all

things" often has a double relation to gender, both critiquing and reifying it—a relation that Shelley seeks to radicalize.

18. For readings of the "Alastor" poet as modeled on (and as a critique of) the Wordsworthian poet, see for example, Francesca Cauchi, "A Rereading of Wordsworth's Presence in Shelley's Alastor"; Yvonne Carothers, "Alastor: Shelley Corrects Wordsworth"; and Paul Mueschke and Earl L. Griggs, "Wordsworth as the Prototype of the Poet in Shelley's Alastor."

19. Also useful in probing this problem is Robert Mitchell's essay on suspended animation in Coleridge and both Shelleys, a kind of ontological and physiological trance. According to Mitchell, such animation describes a vitality that exists without movement, a similar but very different formulation of Shelleyan affect that might be seen as a posthuman vitality that works specifically through movement.

20. See Clark's *Embodying Revolution: The Figure of the Poet in Shelley*. Clark, too, argues for the vacancy in "Alastor" as an emptiness, but more of an existential one, or the absence of a poetic identity.

21. See Baker, Griggs, Blank, and Brown for earlier readings of the veiled maid that signal the Poet's failed imagination—whether of nature or the feminine—which results in despair or suicide. Fischman, as well, provides a condensed summary of pertinent criticism in her article on "Alastor."

22. Sydney Owenson's Luxima from *The Missionary* has been seen as a prototype for the impassioned veiled maid, her Hindu religious beliefs conveyed by a sensual character that reinforces gendered stereotypes. The poet's quest for the veiled maid may represent "an unmasking of Britain's desire for its Indian Other" (Leask, *British East* 123). Although, for Alvey, the Westerner might initially desire not to look upon the East with a scientific, imperialist gaze, ultimately, he falls prey to his "passion for the Orient that images the sensuous female Orient as an object of its desire and conquest" (81). Tilar Mazzeo's essay on Shelley and his circle's interest in Indian music sutures the discourse of feminine sensibility to notions of the feminine East: "*Alastor* is essentially and importantly a poem about the ability of Indian music, especially as performed by a seductive woman, to evoke irrational sympathies and to overpower the will of the listener," demonstrating "the power of Indian culture and its subalterns to seduce the imperialist" (186). In addition to Mazzeo's depiction of the maid's performed Indian music, Susan Fischman's view of the veiled maid as the Echo to the poet's Narcissus engenders a reading of the maid as a poetess, if not a poet.

23. We should not forget Asia, whose long dialogue with Demogorgon can be seen as an act of women's writing. For a discussion of that poem's revolutionary feminist agenda, see Kate Singer, "Stoned Shelley: Revolutionary Tactics and Women under the Influence."

24. For a reading tying together Shelley's interest in electricity, magnetism, and sympathy, see Bonca's *Shelley's Mirrors of Love*, P. M. S. Dawson's "'A Sort of Animal Magic': Shelley and Animal Magnetism," Tim Fulford's "Conducting

The Vital Fluid: The Politics and Poetics of Mesmerism in the 1790s," and Leask, "Shelley's 'Magnetic Ladies': Romantic Mesmerism and the Politics of the Body."

25. Mary Shelley may be the most famous of Percy's female literary companions, but Claire Clairmont was writing journals and short fiction, and Shelley admired Teresa Emilia Viviani for her writing. Harriet Westbrook Shelley's commonplace book attests to the couple's mutual poetic reading, and for some time Westbrook was thought to have authored some of the poems collected in Shelley's early *Esdaile Notebook*. Slightly less ambiguous, Shelley's very first volume, *Poems of Victor and Cazir*, included poems jointly authored with the poet's sister, Elizabeth. Moreover, his early work in *Posthumous Fragments of Margaret Nichols* and select poems in the *Esdaile Notebook* ventriloquize women's voices. See especially Sharon Lynne Joffe's *The Kinship Coterie and the Literary Endeavors of the Women in the Shelley Circle*.

26. In Hartley's pathology, violent passions can be termed a "temporary madness" but frequent recurrences often "transport" such persons "so that they shall not be able to recover themselves, but fall within the limits of the distemper called madness emphatically" (399).

27. According to Clark, Shelley transformed the man of feeling, physiologically sensitive to minute perceptions, into the ideal poet: "It is sensibility whereby, for Shelley, poets become poets, or are better poets than others" (44). Those with an eye on Shelley's interest in medicine and science have likewise attested to his familiarity with vitality debates, his interest in electricity from early youth, his later fascination with mesmerism, as well as his knowledge of miscellaneous medical tracts like those of Thomas Trotter that detailed the physiological extremes of intoxication, madness, and delusion, linking them to embodied sensitivity. Sharon Ruston's *Shelley and Vitality* discusses the poet in the context of vitality debates; Nora Crook and Derek Guiton's *Shelley's Venomed Melody* provides a foundational text for Shelley and medicine; and Timothy Morton's *Shelley and the Revolution in Taste* discusses Shelley, the body, and the natural world.

28. Evan Gottlieb notes, as Jackson had before him, "'nervous vibrunticles' facilitated the internal communication of ideas and feelings" ("Seeing" 148).

29. Allen has argued that the analogies within Hartley's work, for example, those charting the harmonics underlying sound and color, suggest "a potential for a much more extensive unification of phenomena—indeed, for a future integration of all forms of vibrations in one 'grand unified theory'" (102). Early in letters to both Thomas Hogg and Elizabeth Hitchener, Shelley too evinces a unified theory that underlies analogical relations of soul, spirit, and vital materialism: "The word God then, in the sense which you take it analogises with the *universe*, as the soul of man to his body, as the vegetative power to vegetals, the stony power to stones." These powers Shelley articulates not simply as analogy but as Spinozan "synonime for the *existing power of existence*" or "the *essence* of the universe, the universe is the essence of it" (*Letters* 100, 101). If "intelligence & bodily animation" are "conjoined" for Shelley, so are the various sorts of materials that affect

both body and mind. See Shelley's June 11, 1811, letter to Hitchener, but also earlier letters to Hogg on January 6 and 12, 1811.

30. Nigel Leask, for one, has associated this group of abstractions with French Revolutionary catchphrases and the Wollstonecraftian rejection of Rousseauvian sensuality for libertarian rationality. Yet the specific description of the whorls of her song seems much closer to the poetics of sensibility, particularly the version championed by Helen Maria Williams. Shelley was certainly familiar with Williams's *Letters Written in France*, which propounds the infectious virtues of sublime sensibility, "that general sympathy which is caught from heart to heart with irresistible energy, fills every eye with tears, and throbs in every bosom" (90).

31. See, for example, Claudia Johnson's and Barker-Benfield's readings of Wollstonecraft.

32. See Judson's "The Politics of Medusa: Shelley's Physiognomy of Revolution."

33. This projection occurs for both the narrator and the readers of "Alastor," as Tilottama Rajan has argued in *Dark Interpreter*.

34. Here we might see Shelley, as Robinson does in "To Sight," considering philosophical ideas about the existence of a vacuum, a space without matter. Locke argued against the concept of a plenum (or aether-filled space), insisting that there must be these spaces for particles to move within and that body and space are not one and the same. When the "Alastor" poet's mind becomes a vacuum, which then allows him only to see wastes and, alternately, places of roiling materiality, we might read Shelley as critiquing the either/or position of the plenum and the vacuum. This binaristic attitude toward materiality, the poem suggests, comes not simply from this history of philosophy but from sensibility's translation of it into the impulses of excess and absence, which has become seductive through the pursuit of the veiled maiden's eyes—the pursuit of love's material, intersubjective presence, which can only result in failure and the vacuum of absence.

35. We can find good, though circumstantial, evidence in Harriet Westbrook Shelley's commonplace book that Shelley read Smith's sonnets. In it, Harriet recorded poems by Amelia Opie and Charlotte Smith, and the second half of the book contains poetry that "treats women's status in society and the changes needed to improve that," with the last three pages specifically recording poems "on the value of women in both the public and the private spheres" (*CPPBS* II 331). Internal tropic echoes reinforce such connections.

36. I am again referring to John Barrell's seminal essay, "The Uses of Dorothy" and Dorothy as the carrier of the "language of sense."

37. See Francis Ferguson's seminal "Shelley's 'Mont Blanc': What the Mountain Said," Angela Leighton's *Shelley and the Sublime*, and of course Earl Wasserman's interpretation in *Shelley: A Critical Reading*.

38. See Cian Duffy's *Shelley and the Revolutionary Sublime* and Hugo Donnelly, "Beyond Rational Discourse: The 'Mysterious Tongue' of 'Mont Blanc.'" A more equivocal position might be had in seeing the mountain and its loud, lone sound as the voice of Shelleyan skepticism, beginning with C. E. Pulos's *The Deep Truth:*

A Study of Shelley's Scepticism and Donald H. Reiman's *Intervals of Inspiration: The Skeptical Tradition and the Psychology of Romanticism*. See, as well, Son-Moo Ryu's essay on the politics of vacancy and Tim Milnes's more recent *The Truth about Romanticism: Pragmatism and Idealism in Keats, Shelley, Coleridge*.

39. For a pointed reading of the Lucretian echoes in "Mont Blanc," see Jane E. Phillips, "Lucretian Echoes in Shelley's 'Mont Blanc,'" which works from Paul Turner's longer study, "Shelley and Lucretius." Other important Lucretian readings of Shelley's "Epipsychidion" and "Triumph of Life" include Andrew Warren, "Unentangled Intermixture: Love and Materialism in Shelley's 'Epipsychidion,'" Warren's chapter in *The Orient and the Young Romantics*, and Goldstein's "Growing Old Together: Lucretian Materialism in Shelley's 'Poetry of Life.'"

40. Readings in this vein include Anne C. McCarthy's "The Aesthetics of Contingency in the Shelleyan 'Universe of Things,' or, 'Mont Blanc' without Mont Blanc"; Steven Shaviro, *The Universe of Things*; Evan Gottlieb's chapter on Shelley in *Romantic Realities: Speculative Realism and British Romanticism*; and Chris Washington's chapter on Mont Blanc in *Romantic Revelations*.

41. This reading and what follows works in part from notions of materiality culled both from affect studies and from new materialism, both of which tie the human and nonhuman in relation via their exchanges of mutual materiality, "as much force as entity, as much energy as matter" (Bennett 20) and sometimes even through an incorporeal materiality, or all the potential moves the body might make even if it does not actualize them (Massumi 5). Where Bennett and Massumi fall mostly silent on the affective efficacy of language (except perhaps in brief comments on the paradoxical benefits of anthropomorphism), Shelley, I hope to show, gives us a new materialist literary methodology.

42. Goldstein, working from Allewaert, more specifically examines the contiguity between figure and materiality in Shelley's Lucretian physics and the prosopopoeia of "Triumph of Life." She writes, "figures are fractions of the real estranged from their sources, and all bodies, not just verbal ones, are granted the capacity, indeed the necessity, of producing them. Beings transpire into tropes, because to have a physical figure, a body compounded of parts, is to emit figures as those parts fall away" (74).

43. The poem's focus on desire and eros has influenced many studies, including Warren's "Unentangled Intermixture"; William A. Ulmer, "The Politics of Metaphor in Shelley's *Epipsychidion*"; Robert N. Essick, "'A Shadow of Some Golden Dream': Shelley's Language in *Epipsychidion*"; and Ghislaine McDayter, "O'er Leaping the Bounds: The Sexing of the Creative Soul in Shelley's *Epipsychidion*."

44. Kenneth Neill Cameron's classic argument about the biographical basis for "Epipsychidion" can be found in "The Planet-Tempest Passage in *Epipsychidion*."

45. See Ulmer's similar claims about the deconstructive nature of desire to "engender an open-ended dialectic which resists its own final synthesis" (546).

46. O'Malley writes of the synesthesia surrounding Emily as a unity of light, rather than affect, placed through a prism: "Thinking of Emily as an incarnate

ray of the 'great Brightness,' one recalls the supposedly Averroistic concept of the universal soul's being 'a spiritual radiance broken up, coloured and particularized by the prisms of our bodies'" (95).

47. For a longer discussion of Shelley's insight into particle-wave physics, see Mark Lussier's *Romantic Dynamics: The Poetics of Physicality* and his earlier article, "Shelley's Poetics, Wave Dynamics, and the Telling Rhythm of Complementarity," as well as Arkady Plotnitsky's work on Shelley and quantum physics, "All Shapes of Light: The Quantum Mechanical Shelley."

Chapter 4

1. For example, Evan Gottlieb and Francesco Crocco have examined Hemans's conservative patriotic fervor in such early works as *England and Spain* (1808) and *Modern Greece* (1817), while others have just as easily considered her support of a democratic liberalism skeptical of those melancholy sacrifices required of matrons, which Diego Saglia, Nanora Sweet, and Gary Kelly have found in *The Vespers of Palermo* (1823), *The Siege of Valencia* (1823), and *The Forest Sanctuary* (1825). Most recently, in "England and Spain and The Domestic Affections: Felicia Hemans and the Politics of Literature," Juan Sanchez shifts away from ideological critique to explore the "special" ways that Hemans's poetry helps to articulate the perceptions of politics in the nineteenth century. His investigation of "destabilizing literary tropes" in contrast to the more stable narratives of her poems has affinities with this chapter's methodology (400). See as well, Benjamin Kim's thick synopsis of scholarly accounts of Hemans's politics at the start of chapter four, *Wordsworth, Hemans, and Politics, 1800–1830: Romantic Crises*. A swath of scholarship considers Hemans's use of Classical art objects and historiography to various political ends, for example, Westover, Wolfson, Comet, and Williamson, among others.

2. For conflicting views of the more conservative and more liberal Hemans, see Francesco Crocco, "The Ruins of Empire: Nationalism, Art, and Empire in Hemans's Modern Greece," much of Nanora Sweet's work, and Juan Sanchez, "*England and Spain* and the *Domestic Affections*: Felicia Hemans and the Politics of Literature." Claire Knowles, following Angela Leighton's and Stephen Behrendt's earlier arguments, suggests that Hemans, in the course of her career, turns from the more sensational and disturbing vicissitudes of sensibility to a restrained, delicate, feminine, and domesticated sentimentality, a "motherly poetic persona" that leads the way to the Victorian angel in the house (113). Susan J. Wolfson gestures toward a "macrotext" of impassioned revolutionary women, as does McGann's "ideological network," or Diego Saglia's more recent triangulation between the local, regional, and global languages and cultures evoked in her *oeuvre*. See Leighton's *Victorian Women Poets*, Behrendt's "'Certainly Not a Female Pen': Felicia Hemans's Early Public Reception," Wolfson's edition of Hemans's *Selected Poems*

(70), McGann's *Poetics of Sensibility*, and Diego Saglia's "The Society of Foreign Voices: *National Lyrics, and Songs for Music* and Hemans's International Poetics."

3. Early essays, all of which grapple with the interlocking terms of domesticity, the affections, and femininity in Hemans, include Susan J. Wolfson, "'Domestic Affections' and 'the Spear of Minerva': Felicia Hemans and the Dilemma of Gender"; Tricia Lootens, "Hemans and Home: Victorianism, Feminine 'Internal Enemies,' and the Domestication of National Identity"; and Anthony John Harding, "Felicia Hemans and the Effacement of Woman." Sacrifice, death, and social upheaval loom large in these accounts. More recently, in *Sensibility and Female Poetic Tradition, 1780–1860*, Claire Knowles argues that Hemans's poetry marks a shift from sensibility to sentimentality. Hemans certainly featured prominently in McGann's *The Poetics of Sensibility*, and Jason Rudy has discussed Hemans in relation to the terminology of passion. For the way Hemans's poetics and her legacy was shaped by both the literary market of her own day and ensuing scholarship, see Paula Feldman's essays "The Poet and the Profits: Felicia Hemans and the Literary Marketplace" and "Endurance and Forgetting: What the Evidence Suggests." Finally, Helen Luu attempts to deconstruct performances of femininity by Hemans's characters.

4. Wolfson makes the irrevocable connection between "Alastor" and Hemans's poetry from *Tales and Historic Scenes, In Verse*: "Hemans took *Alastor* (1814) to heart, relaying it into her *Tales, and Historic Scenes, in Verse* (1819), even as she tracked the abuses of Shelley's poetry in *The Quarterly Review* and the scandals and controversies roiling across the next decade" (99).

5. Aside from work by Lokke and Kelly on Hemans's German influences in poetry and drama, Lootens has remarked on the similarities between Hegel and Hemans, regarding the contrast between masculine militaristic law and feminine authority. Kelly, in "Death and the Matron," likewise presents Hemans's sense of feminine poetry and knowledge as rescuing history from a masculine oblivion. For discussions of Hemans and religion, spirituality, or transcendence, see Rudy, Anderson, Melnyk, Mason, Nichols, and Stokes, to name a few.

6. In the wake of the Kantian legacy, several philosophers of the early nineteenth century were attempting to bridge the gap between English empiricist doctrine and continental philosophy. In an international debate between English common sense, German speculation, and American pragmatism, the epistemological reliance on sensory experience went toe to toe with those transcendental categories arrived at through subjective reasoning. Rather than discounting perceptual data, G.W.F. Hegel in Germany, Charles Peirce in America, and William Whewell in England all sought to reconcile sensory perception of the world with the mind's ability to conceptualize ideas. As is well known, Hegel was attempting to retool Kantian epistemology by claiming that though conceptual knowledge could not be verified by immediate experiences of the world, sensory data ultimately did shape and prefigure those claims. Richard J. Bernstein makes this point about Peirce in an essay comparing John McDowell to Hegel. McDowell is

a contemporary British philosopher attempting to reconcile Hegel with analytical philosophy, particularly through McDowell's reworking of Kantian receptivity and spontaneity, or the sensory world and the mind's conceptuality. Bernstein points out that McDowell reads Hegel through a post-Kantian lens, much like Peirce's own post-Kantian ideas (19). McDowell is only one of many contemporary philosophers who read Hegel as a post-Kantian, the most important of whom is Robert Pippin. My argument here is that Hegel, along with Peirce, Whewell, and Hemans, were engaged with the epistemological problems that Kant had made so vital. For a good summary of post-Kantian readings of Hegel, see Simon Lumsden's "The Rise of the Non-Metaphysical Hegel."

7. Rudy in "Hemans's Passion" and Julie Melnyk in "Hemans's Later Poetry: Religion and the Vatic Poet" have duly shown that Hemans's later vatic poems lead toward the transcendental experience underwritten by Wordsworth's poems and a newfound spirituality in the wake of her mother's death. What I am calling her middle-period poems mark a midpoint in Hemans's career that develops a type of speculation thinking carefully about what "transcendence" might mean in terms cognitive models.

8. In the second edition, published in 1824, "The Widow of Crescentius" loses the lead spot to "The Abencerrage," perhaps, as Susan J. Wolfson suggests, because the latter poem's subject of Spain would "appeal to contemporary interest in Spanish nationalism" (90). Another reason may be that Hemans had already revised her ideas about revolution, muting the idealistic structure set out by "The Widow" and instead proffering the failures and ambiguities of the multicultural imperial politics set forth in "The Abencerrage." For readings of Hemans sketching gender and racial ambiguities through the Muslim-Spanish conflict in the latter poem, see Saglia's *Poetic Castles in Spain* (279–293) and Sweet's "Gender and Modernity in *The Abencerrage*."

9. Both Wolfson and Lootens have written keen accounts of such violent women, whose recovered stories critique the costs of empire to the domestic hearth. See Wolfson, "'Something Must Be Done': Shelley, Hemans, and the Flash of Revolutionary Female Violence," and Lootens's seminal "Hemans and Home: Victorianism, Feminine 'Internal Enemies,' and the Domestication of National Identity."

10. As Ilana Kurshan remarks in "Mind Reading: Literature in the Discourse of Early Victorian Phrenology and Mesmerism," proponents of phrenology and mesmerism "founded journals to prove and popularize their claims," beginning in the early 1820s (18). Timothy Fulford, P.M.S. Dawson, and Nigel Leask have written about mesmerism in the 1790s, in Blake, and in Shelley, respectively, and Faflak includes a discussion of the psychological theory in *Romantic Psychoanalysis*, though as Brandy Ryan points out in her review of the book, there is oddly no discussion of women writers and the phenomenon in Faflak or in other period scholars.

11. See Richardson (19, 22, 27–28) on the self or "moi" as well as Lawrence's characterization of it as Bentham's internalized overseer in the panopticon.

12. G. S. Rousseau, "Nerves, Spirits, and Fibres: Towards Defining the Origins of Sensibility." See, more recently, Anne C. Villa, *Enlightenment and Pathology: Sensibility in the Literature and Medicine of Eighteenth-Century France*; G. J. Barker-Benfield, *The Culture of Sensibility*; Sarah Knott, *Sensibility and the American Revolution*; and Ildiko Csengei, *Sympathy, Sensibility, and the Literature of Feeling in the Eighteenth Century* on the medical, material roots of the discourse of sensibility.

13. The New York Public Library's Pforzheimer Collection dates this two-volume commonplace book from approximately 1830–1835.

14. For the connection between early brain science and facial expressions, see Richardson's chapter "Facial Expression Theory from Romanticism to the Present" in *Introduction to Cognitive Cultural Studies*, edited by Liza Zunshine.

15. The tenants of materialism, particularly Gall and Spurzheim's doctrines of phrenology, were often viciously discussed in articles throughout the early nineteenth-century, including in the *Edinburgh Review* (1803), *Quarterly Review* (1815), *Monthly Review* (1808, 1815, 1821), and *Blackwood's* (1817, 1819, 1821, 1823).

16. Wolfson suggests that Hemans was quite influenced by "Alastor," and that poem's veiled maid passage furnishes for Richardson a prime example of "cognitive overload" in *The Neural Sublime*. Coleridge's "Kubla Kahn" likewise offers an important account of the cognitive unconscious for Richardson in *Romanticism and Brain Science*, and his play *Remorse* served as one of Hemans's important source texts for her *Forest Sanctuary*, supplying one of its two epigraphs. Frederick Burwick has suggested that the play offers an important reflection on brain science, and as such Hemans may have gained further purchase on such innerworkings of the brain from this and other copious reading.

17. See also Cabanis's comments on "states of trance" (129–130) and on the necessity of sleep to give intellectual men and sensitive women rest from the constant brain processing involved with impressions, imagination, and memory (145).

18. See especially Richardson's chapter on "Coleridge and the New Unconscious" (58–65).

19. As Miller notes, this term was coined by Benjamin Carpenter, whose first works of physiology appeared in 1839.

20. Antonio Damasio, for example, in his widely read *Self Comes to Mind*, distinguishes between emotion and feeling, where emotions are physiological actions carried out by our bodies while feelings are those perceptions that identify particular emotions and codify them into language.

21. Such incendiary moments in *Tales and Historic Scenes* could be framed as what Wolfson describes as "an aesthetic sublime of political fury" ("'Something'" 116). Sweet has also briefly suggested that Hemans revises the aesthetics of the sublime in her reading of "The Abencerrage"—a complement to her earlier discussion of Hemans's refashioning of the category of the beautiful. If they are examples

of the sublime, the explosive moments in *Tales and Historic Scenes* resemble most closely Richardson's dynamic reassessment of what he terms the "neural sublime." See Sweet, "Gender and Modernity" (187–193) and the eponymous chapter from Richardson's *The Neural Sublime*.

22. Patricia Yaeger, "Toward a Feminine Sublime" in *Gender and Theory: Dialogues on Feminist Criticism*, edited by Linda Kauffman; Barbara Claire Freeman, *The Feminine Sublime: Gender and Excess in Women's Fiction*.

23. Colin Jager in "Can We Talk About Consciousness Again?" raises the important question about the relationship between the traditional Romantic concerns over the mind and the world and more recent debates, in both literature and neuroscience, about consciousness and the relationship between mind and brain. Jager also astutely points out that Richardson's research about nineteenth-century brain science often stops short of offering interpretive schemas about how consciousness works in literature, at which point scholars have often reverted to continental philosophy. My argument tries to explain how Hemans proactively uses the way brain science stumps interpretation to rethink certain problems in continental philosophy.

24. The idea of poetry as an intoxicant that provokes thought or challenges habituated ideas is not an uncommon trope in early nineteenth-century writing. Orrin N. C. Wang's *Romantic Sobriety* provides a full-bodied discussion of sobriety, intoxication, and Romanticism. Keats and Shelley use drugs to evacuate old ways of thinking about both Apollo's godliness in *Hyperion* and Asia's submission to Jupiter's tyranny in *Prometheus Bound*. De Quincey famously confessed to opium addiction, which David L. Clark argues may be about the habituations of "infinite deliberation" (281). See Kate Singer, "Stoned Shelley"; Alethea Hayter, *Opium and the Romantic Imagination*; Denise Gigante's chapter on Keats in *Taste: A Literary History*; Florida Hermione de Almeida, *Romantic Medicine and John Keats*, especially "The Pharmacy of Disease"; and David L. Clark, "We 'Other Prussians': Bodies and Pleasures in De Quincey and Late Kant."

25. Though, according to the OED, the participial use of this meaning was obsolete by 1604, the adverbial use, through the phrase "wrought up," was still very much in use. This usage, in fact, has an entry by Hemans from "The Siege of Valencia": "The deep . . . feelings wakening at their voice, / Claim all the wrought-up spirit to themselves."

26. As Wolfson and Sweet note, Hemans asserted in a letter to a clergyman that the recent question of Catholic Emancipation had no bearing on the poem, yet as Sweet suggests, the poem certainly reflects on contemporary religious controversy and political views, as 1823 saw the fall of the Spanish constitution and the restoration of the Inquisition.

27. Hemans and White (whose pseudonym was Don Leucadio Doblado) also corresponded about Spanish literature, though much of this correspondence seems to have been lost. See Wolfson's note on the connections between the two

authors, in her edition of Hemans's *Selected Poems* (296n35) and Sweet's book chapter, "*The Forest Sanctuary*: The Anglo-Hispanic Uncanny in Felicia Hemans and José Maria Blanco White."

28. The nexus of Latin American politics, revolution, empire, and the powers of the mind were clearly paramount for her in 1823 and 1824 when Hemans began composition of *The Forest Sanctuary*. Writing to an unnamed Welsh friend about her disappointment in the stage production of *Vespers of Palermo*, she praises Covent Garden manager John Kemble for his conduct and then writes, "He would, I should think, particularly like to represent an American Indian at the stake, or the Mexican emperor upon the burning coals; and in my opinion, there can be no real grandeur unless *mind* is made the ruling power, and its ascendancy asserted, even amidst the wildest storms of passion" (Chorley I.75; emphasis in original). When discussing Mexican General Iturbide's fate in an 1824 letter, she comments: "The revolutions in a powerful mind, under circumstances so changeful and extraordinary, would, I think, be more impressive than those of an empire" (Chorley I.81).

29. This reading is indebted to Richardson's reading of *Persuasion* and Louisa's blow to the brain in *Romanticism and the Science of the Mind*.

30. For a reading of the Spaniard's journey through the Americas as an uncanny remembrance of his past, see Sweet's "*The Forest Sanctuary*: The Anglo-Hispanic Uncanny in Felicia Hemans and José Maria Blanco White."

31. An early note (n6) to the Spaniard's description of the American forest's "feathery canes" points readers to a passage about Tennessee from Adam Hodgson's *Letters*. The final note to part one (n44) annotates the Spaniard's description of the "high arcades" with a quote from Daniel Webster's bicentenary speech celebrating the Plymouth Rock landing. The first note on the text of part two (n3), however, further describes the "sounding of the torrent-water" with an allusion to a description of upstate New York in Anne Macvicar Grant's *Memoirs of An American Lady*.

32. When the Spaniard finally arrives in the North American wilderness at the end of the poem, his locale is conspicuously evacuated of any people or settlements. Though native populations are nowhere mentioned in Hemans's descriptions of either the South and North American landscapes, neither are the other white settlers. Hemans had certainly read accounts of the Americas that detailed native populations, including Adam Hodgson's *Letters* and Alexander von Humboldt's *Voyage*, both of which she cites in the poem's footnotes. Although Hemans does a disservice to Native Americans, the emptiness of the landscape in a poem about cognition is, I would argue, an attempt to clear the mind more than any guise to erase Native Americans from American history. The poem, from the outset as outlined in the preface, is not meant as a true account of transatlantic immigration but as a "record of the mind."

33. See Sweet's thorough collation of Hemans's sources in "*The Forest Sanctuary*" and Simpson's discussion of Hemans in *Romanticism and the Question of the Stranger* (209–248).

34. It seems unlikely that Hemans would have read about De Soto's travels since the contemporary account, Theodore Irving's *The Conquest of Florida*, was not published until 1835 and noticed by the *Edinburgh* and *Monthly Reviews* that same year.

35. White narrates the *auto-da-fé* of a priest named Gomez and his two sisters, which is a close parallel to Alvar and his sisters, particularly because they join in singing as the final defiant act while they die. These deaths most likely happen in the first or second *auto-da-fé* of Seville, in either 1559 or 1560 (255–256). The Andean consolidation occurs between 1542 and the final battle between the Spanish and the Incas in 1572. So it is likely that the Spaniard leaves Spain at least after 1560 or, at the latest, in the years after 1572 but before the end of Phillip II's reign in 1598.

36. Isaac D'Israeli constructs a similar virtual history in his 1824 essay "Of a History of Events Which Have Not Happened," which discusses historical events that might have changed the religion of nations during the Reformation and Counter-Reformation and which has been labeled the first counterfactual history. Catherine Gallagher makes this claim for D'Israeli's essay in a talk she gave at the University of Jyväskylä (par. 5). The paper had been previously posted on the website of the University's Political Thought and Conceptual Change Centre of Excellence, but she also makes a similar passing comment in her more recent work on counterfactual history, in a chapter in *Practicing Historicism*. Hemans was certainly aware of D'Israeli's exceedingly popular volume *Curiosities of Literature*, Volume I, second series, from which this essay comes. In her commonplace book in the New York Public Library's Pforzheimer collection, she cites a review article discussing the work.

37. Both Žižek's account of self-relating and Catherine Malabou's Hegelian reading of brain plasticity in *The Future of Hegel: Plasticity, Temporality, and Dialectic* laud the potential of self-fashioning that results from the brain's access to an ever-increasing network of data and the neo-Hegelian tendency for the mind to rework and sculpt neural pathways. For Malabou, this potentiality for self-sculpting has direct political consequences, offering the brain the ability to remap democracy aside from capitalist efficiency and to envision a multiplicity of cultures or worlds that overcome the sovereignty of any central power. Although more complicated comparisons could be made, both theorists ultimately assert the ascendancy of the mind to deal with the brain's morass but in hopeful, progressive plans of political action.

38. For a speculative realist reading of Rousseau as formulating a state of nature that is, in fact, hospitable to nonhuman others and their futures, see Chris Washington's "Romantic Post-Apocalyptic Politics: Reveries of Rousseau in a World without Us" in the forthcoming volume *Romanticism and Speculative Realism*.

39. The Spaniard's Daniel Boone mentality goes even further to resist the less explicit appeals to British nationality in discussions of North America, whether endued through Tory insistence on aristocratic civility or Whig demands for new

markets in the New World. In light of the raging debate in British periodicals about the liberal Spanish constitution of 1812, which mitigated monarchical power and sparked the Spanish Civil War during 1820–23, Hemans's depiction of the exile in an unchartered land reiterates her suspicion of transported nationalist attitudes endemic to church, state, and tea table. The Spaniard presents a case of the civilized man tramping through uncultivated forest precisely to outrun national institutions. Gary Kelly, alternatively, argues that Hemans recreates a modern liberal state though freed from material and ideological dependency in "Death and the Matron: Felicia Hemans, Romantic Death, and the Founding of the Modern Liberal State."

40. In "Hemans's 'Red Indians': Reading Stereotypes," Nancy Goslee has argued that the poem tells a story about the consolidation of "an androgynous, nurturing father, and a female sexuality that is displaced and depersonalized in the natural setting" (244). "The Forest Sanctuary" would then depict a male conquistador who assumes a feminine, nurturing position as he flees patriarchal Spain for the vaginal space of a forest sanctuary. Alternately for Sweet the Spaniard engenders what Sweet calls a "new source of male subjectivity" (177), and for Gary Kelly his "feminine masculinity" likewise represents the turn away from state-sanctioned warmongering and mass death. Finally, it would be easy to see Hemans borrowing a technique that Joselyn Almeida excavates in White's letters, the construction of "hybrid identities . . . [which] found a voice within British Romanticism, mirroring in their texts nascent global networks of culture, trade and politics" (440). All these are wonderful readings, yet they do not quite capture the suspension from identity (and its concepts) that Hemans explores with the wandering figure the Spaniard becomes.

41. Her technique may not be too far afield from Emily Dickinson's own use of dashes, which often stymie a reader's cognition when she is forced to traverse the connection between abstract metaphors and particular experiential details. For a summary of scholarship on Dickinson's dash, see Deirdre Fagan's essay, "Emily Dickinson's Unutterable Word," where she argues that the dash represents a linguistic, cognitive blankness.

42. Discussing Hemans's earlier poem "Superstition and Revelation" (1820), Daniel White argues that Hemans's project is wrapped up in a cosmopolitan religiosity that attempts to "see back, through a historical consciousness, to a period when Christian truth was immanent" (275). See his article "'Mysterious Sanctity': Sectarianism and Syncretism from Volney to Hemans."

43. For a reading of Hemans's use of individual voices singing varying creeds, see Diego Saglia's, "'Freedom's Charter'd Air': The Voices of Liberalism in Felicia Hemans's *The Vespers of Palermo*.

Chapter 5

1. The conflict between embodied, habitual sensibility and virtuous intellect echoes Wollstonecraft's formulations in *A Vindication of the Rights of Woman*,

including her critique of Rousseauvian self-absorbed sensuality, which Orrin N. C. Wang explores in his chapter on Wollstonecraft in *Fantastic Modernity*. Susan J. Wolfson's chapter in *Borderlines* addresses Jewsbury's early reading of Wollstonecraft as well as her understanding of gender ideology in the 1820s.

2. See Pascoe, Kelly, and other commentators on Smith's "Beachy Head" and her sonnets, for example.

3. Leask, Indira Ghose, Elizabeth Bohls, Sara Suleri, and others have tackled the question of how the picturesque enabled British women to establish authoritative positions as aesthetic viewing and judging subjects of the Empire. If we agree with these scholars that the feminine gaze replicates Western viewing strategies and sets about ordering, containing, and appropriating landscapes or colonial bodies, then Jewsbury's wandering pictures upend the connections between sight, property, and the body. In other words, the Foucauldian strategy of many scholars of the Western female gaze may place too great an emphasis on middle class women's propensity to consolidate—through acts of viewing and travel writing—the possession of imperial property.

4. See Wang's "Ghost Theory" for a thorough discussion of the phantom in British Romanticism.

5. For a more comprehensive discussion of Jewsbury's relationship to the Wordsworths see Dennis Low's *The Literary Protégés of the Lake Poets*.

6. For a critic who accounts for Wordsworth's conscious skepticism about the impossibility of the imagination to transcend problems of memory or history, see Peter Simonsen's response to McGann and others, "Reading Wordsworth after McGann: Moments of Negativity in 'Tintern Abbey' and the Immortality Ode."

7. See Jewsbury's letter to Dora dated January 4, 1833, and the note on the *Romantic Circles* edition of *The Oceanides*, linked from the reference to Bailey in "The Eden of the Sea."

8. See, for example, Geoffrey Hartman's discussion of the ode in *The Unremarkable Wordsworth*.

9. Sophie Thomas presents Wordsworth's struggle with the reign of the visual as much more complex than any simple fixity or razing of visual production. Passages from Book VII of the *Prelude* are often read as a critique of the sensations and vulgar consumption of urban spectacles. For critics such as W.J.T. Mitchell, Wordsworth's espousal of the visionary gleam in the "Intimations Ode" and the possibilities of the imagination signal his intense iconoclastic stance, rejecting the false visions of mere sensation. Reading the *Guide to the Lakes* and his later ekphrastic poems, however, Simonsen suggests that Wordsworth was increasingly interested in art and the concretely visual aspects of poetry later in his life. Using Thomas's reading, however, when Wordsworth ends the first stanza of the "Intimations Ode" lamenting on "The things which I have seen I now can see no more," we might take this sentiment as a productive blind spot—an "habitual invisibility" (100).

10. Jewsbury's passage almost magically rehearses arguments about the relationship between Wordsworth and Coleridge and the tension between Romanticism and the gothic born through the assembly of the 1798 and 1800 volumes

of *Lyrical Ballads*, which Michael Gamer has presented in his book *Romanticism and the Gothic*.

11. See Castle: "It was common practice in the early nineteenth century to name literary works of a miscellaneous or feuilletonistic nature—collections of tales by divers hands, books of light essays or satirical portraits—after the machinery of the spectre show. The underlying idea seems to have been that the constant shifting of topics and 'scenes' in such works re-created the pleasantly disorienting experience of watching a magic-lantern exhibition. See the Countess of Blessington's satirical sketches of London life, *The Magic Lantern; or, Sketches of Scenes in the Metropolis* (London, 1822), or Maria Jane Jewsbury's *Phantasmagoria; or Sketches of Life and Literature*, 2 vols. (London, 1825)" (56n54).

12. A similar, gothic resurrection of poets occurs in Washington Irving's "Westminster Abbey" from *The Sketch-Book of Geoffrey Canyon, Gent*. Jewsbury cites *The Sketch-Book* covetously and enviously in her essay "A Chapter of Sundries" in *Phantasmagoria*, praising Irving as the "father of the shred and patch school of writing" (306).

13. It also, according to more recent suggestions, may be connected to early instances of the virtual. Botting makes the argument that the Romantic imagination was and has always been "virtual" in his essay, "Virtual Romanticism." More recently, Peter Otto in *Multiplying Worlds: Romanticism, Modernity, and the Emergency of Virtual Reality* argues that the virtual first appears in urban London during the Romantic era.

14. Zahid Chaudhary makes this argument about mystification, using both Marx and Benjamin to reveal how photography of India after the Sepoy Mutiny concealed the physical violence wreaked on human bodies. This paper's ideas of "phantasmagoric aesthetics" seeks to move backwards to a time when the historical apparatus of the phantasmagoria, by the 1830s at least, provided a less realistic and more reflective experience about the illusions created by such technologies.

15. G. C. Mendis, in his *Ceylon Under the British*, documents the British brutal reaction against local rebellion around 1815 as well as the development of commercial agriculture beginning with the Colebrook Commission (1829) and its report (1832).

16. This phantasmagoric exchange—not of things but of images, representations, or ideological value—resembles the circulation of gothic counterfeit signifiers, which Jerold Hogle characterizes as a function of the nineteenth-century gothic. The gothic castle or the cocoa tree both refer to an earlier medieval or primeval past of naturalness and purity that never really existed except through imagined representation. This strategy of signification amounts to both the repression of material realities and the loss of referents that have already been counterfeit. The technologies of the gothic plot and the phantasmagoria effectively denude reality of stable referents even as they put into circulation signs that would otherwise have remained separate and incommensurate. For Hogle, such exchangeability is predicated on women's loss of the body into the signifier of "othered," which allows women to be trafficked easily. See his seminal "Frankenstein as Neo-Gothic."

17. Writing from Ceylon, Fletcher tells Mr. Jewsbury that his daughter is as much at home "as if she had been from amongst them, as curious and lively as a child" (WKF to TJ, January 22, 1833). It is easy to read this description of Jewsbury as a diminutive portrait, what Alan Richardson argues is the child's odd combination of innocence and wildness devoid of worldly experience ("Politics of Childhood" 19). Elsewhere in Fletcher's letters to Mr. Jewsbury, however, he praises his wife for her status as a poet, a friend of Wordsworth, a "good sailor," and a sophisticated conversationalist. This confidence in his new wife's intellectual charms suggests that both partners may have held a more liberal view of childishness.

18. My many thanks to Mark William Fletcher, great-great-great grandson of Jewsbury's husband, for initiating our correspondence and pointing me to Espinasse's text.

19. For a recent meditation on the poetics of sympathetic exchange, metaphorical substitution, and transnational mobility, see Miranda Burgess, "Transport: Mobility, Anxiety, and the Romantic Poetics of Feeling"; for another view of the poetics of mobility, materiality, and the specter of neoliberalism, see Brian McGrath's "Material Excursions."

20. See MJJ to DW, September 19, 1828.

21. One might cite recent queer theorists such as Lee Edelman, who critiques childhood as the possibility of futurity against which queer people are positioned as naysayers refusing to replicate the social and biological order. See his *No Future: Queer Theory and the Death Drive*. Alternately, Kathryn Bond Stockton suggests childhood is always queer, both in terms of sexuality but also as a time suspended before adolescence or adulthood when children might envision other ways of growing besides growing up. See her book chapter, "Growing Sideways, Or Versions of the Queer Child: The Ghost, The Homosexual, the Freudian, the Innocent, and the Interval of Animal."

22. For more on Jewsbury's discussion of "trumpery," her commentary on the commodification of Indian goods, and its model of exchange, see my "Wordsworthian Vision, Moving Picture Shows, and the Ethics of the Moving Image in Maria Jane Jewsbury's *The Oceanides*" (549–550).

Coda

1. The recent *Cambridge Companion to Women's Writing in the Romantic Period* is one such collection—a veritable and important treasury of women's extensive work in a variety of genres and on an array of the most important themes during the period. This important work should, of course, be done; my argument is that we also need to undertake a supple theorizing about gender that tampers with contextual and historical frames to an even more radical degree than has been done within period scholarship.

Works Cited

Abbey, Lloyd. *Destroyer and Preserver: Shelley's Poetic Skepticism*. Lincoln: U of Nebraska P, 1979.
Adelman, Richard. "Idleness and Vacancy in Shelley's 'Mont Blanc.'" *Keats-Shelley Journal: Keats, Shelley, Byron, Hunt, and Their Circles*, vol. 62, 2013, pp. 62–79.
Ahern, Stephen. *Affected Sensibilities: Romantic Excess and the Genealogy of the Novel, 1680–1810*. New York: AMS Press, Inc., 2007.
Allen, Richard C. *David Hartley on Human Nature*. Albany: State U of New York P, 1999.
Allewaert, Monique. "Toward a Materialist Figuration: A Slight Manifesto." *English Language Notes*, vol. 51, no. 2, Fall/Winter 2013, pp. 61–77.
Almeida, Joselyn. "Blanco White and the Making of Anglo-Hispanic Romanticism." *European Romantic Review*, vol. 17, no. 4, 2006, pp. 437–456.
Altick, Richard D. *The Shows of London*. Cambridge, MA: Belknap, 1978.
Alvey, Nahoko Miyamoto. *Strange Truths in Undiscovered Lands: Shelley's Poetic Development and Romantic Geography*. Canada: U of Toronto P, 2009.
Anderson, John M. "Beachy Head: The Romantic Fragment Poem as Mosaic." *Huntington Library Quarterly: Studies in English and American History and Literature*, vol. 63, no. 4, 2000, pp. 547–574.
———. "Icons of Women in the Religious Sonnets of Wordsworth and Hemans." *The Fountain Light: Studies in Romanticism and Religion in Honor of John L. Mahoney*. Edited by J. Robert Barth. New York: Fordham UP, 2002, pp. 90–110.
———. "The Triumph of Voice in Felicia Hemans's *The Forest Sanctuary*." *Felicia Hemans: Reimagining Poetry in the Nineteenth Century*. Edited by Nanora Sweet and Julie Melnyk. United Kingdom: Palgrave, 2001, pp. 55–73.
Armstrong, Isobel. "The Gush of the Feminine: How Can We Read Women's Poetry of the Romantic Period?" *Romantic Women Writers: Voices and Countervoices*. Edited by Paula R. Feldman and Theresa M. Kelley. Lebanon, NH: UP of New England, 1995, pp. 13–32.
———. *The Radical Aesthetic*. New York: John Wiley & Sons, 2000.
Austen, Jane. *Sense and Sensibility*. Edited by Claudia L. Johnson. New York: W.W. Norton & Company, 2001.

Austin, Linda M. "Children of Childhood: Nostalgia and the Romantic Legacy." *Studies in Romanticism*, vol. 42, no. 1, 2003, pp. 75–98.

Backscheider, Paula R. *Eighteenth-Century Women Poets and Their Poetry: Inventing Agency, Inventing Genre*. Baltimore, MD: Johns Hopkins UP, 2010.

Baker, Carlos. *Shelley's Major Poetry: The Fabric of Vision*. Princeton, NJ: Princeton UP, 1948.

Barad, Karen. *Meeting the Universe Halfway: Quantum Physics and the Entanglement of Matter and Meaning*. Chapel Hill, NC: Duke UP, 2007.

———. "Posthumanist Performativity: Toward an Understanding of How Matter Comes to Matter." *Material Feminisms*. Edited by Stacy Alaimo and Susan Hekman. Bloomington: Indiana UP, 2008, pp. 120–156.

———. "Quantum Entanglements and Hauntological Relations of Inheritance: Dis/continuities, SpaceTime Enfoldings, and Justice-to-Come." *Derrida Today*, vol. 3, no. 2, 2010, pp. 240–268.

Barczewski, Stephanie. *Myth and National Identity in Nineteenth-Century Britain: The Legends of King Arthur and Robin Hood*. New York: Oxford UP, 2000.

Barker-Benfield, G. J. *The Culture of Sensibility: Sex and Society in Eighteenth-Century Britain*. Chicago, IL: U of Chicago P, 1992.

Barrell, John. *Poetry, Language, and Politics*. United Kingdom: Manchester UP, 1988.

Behrendt, Stephen C. *British Women Poets and the Romantic Writing Community*. Baltimore, MD: Johns Hopkins UP, 2009.

———. "'Certainly Not a Female Pen': Felicia Hemans's Early Public Reception." *Felicia Hemans: Reimagining Poetry in the Nineteenth Century*. Edited by Nanora Sweet and Julie Melnyk. United Kingdom: Palgrave, 2001, pp. 95–114.

———. "Remapping the Landscape: The Romantic Literary Community Revisited." *Comparative Romanticisms: Power, Gender, Subjectivity*. Edited by Larry H. Peer and Diane Long Hoeveler. Columbia, SC: Camden House, 1998, pp. 11–32.

———. "William Wordsworth and Women Poets." *European Romantic Review*, vol. 23, no. 6, 2012, pp. 635–650.

Bell, Sir Charles. *Idea of a New Anatomy of the Brain: A Facsimile of the Privately Printed Edition of 1811 with a Bio-Bibliographical Introduction*. United Kingdom: Dawsons, 1966.

Bennett, Jane. *Vibrant Matter: A Political Ecology of Things*. Chapel Hill, NC: Duke UP, 2010.

Berlant, Lauren. *The Female Complaint: The Unfinished Business of Sentimentality in American Culture*. Chapel Hill, NC: Duke UP, 2008.

Bernstein, Richard J. "McDowell's Domesticated Hegelianism." *Reading McDowell: On Mind and World*. Edited by Nicholas H. Smith. United Kingdom: Routledge, 2002, pp. 9–24.

Bewell, Alan. "'A Word Scarce Said': Hysteria and Witchcraft in Wordsworth's 'Experimental' Poetry of 1797–98." *ELH*, vol. 53, no. 2, 1986, pp. 357–390.

———. *Wordsworth and the Enlightenment: Nature, Man, and Society in the Experimental Poetry*. New Haven, CT: Yale UP, 1989.

Bialostosky, Don H. *Wordsworth, Dialogics and the Practice of Criticism.* United Kingdom: Cambridge UP, 1992.

Blank, Kim. *Wordsworth's Influence on Shelley: A Study of Poetic Authority.* United Kingdom: Palgrave Macmillan, 2015.

Bode, Christoph. "The Subject of Beachy Head." *Charlotte Smith in British Romanticism.* Edited by Jacqueline Labbe. United Kingdom: Pickering & Chatto, 2008, pp. 57–69.

Bohls, Elizabeth A. *Women Travel Writers and the Language of Aesthetics 1716–1818.* United Kingdom: Cambridge UP, 1995.

Bonca, Teddi Chichester. *Shelley's Mirrors of Love: Narcissism, Sacrifice, and Sorority.* Albany: State U of New York P, 1998.

Booth, Naomi. "Feeling Too Much: The Swoon and the (In)sensible Woman." *Women's Writing*, vol. 21, no. 4, 2014, pp. 575–591.

Botting, Fred. "Virtual Romanticism." *Romanticism and Postmodernism.* Edited by Edward Larrissy. United Kingdom: Cambridge UP, 1999, pp. 98–112.

Boyson, Rowan. *Wordsworth and the Enlightenment Idea of Pleasure.* United Kingdom: Cambridge UP, 2012.

Bradshaw, Penny. "Dystopian Futures: Time-Travel and Millenarian Visions in the Poetry of Anna Barbauld and Charlotte Smith." *Romanticism on the Net: An Electronic Journal Devoted to Romantic Studies*, vol. 21, 2001. Accessed 16 May 2016.

Bray, Matthew. "Removing the Anglo-Saxon Yoke: The Francocentric Vision of Charlotte Smith's Later Works." *The Wordsworth Circle*, vol. 24, no.3, 1993, pp. 155–158.

Brennan, Teresa. *The Transmission of Affect.* Ithaca, NY: Cornell UP, 2004.

Brewer, William D. "Egalitarianism in Mary Robinson's Metropolis." *The Wordsworth Circle*, vol. 41, no. 3, 2010, pp. 146–150.

Broglio, Ron, and Rob Mitchell. *Romanticism and the New Deleuze.* Edited by Ron Broglio and Rob Mitchell. January 2008. *Romantic Circles.* www.rc.umd.edu/praxis/deleuze/index.html. Accessed 11 Dec. 2017.

Bromwich, David. *Disowned by Memory: Wordsworth's Poetry of the 1790s.* Chicago, IL: U of Chicago P, 2000.

Brown, Nathaniel. *Sexuality and Feminism in Shelley.* Cambridge, MA: Harvard UP, 1979.

Bruder, Helen, and Tristanne Connolly. *Queer Blake.* United Kingdom: Palgrave Macmillan, 2010.

Bruhm, Steven. *Gothic Bodies: The Politics of Pain in Romantic Fiction.* Philadelphia: U of Pennsylvania P, 1994.

Buchanan, Ian, and Claire Colebrook, eds. *Deleuze and Feminist Theory.* United Kingdom: Edinburgh UP, 2000.

Bundock, Chris. "Blake's Nervous System: Hypochondria, Judaism, and *Jerusalem*." *Blake: Modernity and Disaster.* Edited by Tilottama Rajan and Joel Faflak. Canada: U of Toronto P, forthcoming.

Burgess, Miranda. "Transport: Mobility, Anxiety, and the Romantic Poetics of Feeling." *Studies in Romanticism*, vol. 49, no. 2, Summer 2010, pp. 229–260.

Burke, Edmund. *A Philosophical Enquiry into the Origin of Our Ideas of the Sublime and Beautiful.* United Kingdom: Oxford UP, 2008.
Burwick, Frederick. "Romanticism as Cognitive Process." *Essays in Romanticism*, vol. 15, no. 1, 2007, pp. 7–32.
Butter, Peter H. *Shelley's Idols of the Cave.* United Kingdom: Edinburgh UP, 1954.
Byron, George Gordon. *Byron's Poetry and Prose.* Edited by Alice Levine. New York: W.W. Norton & Company, 2009.
Byrne, Paula. *Perdita: The Literary, Theatrical, Scandalous Life of Mary Robinson.* New York: Random House, 2007.
Cabanis, Pierre. *On the Relations Between the Physical and Moral Aspects of Man.* Translated by Margaret Duggan Saidi. Edited by George Mora. 2 vols. Baltimore, MD: Johns Hopkins UP, 1981.
Cameron, Kenneth Neill. "The Planet-Tempest Passage in *Epipsychidion*." *PMLA: Publications of the Modern Language Association of America*, vol. 63, no. 3, 1948, pp. 950–972.
Carlson, Julie. "Like Love: The Feel of Shelley's Similes." *Romanticism and the Emotions.* Edited by Joel Faflak and Richard C. Sha. United Kingdom: Cambridge UP, 2014, pp. 76–97.
Carothers, Yvonne. "Alastor: Shelley Corrects Wordsworth." *Modern Language Quarterly*, vol. 42, no. 1, 1981, pp. 21–47.
Castle, Terry. "Phantasmagoria: Spectral Technology and the Metaphorics of Modern Reverie." *Critical Inquiry*, vol. 15, no. 1, 1988, pp. 26–61.
Cauchi, Francesca. "A Rereading of Wordsworth's Presence in Shelley's 'Alastor.'" *SEL: Studies in English Literature, 1500–1900*, vol. 50, no. 4, Autumn 2010, pp. 759–774.
Chandler, James. "The Politics of Sentiment: Notes toward a New Account." *Studies in Romanticism*, vol. 49, no. 4, 2010, pp. 553–575.
———. *An Archeology of Sympathy.* Chicago, IL: U of Chicago P, 2013.
———. *Wordsworth's Second Nature: A Study of the Poetry and Politics.* Chicago, IL: U of Chicago P, 1984.
Chaplin, Susan. *Law, Sensibility, and the Sublime in Eighteenth-Century Women's Fiction: Speaking of Dread.* United Kingdom: Ashgate, 2004.
Chaudhary, Zahid. "Phantasmagoric Aesthetics: Colonial Violence and the Management of Perception." *Cultural Critique*, vol. 59, no. 1, 2005, pp. 63–119.
Cheah, Pheng. "Non-Dialectical Materialism." *New Materialisms: Ontology, Agency, and Politics.* Edited by Diana Coole and Samantha Frost. Chapel Hill, NC: Duke UP, 2009, pp. 70–91.
Cheng, Anne Anlin, *The Melancholy of Race: Psychoanalysis, Assimilation and Hidden Grief.* Princeton, NJ: Princeton UP, 2001.
Chorley, Henry Fothegill. *Memorials of Mrs. Hemans with Illustrations of Her Literary Character from Her Private Correspondence.* Two volumes. London: Saunders and Otley, 1836. Google eBooks. Accessed 3 Dec. 2018.
Cixous, Hélène. "The Laugh of the Medusa." *Signs* vol. 1, no. 4, 1976, pp. 875–893.

Clark, David L, editor. *Romanticism and the Legacies of Jacques Derrida. Studies in Romanticism*, vol. 46, no. 2–3, Summer/Fall 2007, pp. 161–364.

———. "We 'Other Prussians': Bodies and Pleasures in De Quincey and Late Kant." *European Romantic Review*, vol. 14, no. 2, 2003, pp. 261–287.

Clark, Timothy. *Embodying Revolution: The Figure of the Poet in Shelley*. United Kingdom: Oxford UP, 1989.

Class, Monika. *Coleridge and Kantian Ideas in England, 1796–1817: Coleridge's Responses to German Philosophy*. New York: Bloomsbury, 2012.

Colbert, Benjamin. *Shelley's Eye: Travel Writing and Aesthetic Vision*. United Kingdom: Ashgate, 2005.

Coleridge, Samuel Taylor. *Coleridge's Poetry and Prose*. Edited by Nicholas Halmi. New York: W.W. Norton & Company, 2003.

Coleridge, Samuel Taylor, and William Wordsworth. *Lyrical Ballads 1798 and 1800*. Edited by Michael Gamer and Dahlia Porter. Canada: Broadview Press, 2008.

Collings, David. "Rhyming Sensation in 'Mont Blanc.'" *Romanticism and the New Deleuze*. Edited by Ron Broglio and Rob Mitchell. January 2008. *Romantic Circles*. www.rc.umd.edu/praxis/deleuze/collings/collings.html. Accessed 11 Dec. 2017.

———. "Emotion without Content: Primary Affect and Pure Potentiality in Wordsworth." *Romanticism and the Emotions*. Edited by Richard Sha and Joel Faflak. United Kingdom: Cambridge UP, pp. 171–191.

Comet, Noah. "Felicia Hemans and the 'Exquisite Remains' of Modern Greece." *Keats-Shelley Journal*, vol. 58, 2009, pp. 96–113.

———. *Romantic Hellenism and Women Writers*. United Kingdom: Palgrave Macmillan, 2013.

Connolly, Tristanne. *William Blake and the Body*. United Kingdom: Palgrave Macmillan, 2002.

Cooper, Andrew M. *Doubt and Identity in Romantic Poetry*. New Haven, CT: Yale UP, 1988.

Craciun, Adriana. *British Women Writers and the French Revolution: Citizens of the World*. United Kingdom: Palgrave Macmillan, 2005.

———. "Citizens of the World: Emigrés, Romantic Cosmopolitanism, and Charlotte Smith." *Nineteenth-Century Contexts*, vol. 29, no. 2–3, 2007, pp. 169–185.

———. "'Empire Without End': Charlotte Smith at the Limits of Cosmopolitanism." *Women's Writing*, vol. 16, no. 1, 2009, pp. 39–59.

———. *Fatal Women of Romanticism*. United Kingdom: Cambridge UP, 2003.

———. "Mary Robinson, the *Monthly Magazine*, and the Free Press." *Prose Studies: History, Theory, Criticism*, vol. 25, no. 1, 2002, pp. 19–40.

———. "Violence Against Difference: Mary Wollstonecraft and Mary Robinson." *Bucknell Review: A Scholarly Journal of Letters, Arts and Sciences*, vol. 42, no. 1, 1998, pp. 111–141.

Craig, Cairns. "Coleridge, Hume, and the Chains of the Romantic Imagination." *Scotland and the Borders of Romanticism*. Edited by Leith Davis, Ian Duncan, and Janet Sorensen. United Kingdom: Cambridge UP, 2004, pp. 20–37.

———. "'Kant has not answered Hume': Empiricism and the Romantic Imagination." *Romantic Empiricism: Poetics and the Philosophy of Common Sense, 1780–1830*. Edited by Gavin Budge. Lewisburg, PA: Bucknell UP, 2007, pp. 40–63.

Crisman, William. "Psychological Realism and Narrative Manner in Shelley's 'Alastor' and 'The Witch of Atlas.'" *Keats-Shelley Journal*, vol. 35, 1986, pp. 126–148.

Crocco, Francesco. "The Ruins of Empire: Nationalism, Art, and Empire in Hemans's Modern Greece." *Romanticism and Patriotism: Nation, Empire, Bodies, Rhetoric*. Edited by Orrin N. C. Wang. *Romantic Circles*. May 2006. www.rc.umd.edu/praxis/patriotism/index.html. Accessed 8 Mar. 2017.

Crook, Nora. "Shelley and Women." *The Oxford Handbook of Percy Bysshe Shelley*. Edited by Michael O'Neill, Anthony Howe, and Madeleine Callaghan. United Kingdom: Oxford UP, 2013, pp. 65–82.

Crook, Nora, and Derek Guiton. *Shelley's Venomed Melody*. United Kingdom: Cambridge UP, 2010.

Cross, Ashley. "Coleridge and Robinson: Harping on Lyrical Exchange." *Fellow Romantics: Male and Female British Writers, 1790–1835*. Edited by Beth Lau. United Kingdom: Ashgate, 2009, pp. 39–70.

———. "Robert Southey and Mary Robinson in Dialogue." *The Wordsworth Circle*, vol. 42, no. 1, 2011, pp. 10–17.

Cross, Ashley J. "From Lyrical Ballads to Lyrical Tales: Mary Robinson's Reputation and the Problem of Literary Debt." *Studies in Romanticism*, vol. 40, no. 4, 2001, pp. 571–605.

———. "He-She Philosophers and Other Literary Bugbears: Mary Robinson's *A Letter to the Women of England*." *Women's Writing*, vol. 9, no. 1, 2002, pp. 53–68.

———. *Mary Robinson and the Genesis of Romanticism: Literary Dialogues and Debts, 1784–1821*. United Kingdom: Routledge, 2016.

Csengei, Ildiko. *Sympathy, Sensibility, and the Literature of Feeling in the Eighteenth Century*. United Kingdom: Palgrave, 2012.

Curran, Stuart. "Charlotte Smith and British Romanticism." *South Central Review*, vol. 11, no. 2, 1994, pp. 66–78.

———. "Charlotte Smith, Mary Wollstonecraft, and the Romance of Real Life." *The History of British Women's Writing, 1750–1830*. Edited by Jacqueline M. Labbe. United Kingdom: Palgrave Macmillan, 2010, pp. 194–206.

———. "*Epipsychidion*, Dante, and the Renewable Life." *Dante and Italy in British Romanticism*. Edited by Frederick Burwick and Paul Douglass. United Kingdom: Palgrave Macmillan, 2011, pp. 93–104.

———. "Mary Robinson and the New Lyric." *Women's Writing*, vol. 9, no. 1, 2002, pp. 9–22.

———. "Mary Robinson's Lyrical Tales in Context." *Re-Visioning Romanticism: British Women Writers, 1776–1837*. Edited by Carol Shiner Wilson and Joel Haefner. Philadelphia: U of Pennsylvania P, 1994, pp. 17–35.

———. "The Political Prometheus." *Studies in Romanticism*, vol. 25, Fall 1986, pp. 260–284.

———. "Romantic Poetry: The I Altered." *Approaching Literature: Romantic Writings*. Edited by Stephen Bygrave. United Kingdom: Routledge, 1996, pp. 279–293.

Damasio, Antonio. *Self Comes to Mind: Constructing the Conscious Brain*. New York: Vintage, 2012.

Dawson, P.M.S. "'A Sort of Animal Magic': Shelley and Animal Magnetism." *Keats-Shelley Review*, vol. 1, 1986, pp. 15–34.

Deleuze, Gilles. *Difference and Repetition*. Translated by Paul Patton. New York: Columbia UP, 1995.

———. *Francis Bacon: The Logic of Sensation*. Translated by Daniel W. Smith. Minneapolis: U of Minnesota P, 2003.

Deleuze, Gilles, and Felix Guattari. *A Thousand Plateaus: Capitalism and Schizophrenia*. Translated by Brian Massumi. Minneapolis: U of Minnesota P, 1987.

De Almeida, Florida Hermione. *Romantic Medicine and John Keats*. United Kingdom: Oxford UP, 1991.

De Man, Paul. *Aesthetic Ideology*. Edited by Andrzej Warminski. Minneapolis: U of Minnesota P, 1996.

———. *Blindness and Insight: Essays in the Rhetoric of Contemporary Criticism*. 2nd ed. Minneapolis: U of Minnesota P, 1983.

———. "The Epistemology of Metaphor." *Critical Inquiry*, vol. 5, no. 1, 1978, pp. 13–30.

———. *The Rhetoric of Romanticism*. New York: Columbia UP, 1984.

Derrida, Jacques. *Of Hospitality*. Palo Alto, CA: Stanford UP, 2000.

———. *Rogues: Two Essays on Reason*. Palo Alto, CA: Stanford UP, 2005.

———. *Specters of Marx: The State of the Debt, the Work of Mourning and the New International*. United Kingdom: Routledge, 2012.

———. *The Truth in Painting*. Chicago, IL: U of Chicago P, 1987.

———. "Typewriter Ribbon: Limited Ink (2) ('within such limits')." *Material Events*. Edited by Tom Cohen, J. Hillis Miller, and Andrzej Warminski. Minneapolis: U of Minnesota P, 200, pp. 277–360.

D'Israeli, Isaac. *A Second Series of Curiosities of Literature: Consisting of Researches in Literary, Biographical, and Political History; of Critical and Philosophical Inquiries; and of Secret History*. Vol. 1. J. Murray, 1824. Google eBook. Accessed 19 Dec. 2013.

Dolan, Elizabeth A. "British Romantic Melancholia: Charlotte Smith's Elegiac Sonnets, Medical Discourse and the Problem of Sensibility." *Journal of European Studies*, vol. 33, no. 3–4, 2003, pp. 237–253.

———. *Seeing Suffering in Women's Literature of the Romantic Era*. United Kingdom: Ashgate, 2008.

Donnelly, Hugo. "Beyond Rational Discourse: The 'Mysterious Tongue' of 'Mont Blanc.'" *Studies in Romanticism*, vol. 29, no. 4, 1990, pp. 571–581.

Duffy, Cian. *Shelley and the Revolutionary Sublime*. United Kingdom: Cambridge UP, 2005.
Dykstal, Timothy. "The Politics of Taste in the *Spectator*." *Eighteenth Century Theory and Interpretation*, vol. 35, no. 1, 1994, pp. 46–63.
Edelman, Lee. *No Future: Queer Theory and the Death Drive*. Chapel Hill, NC: Duke UP, 2004.
Ellis, Markman. *The Politics of Sensibility: Race, Gender and Commerce in the Sentimental Novel*. United Kingdom: Cambridge UP, 2004.
Emerson, Ralph Waldo. *Emerson's Prose and Poetry*. New York: W.W. Norton & Company, 2001.
Espinasse, Francis. *Lancashire Worthies*. 2nd Series. London: Simpkin, Marshall & Co., 1877. Hathi Trust. Accessed 3 Dec. 2018.
Essick, Robert. "'A Shadow of Some Golden Dream': Shelley's Language in *Epipsychidion*." *Papers in Language and Literature*, vol. 22, 1986, pp. 165–175.
Faflak, Joel. *Romantic Psychoanalysis: The Burden of the Mystery*. Albany: State U of New York P, 2009.
Faflak, Joel, and Richard C. Sha, editors. *Romanticism and the Emotions*. United Kingdom: Cambridge UP, 2014.
Fagan, Deirdre. "Emily Dickinson's Unutterable Word." *Emily Dickinson Journal*, vol. 14, no. 2, 2005, pp. 70–75.
Fairclough, Mary. *The Romantic Crowd: Sympathy, Controversy and Print Culture*. United Kingdom: Cambridge UP, 2013.
Faubert, Michelle. "A Family Affair: Ennobling Suicide in Mary Shelley's *Matilda*." *Essays in Romanticism*, vol. 20, 2013, pp. 101–128.
Favret, Mary. *War at A Distance: Romanticism and the Making of Modern Wartime*. Princeton, NJ: Princeton, 2009.
Fay, Elizabeth. *Becoming Wordsworthian: A Performative Aesthetics*. Amherst: U of Massachusetts P, 1995.
Feldman, Paula R. "Endurance and Forgetting: What the Evidence Suggests." *Romanticism and Women Poets: Opening the Doors of Reception*. Edited by Harriet Kramer Linkin and Stephen C. Behrendt. Lexington: UP of Kentucky, 1999, pp. 15–21.
———. "The Poet and the Profits: Felicia Hemans and the Literary Marketplace." *Women's Poetry, Late Romantic to Late Victorian: Gender and Genre, 1830–1900*. Edited by Isobel Armstrong and Virginia Blain. New York: St. Martin's, 1999, pp. 71–101.
Ferber, Michael. *The Cambridge Introduction to British Romantic Poetry*. United Kingdom: Cambridge UP, 2012.
Ferguson, Frances. "Shelley's 'Mont Blanc': What the Mountain Said." *Romanticism and Language*. Edited by Arden Reed. Ithaca, NY: Cornell UP, 1984, pp. 202–214.
Festa, Lynn. *Sentimental Figures of Empire in Eighteenth-Century Britain and France*. Baltimore, MD: Johns Hopkins UP, 2006.

Fischman, Susan. "'Like the Sound of His Own Voice': Gender, Audition, and Echo in Alastor." *Keats-Shelley Journal*, vol. 43, 1994, pp. 141–169.
Fletcher, Loraine. *Charlotte Smith: A Critical Bibliography*. United Kingdom: Palgrave, 2001.
Fraistat, Neil. "Poetic Quests and Questioning in Shelley's *Alastor* Collection." *Keats-Shelley Journal*, vol. 33, 1984, pp. 161–181.
François, Anne-Lise. "'O Happy Living Things.' Frankenfoods and the Bounds of Wordsworthian Natural Piety." *Diacritics*, vol. 33, no. 2, Summer 2003, pp. 42–70.
Freeman, Barbara Claire. *The Feminine Sublime: Gender and Excess in Women's Fiction*. Berkeley: U of California P, 1995.
Fryckstedt, Monica Correa. "The Hidden Rill: The Life and Career of Maria Jane Jewsbury: I." *Bulletin of the John Rylands University Library of Manchester*, vol. 66, no. 2, 1984, pp. 177–203.
———. "The Hidden Rill: The Life and Career of Maria Jane Jewsbury: II." *Bulletin of the John Rylands University Library of Manchester*, vol. 67, no. 1, 1984, pp. 450–473.
Fulford, Tim. "Conducting the Vital Fluid: The Politics and Poetics of Mesmerism in the 1790s." *Studies in Romanticism*, vol. 43, no. 1, 2013, pp. 57–78.
———. "The Electrifying Mrs. Robinson." *Women's Writing*, vol. 9, no. 1, 2002, pp. 23–35.
———. "Mary Robinson and the Abyssinian Maid: Coleridge's Muses and Feminist Criticism." *Romanticism on the Net: An Electronic Journal Devoted to Romantic Studies*, vol. 13, 1999. Accessed 11 Dec. 2013.
Fulford, Timothy, and Peter J. Kitson. *Romanticism and Colonialism*. United Kingdom: Cambridge UP, 1998.
Gall, Franz Josef. *On the Functions of the Brain and of Each of Its Parts: On the Organ of the Moral Qualities and Intellectual Faculties, and the Plurality of the Cerebral Organs*. Boston: Marsh, Capen & Lyon, 1835. Google eBook. Accessed 8 Mar. 2013.
Gallagher, Catherine. *Nobody's Story: The Vanishing Acts of Women Writers in the Marketplace, 1670–1820*. Berkeley: U of California P, 1995.
Galperin, William H. *The Return of the Visible in British Romanticism*. Baltimore, MD: Johns Hopkins UP, 1993.
Gamer, Michael. *Romanticism and the Gothic: Genre, Reception, and Canon Formation*. United Kingdom: Cambridge UP, 2000.
Garnai, Amy. *Revolutionary Imaginings in the 1790s: Charlotte Smith, Mary Robinson, Elizabeth Inchbald*. United Kingdom: Palgrave Macmillan, 2009.
Garofalo, Daniela. *Women, Love, and Commodity Culture in British Romanticism*. United Kingdom: Ashgate, 2012.
Gasché, Rodolphe. *The Idea of Form: Rethinking Kant's Aesthetics*. Palo Alto, CA: Stanford UP, 2003.
Ghose, Indira. *Women Travellers in Colonial India*. United Kingdom: Oxford UP, USA, 1999.

Gigante, Denise. *Taste*. New Haven, CT: Yale UP, 2005.
Gillett, Eric. *Maria Jane Jewsbury. Occasional Papers, Selected with a Memoir*. United Kingdom: Oxford UP, 1932.
Godwin, William. *An Enquiry Concerning Political Justice*. United Kingdom: Oxford UP, 2013.
———. *Fleetwood*. Edited by Gary Handwerk and A. A. Markley. Canada: Broadview Press, 2001.
Goldsmith, Steven. *Blake's Agitation: Criticism and the Emotions*. Baltimore, MD: Johns Hopkins UP, 2013.
Goldstein, Amanda Jo, "Growing Old Together: Lucretian Materialism in Shelley's 'Poetry of Life'." *Representations*, vol. 128, Fall 2014, pp. 60–92.
Goode, Mike. *Sentimental Masculinity and the Rise of History, 1790–1890*. United Kingdom: Cambridge UP, 2009.
Goodman, Kevis. "Conjectures on Beachy Head: Charlotte Smith's Geological Poetics and the Grounds of the Present." *ELH*, vol. 81, no. 3, 2014, pp. 983–1006.
———. *Georgic Modernity and British Romanticism: Poetry and the Mediation of History*. United Kingdom: Cambridge UP, 2004.
Goslee, Nancy Moore. "Dispersoning Emily: Drafting as Plot in *Epipsychidion*." *Keats-Shelley Journal*, vol. 42, 1993, pp. 104–119.
———. "Hemans's 'Red Indians': Reading Stereotypes." *Romanticism, Race, and Imperial Culture, 1780–1834*. Edited by Alan Richardson and Sonia Hofkosh. Indianapolis: Indiana UP, 1996, pp. 237–261.
Gottlieb, Evan. "Fighting Words: Representing the Napoleonic Wars in the Poetry of Hemans and Barbauld." *European Romantic Review*, vol. 20, no. 3, 2009, pp. 327–343.
———. *Romantic Realities: Speculative Realism and British Romanticism*. United Kingdom: Edinburgh UP, 2016.
———. "Seeing into the Life of Things: Re-Viewing Early Wordsworth through Object-Oriented Philosophy." *Beyond Sense and Sensibility: Moral Formation and the Literary Imagination from Johnson to Wordsworth*. Lewisburg, PA: Bucknell UP, 2015, pp. 145–162.
Grant, Anne Macvicar. *Memoirs of an American Lady with Sketches of Manners and Scenes as They Existed Previous to the Revolution*. New York: D. Appleton & Co., 1846. Internet Archive. Accessed 3 Dec. 2018.
Grant, Edward. *Much Ado About Nothing: Theories of Space and Vacuum from the Middle Ages to the Scientific Revolution*. United Kingdom: Cambridge UP, 1981.
Gravil, Richard. *Wordsworth and Helen Maria Williams; or, the Perils of Sensibility*. Tirril, Penrith: Humanities-Ebooks, 2010. Accessed 15 Mar. 2014.
Gray, Erik. *The Poetry of Indifference*. Amherst: U of Massachusetts P, 2005.
Greville, Frances. "A Prayer for Indifference." *Eighteenth-Century Women Poets: An Oxford Anthology*. Edited by Roger Lonsdale. United Kingdom: Oxford, 1989.
Griggs, Earl Leslie. "Coleridge and Mrs. Mary Robinson." *Modern Language Notes*, vol. 45, no. 2, 1930, pp. 90–95.

Groom, Nick. *The Making of Percy's Reliques*. New York: Clarendon Press, 1999.
Grosz, Elizabeth. *Volatile Bodies: Toward a Corporeal Feminism*. Indianapolis: Indiana UP, 1994.
Grusin, Richard, ed. *The Nonhuman Turn*. Minneapolis: U of Minnesota P, 2015.
Guest, Harriet. "Charlotte Smith, Mary Robinson and the First Year of the War with France." *The History of British Women's Writing, 1750–1830*. Edited by Jacqueline M. Labbe. United Kingdom: Palgrave Macmillan, 2010, pp. 207–230.
Gurton-Wachter, Lily. "Blake's Blush." *Blake: Modernity and Disaster*, edited by Tilottama Rajan and Joel Faflak. Canada: U of Toronto P, forthcoming.
Harding, Anthony J. "Felicia Hemans and the Effacement of Women." *Romantic Women Writers: Voices and Countervoices*. Edited by Paula R. Feldman and Theresa M. Kelley. Lebanon, NH: UP of New England, 1995, pp. 138–149.
Hargreaves-Mawdsley, W. N. *The English Della Cruscans and Their Time, 1783–1828*. Netherlands: Martinus Nijhoff, 1967.
Hart, Monica Smith. "Charlotte Smith's Exilic Persona." *Partial Answers: Journal of Literature and the History of Ideas*, vol. 8, no. 2, 2010, pp. 305–323.
Hartley, David. *Observations on Man: His Frame, His Duty, and His Expectations. In Two Parts*. 6th ed. United Kingdom: Thomas Tegg and Son, 1834.
Hartman, Anne. "Hemans, Hume, and Philosophical Skepticism." *The Sceptic: A Hemans-Byron Dialogue*. Edited by Nanora Sweet and Barbara Taylor. *Romantic Circles*. January 2004. Accessed 8 Mar. 2013.
Hartman, Geoffrey H. *The Unremarkable Wordsworth*. Minneapolis: U of Minnesota P, 1987.
Hatherell, William. "'Words and Things': Locke, Hartley and the Associationist Context for the Preface to *Lyrical Ballads*." *Romanticism*, vol. 12, no. 3, 2008, pp. 223–235.
Hawley, Judith. "Charlotte Smith's Elegiac Sonnets, Losses and Gains." *Women's Poetry in the Enlightenment: The Making of a Canon, 1730–1820*. Edited by Isobel Armstrong and Virginia Blain. New York: St. Martin's, 1999, pp. 184–198.
———. "Romantic Patronage: Mary Robinson and Coleridge Revisited." *British Women's Writing in the Long Eighteenth Century: Authorship, Politics and History*. Edited by Jennie Batchelor and Cora Kaplan. United Kingdom: Palgrave Macmillan, 2005, pp. 62–75.
Hayter, Alethea. *Opium and the Romantic Imagination*. Berkeley: U of California P, 1968.
Hemans, Felicia. *Felicia Hemans Commonplace Books*. Ms. FH 0050. The Carl H. Pforzheimer Collection. New York Public Library, New York.
———. *Felicia Hemans: Selected Poems, Letters, Reception Materials*. Edited by Susan J. Wolfson. Princeton, NJ: Princeton UP, 2000.
———. Letter to James Simpson. 12 April 1824. Ms. FH 0053. The Carl H. Pforzheimer Collection. New York Public Library, New York.
———. *The Sceptic: A Hemans-Byron Dialogue*. Edited by Nanora Sweet and Barbara Taylor. Jan. 2004. *Romantic Circles*. Accessed 8 Mar. 2013.

Henderson, Andrea. *Romanticism and the Painful Pleasures of Modern Life.* United Kingdom: Cambridge UP, 2007.

Hilbish, Florence M. A. *Charlotte Smith, Poet and Novelist (1749–1806).* Philadelphia: U of Pennsylvania P, 1941.

Hitt, Christopher. "Shelley's Unwriting of Mont Blanc." *Texas Studies in Literature and Language*, vol. 47, no. 2, 2005, pp. 139–166.

Hoagwood, Terence Allan. *Skepticism & Ideology: Shelley's Political Prose and Its Philosophical Context from Bacon to Marx.* Iowa City: U of Iowa P, 1988.

Hodgson, Adam. *Letters from North America Written during a Tour in the United States and Canada.* Two volumes. United Kingdom: Hurst, Robinson, & Co., 1824. Internet Archive. Accessed 3 Dec. 2018.

Hoeveler, Diane Long. Romantic Androgyny: *The Women Within.* Philadelphia: U of Pennsylvania P, 1991.

Hofkosh, Sonia. "A Woman's Profession: Sexual Difference and the Romance of Authorship." *Studies in Romanticism*, vol. 32, no. 2, 1993, pp. 245–272.

———. *Sexual Politics and the Romantic Author.* United Kingdom: Cambridge UP, 1998.

———. "The Writer's Ravishment: Women and the Romantic Author—the Example of Byron." *Romanticism and Feminism.* Edited by Anne K. Mellor. Bloomington: Indiana UP, 1988, pp. 93–114.

Hogle, Jerrold E. "Frankenstein as Neo-Gothic: From the Ghost of the Counterfeit to the Monster of Abjection." *Between Cultures: Transformations of Genre in Romanticism.* Edited by Tilottama Rajan and Julia Wright. United Kingdom: Cambridge UP, pp. 176–210.

———. *Shelley's Process: Radical Transference and the Development of His Major Works.* New York: Oxford UP, 1988.

Hogsette, David S. "Eclipsed by the Pleasure Dome: Poetic Failure in Coleridge's 'Kubla Khan.'" *Romanticism on the Net: An Electronic Journal Devoted to Romantic Studies*, vol. 5, 1997. Accessed 11 Dec. 2013.

Holmes, Richard. *Shelley: The Pursuit.* New York: New York Review Books, 2003.

Homans, Margaret. *Women Writers and Poetic Identity: Dorothy Wordsworth, Emily Brontë, and Emily Dickinson.* Princeton, NJ: Princeton UP, 1980.

Hume, David. *An Inquiry Concerning Human Understanding.* Edited by Charles W. Hendel. Upper Saddle River, NJ: Prentice Hall, 1995.

———. *Selected Essays.* United Kingdom: Oxford UP, 1993.

———. *A Treatise of Human Nature.* New York: Penguin Classics, 1985.

Irving, Theodore. *The Conquest of Florida by Hernando de Soto.* New York: George P. Putnam, 1851. HathiTrust. Accessed 3 Dec. 2018.

Irving, Washington. *The Sketch-Book of Geoffrey Crayon, Gent.* Edited by Susan Manning. United Kingdom: Oxford UP, 1998.

Jacobus, Mary. *Romanticism, Writing, and Sexual Difference: Essays on The Prelude.* United Kingdom: Oxford UP, 1995.

———. *Romantic Things: A Tree, A Rock, A Cloud.* Chicago, IL: U of Chicago P, 2012.

Jackson, Noel. *Science and Sensation in Romantic Poetry*. United Kingdom: Cambridge UP, 2008.

Jackson, Virginia, and Yopie Prins. "Lyrical Studies." *Victorian Literature and Culture*, vol. 27, no. 2, 1999, pp. 521–530.

Jager, Colin. "Can We Talk About Consciousness Again? (Emergence, Natural Piety, Wordsworth)." *Romantic Frictions*. Edited by Theresa M. Kelley. September 2011. *Romantic Circles*. www.rc.umd.edu/praxis/frictions/HTML/praxis.2011.jager.html. Accessed 8 Mar. 2017.

Jarvis, Simon. *Wordsworth's Philosophic Song*. United Kingdom: Cambridge UP, 2007.

Jewsbury, Maria Jane. "Extracts from a Lady's Log-Book." *Athenaeum*, 1 December 1832, pp. 777–778. *The Oceanides*. Edited by Judith Pascoe. *Romantic Circles Editions*. Accessed 23 Feb. 2013.

———. "Extracts from a Lady's Log-Book." *Athenaeum*, 22 December 1832, pp. 824–825. *The Oceanides*. Edited by Judith Pascoe. *Romantic Circles Editions*. Accessed 23 Feb. 2013.

———. *Letters to the Young*. New York: D. Appleton & Co., 1835. Accessed 8 Dec. 2013.

———. "The Nature and Dignity of Christ. By Joanna Baillie." Review of "The Nature and Dignity of Christ" by Joanna Baillie. *Athenaeum*, 28 May 1831.

———. "On Modern Female Cultivation, No. 1." *Athenaeum*, 4 February 1832, pp. 79–80.

———. "On Modern Female Cultivation, No. 2." *Athenaeum*, 11 February 1832, pp. 95–96.

———. "On Modern Female Cultivation, No. 3." *Athenaeum*, 25 February 1832, p. 129.

———. "On Modern Female Cultivation, No. 4." *Athenaeum*, 11 August 1832, pp. 521–522.

———. *The Oceanides*. Edited by Judith Pascoe. *Romantic Circles Editions*. College Park, MD, U of Maryland P. Accessed 23 Feb. 2013.

———. *Phantasmagoria; Or, Sketches of Literature*. Two volumes. United Kingdom: Hurst, Robinson and Company and Archibald Constable and Company, 1825.

———. Rylands English MS 1320. United Kingdom: John Rylands Library, University of Manchester.

———. "Shelley's 'Wandering Jew.'" Review of "Wandering Jew" by Percy Bysshe Shelley. *Athenaeum*, 1831, pp. 456–457.

———. WLMS A. The Wordsworth Trust. Dove Cottage, Cambria, UK.

Joffe, Sharon Lynne. *The Kinship Coterie and the Literary Endeavors of the Women in the Shelley Circle*. New York: Peter Lang, 2007.

Johnson, Claudia. *Equivocal Beings: Politics, Gender, and Sentimentality in the 1790s*. Chicago, IL: U of Chicago P, 1995.

Jones, Christopher. *Radical Sensibility: Literature and Ideas in the 1790s*. United Kingdom: Routledge, 1993.

Judson, Barbara. "The Politics of Medusa: Shelley's Physiognomy of Revolution." *ELH*, vol. 68, no. 1, 2001, pp. 135–154.

———. "Under the Influence: Owenson, Shelley, and the Religion of Dreams." *Modern Philology: Critical and Historical Studies in Literature, Medieval Through Contemporary*, vol. 104, no. 2, 2006, pp. 202–223.

Jump, Harriet Devine. "'My Dearest Geraldine': Maria Jane Jewsbury's Letters." *Bulletin of the John Rylands University Library of Manchester*, vol. 81, no. 1, 1999, pp. 63–72.

Jung, Sandro. "Some Notes on the 'Single Sentiment' and Romanticism of Charlotte Smith." *Connotations: A Journal for Critical Debate*, vol. 9, no. 3, 1999, pp. 269–284.

Kant, Immanuel. *Critique of Judgment*. Translated by Paul Guyer and Eric Matthews. United Kingdom: Cambridge UP, 2001.

———. *Perpetual Peace and Other Essays on Politics, History, and Morals*. Translated by Ted Humphrey. Indianapolis: Hackett Publishing Company, 1983.

Kaufman, Robert. "Legislators of the Post-Everything World: Shelley's Defence of Adorno." *English Literary History*, vol. 63, no. 3, Fall 1996, pp. 707–733.

———. "Negatively Capable Dialectics: Keats, Vendler, Adorno, and the Theory of the Avant-Garde." *Critical Inquiry*, vol. 27, no. 2, Winter 2001, 354–384.

———. "Red Kant: or, the Persistence of the Third Critique in Adorno and Jameson." *Critical Inquiry*, vol. 26, no. 4, 2000, 710–712.

Keach, William. *Shelley's Style*. United Kingdom: Routledge, 1984.

Keats, John. *John Keats's Poetry and Prose*. Edited by Jeffrey N. Cox. New York: W.W. Norton & Company, 2008.

Kelley, Theresa M. *Clandestine Marriage: Botany and Romantic Culture*. Baltimore, MD: Johns Hopkins UP, 2012.

———. "Romantic Exemplarity: Botany and 'Material' Culture." *Romantic Science: The Literary Forms of Natural History*. Edited by Noah Heringman. Albany: State U of New York P, 2003, pp. 223–254.

———. "Romantic Histories: Charlotte Smith and *Beachy Head*." *Nineteenth-Century Literature*, vol. 59, no. 3, 2004, pp. 281–314.

Kelly, Gary. "Death and the Matron: Felicia Hemans, Romantic Death, and the Founding of the Modern Liberal State." *Felicia Hemans: Reimagining Poetry in the Nineteenth Century*. Edited by Nanora Sweet and Julie Melnyk. United Kingdom: Palgrave, 2001, pp. 196–211.

———. "Felicia Hemans, Schillerian Drama, and the Feminization of History." *Women's Romantic Theater and Drama: History, Agency, and Performativity*. Edited by Lilla Maria Crisafulli and Keir Elam. United Kingdom: Ashgate, 2010, pp. 85–99.

Kerr, Heather. "Melancholy Botany: Charlotte Smith's Bioregional Poetic Imaginary." *The Bioregional Imagination: Literature, Ecology, and Place*. Edited by Tom Lynch, Cheryll Glotfelty, and Karla Armbruster. Athens: U of Georgia P, 2012, pp. 181–199.

Khalip, Jacques. *Anonymous Life: Romanticism and Dispossession*. Palo Alto, CA: Stanford UP, 2008.

Kim, Benjamin. *Wordsworth, Hemans, and Politics, 1800–1830: Romantic Crises*. Lewisburg, PA: Bucknell UP, 2013.

Kitson, Peter J. *Romantic Literature, Race, and Colonial Encounter*. United Kingdom: Palgrave Macmillan, 2007.

Knott, Sarah. *Sensibility and the American Revolution*. Chapel Hill: U of North Carolina P, 2009.

Knowles, Claire. Sensibility and Female Poetic Tradition, 1780–1860: The Legacy of Charlotte Smith. United Kingdom: Ashgate, 2009.

Kowalski-Wallace, Elizabeth. *Consuming Subjects: Women, Shopping, and Business in the Eighteenth Century*. New York: Columbia UP, 1997.

Kristeva, Julia. *Nations without Nationalism*. New York: Columbia UP, 1993.

Kurshan, Ilana. "Mind Reading: Literature in the Discourse of Early Victorian Phrenology and Mesmerism." *Victorian Literary Mesmerism*. Edited by Martin Willis and Catherine Wynne. Amsterdam: Rodopi, 2006, pp. 17–37.

Labbe, Jacqueline M. *Charlotte Smith: Romanticism, Poetry and the Culture of Gender*. United Kingdom: Manchester UP, 2003.

———. "The Hybrid Poems of Smith and Wordsworth: Questions and Disputes." *European Romantic Review*, vol. 20, no. 2, 2009, pp. 219–226.

———. "Revisiting the Egotistical Sublime: Smith, Wordsworth, and the Romantic Dramatic Monologue." *Fellow Romantics: Male and Female British Writers, 1790–1835*. Edited by Beth Lau. United Kingdom: Ashgate, 2009, pp. 17–38.

———. "Romance and Violence in Mary Robinson's Lyrical Tales and Other Gothic Poetry." *"A Natural Delineation of Human Passions": The Historic Moment of Lyrical Ballads*. Edited by C. C. Barfoot. Netherlands: Rodopi, 2004, pp. 137–156.

———. "Selling One's Sorrows: Charlotte Smith, Mary Robinson, and the Marketing of Poetry." *The Wordsworth Circle*, vol. 25, no. 2, 1994, pp. 68–71.

———. "'Transplanted into More Congenial Soil': Footnoting the Self in the Poetry of Charlotte Smith." *Ma(r)king the Text: The Presentation of Meaning on the Literary Page*. Edited by Joe Bray et al. United Kingdom: Ashgate, 2000, pp. 71–86.

———. *Writing Romanticism: Charlotte Smith and William Wordsworth, 1784–1807*. United Kingdom: Palgrave Macmillan, 2011.

Lanser, Susan. "'Put to the Blush': Romantic Irregularities and Sapphic Tropes." *Historicizing Romantic Sexuality*. Edited by Richard Sha. January 2006. *Romantic Circles*. www.rc.umd.edu/praxis/sexuality/lanser/lanser.html. Accessed 11 Dec. 2013.

Laqueur, Thomas. *Making Sex: Body and Gender from Greeks to Freud*. Cambridge, MA: Harvard UP, 1990.

Lau, Beth. *Fellow Romantics: Male and Female British Writers, 1790–1835*. United Kingdom: Ashgate, 2009.

Lawrence, William. *Lectures on Physiology, Zoology, and the Natural History of Man.* J. United Kingdom: Callow, 1819.

Leask, Nigel. *British Romantic Writers and the East: Anxieties of Empire.* United Kingdom: Cambridge UP, 1993.

———. *Curiosity and the Aesthetics of Travel-Writing, 1770–1840: "From an Antique Land."* United Kingdom: Oxford UP, 2004.

———. "Shelley's 'Magnetic Ladies': Romantic Mesmerism and the Politics of the Body." *Beyond Romanticism: New Approaches to Texts and Contexts, 1780–1832.* Edited by Stephen Copley and John Whale. Syracuse, NY: Syracuse UP, 1991, pp. 53–78.

Ledbetter, Kathryn. "A Woman of Undoubted Genius: Mary Robinson and S. T. Coleridge." *Postscript*, vol. 11, no. 1, 1994, pp. 43–49.

Leighton, Angela. *Shelley and the Sublime: An Interpretation of the Major Poems.* United Kingdom: Cambridge UP, 1984.

———. *Victorian Women Poets: Writing Against the Heart.* Charlottesville: U of Virginia P, 1992.

Levinson, Marjorie, "'A Motion and A Spirit: Romancing Spinoza." *Studies in Romanticism*, vol. 46, 2007, pp. 367–408.

Levy, Martin J. "Coleridge, Mary Robinson and Kubla Khan." *Charles Lamb Bulletin*, vol. 77, 1992, pp. 156–166.

Leys, Ruth. "The Turn to Affect: A Critique." *Critical Inquiry*, vol. 37, no. 3, Spring 2011, pp. 434–472.

Linkin, Harriet Kramer. "Romantic Aesthetics in Mary Tighe and Letitia Landon: How Women Recuperate the Gaze." *European Romantic Review*, vol. 7, 1997, pp. 25–39.

Liu, Alan. *Wordsworth: The Sense of History.* Palo Alto, CA: Stanford UP, 1991.

Livingston, Donald W. "David Hume and the Conservative Tradition." *Intercollegiate Review*, vol. 44, no. 2, Fall 2009, pp. 30–41.

Locke, John. *An Essay Concerning Human Understanding.* 2nd ed. New York: Penguin, 1998.

Locke, Don. *A Fantasy of Reason.* United Kingdom: Routledge, 2013.

Lokash, Jennifer. "Shelley's Organic Sympathy: Natural Communitarianism and the Example of Alastor." *Wordsworth Circle*, vol. 28, no. 3, 1997, pp. 177–183.

Lokke, Kari. "Embodied Compassion: The Figure of the Hermit in Charlotte Smith's *Beachy Head*." *Charlotte Smith in British Romanticism.* Edited by Jacqueline Labbe. United Kingdom: Pickering and Chatto, 2008, pp. 45–56.

———. "The Figure of the Hermit in Charlotte Smith's Beachy Head." *Wordsworth Circle*, vol. 39, nos. 1–2, 2008, pp. 38–43.

———. "'The Mild Dominion of the Moon': Charlotte Smith and the Politics of Transcendence." *Rebellious Hearts: British Women Writers and the French Revolution.* Edited by Adriana Craciun, Kari E. Lokke, and Madelyn Gutwirth. Albany: State U of New York P, 2001, pp. 85–106.

———. "Poetry as Self-Consumption: Women Writers and Their Audiences in British and German Romanticism." *Romantic Poetry*. Edited by Angela Esterhammer. Netherlands: Benjamins, 2002, pp. 91–111.

Looser, Devoney, editor. *The Cambridge Companion to Women's Writing in the Romantic Period*. United Kingdom; Cambridge UP, 2016.

Lootens, Tricia. "Hemans and Home: Victorianism, Feminine 'Internal Enemies,' and the Domestication of National Identity." *PMLA: Publications of the Modern Language Association of America*, vol. 109, no. 2, 1994, pp. 238–253.

Low, Dennis. "Gold and Silver Fishes in a Vase: A Portrait of Wordsworth and Maria Jane Jewsbury." *Coleridge Bulletin: The Journal of the Friends of Coleridge*, vol. 25, 2005, pp. 61–70.

———. *The Literary Protégées of the Lake Poets*. United Kingdom: Ashgate, 2006.

Lumsden, Simon. "The Rise of the Non-Metaphysical Hegel." *Philosophy Compass*, vol. 3, no. 1, 2007, pp. 51–65.

Lussier, Mark. *Romantic Dynamics: The Poetics of Physicality*. United Kingdom: Palgrave Macmillan, 2000.

———. "Shelley's Poetics, Wave Dynamics, and the Telling Rhythm of Complementarity." *The Wordsworth Circle*, vol. 34, no. 2, 2003, pp. 91–95.

Luther, Susan. "A Stranger Minstrel: Coleridge's Mrs. Robinson." *Studies in Romanticism*, vol. 33, no. 3, 1994, pp. 391–409.

Luu, Helen. "Fantasies of 'Woman': Hemans's Deconstruction of 'Femininity' in Records of Woman." *Women's Writing*, vol. 21, no. 1, 2014, pp. 41–57.

Mackie, Erin, ed. *The Commerce of Everyday Life*. New York: Bedford/St. Martin's Press, 1998.

———. *Market à la Mode: Fashion, Commodity and Gender in* The Tatler *and* The Spectator. Baltimore, MD: Johns Hopkins UP, 1997.

Makdisi, Saree, and Felicity Nussbaum, eds. *The Arabian Nights in Historical Context: Between East and West*. United Kingdom: Oxford UP, 2009.

Malabou, Catherine. *The Future of Hegel: Plasticity, Temporality and Dialectic*. United Kingdom: Routledge, 2004.

Manning, Peter J. *Reading Romantics: Texts and Contexts*. New York: Oxford UP, 1990.

Marshall, Peter H. *William Godwin*. New Haven, CT: Yale UP, 1984.

Marx, Karl. *Capital: A Critique of Political Economy*. Translated by Ben Fowkes. New York: Penguin, 1992.

Mason, Emma, and Jonathan Roberts. "Felicia Hemans's Sonnets on Female Characters of Scripture." *Yearbook of English Studies*, vol. 39, nos. 1–2, 2009, pp. 72–83.

———. *Women Poets of the Nineteenth Century*. United Kingdom: Northcote House Publishers, 2006.

Massumi, Brian. *Parables for the Virtual: Movement, Affect, Sensation*. Chapel Hill, NC: Duke UP, 2002.

———. *Politics of Affect*. New York: Polity, 2015.

Mazzeo, Tilar. "The Strains of Empire: Shelley and the Music of India." *Romantic Representations of British India*. Edited by Michael J. Franklin. United Kingdom: Routledge, 2006.

McCarthy, Anne C. "The Aesthetics of Contingency in the Shelleyan 'Universe of Things,' or, 'Mont Blanc' without Mont Blanc." *Studies in Romanticism*, vol. 54, no. 3, 2015, pp. 355–375.

McDayter, Ghislaine. "O'er Leaping the Bounds: The Sexing of the Creative Soul in Shelley's *Epipsychidion*." *Keats-Shelley Journal*, vol. 52, 2003, pp. 21–49.

McGann, Jerome. "Literary History, Romanticism, and Felicia Hemans." *Re-Visioning Romanticism: British Women Writers, 1776–1837*. Edited by Carol Shiner Wilson and Joel Haefner. Philadelphia: U of Pennsylvania P, 1994, pp. 210–227.

———. "Mary Robinson and the Myth of Sappho." *Eighteenth-Century Literary History: An MLQ Reader*. Edited by Marshall Brown. Chapel Hill, NC: Duke UP, 1999, pp. 114–135.

———. "Mary Robinson and the Myth of Sappho." *Modern Language Quarterly: A Journal of Literary History*, vol. 56, no. 1, 1995, pp. 55–76.

———. *The Poetics of Sensibility: A Revolution in Literary Style*. United Kingdom: Oxford UP, 1998.

———. *Romantic Ideology: A Critical Investigation*. Chicago, IL: U of Chicago P, 1985.

McGrath, Brian. "Material Excursions." *Romantic Materialities*. Edited by Sara Guyer and Celeste Langan. February 2015. Romantic Circles. www.rc.umd.edu/praxis/materialities/index.html. Accessed 31 May 2017.

McLane, Maureen N. *Balladeering, Minstrelsy, and the Making of British Romantic Poetry*. United Kingdom: Cambridge UP, 2008.

Mellor, Anne K. *Romanticism and Feminism*. Bloomington: Indiana UP, 1988.

———. *Romanticism and Gender*. United Kingdom: Routledge, 1992.

Mellor, Anne K., and Richard E. Matlak. *British Literature 1780–1830*. San Diego, CA: Harcourt Brace College Publishers, 1996.

Melnyk, Julie. "Hemans's Later Poetry: Religion and the Vatic Poet." *Felicia Hemans: Reimagining Poetry in the Nineteenth Century*. Edited by Nanora Sweet and Julie Melnyk. United Kingdom: Palgrave, 2001, pp. 74–92.

———. "William Wordsworth and Felicia Hemans." *Fellow Romantics: Male and Female British Writers, 1790–1835*. Edited by Beth Lau. United Kingdom: Ashgate, 2009, pp. 139–158.

Melville, Peter. *Romantic Hospitality and the Resistance to Accommodation*. Canada: Wilfrid Laurier UP, 2007.

Mendis, G. C. *Ceylon Under the British*. Asian Educational Services, 2005. Google eBook. Accessed 8 Dec. 2013.

———. *The Early History of Ceylon and Its Relations with India and Other Foreign Countries*. India: Asian Educational Services, 1996. Google eBook. Accessed 8 Dec. 2013.

Mergenthal, Silvia. "Charlotte Smith and the Romantic Sonnet Revival." *Feminist Contributions to the Literary Canon: Setting Standards of Taste*. Edited by Susanne Fendler. Lewiston, NY: Mellen, 1997, pp. 65–79.

Miller, Jonathan. "Going Unconscious." *The New York Review of Books*, 20 April 1995. www.nybooks.com/articles/1995/04/20/going-unconscious. Accessed 12 Dec. 2017.

Milnes, Tim. *The Truth about Romanticism. Pragmatism and Idealism in Keats, Shelley, Coleridge*. United Kingdom: Cambridge UP, 2010.

Mitchell, Robert. "Suspended Animation, Slow Time, and the Poetics of Trance." *PMLA*, vol. 126, no. 1, 2011, pp. 107–122.

———. *Sympathy and the State in the Romantic Era: Systems, State Finance, and the Shadows of Futurity*. United Kingdom: Routledge, 2007.

———. "The Transcendental: Deleuze, P. B. Shelley, and the Freedom of Immobility." *Romanticism and the New Deleuze*. Edited by Ron Broglio and Rob Mitchell. January 2008. *Romantic Circles*. www.rc.umd.edu/praxis/deleuze/mitchell/mitchell.html. Accessed 11 Dec. 2013.

Mitchell, W.J.T. *Iconology: Image, Text, Ideology*. Chicago, IL: U of Chicago P, 1986.

Mole, Tom. "Mary Robinson's Conflicted Celebrity." *Romanticism and Celebrity Culture, 1750–1850*. Edited by Tom Mole. United Kingdom: Cambridge UP, 2009, pp. 186–205.

Moore, Hannah. "Sensibility: A Poetical Epistle to the Hon. Mrs. Boscawen." *Romanticism: An Anthology*. Edited by Duncan Wu. 4th ed. Hoboken, NJ: Wiley-Blackwell, 2012.

Moore, Mary B. *Desiring Voices: Women Sonneteers and Petrarchism*. Carbondale, IL: Southern Illinois UP, 2000.

Morton, Timothy. *Shelley and the Revolution in Taste*. United Kingdom: Cambridge UP, 1994.

Mueschke, Paul, and Earl L. Griggs. "Wordsworth as the Prototype of the Poet in Shelley's *Alastor*." *PMLA: Publications of the Modern Language Association of America*, vol. 49, no. 1, 1934, pp. 229–245.

Mullan, John. *Sentiment and Sociability: The Language of Feeling in the Eighteenth Century*. United Kingdom: Oxford UP, 1988.

Mulrooney, Jonathan. "How Keats Falls." *Studies in Romanticism*, vol. 50, no. 2, Summer 2011, pp. 251–273.

———. "Keats's Avatar." *European Romantic Review*, vol. 22, no. 3, 2011, pp. 313–321.

Myers, Anne. "Charlotte Smith's Androgynous Sonnets." *European Romantic Review*, vol. 13, no. 4, 2002, pp. 379–382.

Myers, Mary Anne. "Unsexing Petrarch: Charlotte Smith's Lessons in the Sonnet as Social Medium." *Studies in Romanticism*, vol. 53, no. 2, 2014, pp. 239–263.

Nagle, Christopher. *Sexuality and the Culture of Sensibility in the British Romantic Era*. United Kingdom: Palgrave, 2007.

Najarian, James. *Victorian Keats: Manliness, Sexuality and Desire*. United Kingdom: Palgrave Macmillan, 2002.

Ngai, Sianne. *Ugly Feelings*. Cambridge, MA: Harvard UP, 2007.

Nichols, Anne. "Glorification of the Lowly in Felicia Hemans' Sonnets 'Female Characters of Scripture.'" *Victorian Poetry*, vol. 48, no. 4, 2010, pp. 559–575.

Noggle, James. "Unfelt Affect." *Beyond Sense and Sensibility: Moral Formation and the Literary Imagination from Johnson to Wordsworth*. Lewisburg, PA: Bucknell UP, 2015, pp. 125–144.

Olkowski, Dorothea. "Deleuze's Aesthetics of Sensation." *The Cambridge Companion to Deleuze*. Edited by Daniel Smith and Henry Somers-Hall. United Kingdom: Cambridge UP, 2012, pp. 265–306.

O'Malley, Glenn. *Shelley and Synesthesia*. Evanston, IL: Northwestern UP, 1964.

O'Neill, Michael. *The Cambridge History of English Poetry*. United Kingdom: Cambridge UP, 2010.

———. "'A Deeper and Richer Music': Felicia Hemans in Dialogue with Wordsworth, Byron and Shelley." *Charles Lamb Bulletin*, vol. 145, 2009, pp. 3–12.

Ostas, Magdalena. "Kant with Michael Fried: Feeling, Absorption, and Interiority in the *Critique of Judgment*." *symploke* vol. 18, no. 1, 2010, pp.15–31.

Otto, Peter. *Multiplying Worlds: Romanticism, Modernity, and the Emergence of Virtual Reality*. United Kingdom: Oxford UP, 2011.

Owensen, Sydney. *The Missionary: An Indian Tale*. Edited by Julia M. Wright. Orchard Park, NY: Broadview Press, 2002.

Özdemir, Erinç. "Charlotte Smith's Poetry as Sentimental Discourse." *Studies in Romanticism*, vol. 50, no. 3, 2011, pp. 437–473.

Pascoe, Judith. "Female Botanists and the Poetry of Charlotte Smith." *Re-Visioning Romanticism: British Women Writers, 1776–1837*. Edited by Carol Shiner Wilson and Joel Haefner. Philadelphia: U of Pennsylvania P, 1994, pp. 193–209.

———. "Mary Robinson and the Literary Marketplace." *Romantic Women Writers: Voices and Countervoices*. Edited by Paula R. Feldman and Theresa M. Kelley. Lebanon, NH: UP of New England, 1995, pp. 252–268.

———. "Mary Robinson and Your Brilliant Career." *Romanticism on the Net: An Electronic Journal Devoted to Romantic Studies*, vol. 19, 2000.

———. *Romantic Theatricality: Gender, Poetry, and Spectatorship*. Ithaca, NY: Cornell UP, 1997.

———. "The Spectacular Flâneuse: Mary Robinson and the City of London." *The Wordsworth Circle*, vol. 23, no. 3, 1992, pp. 165–171.

———. "'Unsex'd Females': Barbauld, Robinson, and Smith." *The Cambridge Companion to English Literature 1740–1830*. Edited by Thomas Keymer and Jon Mee. United Kingdom: Cambridge UP, 2004, pp. 210–226.

Pfau, Thomas. *Romantic Moods: Paranoia, Trauma, and Melancholy, 1790–1840*. Baltimore, MD: Johns Hopkins UP, 2005.

———. "Tropes of Desire: Figuring the 'Insufficient Void' of Self-Consciousness in Shelley's *Epipsychidion*." *Keats-Shelley Journal*, vol. 40, 1991, pp. 99–126.

Phillips, Jane E. "Lucretian Echoes in Shelley's 'Mont Blanc.'" *Classical and Modern Literature*, vol. 2, no. 2, 1982, pp. 71–93.

Pinch, Adela. *Strange Fits of Passion*. Palo Alto, CA: Stanford UP, 2006.

Plotnitsky, Arkady. "All Shapes of Light: The Quantum Mechanical Shelley." *Shelley: Poet and Legislator of the World*. Edited by Stuart Curran and Betty T. Bennett. Baltimore, MD: Johns Hopkins UP, 1995, pp. 263–273.

Plotz, Judith. *Romanticism and the Vocation of Childhood*. United Kingdom: Palgrave, 2001.

Pratt, Kathryn. "Charlotte Smith's Melancholia on the Page and Stage." *SEL: Studies in English Literature, 1500–1900*, vol. 41, no. 3, 2001, pp. 563–581.

Pulos, C. E. *The Deep Truth: A Study of Shelley's Skepticism*. Lincoln: U of Nebraska P, 1954.

Pyle, Forest. "Kindling and Ash: Radical Aestheticism in Keats and Shelley." *Studies in Romanticism*, vol. 42, no. 4, 2003, pp. 427–459.

Quillin, Jessica K. *Shelley and the Musico-Poetics of Romanticism*. United Kingdom: Ashgate, 2012.

Quinn, Mary A. "The Daemon of the World: Shelley's Antidote to the Skepticism of Alastor." *SEL: Studies in English Literature, 1500–1900*, vol. 25, no. 4, 1985, pp. 755–774.

Quinney, Laura. *The Poetics of Disappointment: Wordsworth to Ashbery*. Charlottesville: UP of Virginia, 1999.

———. *William Blake on Self and Soul*. Harvard UP, 2009.

Rajan, Tilottama. *Dark Interpreter: The Discourse of Romanticism*. Ithaca, NY: Cornell UP, 1980.

———. *Romantic Narrative: Shelley, Hays, Godwin, Wollstonecraft*. Baltimore, MD: Johns Hopkins UP, 2010.

Raycroft, Brent. "From Charlotte Smith to Nehemiah Higginbottom: Revising the Genealogy of the Early Romantic Sonnet." *European Romantic Review*, vol. 9, no. 3, 1998, pp. 363–392.

Redfield, Marc. *The Politics of Aesthetics: Nationalism, Gender, Romanticism*. Palo Alto, CA: Stanford UP, 2003.

———, ed. *Legacies of Paul de Man*. May 2005. *Romantic Circles*. Accessed 11 Dec. 2013.

Reiman, Donald H. "The Beauty of Buttermere as Fact and Romantic Symbol." *Criticism: A Quarterly for Literature and the Arts*, vol. 26, no. 2, 1984, pp. 139–170.

———. *Intervals of Inspiration: The Skeptical Tradition and the Psychology of Romanticism*. Greenwood, FL: Penkevill Publishing Company, 1988.

Richardson, Alan. *British Romanticism and the Science of the Mind*. United Kingdom: Cambridge UP, 2001.

———. "Facial Expression Theory from Romanticism to the Present." *Introduction to Cognitive Cultural Studies*. Edited by Liza Zunshine. Baltimore, MD: Johns Hopkins UP, 2010, pp. 65–83.

———. *Literature, Education, and Romanticism: Reading as Social Practice, 1780–1832*. United Kingdom: Cambridge UP, 1994.

———. *The Neural Sublime: Cognitive Theories and Romantic Texts*. Baltimore, MD: Johns Hopkins UP, 2010.

———. "The Politics of Childhood: Wordsworth, Blake, and Catechistic Method." *ELH*, vol. 56, no. 4, 1989, pp. 853–868.

———. "Romanticism and the Colonization of the Feminine." *Romanticism and Feminism*. Edited by Anne K. Mellor. Bloomington: Indiana UP, 1988, pp. 13–25.

———. "Spiritual Converse: Hemans's *A Spirit's Return* in Dialogue with Byron and Shelley." *Fellow Romantics: Male and Female British Writers, 1790–1835*. Edited by Beth Lau. United Kingdom: Ashgate, 2009, pp. 123–138.

Richman, Jared. "Charlotte Smith and the Spectre of America." *Transatlantic Literary Exchanges, 1790–1870: Gender, Race, and Nation*. Edited by Kevin Hutchings and Julia M. Wright. United Kingdom: Ashgate, 2011, pp. 17–37.

Riskin, Jessica. *Science in the Age of Sensibility: The Sentimental Empiricists of the French Enlightenment*. Chicago, IL: U of Chicago P, 2002.

Robinson, Daniel. "Coleridge, Mary Robinson, and the Prosody of Dreams." *Dreaming: Journal of the Association for the Study of Dreams*, vol. 7, no. 2, 1997, pp. 119–140.

———. "Della Crusca, Anna Matilda, and Ludic Sensibility." *The Wordsworth Circle*, vol. 42, 2011, pp. 170–175.

———. "The Duchess, Mary Robinson, and Georgiana's Social Network." *The Wordsworth Circle*, vol. 42, no. 3, 2011, pp. 193–197.

———. "Elegiac Sonnets: Charlotte Smith's Formal Paradox." *Papers on Language and Literature: A Journal for Scholars and Critics of Language and Literature*, vol. 39, no. 2, 2003, pp. 185–220.

———. "From 'Mingled Measure' to 'Ecstatic Measures': Mary Robinson's Poetic Reading of 'Kubla Khan.'" *The Wordsworth Circle*, vol. 26, no. 1, 1995, pp. 4–7.

———. "Mary Robinson and the Trouble with Tabitha Bramble." *The Wordsworth Circle*, vol. 41, no. 3, 2010, 142–146.

———. *The Poetry of Mary Robinson: Form and Fame*. United Kingdom: Palgrave Macmillan, 2011.

———. "The Poets 'Perplext': Southey and Robinson at Work on the *Morning Post*." *The Wordsworth Circle*, vol. 42, no. 1, 2011, pp. 5–9.

———. "Reviving the Sonnet: Women Romantic Poets and the Sonnet Claim." *European Romantic Review*, vol. 6, no. 1, 1995, pp. 98–127.

Robinson, Jeffrey C. "The Poetics of Expiration: Felicia Hemans." *Romanticism on the Net: An Electronic Journal Devoted to Romantic Studies*. February 2003. Accessed 8 Mar. 2013.

———. *Unfettering Poetry: Fancy in British Romanticism*. United Kingdom: Palgrave Macmillan, 2006.

Robinson, Mary. *A Letter to the Women of England, on the Injustice of Mental Subordination*. Edited by Adriana Craciun, Anne Irmen Close, Megan Musgrave, and Orianne Smith. May 1998. *Romantic Circles*. Accessed 18 Dec. 2013.

———. *Mary Robinson: Selected Poems*. Edited by Judith Pascoe. Canada: Broadview Press, 1999.

———. *Walsingham: Or, the Pupil of Nature*. Canada: Broadview Press, 2003.

———. *The Works of Mary Robinson*. Edited by William D. Brewer. 6 vols. United Kingdom: Pickering & Chatto, 2009.

Ronell, Avital. *Stupidity*. Champaign, IL: U of Illinois P, 2002.

Ross, Marlon Bryan. *The Contours of Masculine Desire: Romanticism and the Rise of Women's Poetry*. United Kingdom: Oxford UP, 1990.

Rousseau, G S. "Nerves, Spirits, and Fibres: Towards Defining the Origins of Sensibility." *Studies in the Eighteenth Century III: Papers Presented at the Third David Nichol Smith Memorial Seminar, Canberra 1973*. Edited by R. F. Brissenden and J. C. Eade. Canada: Toronto UP, 1976, pp. 137–157.

Rowe, Samuel. "The Negative Turn: Smith's *Elegiac Sonnets* and the Right not to Communicate." *Romanticism and the Rights of the Negative*. Edited by Tilottama Rajan. *Romantic Circles*. www.rc.umd.edu/praxis/negative/praxis.2017.negative.rowe.html. Accessed 18 Dec. 2018.

Royle, Edward, and James Walvin. *English Radicals and Reformers, 1760–1848*. Lexington: UP of Kentucky, 1982.

Ruderman, D. B. *The Idea of Infancy in Nineteenth-Century British Poetry: Romanticism, Subjectivity, Form*. United Kingdom: Routledge, 2016.

Rudy, Jason R. "Hemans' Passion." *Studies in Romanticism*, vol. 45, no. 4, 2006, pp. 543–562.

Ruston, Sharon. *Shelley and Vitality*. United Kingdom: Palgrave, 2012.

Ruwe, Donelle R. "Charlotte Smith's Sublime: Feminine Poetics, Botany, and *Beachy Head*." *Prism(s): Essays in Romanticism*, vol. 7, 1999, pp. 117–132.

Ryan, Brandy. Review of *Romantic Psychoanalysis: The Burden of the Mystery*, by Joel Faflak. *University of Toronto Quarterly*, vol. 80, no. 2, 2011, p. 351.

Ryu, Son-Moo. "Shelley's 'Mont Blanc'—The Politics of Vacancy." *Nineteenth Century Literature in English*, vol. 11, no. 2, 2007, pp. 87–112.

Saglia, Diego. "Commerce, Luxury, and Identity in Mary Robinson's Memoirs." *SEL Studies in English Literature, 1500–1900*, vol. 49, no. 3, 2009, pp. 717–736.

———. "The Dangers of Over-Refinement: The Language of Luxury in Romantic Poetry by Women, 1793–1811." *Studies in Romanticism*, vol. 38, no. 4, 1999, pp. 641–672.

———. "'A Deeper and Richer Music': The Poetics of Sound and Voice in Felicia Hemans's 1820s Poetry." *ELH*, vol. 74, no. 2, 2007, pp. 351–370.

———. "'Freedom's Charter'd Air': The Voices of Liberalism in Felicia Hemans's *The Vespers of Palermo*." *Nineteenth-Century Literature*, vol. 58, no. 3, 2003, pp. 326–367.

———. "Other Homes: Exoticism and Domesticity in Maria Jane Jewsbury's *Oceanides*." *Women's Writing*, vol. 12, no. 2, 2005, pp. 205–223.

———. *Poetic Castles in Spain. British Romanticism and Figurations of Iberia*. Netherlands: Rodopi, 2000.

———. "The Society of Foreign Voices: *National Lyrics, and Songs for Music* and Hemans's International Poetics." *Women's Writing*, vol. 21, no. 1, 2014, pp. 110–127.

Sanchez, Juan. "England and Spain and The Domestic Affections: Felicia Hemans and the Politics of Literature." *Studies in Romanticism*, vol. 53, no. 3, Fall 2014, pp. 416.

Schulkins, Rachel. *Keats, Modesty and Masturbation*. United Kingdom: Ashgate, 2014.

Scrivener, Michael. *Cosmopolitan Ideal in the Age of Revolution and Reaction, 1776–1832*. United Kingdom: Pickering and Chatto, 2007.

Sha, Richard. "The Motion behind Romantic Emotion: Towards a Chemistry and Physics of Feeling." *Romanticism and the Emotions*. Edited by Joel Faflak and Richard C. Sha. United Kingdom: Cambridge UP, 2014, pp. 19–47.

Shaffer, Julie. "*Walsingham*: Gender, Pain, Knowledge." *Women's Writing*, vol. 9, no. 1, 2002, pp. 69–85.

Shaviro, Steven. *The Universe of Things: On Speculative Realism*. Minneapolis: U of Minnesota P, 2014.

Shaw, Peter Knox. *Jane Austen and the Enlightenment*. United Kingdom: Cambridge UP, 2004.

Sheldon, Rebekah. "Form / Matter / Chora: Object-Oriented Ontology and Feminist New Materialism." *The Nonhuman Turn*, edited by Richard Grusin. Minneapolis: U of Minnesota P, 2015, pp. 193–222.

Shelley, Bryan Keith. "The Synthetic Imagination: Shelley and Associationism." *Wordsworth Circle*, vol. 14, no. 1, Winter 1983, pp. 68–73.

Shelley, Percy Bysshe. *The Complete Poetry of Percy Bysshe Shelley*. Edited by Donald H. Reiman and Neil Fraistat. Three volumes. Baltimore, MD: Johns Hopkins UP, 1999.

———. *The Letters of Percy Bysshe Shelley*. Two volumes. Edited by Fredrick L. Jones. United Kingdom: Oxford UP, 1964.

———. *Shelley's Poetry and Prose*. Edited by Donald H. Reiman and Neil Fraistat. New York: W.W. Norton & Company, 2002.

Simonsen, Peter. "Reading Wordsworth after McGann: Moments of Negativity in 'Tintern Abbey' and the Immortality Ode." *NJES: Nordic Journal of English Studies*, vol. 4, no. 1, 2005, pp. 79–99.

———. *Wordsworth & Word-Preserving Arts: Typographic Inscription, Ekphrasis and Posterity in the Later Work*. United Kingdom: Palgrave Macmillan, 2007.

Simpson, David. *Romanticism and the Question of the Stranger*. Chicago, IL: U of Chicago P, 2012.

———. *Romanticism, Nationalism, and the Revolt Against Theory*. Chicago, IL: U of Chicago P, 1993.

Singer, Kate. "Limpid Waves and Good Vibrations: Charlotte Smith's New Materialist Affect." *Essays in Romanticism*, vol. 23, no. 2, 2016, pp. 175–192.

———. "Mary Robinson and the Idiot's Guide to Suicide and Oblivion." *Literature Compass*, vol. 12, 2015, pp. 667–674.

———. "Stoned Shelley: Revolutionary Tactics and Women Under the Influence." *Studies in Romanticism*, vol. 48, no. 4, 2009, pp. 687–707.

———. "Surfing the Crimson Wave: Romantic New Materialisms and Speculative Feminisms." *Romanticism and Speculative Realism*. Edited by Chris Washington and Anne C. McCarthy. New York: Bloomsbury, 2019.

———. "Wordsworthian Vision, Moving Picture Shows, and the Ethics of the Moving Image in Maria Jane Jewsbury's The Oceanides." *European Romantic Review*, vol. 23, no. 5, 2012, pp. 533–553.

Smith, Adam. *The Theory of Moral Sentiments*. Edited by Ryan Patrick Hanley. New York: Penguin, 2009.

Smith, Charlotte. *Old Manor House*. Edited by Jacqueline M. Labbe. Canada: Broadview, 2002.

———. *The Poems of Charlotte Smith*. Editor, Stuart Curran. United Kingdom: Oxford UP, 1993.

Smith, Orianne. *Romantic Women Writers, Revolution, and Prophecy: Rebellious Daughters, 1786–1826*. United Kingdom: Cambridge UP, 2013.

Sodeman, Melissa. "Charlotte Smith's Literary Exile." *ELH*, vol. 76, no. 1, 2009, pp. 131–152.

Spacks, Patricia Meyer. "Oscillations of Sensibility." *New Literary History: A Journal of Theory and Interpretation*, vol. 25, no. 3, 1994, pp. 505–520.

Spratley, Peter. "Wordsworth's Sensibility Inheritance: The Evening Sonnets and the 'Miscellaneous Sonnets.'" *European Romantic Review*, vol. 20, 2009, pp. 95–115.

Spurzheim, Johann Gaspar. *The Physiognomical System of Drs. Gall and Spurzheim: Founded on an Anatomical and Physiological Examination of the Nervous System in General, and of the Brain in Particular; and Indicating the Dispositions and Manifestations of the Mind*. United Kingdom: Baldwin, Cradock, and Joy, 1815. Google eBook. Accessed 7 Mar. 2013.

Stelzig, Eugene. "'Spirit Divine! With Thee I'll Wander': Mary Robinson and Coleridge in Poetic Dialogue." *The Wordsworth Circle*, vol. 35, no. 3, 2004, pp. 118–122.

Stewart, Susan. *Poetry and the Fate of the Senses*. Chicago, IL: U of Chicago P, 2001.

Stockton, Kathryn Bond. "Growing Sideways, Or Versions of the Queer Child: The Ghost, the Homosexual, the Freudian, the Innocent, and the Interval of Animal." *Curiouser: On the Queerness of Children*. Edited by Steve Bruhm and Natasha Hurley. Minneapolis: U of Minnesota P, 2004, pp. 277–316.

Stokes, Christopher. "Lorn Subjects: Haunting, Fracture and Ascesis in Charlotte Smith's Elegiac Sonnets." *Women's Writing*, vol. 16, no. 1, 2009, pp. 143–160.

Suleri, Sara. *The Rhetoric of English India*. Chicago, IL: U of Chicago P, 1992.

Sussman, Charlotte. "The Art of Oblivion: Charlotte Smith and Helen of Troy." *Studies in Eighteenth-Century Culture*, vol. 27, 1998, pp. 131–146.

———. "Epic, Exile, and the Global: Felicia Hemans's 'The Forest Sanctuary.'" *Nineteenth-Century Literature*, vol. 65, no. 4, 2011, pp. 481–512.

Sweet, Nanora. "'A Darkling Plain': Hemans, Byron and The Sceptic; A Poem." *The Sceptic; A Poem: A Hemans-Byron Dialogue*. Edited by Nanora Sweet and Barbara Taylor. January 2004. *Romantic Circles*. Accessed 8 March 2013.

———. "Felicia Hemans' 'A Tale of the Secret Tribunal': Gothic Empire in the Age of Jeremy Bentham and Walter Scott." *European Journal of English Studies*, vol. 6, no. 2, 2002, pp. 159–71.

———. "*The Forest Sanctuary*: The Anglo-Hispanic Uncanny in Felicia Hemans and José María Blanco White." *Romanticism and the Anglo-Hispanic Imaginary*. Edited by Joselyn M. Almeida. Netherlands: Rodopi, 2010, pp. 159–182.

———. "Gender and Modernity in *The Abencerrage*: Hemans, Rushdie, and 'The Moor's Last Sigh.'" *Felicia Hemans: Reimagining Poetry in the Nineteenth Century*. Edited by Nanora Sweet and Julie Melnyk. United Kingdom: Palgrave, 2001, pp. 181–195.

———. "Hemans's 'The Widow of Crescentius': Beauty, Sublimity, and the Woman Hero." *Approaches to Teaching British Women Poets of the Romantic Period*. Edited by Stephen C. and Harriet Kramer Linkin. New York: Modern Language Association of America, 1997, pp. 101–105.

———. "'Hitherto Closed to British Enterprise': Trading and Writing the Hispanic World, Circa 1815." *European Romantic Review*, vol. 8, no. 2, 1997, pp. 139–147.

———. "'Lorenzo's' Liverpool and 'Corinne's' Coppet: The Italianate Salon and Romantic Education." *Lessons of Romanticism: A Critical Companion*. Edited by Thomas Pfau and Robert F. Gleckner. Chapel Hill, NC: Duke UP, 1998, pp. 244–260.

———. "'Those Syren-Haunted Seas Beside': Naples in the Work of Staël, Hemans, and the Shelleys." *Romanticism's Debatable Lands*. Edited by Claire Lamont and Michael Rossington. United Kingdom: Palgrave Macmillan, 2007, pp. 160–171.

———. "'Under the Subtle Wreath': Louise Bogan, Felicia Hemans, and Petrarchan Poetics." *Romanticism on the Net: An Electronic Journal Devoted to Romantic Studies*, vols. 29–30, Feb. 2003. Accessed 8 Mar. 2013.

Sweet, Nanora, Julie Melnyk, and Marlon B. Ross, editors. *Felicia Hemans: Reimagining Poetry in the Nineteenth Century*. United Kingdom: Palgrave, 2001.

Tayebi, Kandi. "Charlotte Smith and the Quest for the Romantic Prophetic Voice." *Women's Writing*, vol. 11, no. 3, 2004, pp. 421–438.

———. "Undermining the Eighteenth-Century Pastoral: Rewriting the Poet's Relationship to Nature in Charlotte Smith's Poetry." *European Romantic Review*, vol. 15, no. 1, 2004, pp. 131–150.

Terada, Rei. *Feeling in Theory*. Cambridge, MA: Harvard UP, 2001.

———. "Living a Ruined Life: De Quincey's Damage." *Romanticism and the Emotions*. Edited by Joel Faflak and Richard C. Sha. United Kingdom: Cambridge UP, 2014, pp. 215–240.

Thomas, Sophie. "Making Visible: The Diorama, the Double and the (Gothic) Subject." *Gothic Technologies: Visuality in the Romantic Era*. Edited by Robert Miles. December 2005. *Romantic Circles*. Accessed 25 Dec. 2013.

———. *Romanticism and Visuality: Fragments, History, Spectacle*. United Kingdom: Routledge, 2007.

Turner, Paul. "Shelley and Lucretius." *Review of English Studies*, New Series vol. 20, 1959, pp. 269–282.

Todd, Janet M. *Sensibility: An Introduction*. United Kingdom: Methuen, 1986.

Ulmer, William A. "The Politics of Metaphor in Shelley's *Epipsychidion*." *Journal of English and Germanic Philology*, vol. 87, 1988, pp. 535–557.

———. "William Wordsworth and Philosophical Necessity." *Studies in Philology*, vol. 110, no. 1, Winter 2013, pp. 168–198.

Underwood, Ted. "Romantic Historicism and the Afterlife." *PMLA: Publications of the Modern Language Association of America*, vol. 117, no. 2, 2002, pp. 237–251.

Van Sant, Ann Jessie. *Eighteenth-Century Sensibility and the Novel*. United Kingdom: Cambridge UP, 2004.

Vargo, Lisa. "The Claims of 'Real Life and Manners': Coleridge and Mary Robinson." *The Wordsworth Circle*, vol. 26, no. 3, 1995, pp. 134–137.

———. "Tabitha Bramble and the Lyrical Tales." *Women's Writing*, vol. 9, no. 1, 2002, pp. 37–52.

Vila, Anne C. *Enlightenment and Pathology: Sensibility in the Literature and Medicine of Eighteenth-Century France*. Baltimore, MD: Johns Hopkins UP, 1998.

Viscomi, Joseph. "Wordsworth, Gilpin, and the Vacant Mind." *The Wordsworth Circle*, vol. 38, nos. 1–2, 2007, pp. 40–49.

Von Humboldt, Alexander. *Personal Narrative of a Journey to the Equinocital Regions of the New Continent*. Edited by Jason Wilson. New York: Penguin, 1996.

Wallace, Anne D. "Picturesque Fossils, Sublime Geology? The Crisis of Authority in Charlotte Smith's *Beachy Head*." *European Romantic Review*, vol. 13, no. 1, 2002, pp. 77–93.

Wang, Orrin N. C. *Fantastic Modernity*. Baltimore, MD: Johns Hopkins UP, 1996.

———. "Ghost Theory." *Studies in Romanticism*, vol. 46, no. 2, Summer 2007, pp. 203–225.

———. "Romantic Sobriety." *Modern Language Quarterly: A Journal of Literary History*, vol. 60, no. 4, 1999, pp. 469–493.

———. *Romantic Sobriety: Sensation, Revolution, Commodification, History*. Baltimore, MD: Johns Hopkins UP, 2011.

Warren, Andrew. *The Orient and the Young Romantics*. United Kingdom: Cambridge UP, 2014.

———. "Unentangled Intermixture: Love and Materialism in Shelley's 'Epipsychidion.'" *Keats-Shelley Journal*, vol. 59, 2010, pp. 78–95.

Washington, Chris. "Romantic Post-Apocalyptic Politics: Reveries of Rousseau in a World without Us." *Romanticism and Speculative Realism*. Edited by Anne McCarthy and Chris Washington. New York: Bloomsbury, 2019.

———. *Romantic Revelations: Visions of Post-Apocalyptic Life and Hope in the Anthropocene*. Canada: U of Toronto P, 2019.

Wasserman, Earl R. *Shelley: A Critical Reading*. Baltimore, MD: Johns Hopkins UP, 1977.

Waters, Mary A. *British Women Writers of the Romantic Period: An Anthology of Their Literary Criticism*. United Kingdom: Palgrave Macmillan, 2009.

Watkins, Daniel P. *Anna Letitia Barbauld and Eighteenth-Century Visionary Poetics*. Baltimore, MD: Johns Hopkins UP, 2012.

Webb, Timothy. "Listing the Busy Sounds: Anna Seward, Mary Robinson and the Poetic Challenge of the City." *Romantic Women Poets: Genre and Gender*. Edited by Lilla Maria Crisafulli and Cecilia Pietropoli. Netherlands: Rodopi, 2007, pp. 80–111.

Wellmann, Janina. *The Form of Becoming: Embryology and Epistemology of Rhythm, 1760–1830*. Translated by Kate Sturge. Brooklyn: Zone Books, 2017.

Weiss, Deborah. "Suffering, Sentiment, and Civilization: Pain and Politics in Mary Wollstonecraft's 'Short Residence.'" *Studies in Romanticism*, vol. 45., no. 2, Summer 2006, pp. 199–221.

Weisman, Karen. *Imageless Truths: Shelley's Poetic Fictions*. Philadelphia: U of Pennsylvania P, 1994.

West, Cornel. *The American Evasion of Philosophy: A Genealogy of Pragmatism*. Madison: U of Wisconsin P, 1989.

Westover, Paul. "Imaginary Pilgrimages: Felicia Hemans, Dead Poets, and Romantic Historiography." *Literature Compass*, vol. 2, no. 1, 2005. Accessed 8 Mar. 2013.

———. *Necromanticism: Travelling to Meet the Dead, 1750–1860*. United Kingdom: Palgrave Macmillan, 2012.

White, Daniel E. "'Mysterious Sanctity': Sectarianism and Syncretism from Volney to Hemans." *European Romantic Review*, vol. 15, no. 2, 2004, pp. 269–276.

White, Joseph Blanco. *Letters from Spain*. United Kingdom: Henry Colburn and Co., 1822.

———. "Review of *A Visit to Spain* by Michael J. Quin." *Quarterly Review*, vol. 29, 1823, pp. 240–276.

Williams, Helen Maria. *Letters Written in France*. Edited by Neil Fraistat and Susan Lanser. Canada: Broadview, 2001.

———. "To Sensibility." *British Literature, 1780–1830*. Edited by Anne K. Mellor and Richard E. Matlak. San Diego, CA: Harcourt Brace & Company, 1996.

Wiley, James. *Theory and Practice in the Philosophy of David Hume*. United Kingdom: Palgrave Macmillan, 2012.

Wiley, Michael. "The Geography of Displacement and Replacement in Charlotte Smith's *The Emigrants*." *European Romantic Review*, vol. 17, no. 1, 2006, pp. 55–68.

Wilkie, Brian. *Romantic Poets and the Epic Tradition*. Madison: U of Wisconsin P, 1965.

Williamson, Michael T. "Felicia Hemans's Public Poetry, Winckelmann's History of the Art of Antiquity and the Imaginative Plenitude of the Victory Ode." *Women's Writing*, vol. 21, no. 1, 2014, pp. 25–40.

Wolfson, Susan J. *Borderlines: The Shiftings of Gender in British Romanticism*. Palo Alto, CA: Stanford UP, 2006.

———. "Charlotte Smith's *Emigrants*: Forging Connections at the Borders of a Female Tradition." *Huntington Library Quarterly: Studies in English and American History and Literature*, vol. 63, no. 4, 2000, pp. 509–546.

———. "Charlotte Smith: 'To Live Only to Write & Write Only to Live.'" *Huntington Library Quarterly: Studies in English and American History and Literature*, vol. 70, no. 4, 2007, pp. 633–659.

———. "'Domestic Affections' and 'the Spear of Minerva': Felicia Hemans and the Dilemma of Gender." *Re-Visioning Romanticism: British Women Writers, 1776–1837*. Edited by Carol Shiner Wilson and Joel Haefner. Philadelphia: U of Pennsylvania P, 1994, pp. 128–166.

———. "Editing Felicia Hemans for the Twentieth-Century." *Romanticism on the Net: An Electronic Journal Devoted to Romantic Studies*, vol. 19, August 2000. Accessed 13 May 2015.

———. "Felicia Hemans and the Revolving Doors of Reception." *Romanticism and Women Poets: Opening the Doors of Reception*. Edited by Harriet Kramer Linkin and Stephen C. Behrendt. Lexington: UP of Kentucky, 1999, pp. 214–241.

———. "Hemans and the Romance of Byron." *Felicia Hemans: Reimagining Poetry in the Nineteenth Century*. Edited by Nanora Sweet and Julie Melnyk. United Kingdom: Palgrave, 2001, pp. 155–180.

———. "Introduction: Representing Felicia Hemans." *European Romantic Review*, vol. 17, no. 1, 2006, pp. 89–109.

———. "Keats and the Manhood of the Poet." *European Romantic Review*, vol. 6, no. 1, 1995, pp. 1–37.

———. "*Lyrical Ballads* and the Language of (Men) Feeling: Wordsworth Writing Women's Voices." *Men Writing the Feminine: Literature, Theory, and the Question of Genders*. Edited by Thaïs E. Morgan. Albany: State U of New York P, 1994, pp. 29–57.

———. *Romantic Interactions: Social Being and the Turns of Literary Action*. Baltimore, MD: Johns Hopkins UP, 2010.

———. "'Something Must Be Done': Shelley, Hemans, and the Flash of Revolutionary Female Violence." *Fellow Romantics: Male and Female British Writers, 1790–1835*. Edited by Beth Lau. United Kingdom: Ashgate, 2009, pp. 99–122.

———. "'Their She Condition': Cross-Dressing and the Politics of Gender in *Don Juan*." *ELH*, vol. 54, no. 3, 1987, pp. 585–617.

Wollstonecraft, Mary. *A Vindication of the Rights of Woman: An Authoritative Text*. New York: W.W. Norton & Company, 1988.

———, and Mary Shelley. *Mary and Maria, by Mary Wollstonecraft and Matilda by Mary Shelley*. Edited by Janet Todd. New York: Penguin Classics, 1992.

Wood, Allen W. "Kant's Project for Perpetual Peace." *Cosmopolitics: Thinking and Feeling Beyond the Nation*. Edited by Pheng Cheah and Bruce Robbins. Minneapolis: U of Minnesota P, 1998, pp. 59–76.

Wordsworth, William. *The Excursion*. Edited by Sally Bushell, James A. Butler, and Michael C. Jaye. Ithaca, NY: Cornell UP, 2007.

———. *Lyrical Ballads, and Other Poems, 1798–1800*. Edited by James Butler and Karen Green. Ithaca, NY: Cornell UP, 1992.

———. *The Prelude: 1799, 1805, 1850*. New York: W.W. Norton & Company, 1979.

Wroe, Ann. "Shelley's Good Vibrations: His Marginal Notes to Hartley's *Observations on Man*." *Wordsworth Circle*, vol. 41, no. 1, Winter 2010, pp. 36–41.

Wu, Duncan. *Romantic Women Poets: An Anthology*. Hoboken, NJ: Blackwell Publishers, 1997.

———. "Wordsworth and Sensibility." *The Oxford Handbook of William Wordsworth*. Edited by Richard Gravil and Daniel Robinson. United Kingdom: Oxford UP, 2015, pp. 467–481.

Yaeger, Patricia. "Toward a Female Sublime." *Gender and Theory: Dialogues on Feminist Criticism*. Edited by Linda Kauffman. United Kingdom: Basil Blackwell, 1989, pp. 191–212.

Yearsley, Ann. "To Indifference." *The Broadview Anthology of Romantic Poetry*. Edited by Joseph Black et al. Canada: Broadview Press, 2016.

Yousef, Nancy. *Isolated Cases: The Anxieties of Autonomy in Enlightenment Philosophy and Romantic Literature*. Ithaca, NY: Cornell UP, 2004.

———. *Romantic Intimacy*. Palo Alto, CA: Stanford UP, 2013.

Zimmerman, Sarah M. "'Dost Thou Not Know My Voice?': Charlotte Smith and the Lyric's Audience." *Romanticism and Women Poets: Opening the Doors of Reception*. Edited by Harriet Kramer Linkin and Stephen C. Behrendt. Lexington: UP of Kentucky, 1999, pp. 101–124.

———. *Romanticism, Lyricism, and History*. Albany: State U of New York P, 1999.

———. "Varieties of Privacy in Charlotte Smith's Poetry." *European Romantic Review*, vol. 18, no. 4, 2007, pp. 483–502.

Žižek, Slavoj. *The Ticklish Subject: The Absent Centre of Political Ontology (The Essential Žižek)*. New York: Verso, 2009.

———. *The Parallax View (Short Circuits)*. Cambridge, MA: MIT Press, 2009.

———. *The Sublime Object of Ideology*. New York: Verso, 1989.

Index

Abbey, Lloyd Robert, 158n23
abstraction, xxxi, xxxix, xli, 15–16, 20, 54–55, 59–61, 65–66, 83, 86, 122; consuming, 14; linguistic, 89; mind's powers of, 96, 102–07; and vacancy, 159n31
abyss, 38, 71, 108. *See also* oblivion; void
Addison, Joseph, 12, 161n10
aether, 74, 85, 143, 175n34
affect: circulation/transmission of, 72–74, 82, 84–90, 92–93, 151, 159n31; cognitive theories of, 97; dangerous, 108; material, xxviii, xlii, 82, 84, 121, 146, 166n13; and movement, 34, 66, 81–93, 97, 108–10, 113, 122, 125, 139–40, 151–52, 155n2, 156n11; impersonal, xxxii, 3, 58, 82–83, 85, 88, 156n11; and loss, 172n16, 172–73n17; nongendered, 92; overwhelming, 72, 103, 108; and protest, xxxvi, 157–58n19; relation to language, xv, xviii, xxxii, xxxv–xxxvi, 87, 165n5, 176n41; and sensibility, xxviii; shared, xxxiv, 10, 53, 83–84, 89; and the soul, 121–22; speculative, xlii; theory, xix; and vacancy, xv–xvi, xviii, xxv, xxx–xxxii, 158n20, 158n27
Ahern, Stephen, xx
Alien Act of 1793, 28, 162n18, 163n26
Allen, Richard C., 74, 174–75n29
Allewaert, Monique, 89, 176n42
Almeida, Joselyn, 111, 184n40
Altick, Richard, 134, 136
Alvey, Nahoko Miyamoto, 71, 173n22

Anderson, John, 164n29
aporia, xiv, xviii, xl, 4, 9, 14–19, 31, 34, 60, 122, 151–52; of consumption, 30; linguistic, xxxix, 2; movement of, xxxii, 9; of unconditional hospitality, 30, 164n30
Armstrong, Isobel, 95, 157–58n19
Arnold, Matthew, 161n10
Arve River, 66, 82–83, 86
atoms, 82, 84
aural, 36, 41, 48, 54, 58–59, 69, 92. *See also* hearing; music; singing
Austen, Jane, 20, 42, 156n8, 156–57n14
Austin, Linda, 141
autonomy, 138, 157n18

Bacscheider, Paula, 157n15
Baily, Revered Benjamin, 132, 185n7
Baker, Carlos, 173n21
Bakhtin, Mikhail, 160n4
ballad: collecting, 166n14; repetition and refrain, xxx, xl, 36, 47–58, 60, 68, 142–43
Barad, Karen, xxxvii, 139, 159n30, 170n36
Barbauld, Anna, 156–57n14
Barczewski, Stephanie, 166n14
Barker-Benfield, G. J., xx–xxi, 12, 76, 155n4, 156n8, 156n9, 172n12, 175n31, 180n12
Barrell, John, 171n8, 175n36
Battle of Trafalgar (1805), 33
Baucaom, Ian, 158n27
"Beachy Head" (Smith), xxxiii–xxxiv, xl, 19–34, 160–61n7, 161n8, 162n20,

"Beachy Head" (*continued*)
163n26; and geology, 21–23, 25; hermit, xl, 3–4, 19–20, 25–33, 164n29, 164n32; and history, 21–25, 32–33, 162n21, 163n22, 164n32; and missing epitaph, 31–32, 164n29; and the national body, 3–4, 19
beauty, xl, 3, 14–16, 134, 137, 180–81n21
Behrendt, Stephen, xxv, 157n15, 160n2, 177–78n2
Bell, Charles, 101
Benjamin, Walter, 186n14
Bennett, Jane, xviii, xxxii, 3, 58, 82, 156n11, 166n13, 176n41
Bentham, Jeremy, 180n11
Berlant, Lauren, 160n1
Berlin Decree of 1806, 33
Bernstein, Richard J., 178–79n6
Bewell, Alan, 68, 167n20, 168n28, 171n7
Bialostosky, Don H., 172n15
binary: gender, xxv, xxxii, 2, 17, 37, 53, 152. *See also* nonbinary
Blake, William, xxxviii, 73, 84; and the hysterical male, 159n34; and mesmerism, 179n10
Blank, Kim, 173n21
blood, xx, 73–74, 80, 84; circulation of, 74–75
Bode, Christoph, 22, 157n17, 160n4
body, 19–20, 58, 102, 113, 131, 147, 151, 155n2, 176n42; and affect, 74–75, 87, 125; disruptive, 166n13; empirical, 165n4; emptying of, 161n12; gendered, 5, 12, 29, 31, 40, 47–48, 72, 95, 124, 139, 186–87n16; and history, xlii; and movement, 3, 8, 33–35, 42, 64–69, 82, 171–72n10, 175n34, 176n41; nongendered, 72; outside of, 34–36, 41, 55–56, 74, 85–86, 159n33, 160–61n7, 166n13; and sensation, 13, 16, 36–37, 44–47, 63–65, 128, 158n20; and soul, 174–75n29
Bohls, Elizabeth, 185n3
Bonca, Teddi Chichester, 71, 171n2, 173–74n24
Booth, Naomi, 157–58n19
Botting, Fred, 186n13
Boyson, Rowan, 168n28

Bradshaw, Penny, 157n16
brain, 44; and cognitive theories, 97; and concussion, 20; materialist, 100–03; overwhelmed, 67, 113–14; paralysis of, 95–106; and politics, 183n37; relationship to mind, 100–04, 107–10, 181n23; ruination, xli, 111, 117, 121; science of, xxvii, xli, 75, 96, 99–106, 180n14, 180n16, 180n17, 181n23; and sensation, 49; and soul, xx; vacant, xli, 47, 63, 78–79, 85, 92, 96. *See also* mind
Bray, Matthew, 164n32
Brennan, Teresa, xxxii, 74–75, 84, 159n31
Brewster, Sir David, 135
Bromwich, David, 168n28
Brown, Nathaniel, 173n21
Bruder, Helen, 159n34
Buchanan, Ian, 165n4
Bundock, Chris, 159n34
Burgess, Miranda, xxi, 187n19
Burke, Edmund, xxi–xxii, 36, 105; and custom/habit, xli, 68, 167n22, 168n28; and the sublime, xxvii, 65, 79, 106
Burwick, Frederick, 180n16
Butler, Marilyn, 100
Byrne, Paula, 167–68n23, 169n31
Byron, Lord (George Gordon), xxix, xxxix, 117, 160n38, 171n6

Cabanis, Pierre-Jean-George, 100, 102, 180n17
caesura, 51, 54–55, 113, 120; visual, 144
Cameron, Kenneth Neill, 176n44
canon: literary, xxiv, 135, 149, 187n1. *See also* history, literary
Carlson, Julie, 65–66, 84, 88–89
Carothers, Yvonne, 173n18
Carpenter, Benjamin, 180n19
Castle, Terry, 134–35, 186n11
Catholicism, 111, 117, 181n26
Cauchi, Francesca, 173n18
Ceylon (Sri Lanka), 124, 131–46, 186n15, 187n17
Chandler, James, 64, 155n7, 158n24, 167n22, 168n28
Channing, William Ellery, 116
Chaplin, Susan, 155n7
Chaudhary, Zahid, 186n14

INDEX

Cheah, Pheng, xxxvii, 19
Cheng, Anne Anlin, 172n14
Cheyne, George, xx
childhood, 140–47, 172n16, 187n17, 187n21
chivalry, 67
Cixous, Hélène, xxv
Clairmont, Claire, 174n25
Clark, David L., 181n24
Clark, Timothy, 71, 75, 171n2, 173n20, 174n27
class, 12, 106, 161n10, 163n23, 185n3
Class, Monika, 169n31
cocoa tree, xlii, 124–25, 132–40, 144, 186n16
Colebrook, Claire, 165n4
Colebrook Commission, 186n14
Coleridge, Samuel Taylor, xxv, xxxviii, 27, 48, 102, 140, 167n16, 173n19, 185–86n10; "Christabel," 133, 140; "Kubla Khan," xvii, xxx, 56–57, 61, 101, 169n31, 169n32, 170n33; poetic conversation with Robinson, 55–59, 159n33, 165n2, 167n15, 167–68n23, 168–69n30, 169n31
Collings, David, xxxiii, 70, 158n25, 170n34, 170–71n17, 172n16, 172n16, 172–73n17
colonialism/colonization, xxxv, xli–xlii, 23–24, 69–70; India, 123–47, 186n13, 186n14; invisibility of Indian subjects 145–46; New World, 97, 115–17, 182n32, 183–84n39, 184n40; and the Western gaze, 185n3
color-blindness: ideology of, 145–46
Combe, George, 101
Comet, Noah, 177n1
commodification: of Indian goods, 187n22
commodities, xxvi, xxxix, xlii, 12, 124–25, 131–34, 137–40; language of, 146–47; luxury, xxxvii, 125, 150; women's bodies, 138–39
Connolly, Tristanne, xxxviii, 159n34
consciousness, xiv, xx, xli, 101–06, 109, 112–15, 118, 120–21, 165n6, 181n23; loss of, xxiii, xxv–xxvi, xxix, 3, 113, 157–58n19

consumerism, xiv, 5–6, 12, 17; imperial, 20–21, 138, 161n10; and women, xxvi–xxvii. *See also* commodities; commodification
Cooper, Andrew M., 172n15
Corresponding Acts Society of 1799, 53
cosmopolitanism, xlii, 4, 20, 25, 27–29, 32, 118, 163n27, 164n28, 164n32, 184n42
Countess of Blessington, 186n11
Cowper, William, xxviii–xxix, 5
Craciun, Adriana, 156–57n14, 168n24, 170–71n1
Craig, Cairns, 49, 167n19
Crocco, Francesco, 177n1, 177–78n2
Crook, Nora, 71–72, 174n27
Cross, Ashley, 38, 40, 56, 156n8, 159n33, 164–65n1, 165n2, 165n8, 165–66n9, 167n15, 167n16, 168n26, 168–69n30, 169n31, 170–71n1
cross-dressing, 108–9
Crowley, Hannah, 38
Csengei, Ilddiko, xxvi, 155n4, 157–58n19, 159n32, 160n1, 180n12
Curran, Stewart, 3, 160n3, 160n6, 166n10, 167n17
custom, xxii, xxxix, xl–xli, 35–40, 48, 61, 146, 167n22; resistance to poetic, 57

Daguerre, Louis, 134, 136
Damasio, Antonio, 180n20
Darby, Parson, 27, 33
Darwin, Erasmus, 100
Dawson, P. M. S., 173–74n24, 179n10
de Almeida, Florida Hermione, 181n24
de Man, Paul, xxxii, xxxvi, 92, 158n28, 159n29, 163n24
de Quincey, Thomas, 181n24
de Soto, Hernando, 116, 183n34
de Staël, Madame, 156–57n14
death, xv, 8, 14, 19, 24, 30, 32, 35, 40, 80–81, 85, 107, 109, 113, 118, 134, 166n11, 178n3, 183n35, 184n40; living, 75. *See also* suicide; violence
deconstruction, xix, xxxii, 4, 147, 150, 152, 160n4, 162n20, 171n3, 171–72n10; and desire, 176n45; and emotions, 18; and epistemology, 108;

deconstruction (*continued*)
of femininity, 178n3; and language, xxxv–xxxvi, 82, 87
Deleuze, Gilles, 37, 165n4, 166n13, 170n34, 170n36; and difference, 44–45; influence on Romantic critics, 170n36; and intensity, 52, 54, 156n11; and repetition, 40, 42–43, 48, 164–65n1, 168n27; and sensation, 59–60
Della Cruscan poets, xxv, 38
Derrida, Jacques, xxxvi–xxxvii, xl, 14–15, 131, 159n29; and commodities, 138; and hauntology, 125, 127, 139; and hospitality, 29–31, 164n28, 164n30; and messianic spirit, 146
desire, xxxix, 78–79, 90, 112, 129, 176n43; commodified, 134; consumer, 138–39; deconstructive nature of, 176n45; for exotic Other, 173n22; material, 24–25; patriarchal, 110; Western, 134
despair, 40, 79, 99, 103, 173n21
Dickenson, Emily, 184n41
diorama, 134, 136,
D'Israeli, Isaac, 183n35, 183n36
Doblado, Don Leucadio, 181–82n27
Dolan, Elizabeth, 156n12, 158n21, 160n1
domesticity, xxiv, xxviii, 64, 67–69, 98, 124–28, 145, 178n3, 179n9; English, 125–26, 142
Donnelly, Hugo, 82, 175–76n38
doubt, 172n15
dreams, xiv–xv, xxiii, 31, 45, 71–72, 76–78, 102, 126–27, 133, 135, 141, 169n31. *See also* sleep
Duffy, Cian, 82, 175–76n38
Dykstal, Timothy, 161n10

ecology, xxxii, xli, 4, 24, 82–87, 90; affective, 82–85, 151
Edelman, Lee, 187n21
Eden, 12, 16, 120, 132, 140–41
Edgeworth, Maria, 156n8
education, xxxv, 7, 161n10, 165n3
electricity, 173–74n24, 174n27
Elegiac Sonnets (Smith), xviii, xl, 67; fame of, 2–4; and impossible consumption, xiv–xv, xvii, 2–5, 8–10, 14–15, 17, 19; Robinson's critique of, 43–44; and taste, 4–19; and vacancy from passions, xiii–xv, xviii, 1–2, 9, 15–17
Ellis, Markman, 155n4, 155n7, 159n32
embodiment, xxxix, 13, 18–19, 76, 125, 143: empirical, xx–xxi; and gender, xxxv, 6, 70, 72, 79, 103, 149; and identity, 30; material, xxvii; poetics of, 92
Emerson, Ralph Waldo, 146
emotions, xli, xxvi–xxviii, 18–19, 35, 51, 52, 54–55, 73, 95–96, 102–05, 128, 149–50, 156n11, 168n29, 180n20; and affect, xxxi–xxxii, 83, 87–89; embodies, 18; excessive, xxv; and gender, xvii, xix, xxxiii, xxxix, 64, 68, 91, 97, 172n11; overwhelming, xxiii, 20, 69; physics of, 170n35; and reason, xxii; relationship to feelings, 180n20; and sensation, xvi, 5; and taste, 13; undue, xxiv
empiricism: and affect, xxxi; critique of, 13, 38; and epistemology, 151; and feeling, 157n15; gendered critique of, xix–xxvii, 35–37, 40–41; and history, xxxiii–xxxiv; Kantian, 178–79n6; and the passive mind, 100; radical, 47; rejection of, 167n22, 168n28, 169n32; and Romanticism, xxii–xxiii; and sensibility, xvi, xxi–xxiii, xxxiv, 44, 149–50, 156n9; and taste, xxxix, 3–4, 10–11
entrainment, 74–75, 78, 81–82, 84, 92
epic, 22, 24, 163n22
epistemology, xxv, 4, 22, 45–48, 61, 104–10, 150, 152, 164–65n1, 169n32, 178–79n6, 179n6; of affect, xxviii; blindness to, 162n16; empirical/empiricist, xxi, xxxv, xlii; 9, 56, 88, 169n31; Enlightenment, 37–40; and freedom, 45–46, 121; gendered, xvii, xx, 67; Kantian, 178–79n6 Lokean, xxvi, 165n3; problems of, xxxvii, 178–79n6; of taste, 9, 13; transcendental, 96; visual, 126, 132, 134, 137–40. *See also* knowledge; empiricism
Espinasse, Francis, 141, 187n18
Essick, Robert N., 176n43
euporia, xl, 34

INDEX

Fagan, Deirdre, 184n41
Faflak, Joel, 179n10
Fairclough, Mary, 106
Faubert, Michelle, 166n11
Favret, Mary, xxviii, xxxi, 64, 155n1, 158n22, 158n24, 158n27, 166n13
Fay, Elizabeth, 170–71n1
feeling/s, 35–40, 44, 66–72, 79, 87–90, 174n28; and affect, xxxi, 92, 103; and caesura, 54–55, 120; contagious, xli; cult of, xx–xxi, 40, 156n8; embodied, 119; and emotion, 156n11, 180n20; empirical, xix–xxviii, 15; and gender, xvii, 40, 47–48, 124, 129–30, 145, 172n16; habitual, 167n22, 168n28; Kantian, 18; language of, 87; as a mode of thought, 157n15; phantom, 131, 146–47; repetitive, 39, 42; and sensibility, xv; subject, xxix, 3–4, 39, 47, 157n17; and taste, 13; unrepresentable, 157–58n19
Feldman, Paula, 178n3
Ferber, Michael, xxiii–xxiv
Ferguson, Francis, 175n37
Festa, Lynn, 155n7
fever, xiii, xv, xxiii, xli
Fischman, Susan, 173n21, 173n22
Fletcher, Loraine, 26, 163n23, 187n17
Fletcher, Mark William, 187n18
forgetting, xiv, xviii, xxiii, 3, 8, 46, 81, 162n21, 165n6. *See also* oblivion
Fraistat, Neil, 78, 156–57n14
François, Anne-Lise, 172n11
freedom, 104, 117, 121, 166n11; cognitive, 88, 119; Enlightenment, 28, 30–31; epistemological, 45–46, 121; from sensation, 17–18; of the soul, 102; universal, 20; women's, 71. *See also* liberty
Freeman, Barbara Claire, xxvii, 106, 181n22
French Revolution, xxxv, 27–28, 53, 107, 156n8, 156–57n14, 163n26, 164n32, 175n30
Freud, Sigmund, 100, 163n27
Fulford, Tim, 168–69n30, 170n37, 170–71n1, 173–74n24, 179n10

Gall, F. J., 99–102, 180n15
Gallagher, Catherine, 183n36
Galperin, Thomas, 136
Galperin, William, 136
Gamer, Michael, 185–86n10
Garnai, Amy, 163n26
Garofalo, Daniela, 160n39
Gasche, Rodolphe, 161n15
gaze: colonial, xlii, 134, 137, 141, 173n22, 185n3; feminine, 185n3
Ghose, Indira, 185n3
ghosts. *See* phantoms
Gibbon, Edward, 163n23
Gifford, William, xxv
Gigante, Denise, 161n11, 161n12, 181n24
God, 28, 96, 111, 120–21
Godwin, William, 166n11, 167–68n23, 168n26, 171n6
Goldsmith, Steven, xxxviii, 73, 84, 103, 105, 158n24
Goldstein, Amanda Jo, 66, 89, 176n39, 176n42
Goodman, Kevis, xxviii, 23, 155n1, 158n22, 158n24, 158n27, 161n8
Goslee, Nancy, 184n40
gothic, 136–39, 160n1, 185–86n10, 186n12, 186n16; phantoms, 133–36; violence, 53, 167n21
Gottlieb, Evan, 174n28, 176n40, 177n1
Grant, Anne, 116
Grant, Edward, 165n7
Greville, Frances, xiv, 10
grief, xxiv
Griggs, Earl L., 173n18, 173n21
Groom, Nick, 166n14
Grosz, Elizabeth, 53
groupthink, 53
Guattari, Felix, 48, 60
Guest, Harold, 168n24
Guiton, Derek, 174n27
Gurton-Wachter, Lily, 159n34

habit, xxii, 35–48, 57, 61, 164–65n1, 167n22, 168n28; Burkean, 168n28; of feeling, 168n28; poetic, 69–70
Hades, xiv

Hamilton, Elizabeth, 156–57n14
Harding, Anthony John, 178n3
Hart, Monica Smith, 30, 163n27
Hartley, David, xxiii, 66, 74, 82, 169n32, 174n25, 174–75n29
Hartman, Anne, 111
Hartman, Geoffrey, 69, 185n8
Hatherell, William, 169n32
Hawley, Judith, 160n1, 168–69n30
Hays, Mary, 156–57n14
Hayter, Alethea, 181n24
Hazlitt, William, 66
hearing, 39, 58–59. *See also* aural; music
Hegel, G. W. F., 100, 105, 108, 114–15, 120, 178n5, 178–79n6, 183n37, 183n37
Hemans, Felicia, xv, xxii–xxiii, xxv, xxxiii, xxxv, xxxvii–xxxviii, xli–xlii, 95–122, 129, 139, 151, 155n1, 158n20, 178n3, 178n4, 180n16, 181n25, 181–82n27, 183n34, 184n42, 184n43; "The Forest Sanctuary," xli–xlii, 97, 103, 105, 110–22, 180n16, 182n28, 182n30, 182n31, 182n32, 182n33, 183–84n39, 184n40; German influences, 178n5; interest in science of brain and mind, 96–103, 181n23; and religion, 181n26; and the ruined brain/mind, 96–98, 102–11, 114, 117, 121; politics of, 177n1, 177–78n2, 182n28; and the sublime, 180–81n21; and transcendentalism, 179n7 ; "The Widow of Crescentius," xxiii, xli, 95–110, 179n8; use of dashes, 184n41
Hilbish, Florence, 164n29
history, xxv, xxxiii–xxxiv, xxxv, xlii, 4, 18–27, 97, 106, 111, 115–17, 122, 131, 135, 158n27, 162n21, 163n23, 164n31, 178n5, 185n6; affective, 158n27; American, 182n32; British, 163n22, 164n32; counterfactual, 116–17, 183n36; geologic/natural, 22–23; literary, xxxiii, 31, 33, 135, 149, 151; as narrative erasure, 163n24
Hitchener, Elizabeth, 174–75n29
Hitt, Chrisopher, 88
Hodgson, Adam, 116, 182n31, 182n32

Hoeveler, Diane Long, 170–71n1
Hofkosh, Sonia, 170–71n1
Hogg, Thomas, 174–75n29
Hogle, Jerrold E., 83, 171n3, 186n16
Hogsette, David S., 169n32
hormones, 75
hospitality, xl, 20, 24–32; Kantian, 4; unconditional/universal, xl, 163n26, 164n28, 164n30
Hume, David, xxi–xxii, xxxi, 3, 68, 161n11; and custom, 36; and identity, 7–8, 10, 12–13
hyperfeminine, xxi
hypnosis, 99, 101–02
hysteria, xli, 13, 67–68, 78, 160n1, 171n7

idealism, xxii, 4, 82, 96
identity, xxiii, 7–11, 17, 29–30, 111–12, 118, 149–50, 164n28, 173n20; lack of, 121; resistance to, 53–54; suspension from, 184n40
ideology, xxxv, xlii, 30, 145–46; colonial, 137; gender, xvi, xviii, xix–xxiv, xxxiii, 8, 19, 36–37, 70, 72, 77, 81, 105–14, 131–32, 150, 152, 184–85n1; imperialism, xxxv; national, 20; of the Other, xxxv; Romantic, xxiv; and sensibility, xvii, 40, 88, 122; visual, 134, 137; and women's writing, 64–65, 72, 76–77, 79, 85
idiot/idiocy, 35–37, 41–42, 47–50, 53–56; Romantic, 168n27
images, xlii, 7, 75, 84, 113, 123–47, 186n16; ideology of, 137
imagination, xxix, 3, 7–8, 11, 16–18, 36, 43, 49, 69, 86, 129–30, 135, 162n13, 185n6, 185n9, 186n13; failed, 173n21; Kantian, 169n32; tension with hysteria, 171n7; and the virtual, 186n13
immigration, 116, 162n17, 182n32
India, xxxv, xliii, 123–47, 186n14; British, 125, 131, 138, 141; landscape of, 124, 134, 145
indifference, xiv, xvi, xxv–xxvi, 10
inequality, 52–53; gender, xvii, xxxix, 110, 156n10
infant. *See* childhood

innocence, 140–42, 144, 187n17
inquisition, 97, 111–12, 181n26
insensibility, xvi, xxv, xxviii, 32, 73, 157–58n19, 161n11, 171n6
intoxication, 174n27, 181n24
Irving, Theodore, 183n34
Irving, Washington, 116, 186n12
Iturbide, Augustín de, 182n28

Jackson, Noel, 67–68, 158n24, 174n28
Jackson, Virginia, 157n17
Jacobus, Mary, 137, 170–71n1, 171–72n10
Jager, Colin, 181n23
Jarvis, Simon, 146
Jewsbury, Maria Jane, xv, xxiii, xxxiii, xxxviii, xli–xlii, 34, 93, 123–49, 151, 184–85n1, 186n12, 187n17, 187n22; *The Oceanides*, xxxv, xlii, 123–47, 185n7, 185–86n10; and ghouls of passion, 123–24, 130; letters, 129–30, 132, 145, 185n7; relationship with Wordsworth, 185n5
Joffe, Sharon Lynne, 174n25
Johnson, Claudia, xxi, 152, 156n8, 160n1, 175n31
Jones, Chris, xxi, 155n7
Judson, Barbara, 77, 175n32
Jung, Sandro, 166n10

Kant, Immanuel, xxvii, xl, 3–4, 16–18, 169n32, 178–79n6; *apatheia*, xxviii, 18; critique of taste, 13–14; and hospitality, 25, 28–30; reason, xxii, xxxix; and the sublime, 7, 100, 106; transcendence, xxxi, 150
Kaufman, Robert, 18
Keach, William, 73
Keats, John, xvi–xvii, xxix, xxxviii–xxxix, 18; and affect, 159n37; ambivalence about gender, 159n35; use of drugs, 181n24
Kelley, Theresa M., 21, 162n19
Kelly, Gary, 177n1, 178n5, 183–84n39, 184n40
Kemble, John, 182n28
Khalip, Jacques, xxxix, 156–57n14, 158n21, 158n24

Kim, Benjamin, 177n1
kinesis, xlii, 124–25, 139, 147
Knott, Sarah, 180n12
knowledge, 8, 34, 45–47, 78, 105, 130, 178–79n6; boundaries of, 60; empirical, 21, 30; gendered, xvii, xix, xxxv, 36, 68, 150, 170–71n1; feminine, 178n5; and figural movements of language, xvi, xxvii; Lockean, xxii, 38, 165n3; new, 44, 128–29; non–, 9–10, 18–19; overwhelming, 104–05; and sensation, xxxi, 1, 36–40, 158n20; theories of, xlii; transcendental, 92, 96; universal, 104; visual, 125, 145
Knowles, Claire, xxiv, 156n12, 177–78n2, 178n3
Knox-Shaw, Peter, 156–57n14
Kowaleski-Wallace, Elizabeth, xxvi
Kristeva, Julia, 157–58n19, 163n27
Kurshan, Ilana, 179n10

Labbe, Jacqueline, 4, 13, 21, 157n17, 160n4, 160n5, 164n29, 167n21, 170–71n1
Landon, Letitia, xxxix, 160n39
landscape, xiv, xxxiii–xxxiv, 2, 11, 14–21, 25, 31, 33, 61, 69, 79–80, 82–88, 113, 115–18, 124, 126–36, 143–47, 151; colonial, 131–34, 182n32, 185n3; and female sexuality, 184n40; mental, 19, 57, 127–28; pastoral, 10–11, 15, 17, 162n20; winter, 15–17
Laqueur, Thomas, 156n10
Lanser, Susan, 64, 92, 156–57n14
Lau, Beth, 170–71n1
laughter, 69
Lawrence, William, 100, 180n11
Leask, Nigel, 173–74n24, 175n30, 179n10, 185n3
Ledbetter, Kathryn, 168–69n30
Leighton, Angela, 175n37, 177–78n2
Lethe, xiv–xvii, xxix, 2, 6, 8–10, 17, 20, 34, 45–46. *See also* Robinson, Mary; *Sappho and Phaon*
Levinson, Marjorie, 172–73n17
Levy, Martin, 169n31
Leys, Ruth, 165n5

liberalism: democratic, 177n1
liberty, 36, 39, 43, 46, 117, 146; from British imperialism, 146; from tyranny, 71. *See also* freedom
light, 38, 84–87, 91, 107, 120, 134, 136, 144; metaphor for knowledge, 38, 104; rays, 74; of reason, 40, 107; and synesthesia, 176–77n46
Linkin, Harriet Kramer, 160n39
literati, 134–35
Liu, Alan, 164n31
Locke, John, xx, xxii–xxiii, xxvi, xxxi, 3, 7, 36, 38–39, 52, 125–27, 165n3; and interrupted consciousness, 156n6; and liberty, 46, 166n11; and plenum, 175n34; and the void, 165n7
Lokash, Jennifer, 171n2
Lokke, Kari E., xxv, 27, 163n25, 178n5
Lootens, Tricia, 178n3, 178n5, 179n9
loss, xxviii, xxxix; 56, 70–71, 105, 107, 129, 132, 169n32; of mother, xxxiii, 172n16; of self, xxvi; of sensation, 39; wartime, xxxv, 158n27; and women, 172–73n17, 186n16. *See also* consciousness, loss of
love, xv, xxiii, 31, 39–40, 42, 45, 65, 73, 84, 89–90, 175n34
Low, Dennis, 185n5
Lucretius/Lucretian: 66, 82–84, 87, 176n39, 176n42
Lumsden, Simon, 178–79n6
Lussier, Mark, 177n47
Luther, Susan, 168–69n30
Luu, Helen, 178n3
lyric, xxxviii, 21, 31, 48–49, 162n21; gendered, 64, 79–81; feminine, 66–71; as a public genre, 167n18; subject, 17; and vacancy, 54

Mackie, Erin, 161n9
Macvicar, Grant, 182n31
madness, 41–42, 66–68, 73, 174n26, 174n27
magic lantern show, 135–36, 186n11
magnetism, 92, 99, 173–74n24
Malabou, Catherine, 183n37
Manning, Peter J., 172n13

Marz, Karl, 138, 186n14
Massumi, Brian, xviii, xxviii, xxxi–xxxii, 52, 87, 89, 102–03, 113, 117, 119–20, 155n2, 156n11, 166n13, 170n36, 176n41
masturbation, 159n35
materialism, xxxviii, 66, 72, 100–01, 174–75n29 180n15; historical, xxxv. *See also* materiality; new materialism
materiality, xxix, xxxv–xxxviii, xl, xlii, 10, 21, 23–27, 58–61, 65–66, 81–93; 151–53, 166n13, 176n42; cognitive, 113–15, 118–20; human and non-human, 176n41; and language, xxxii, 60; and movement, xxxi, 3, 10, 14, 150–51; nongendered, 56; outside the subject, 162n16; pictures, 131; post-human, 31, 97; in Robinson, 167n17; and seascape, 160–61n7; shared, 58; vital, 174–75n29. *See also* new materialism
Mazzeo, Tilar, 71, 173n22
McCarthy, Anne C., 82, 176n40
McDayter, Ghislaine, 176n43
McDowell, John, 178–79n6
McGann, Jerome, xxii, xxiv–xxvi, xxviii, xxxviii, 36, 145, 160n38, 164n31, 165n2, 165n8, 177–78n2, 178n3
McGrath, Brian, 187n19
Medea, 80–81
melancholy, xxvii, 13, 37, 69–70, 99, 142, 158n21, 159n37, 177n1; and race, 172n14
Mellor, Anne K., xxiv, 170–71n1
Melnyk, Julie, 179n7
Melville, Peter, 29
memory/memories, xiv, 5–11, 48–49, 112–13, 123–24, 143, 146, 162n21, 180n17, 185n6; childhood, 141, 165n3; ghostly, 124; historical, 22; and imagination, 185n6; picture, 125–31; and sensation, xxix, 7
memsahib, 141, 147
Mendis, G. C., 186n15
Mergenthal, Silvia, 166n10
Merry, Robert, 38
Mesmer, Franz, 99, 101

mesmerism, 99, 102, 174n27, 179n10
Mill, John Stuart, 117, 167n18
Miller, Jonathan, 100–02, 106, 180n19
Milnes, Tim, 175–76n38
mind: breakdown of, 18–20, 26; clearing of, 182n30; deadening/emptying of, xxviii, xli–xlii, 7, 18–20, 26, 33–48, 63–65, 68, 72, 75, 92, 165n6; and epistemology, xxvi; gendered, xvi, xxxiii, 35–37; habits of, xxii, 11; and impossibility, 7; and linguistic impossibility, xxxii; movement of, xxvii, 2, 14, 107–08, 113, 171n3; and negation, 157–58n19; passive, xxiii; paralysis of, xxiii, 9, 13, 100; and politics, 183n37; rational, 3; relationship to body, xiv–xv, 55; relationship to brain, 100–04, 107–10, 181n23; at rest, 119–21; ruined, 96–121; and sensation, 18; vacant, xxxix, xl–xli, 47, 49–63, 71–81, 85, 88, 92, 168n28. *See also* brain
miscellany, 135, 186n11
Mitchell, Robert, 58, 155n7, 170n34, 171n2, 173n19
Mitchell, W. J. T., 185n9
monomania, xxiii, xxxvii, 35–36, 41–43, 77, 150
"Mont Blanc" (Shelley), xvii, xxxii, 65–66; as analogy of the mind, 81–82, 84; ecology of, 82–87, 90; and Lucretian echoes, 176n39; movement/flow in, 83–85, 90; repetition in, 85, 87–88; and skepticism, 175–76n38
More, Hannah, xiv, 10, 156n11
Morton, Timothy, 174n27
motherese, 170–71n1
Mueschke, Paul, 173n18
Mullan, John, xx, 76
Mulrooney, Jonathan, 159n37
music, 54, 57–58, 63–93, 108–10, 114, 126; as allegories about vacant stasis, 71–81; Indian, 173n22
Myers, Anne, 162n14

Nagle, Christopher, xxv, 155n7, 171n4
Napoleon, 33, 53, 98
negation, xvi, 8, 15, 46, 157–58n19

nerves, xix–xx, 65, 73–74, 93, 156n9; feminine, 56; theory of, 96, 100, 156n9
new materialism/materiality, xix, xxxii, xxxiv–xxxviii, xli, 58, 60, 83, 93, 150, 153, 176n41
The New World, xxxv, 97, 110–22, 183–84n39; mind, 112, 118; Spanish presence in, 116
newspaper: verse, 47, 166n14, 167n15, 167n16, 169n31
Ngai, Sianne, xxvii, 168n27
Noggle, James, xxviii
nonbinary: gender, xvii, xxiv, xxxii, xxxiii, 53, 82, 108, 152
nonhuman, xv, xviii, xxxii, xl–xli, 18–19, 25–26, 33, 62, 65–66, 72, 74, 81, 83, 86–93, 139, 150, 176n41, 183n38
Norton, Andrew, 116
nostalgia, xlii, 27, 70, 79, 123–31, 138, 142, 145, 151
nursing, 67

oblivion, xvi–xviii, xxiii, xxv, xxxix, xl, 3, 8–10, 18–19, 32, 35, 37–47, 68, 78–79, 81, 88, 149, 152; masculine, 178n5
O'Malley, Glenn, 86–87, 176–77n46
O'Neill, Henrietta, 162n17
O'Neill, Michael, xxiv, 120, 156n13
ontology, xv, xix, xxxvii, 66, 88, 110, 150, 152, 162n16, 170n36; and commodities, 138; and epistemology, 22, 46, 48, 61; and landscape, 112
Opie, Amelia, 175n35
opium, 162n17, 169n31, 181n24
Ostas, Magdalena, 18
Otto, Peter, 186n13
Ovid, 88
Owenson, Sydney, 173n22
Oxford English Dictionary (OED), 181n25
Özdemir, Erinç, 2–3, 160n2, 160n4

panorama, 136
paralysis, xxxvii, 79, 150, 152; feminine, 70; mental, xli, 64, 72, 96–105
particles, 73–74, 82, 86, 175n34; and wave physics, 90, 177n47

Pascoe, Judith, 21, 162n19, 165n2
passion/s, 88, 178n3, 182n28; and affect, xxxi; empiricist, 68; exotic, 71, 173n22; and gender, xvi–xvii, xxiii, 35, 66–67, 95–96, 98, 161n11, 179n9; ghoulish, 123, 130; frenzied, xiii–xiv, xviii; "loftier," xv, 35–36, 47, 61; monomaniacal, 41–45; sensible, xxii; and taste, 12–13, 161n11; violent, 174n25
pastoral, xxxiii, 3, 5–7, 9–17, 20–21, 31, 68, 123, 131–33, 162n20
Peirce, Charles, 178–79n6
Percy, Thomas, 166n14
Peterloo massacre, 98, 106
Pfau, Thomas, xxxv, 158n24, 159n37
phantasmagoria, 124–25, 133–40, 147, 186n16; aesthetics of, 186n14
phantoms, 123–47, 185n4; of colonized subjects, 137; commodities as, 138; gothic, 133–36; of home, 126–31, 133; language of, xlii; of the past, 125, 127; woman as, 149
pheromones, 75, 84
Phillips, Jane E., 84, 176n39
philosophy, xxiv, xxix, xxxiv, xxxviii, 5, 107, 161n11, 169n31, 169n32, 181n23; of association, 168n28; and consciousness, 181n23; discourse of, xxvi; and empiricism, xix, 13, 38, 150; Enlightenment, 156–57n14; history of, 175n34; and insensibility, 161n11; post-Kantian, 99–100, 178–79n6; and sensation, 36
phrenology, 99–102, 179n10, 180n15
Pinch, Adela, xxv, 3, 12, 66, 155n1, 158n24, 160n4, 171n8
Pippin, Robert, 178–79n6
pleasure, 5, 7, 11–14, 123, 168n28; ironic, 160n38; sensory, xxxviii; of vacancy, xxxix; and women, 17, 70
plenum, 55, 175n34
Plotnitsky, Arkady, 177n47
poeisis, 39, 121; and science, 159n31
poetics: deconstructive, 160n4; feminine, xvii, xxiii, xxx, 2, 63–64, 71–72, 75–81, 85, 90–92, 171n5, 171n9; of mobility, 187n19; new, 41, 47, 56, 81, 143; posthuman, 31; revolutionary, 77; and science, 159n31; and sensibility, 95, 156n12, 175n30; speculative, xvi, xxiv, xlii, 34; of vacancy, xix, xxxvii, 20, 55, 61, 110; visual, 126, 132, 152
Pope, Alexander, 88
posthumanism, xxiii, xxxiv, xxxvii, 20, 37; affect, 65, 97, 120, 151, 171–72n10; poetics of, 31; vitality, 173n19; and vacancy, xviii, xxxii
power, xxiv, xli, 36–37, 39, 46, 106, 155n2, 174n29, 182n28
Pratt, Kathryn, 158n21
Prins, Yopie, 157n17
Protestantism, 97, 111–12, 116, 118, 120
Puloss, C. E., 175–76n38
Pyle, Forest, 158n23

queer, 108; and childhood, 187n21; panic, 168n26; theory, 187n21
Quillin, Jessica, 71
Quin, Michael J., 111
Quinney, Laura, 126, 172n15

Rajan, Tilottama, 80, 82, 85, 156–57n14, 175n33
rationality, xxi–xxii, xxvii, 14, 158n21, 175n30
Raycroft, Brent, 171n5
reason, 38, 40, 42, 45, 156–57n14, 178–79n6; and emotion, xxii, 96; empiricist, 1; Enlightened, 30, 54, 120–22, 156n8, 164n30; and idiocy, 42; Kantian, xxvii, xxxix; loss of, 107; and oblivion, 38; revolutionary, 77, 165n2
receptivity, 44–45, 91; and affect, xxxviii; impossible, 4, 19–34; Kantian, 178–79n6; material, 121, 158n28; passive, 54
Redfield, Marc, 161n10
reflection, 60, 75, 103, 126, 158n21, 167n18; self, 18; and sensation, xx, xxii, xxxi, xl, 36–38, 149, 157n15; and Wordsworth, 171n8
Reiman, Donald H., 175–76n38

INDEX

repetition, xviii, 5, 10, 14, 19, 33–43, 49–51, 57–58, 68, 87–88, 122, 127, 142–44, 164–65n1, 167n17; as productive, 47–62; as stunting, 37–47; with difference, xvii–xviii, xxx, xl, 34–37, 41–44, 52–62, 164–65n1
reproduction, 128, 141–44
revolution, xxv, 95–98, 107–08, 111, 179n8; bottom–up, 105–06. *See also* French Revolution
rhythm, 37, 48, 52, 54–55, 57–60, 69, 75, 89, 159n31, 170n33
Richardson, Alan, xxvii, 20, 69, 75, 99–100, 102, 106, 144, 170–71n1, 180n11, 180n14, 180n16, 180n18, 180–81n21, 181n23, 182n29, 187n17
Richardson, Samuel, xx
Richman, Jared, 163n26
Riskin, Jessica, 155n5
Ritson, Joseph, 166n14
Robinson, Daniel, 36, 40, 56, 88, 156n8, 165n8, 165–66n9, 167n15, 168–69n30, 169n31, 170n33, 172n13
Robinson, Jeffrey, 16–17, 162n13, 165n2
Robinson, Mary, xvii–xviii, xxii, xxvi, xxx, xxxiii, xxxvii–xxxix, xl–xlii, 27, 34, 79, 92, 96, 109, 113, 118, 140, 143, 155n1, 156n8, 158n20, 165n2, 165n3, 167n16, 168n26; and the ballad, 47–58, 68, 166n14; celebrity of, 168–69n30; critique of empiricism, 38–40, 167n22; "To the Poet Coleridge," xxx, 36, 54–62, 170n33; poetic conversation with Coleridge, 55–59, 159n33, 165n2, 167n15, 167–68n23, 168–69n30, 169n31; and postmodern texture, 167n17; and radical immersion, xv, 110; and radical political affiliations, 167–68n23, 168n24; and repetition, xl, 34–51, 56–62, 140, 143, 151, 164–65n1; rivalry with other women poets, 165–66n9; *Sappho and Phaon*, xiii–xv, xxii–xxiii, xl, 35–47, 165n8; "The Savage of Aveyron," 36, 49–55, 57, 113, 167n18; "Sight," 37–39; use of opium, 169n31. *See also Sappho and Phaon*

Roman Empire, 104, 163n23; invasion of Britain, 22–24
Ronell, Avital, 54, 168n27
Ross, Marlon, 159n35, 170–71n1
Rousseau, G. S., xx, 159n34, 180n12, 183n38
Rowe, Samuel, 4, 8
Royle, Edward, 168n25
Ruderman, D. B., 141, 143
Rudy, Jason, xxv, 178n3, 179n7
Ruston, Sharon, 75–76, 174n27
Ruwe, Donnell R., 162n19, 162n20
Ryan, Brandy, 179n10
Ryu, Son-Moo, 175–76n38

Saglia, Diego, xxv, 165n2, 177n1, 177–78n2, 179n8, 184n43
Sanchez, Juan, 177n1, 177–78n2
Sappho and Phaon (Robinson), xvii, xl, 35–47; critique of sonnet of sensibility, 43–44; and gendered passion, xxii–xxiii; and "loftier passions," xv, 35–36, 47; and movement of waves, xiv–xv, 8–10, 46; and repetition, 35–47; and vacancy from passions, xiii–xv, xviii, 35. *See also* Lethe; Robinson, Mary
Schulkins, Rachel, 159n35, 170–71n1
seeing. *See* sight
self, xxiii, 3, 6, 22, 54, 109, 114, 121, 147, 150, 152, 180n11, 183n37; determination, 104–05; empirical, xxi; feeling, 2; feminine representation, 2; gendered, xxvii; and infancy, 143; inhabiting other ontologies, 88; loss of, xxvi; and memory, 113; and the past, 115, 117; reflection, 18, 103; sense of, xxiii, xxvi, 6–7; unrecognizable, 96–97; voiding, xxxix
sensation, xxx–xxxi; absence of, xiii–xvii, 125, 130; critique of, 185n9; gendered, 150; embodied, xlii, 39; empiricist, 165n2; and ideas, 164–65n1; language of, 45–46, 87; and movement, 36; nonempirical, 47; outside the body, 158n20, 159n33; passive, 165n2; past, 127; problems of, 36–39; and reflection, 157n15; and visibility, 129

sensibility: as a contagion/disease, xli, 64–65, 71, 76, 81, 85, 92, 108, 150–51; critiques of, xxv–xxviii, xxxix, 10–11, 38–40, 64–66, 77, 156n8, 165n2; definition of, 156n11; discourse of, xiv, xvii, 71, 74, 76, 83, 156n9; and empiricism, xxi–xxiii; evolution of, xx–xxii; excessive, 63, 66–69, 72–73, 76, 78, 81, 85, 150, 175n34; failure as a revolutionary force, 77–78; feminization of, xvi–xvii, xix–xxv, 72; history of, xv, xix, xxi; and insects, 167n15; language of, 4, 44, 63, 65, 67, 75–76, 80, 87–88, 138, 175n30; male, 67; and medicine, 180n12; phantoms of, 124–47; philosophical problems with, xv–xvi, xix–xx, xxxvii–xxxviii; poetess of, 35, 63, 79, 149–50, 173n22; revolutionary aspects of, 155n7, 156n8; and science, 155n5; transmission of, 69–70, 72–74, 78–79; and vacancy, xiv–xvi, xix, xxv–xxvi

sentiment/sentimentalism, 3, 43, 52, 125, 160n4; colonial, 138, 147, 151; embodied, xxiv, 26, 139, 147; and gender, 172n11; gothic, 167n21; in Hemans, 177–78n2, 178n3; language of, 67; negativity towards, 160n2; novels of, xxi, 12; poetry, 4, 88, 95; subjectivity, 118; and visibility, 129–31, 140; and women's writing, xxiii, xxiv

Sha, Richard, 55, 74, 109, 168n29, 170n35

Shaffer, Julie, 165n3

Shaftesbury, Lord (Anthony Ashley-Cooper), 161n12

Shaviro, Steven, 176n40

Sheldon, Rebekah, 119

Shelley, Elizabeth, 174n25

Shelley, Harriet Westbrook, 174n25, 175n35

Shelley, Mary, xxix, 71, 156–57n12, 173n19, 174n25

Shelley, Percy Bysshe, xv, xvii–xviii, xxii, xxix, xxxvii–xxxviii, xli, 61–66, 70, 81–93, 118, 123, 151, 158n20, 158n23, 172–73n17, 173n19; "Alastor," xxii, xli, 63, 71–81, 84, 90, 95, 110–11, 114, 173n18, 173n20, 173n21, 173n22, 173n23, 175n33, 175n34, 178n4, 180n16; "Epipsychidion," 87, 90–92, 121, 176n39, 176n43, 176n44; interest in science, 173–74n24, 174n27, 174–75n29, 177n47; and materiality, 65–66, 85–87, 176n41, 176n42; "Mont Blanc," xvii, xxxii, 65–66, 81–90, 175–76n38, 176n39; radical poetics and politics of, 62, 64, 71–72, 76, 84, 90–93, 175–76n38, 176n39; and rhyme, 170n34; support of women writers, 71–72, 174n25, 175n35; use of drugs, 181n24. *See also* "Mont Blanc"

sight, 2, 37–39, 60, 76, 119, 124–33, 137–46; and colonialism, 185n3; phantoms of, 123–24

silence, xiv, xxvi, 32, 35, 48, 65–66, 85–88, 102, 119; mental, 55

Simonsen, Peter, 185n6, 185n9

Simpson, James, 101, 116, 182n33

simulacra, 66, 84–85

Singer, Kate, 166n11, 173n23, 181n24, 187n22

singing, 42, 44, 48, 97, 183n35, 184n43; women, xli, 63–93, 114

skepticism, xxiii, xxvi, 7, 82, 85, 149, 158n21, 175–76n38, 185n6

sleep, xxiii, xxvi, xl, 3, 5, 19, 32, 78, 85, 88, 102, 135, 165n6, 180n17

Smith, Adam, xxi, 27, 155n5, 156n11

Smith, Charlotte, xviii, xxii, xxv–xxvi, xxvi, xxxvii–xlii, 1–35, 38, 67, 79, 96, 139, 150–51, 155n1, 160n1, 160n4, 161n11, 162n14, 162n16, 163n22, 163n26, 166n10, 175n35; "Beachy Head," xxxiii–xxxiv, xl, 19–34, 160–61n7, 161n8, 162n20, 162n21, 163n26, 164n29, 164n32; creating new forms of affect, 3–4; and displacement, 163n27; *Elegiac Sonnets*, xiii–xv, xl, 1–19, 43–44, 67; and figuration and form, 161n8; and impossible consumption, xiv, xv, 2–3, 17, 19, 110, 139, 151; use of opium, 162n17; and Mary Robinson, 165–66n9. See also *Elegiac Sonnets*

Smith, Orianne, 157n16
song. *See* music
soul, xx, 72, 102, 104–05, 108–10, 114, 119–21, 176–77n46; and Hegel, 100, 114; and unified theory, 174–75n29. *See also* spirit
Southey, Robert, 167n15, 167n16, 168–69n30
Spacks, Patricia, xxv
specters. *See* phantoms
speculative: affect, xlii, 147; imagination, 7; realism, 150, 162n16, 183n38; thinking, xv–xvi, xix–xx, xxiv, xxxv, xxxviii, xli, 98, 165n2
Spinoza, Baruch, xviii, 66, 82–83, 155n2, 174–75n29; and affect, 3, 172–73n17; definition of body, 155n2
spirit, xiv, 32, 65, 104, 109, 121, 146; affective, 91–93; animal, xx; avenging, 79; divine, xxx, 59; nongendered, 92; poetic, 59, 61; and sensibility, xxii; and unified theory, 174–75n29. *See also* soul
Spratley, Peter, 171n9
Spurzheim, Johann, 99–100, 180n15
Steele, Richard, 12
Stelzig, Eugene, 168–69n30
Stewart, Susan, 39
Stockton, Kathryn Bond, 187n21
Stokes, Christopher, xxvi, 4, 160n1
stuplinity, 168n27
subjectivity, xviii, xix, xxvi–xxvii, xxix, xlii, 18, 29–32, 46, 52–53, 84–85, 108, 115, 120–22, 156n11, 158n21, 162n16, 164n29, 166n13; emotional, xvi; Enlightenment, 41, 166n13; gendered, 4–5, 31, 97, 106, 110, 184n40; Romantic, 159n37; and sensation, 26; and the void, 8
sublime, xxv, xxvii–xxviii, xxix, 2–3, 21, 65, 79, 88, 106, 158n21, 160n2, 162n20, 180–81n21; Kantian, xxvii, 7, 100, 106; neural, xxvii, 75, 100, 106, 181n21; sensibility, 175n30; transcendence, 3, 7, 25
succubi, 159n35
suffering, xix, xxv, xxviii, 27, 68, 76, 96

suicide, 40–41, 45–47, 98, 108, 166n11, 173n21; *sati*, 107
Suleri, Sara, 185n3
Sweet, Nanora, 107, 111, 116, 177n1, 177–78n2, 179n8, 180–81n21, 181n26, 181–82n27, 182n30, 182n33, 184n40
sympathy, xxi, xxvi, 4, 20, 27, 29–30, 50–53, 69, 156n11, 173–74n24, 175n30; intersubjective, 72, 76–77; language of, 69; radical, 64; rational, 172n11
syncope, xxvi, 54, 157–58n19
synesthesia, 61, 83, 85–93, 176–77n46

taste, xviii, xl, 161n10, 161n11, 161n12; discourse of, xiv–xv, xxxix, 3, 13, 35; empiricist, 30; and fashion, 161n9; impossibility of, 4–19
technologies: visual, 125, 134–36, 186n14, 186n16
Terada, Rei, xxviii, xxxiii, xxxv, 18, 108
Thomas, Sopie, 136, 185n9
Tighe, Mary, xxxix, 160n39
Todd, Janet, 155n7
trade, 20, 29–30, 131, 137, 139, 184n40; Anglo-Indian routes, 146
trance, 96, 99–102, 106, 173n19, 180n17
transcendence/transcendentalism, xxv, xxxviii, xli–xlii, 37, 44, 53, 82, 88, 110, 120–21, 143, 160n2, 178n5, 178–79n6, 179n7, 185n6; divine, 91; Kantian, xxvii, xxxi, 7, 13, 150; knowledge, 92, 96, 104; sublime, 3, 7, 25. *See also* sublime
trauma, 20, 49, 77, 113, 159n37
travelogue, 116, 124, 127
trope/tropology, xix, xxiii, xxviii–xxxii, 9–10, 33, 38, 58–61, 142–47, 166n14, 176n42; and affect, xxviii, destabilizing, 177n1; 37; of infant, 142–46, 151, 153; movement of, xviii, xxix, 2, 125, 146–47; and repetition, 47; turning of, xl, xlii; of vacancy, xxxvii, 55, 64–65, 81, 88, 92, 121, 137, 140, 153
Trotter, Thomas, 174n27
Turner, Paul, 176n39
Tyebi, Kandi, 162n19, 162n20

Ulmer, William A., 90, 168n28, 176n43, 176n45
unconscious, 3, 11, 20, 57, 100–03, 106, 112–19, 169n31, 180n16; textual, 117
universality, 28–29, 53

vacuum, xxx, 38, 55, 78, 175n34
van Goethe, Johann, 166n12
van Sant, Ann Jessie, xxv
vibration/s, xiv, xxii–xxiii, 56, 58–61, 65–66, 72–75, 82–85, 87, 113, 115, 151; and grand unifying theory, 174–75n29; and synonym "thrill," 172n12
Villa, Anne C., 180n12
violence, 53, 60, 105, 109, 112–13; colonial subjects, 24, 137, 186n14; female, 179n9; gothic, 53, 167n21; of sensation, 55
virtual, the, 156n11, 186n13
Viscomi, Joseph, 168n28, 171–72n10
vision/s, xlii, 7–8, 31, 45, 56–57, 63, 71, 76–80, 90, 112, 123–47, 151, 185n9; loss of, 56, 76. *See also* dreams; phantoms; sight
vitality, 92, 147, 173n19; debates, 174n27; material, 85
Viviani, Teresa Emilia, 174n25
voice, 58–59, 65, 67, 69–73, 86–87, 91–92, 121, 168–69n30, 171n8, 174n25, 184n43; poetic, 56, 169n32
void, xxvi, xxx, 3, 8, 22, 38–39, 45–46, 54, 59, 78–79, 137, 165n7; mental, xxix, 42; of the self, xxxix; sensory, xxiii, 78, 85. *See also* oblivion
von Humboldt, Alexander, 116, 182n32

Wallace, Anne D., 23, 162n19
Walvin, James, 168n25
Wang, Orrin N. C., 155n3, 156–57n14, 181n24, 184–85n1, 185n4
war, xxviii, 20, 29, 33, 53, 97, 158n27, 164n32, 183n35, 184n40
Warren, Andrew, 87, 176n39, 176n43
Washington, Chris, 176n40, 183n38
Wasserman, Earl, 175n37
water, xiv, xviii, 1–2, 8, 22, 27–28, 30, 33, 57–58, 73, 80, 84–85, 93, 143–44, 147, 151. *See also* Arve River; Lethe; waves
Watkins, Daniel P., 157n16
waves, 1, 27, 30, 40, 45–46, 73, 83; limpid, 8–9, 17, 160–61n7; movement of, xiv–xvi, xviii, 8–10, 46; and particle physics, 91, 177n47; poisonous, 82
Webb, Timothy, 165n2
Webster, Daniel, 182n31
weeping, 63, 73
Weisman, Karen, 82
Wellmann, Janina, 159n31
West, Cornel, 146
Westover, Paul, 177n1
Whewell, William, 178–79n6
White, Daniel, 184n42
White, José Maria Blanco, 111, 116, 183n35, 184n40
Wilkie, Brian, 163n22
Williams, Helen Maria, xvii, 10, 67, 156–57n14, 175n30
Williamson, Michael T., 177n1
Wily, Michael, 163n27
wind, xxix–xxx, 57, 72–73, 83–87, 91, 93, 103, 113, 151, 160–61n7
Wolfson, Susan, 67, 95, 98, 111, 152, 156–57n12, 159n35, 159n36, 170–71n1, 171n8, 177n1, 177–78n2, 178n3, 178n4, 179n8, 179n9, 180n16, 180–81n21, 181n26, 181–82n27, 184–85n1
Wollstonecraft, Mary, xxxix, 40, 42, 64, 66, 79, 123, 156–57n14, 175n31, 184–85n1
womb, 26, 119
Wordsworth, Dora, 126, 132, 145, 185n7
Wordsworth, William, xv, xvii, xxviii–xxix, xxxvii–xxxviii, xli, 5–7, 21, 32, 63–71, 80, 123, 125–27, 129–30, 132, 137, 151, 164n31, 167n16, 167n22, 172n15, 173n18, 185n5; aesthetics of, 171–72n10; and affect, 172n16; and idiot boys, 168n27; and imagination, 185n6; "The Intimations Ode," 132–33, 144, 146, 185n9; *Lyrical Ballads*, 5, 49, 66–67, 69, 92, 185–86n10; "The

Mad Mother," 66–68; natural piety of, 62, 69, 172n11; and sensibility, 171n4, 171n5, 171n9, 172n11; "The Solitary Reaper," 64, 69–70; "The Thorn," 64, 67–68; and vacancy, 168n28; and the visual, 185n9; and women's language, 171n8
Wroe, Ann, 74
Wu, Duncan, 171n5

Yaeger, Patricia, 106, 181n22
Yearsley, Ann, xvi
Yousef, Nancy, xxvi, xxxi, 145, 157n18

Zimmerman, Sarah, xxvi, 162n21, 167n18
Žižek, Slavo, 77, 96–97, 105; and freedom, 117; and self–relating, 183n37; and subjectivity, 114–15
Zunshine, Liza, 180n12

www.ingramcontent.com/pod-product-compliance
Lightning Source LLC
Chambersburg PA
CBHW070757230426
43665CB00017B/2391